Web Technologies

by

Dr. Shruti Kohli

BPB PUBLICATIONS
B-14 Connaught Place, New Delhi-110 001

FIRST EDITION 2015

Copyright © BPB Publications, India

ISBN : 978-81-8333-575-1

Distributors:

COMPUTER BOOK CENTRE
12, Shrungar Shopping Centre,
M.G. Road, BENGALURU-560001
Ph: 25587923, 25584641

MICRO BOOKS
Shanti Niketan Building,
8, Camac Street, KOLKATA-700017
Ph: 22826518/22826519

MICRO MEDIA
Shop No. 5, Mahendra Chambers,
150 DN Rd. Next to Capital Cinema,
V.T. (C.S.T.) Station, MUMBAI-400 001
Ph: 22078296/22078297

DECCAN AGENCIES
4-3-329, Bank Street,
HYDERABAD-500195
Ph: 24756967/24756400

BPB PUBLICATIONS
B-14, Connaught Place,
NEW DELHI-110001
Ph:23325760/43526249

BPB BOOK CENTRE
376, Old Lajpat Rai Market,
DELHI-110 006,
Ph: 23861747

INFOTECH
G-2, Sidhartha Building,
96 Nehru Place,
NEW DELHI-110 019
Ph: 26438245

BPB PUBLICATIONS
20, Ansari Road, Darya Ganj,
NEW DELHI-110002
Ph: 23254990/23254991

Published by Manish Jain for BPB Publications, B-14, Connaught Place, New Delhi – 110001 and Printed by him at Repro India Ltd.

Dedications

I dedicate this book to my mom and dad (Mrs Veena and N.K Sondhi), who inspired me to believe that I was capable of authoring a book.

Acknowledgement

I would like to express my gratitude to the many people who saw me through this book; to all those who provided support, talked things over, read, wrote, offered comments, allowed me to quote their remarks and assisted in the editing, proofreading and design.

I would like to thank my parents for inspiring me to publish this book. Above all I want to thank my husband (Amit), my kids (Kanchi and Gauri) and my in laws who provided me the congenial environment for authoring this book . They supported and encouraged me in spite of all the time it took me away from them. Specially, my mother in law(Renu Kohli) and Aunt (Mrs Satish Nelson) who had been supporting all my career moves. It was a long and difficult journey for them. Not to forget my younger sister, Richa Sondhi who had been boosting me and encouraging me to achieve higher avenues in life.

I would like to thank Himani, Vijay,Shashi,Sonia,Ankit for helping me in the process of selection and editing. Thanks to Vijay for his consistent feedback that helped me in giving final shape to the book. Thanks to Pankaj who act as a catalyst for motivating me to write for BPB. Thanks to my publisher who encouraged me to pin down my skills which could be used for the development of the students.

Last and not least: I beg forgiveness of all those who have been with me over the course of the years and whose names I have failed to mention."

Preface

Book encapsulates from rich practical hands-on experience of developing Web applications, bundled with teaching of the subject for graduate/post-graduate students. It's an endeavor to put things together, what has been both practiced as well as preached, which is the one of the most compelling differentiators of this book.

It's enlightens how Web has evolved over a period of time. It's changing the world since it influences all spheres of our lives now. As a matter of fact, it changes the world, and changes itself too! Each such change is perceived as if it's just the beginning of the Web. Over the course of many generations of the Web, every added set of functions adds a layer of abstraction to it, because that is how any software development takes place. Each such abstraction makes it simpler to use, but the flip side is that the fundamentals tend to be forgotten by those who have joined the bandwagon late. This book attempts to bridge the fundamentals, how it has evolved and how it's in present form. The book can be used by students to get a gasp of the fundamentals and also by professionals who want to brush up with the basics of the technology. It is written as concise as possible so that the reader need not skip any section, at the same time, can finish reading the book like a novel.

The reader may wonder that Web world related technology are changing much faster than ever before. And then there are so many books on Web technology. So why go through the trouble of reading another book ? Well, it's true that technologies are changing fast but if one observes closely there is a pattern on "how it changes". For instance, an abstraction of such a pattern is that most of the new advancements are happening by combining a few things together and all of those things already exist. As a corollary and a direct proof of it, these innovations are observed to happen in waves rather than by sharp turns. So it actually makes sense for someone to take a snapshot of the current state which will be useful for extrapolation.

The first wave of the Web (retrospectively termed Web 1.0, though there is no such term officially) brought about interconnecting computers together. The subsequent waves (Web 2.0 and 3.0) focused on bringing about people together. The phenomenon of Web 2.0 happened in stages and was not discovered or invented in one day. This holds true for Web 3.0 as well. The power of collaboration among people is not to be underestimated. It is counterpart in the world of innovation, where it has been proven that enabling interaction among people brings in remarkable progress in innovation. Similarly, the Web will continue to change and the pace of change will only get faster. To catch up with it becomes a continuous process throughout one's life but to understand its mechanics is something that is a more lasting skill or achievement, giving rather a brief reprieve to forecasting trends. During the time the book is written and published, the world is already talking of the sixth sense !

Well, this is almost true when one considers the ubiquitous Web - being not only on the browser but also on mobile phones, electronic gadgets like ipads, tablets, GPS, credit cards and a host of such day-to-day stuff. The way people interact and collaborate using these devices is no longer dependent on logging on to a computer and browsing through, it is being made possible to directly connect to the servers and get the results without going through a browser.

The Intended Audience

- Graduate/post-graduate students in IT or Computer Science as a textbook providing an all-round perspective of the various technologies involved.
- An aspiring IT architect who would like to understand or get refreshed with the fundamentals.
- A business person or manager of an IT firm who would like to glance over certain topics in this book as a starting point for getting hands-on experience.

Organization of the Book

This book covers the fundamentals of the main technologies that make up the Web. The topics of the book is cumulated and represented by Figure 1.

The book is structured along the lines of the representation shown in the figure. Starting from Internet Fundamentals in the top middle, it follows clockwise through, to Web Services. As technologies are changing very fast, specific areas of technology go obsolete faster than ever before. They are replaced by new areas of technology but the base concepts will remain more or less the same, so an understanding of these will be useful. For example, when we refer communication among systems connected to the internet, the protocol by default is TCP/IP. This will not change often, but, how this is used to service an application will change fast enough. Also, another example is in Ajax which is a technology that has brought in rich interfaces into the Web, thus opening up new business possibilities. The question that might come to the reader at this point is how Web technologies are relevant in the current times. As a matter of fact, Web technology has revolutionized the usage surpassing all other innovation cycles. Economists have come out with a theory of innovation cycles and its relation to the economy.

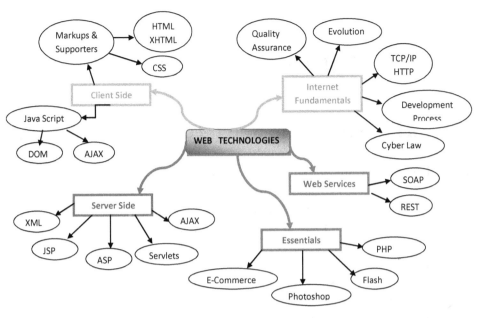

Figure 1

Special Features

This book captures the essence of the various technologies that constitute the Web. Rather than just focus on theory, the book brings out the concepts in the form of examples and illustrations. Just like how the Web is linked to many resources, the exercises aid the reader. The book is self-contained in the sense that the section on essentials provides a useful guide to the basics of the topics. Photoshop helps in designing User Interface and Flash helps to develop animated tools. Similarly PHP and E-commerce help to enhance the knowledge on upcoming trends. It provides almost the complete ecosystem for developing Web applications.

Table of Contents

Chapter 1

An Introduction to Web Technology

Key Topics

- *World Wide Web Fundamentals*
- *Web Development Process*
- *Accessing Internet*
- *Quality Assurance*
- *Frequent Terms in Web World*
- *Web Servers*

1. Introduction

WWW (World Wide Web) was developed by Tim Berners-Lee of Massachusetts's Institute of Technology and released by the Centre for European Nuclear Research (CERN), Switzerland. The Web servers are interconnected in the formation of a Web and as they are spread across the globe, it is popular as World Wide Web. Any unique file on Web server that can be downloaded is known as a Web page and moving further bundle of Web pages constitute a Website. When we start browsing any Website, first page is called home page. The domain name of the World Wide Web servers begins with 'www', for example www.yahoo.com. WAIS, Gopher and WWW were the pioneering servers and they registered phenomenal growth. Key tool after Internet connection to see Website is a browser software. Users use browser software, such as Internet Explorer, Netscape, Google Chrome, Mozilla, Firefox, etc., which eventually help to navigate the Web. WWW also makes valuable use of hypertext along with high quality graphics. As against text-based services like FTP and telnet the Web is a graphic medium with most Web pages having some amount of images. Today we also have Web pages that have sound and video embedded in them. Before learning about WWW it is important to understand Internet and how it is different from WWW.

1.1 World Wide Web Fundamentals

Do You Know?
Tim Berners-Lee is known as father of WWW.

1.2   Internet Fundamentals

Let's start with basics!!

1.2.1   What is Internet ?

The Internet can be defined as a global system of interconnected computer networks that use the standard Internet protocol suite (TCP/IP) to link several billion devices worldwide. It is a network of networks that flourish across hundreds / millions of private, public, academic, business and government networks of local to global scope. They are connected via a fleet of electronic, wireless, wired and optical networking technologies. The Internet hosts an exhaustive range of information resources and services, for example inter-linked hypertext documents and applications of the World Wide Web (WWW), the infrastructure to support corporate organization and Peer-to-Peer networks for file sharing.

How it is different from WWW ?

Internet	WWW
The Internet is a gigantic network of networks. It connects billions of mobile devices, computers together globally, forming a cloud in which these devices can exchange information / communicate as long as they are both connected to the Internet. Suffix to physical platform, it is vital to note Internet also rely heavenly on variety of languages known as protocols.	The World Wide Web, or simply Web, is a way of accessing information over the medium of the Internet. It is an information-sharing model that is built on top of the Internet.
The Internet, not the Web is also used for e-mail which still today is large piece of Internet activity, it relies on SMTP, then Usenet news groups, instant messaging and FTP. So the Web is just a portion of the Internet, albeit a large portion, but the two terms are not synonymous and should not be confused.	WWW uses HTTP Protocol to transmit data. The Web also utilizes browsers, such as Internet Explorer or Firefox, to access Web documents called Web pages that are linked to each other via hyperlinks.

Internet is also called as *information superhighway* or cyberspace. As you travel the highway, you will encounter many different information communities. Information and its accessibility is actual treasure on the Internet!!

The Internet has changed ecosystem among mobile devices, computers and communications world. In past invention of the legacy systems telegraph, telephone, radio, and computers had laid foundation for this unprecedented integration of capabilities. The Internet is looked at helm of global broadcasting company, a medium for collaboration and interaction between individuals and their devise irrespective of geographic location. The Internet also represents one of the most successful examples of the benefits of sustained investment and commitment to research and development of information infrastructure.

The Internet is based upon client/server model as depicted in Figure 1.1. It basically contains two types of computers:

1. **Servers:** Servers are computers which provide services or information required by other computers. Servers run special software called Web Server software to respond to client's request. You will learn about them in the later Section of this Unit.

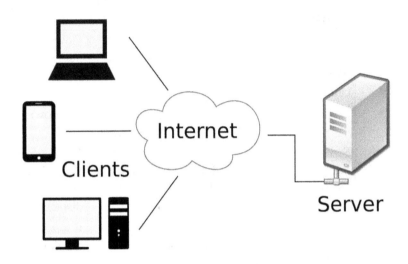

Figure 1.1: Client/Server Model

2. **Clients:** Computers that request information from the server are called Clients.

Do You Know?
Steve Wilhite of Compuserve debuted the GIFs in June 1987. But he didn't foresee this.

1.2.1.1 Understanding Internetwork

We use the term "internetwork," or sometimes just "Internet" with a lowercase " i " , to refer to an arbitrary collection of networks interconnected to provide some sort of host-to-host information delivery service. For example, a corporation with many sites might construct a private internetwork by interconnecting the LANs at their different sites with point-to-point links leased from the service provider. When we are talking about the global internetwork to which a comprehensive percentage of devices/networks are now connected, we call it the "Internet" with a capital "I". As we know basics first thing first, it is vital for you to learn about the principles of "lowercase i" internetworking, but we illustrate these ideas with real-world examples from the "big I" Internet.

An internetwork is an interconnected collection of such networks. Sometimes, to avoid ambiguity, we refer to the underlying networks that we are interconnecting as physical networks.

The Internet is a logical network built out of a collection of physical networks. In this context, a collection of Ethernets links connected via set of devices like bridges or switches would still be viewed as a single network.

1.2.1.2 Types of Networks

Parameter	Local Area Network (LAN)	Metropolitan Area Network (MAN)	Wide Area Network (WAN)
Definition	Covers a small geographical area like office, building, campus	Its size is between a LAN and WAN, and covers area inside a town or city	Covers a large geographical area
	Privately owned	Both privately owned and publically owned	Multiownership
Diameter	Size limited to few kilometres. Maximum distance=1.3km	Covers hundreds of kilometres. Maximum distance is less than 30-50km.	Diameter more than 100km. Maximum distance=30-50km
Topology	Commonly used symmetric topologies are bus, ring and star.	It has irregular topologies.	It has irregular topologies.
Data Rate Mbps	Data rate is typically 4-16Mbps in range. Speed is normally 100 or 1000Mbps	Data rate is in Mbps but less than that of LAN.	WANs have a lower data transfer rate compared to LANs
Channel links	They are multi access links.	They use broadcast channel.	They use point to point link.
Error	Error rate is less.	Error rate is higher than LAN but less than WAN	Error rate is thousand times that of LAN
Reliability	LAN cables are reliable	MAN cables are moderately reliable	WAN cables are less reliable
Protocols	Simple	Simple	Complex Example TCP/IP

1.2.1.3 Internet Servers

A prerequisite for the commercialization of the Internet was its ability to provide data in a user friendly manner and to store large volumes of data. It was essential that the contents of a file be displayed directly on the users' terminal instead of them having to download the file onto his computer and then view it. In today's era its popularly known as "cloud" setup where are applications running on the host computer and primarily wait for the users requests for providing data stored on it. The path breaking developments in the early 1990s that played a significant role in shaping of the Internet today are:

WAIS (Wide Area Information Server) : This was invention by Brewster Kahle and released by Thinking Machine Corporation. It is a distributed information system that allows simple natural language input, indexed searching and relevance feedback.

Gopher: Gopher was invented by Paul Linder and Marc McCahill of the University of Minnesota. It is a distributed information system that provides information to the user in the form of hierarchal menus. Handshake between the multiple Gophers on the Internet allows users to search information on different host computers using the same interface.

1.2.2 History of Internet

In 1969, Department of Defense (DoD) of United States started a network called ARPANET (Advanced Research Project Administration Network). It was an experiment carried out to reveal whether networking could be reliable or not. Objective of this network was setup for military to ensure that communication did not break down in the events of war. The DoD wanted to maintain contacts with military research contractors and universities in the event of war. The DoD also wanted these agencies to share software and hardware resources that they could not afford! Later, the military allowed universities to join the network. Students at these universities caught on to the network and developed much of the software that its present shapes.

APARNET was quickly agree to cover the entire American continent and became a big success. Every university in the country wanted to be part of this cloud! To better structure out things, network was diversified MILNET for managing military sites and APARNET for managing non military sites.

1.2.3 Growth of Internet

Internet has been found to doubles each year. Reasons for success:

1. Decisions not politically based
2. Internet is distributed in operations
3. Open standards, free (or inexpensive) software
4. Easy to operate

Figure below shows the growth of Internet.

	2005	2010	2013[a]
World population	6.5 billion	6.9 billion	7.1 billion
Not using the Internet	84%	70%	61%
Using the Internet	16%	30%	39%
Users in the developing world	8%	21%	31%
Users in the developed world	51%	67%	77%

1.2.4 Working of Internet

The most peculiar thing about the Internet is the way data is transferred from one computer to another.

This is what happens with every type of data (e.g. a Web page / e-mail) when it is transferred over the Internet:

● It is broken up into a whole lot of **same-sized pieces** (technically speaking **packets**).

● A **header** is added to each packet. This header explains the source and destination of the packet. Also how it will fit among the rest of the packets.

● Each packet is **sent from computer to computer** until it finds its way to its desired destination. During the movement, each computer decides where to send next packet. This could depend on number of things like how busy the other computers are when the packet was received. It is quite possible that packets may not all take the same route, but reach safely!

● At the destination, the **packets are examined**. In case any packet is missing or partially damaged, a message is sent asking for those packets to be sent again. This cycle continues until all desired packets have been received intact and message/data is complete.

● The packets are **reassembled** into their original form and presented further.

Do You Know?

In 2009, Satoshi Nakamoto released the first Bitcoin client and issued the first Bitcoins.

Figure 1.2 below depicts routing of packets in Internet.

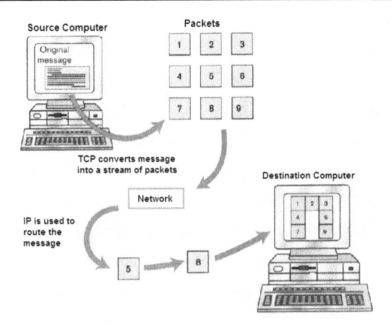

Figure 1.2: Working of Internet

Internet uses TCP/IP protocol for communication. TCP/IP (Transmission Control Protocol/Internet Protocol) specifies how computers connect, send, and receive information whereas IP specifies how packets are routed between two computers. Message is split into IP packets which contain following information:

● Pieces of message

● Information about sender

● Information about receiver

● Sequence number

● Error checking information

When the packet has been received by destination computer, it reassembles the message. In case any packet gets corrupted receiving computer sends request for corrupt packets back to the sender. Advantages of using packets can be summarized as follows:

● Error recovery

● Load distribution

● Flexibility

Do You Know?

The TCP/IP model does not have session or presentation lagers.

Lets discuss how an e-mail is delivered over Internet.

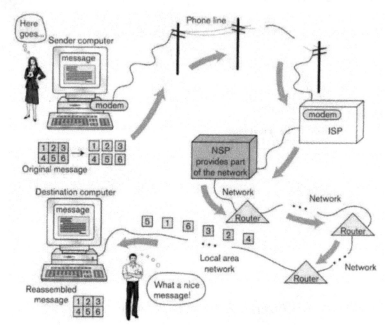

Figure 1.3: Delivery of E-mail on Internet

Figure 1.3 explains, detailed path e-mail message takes from one computer to another. Figure 1.3 illustrates the process of delivering of e-mail in which a message is split into packets, routed to destination through an Internet Service Provider (ISP), and an NSP, and reassembled.

1.2.5 Overview of TCP/IP and its Services

TCP/IP (Transmission Control Protocol/Internet Protocol) is the basic communication language or protocol of the Internet which has been used as a communications protocol. It can be understood as a two-layer program. The work of the higher layer (TCP layer) is to manage manages the assembling of a message or file into smaller packets that are transmitted over the Internet, and received by a TCP layer that reassembles the packets into the original message. Whereas the lower layer (Internet Protocol) handles the address part of each packet so that it gets to the right destination. As already discussed Internet is based on client/server model so TCP/IP uses the client/server model of communication in which a computer user (a client) requests and is provided a service (such as sending a Web page) by another computer (a server) in the network.

Communication of TCP/IP could be understood as a primarily point-to-point communication as each communication is from one point (or host computer) in the network to another point or host computer. We can visualize TCP/IP and the higher-level applications as "stateless" because each client request is considered as a new request unrelated to any previous one. This is quite different from an ordinary phone conversations where a dedicated connection is required for the whole call duration). Being stateless network paths are built on demand so that everyone can use them as per need. It is vital to highlight TCP layer itself is not stateless as far as any one message is concerned. Its connection remains in like fixed path until all packets in a message have been received.

Many Internet users are familiar with the even higher layer application protocols that use TCP/IP to get to the Internet. HyperText Transfer Protocol (HTTP), File Transfer Protocol (FTP), Telnet (Telnet), etc., let you logon to remote computers and the Simple Mail Transfer Protocol (SMTP) used for handling e-mails. These and other protocols are often packaged together with TCP/IP as a "suite."

Personal computer users with an analog phone modem connection to the Internet usually get to the Internet through the Serial Line Internet Protocol (SLIP) or the Point-to-Point Protocol (PPP). These protocols encapsulate the IP packets so that they can be sent over the dial-up phone connection to an access provider's modem.

Protocols related to TCP/IP include the User Datagram Protocol (UDP), which is used in place of TCP for special purposes. Also, note there are bunch of protocols used by devices/networks/host computers for exchanging router information. To name a few the Interior Gateway Protocol (IGP), the Exterior Gateway Protocol (EGP), Internet Control Message Protocol (ICMP) and the Border Gateway Protocol (BGP).

TCP/IP and its protocols at different layers have been depicted in figure 1.4.

You can see that TCP/IP has 4 layers as compared to OSI which had 7 layers. Like OSI network model, TCP/IP also has a network model. TCP/IP was on the path of development when the OSI standard was published and there was interaction between the designers of OSI and TCP/IP standards. The TCP/IP model is not same as OSI model. OSI is a seven-layered standard, but TCP/IP is a four-layered standard. The

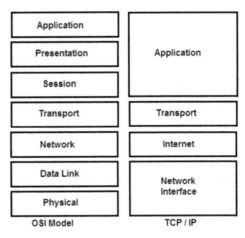

Figure 1.4: OSI and TCP/IP

OSI model has been very influential in the growth and development of TCP/IP standard, and that is why much OSI terminology is applied to TCP/IP. The Figure 1.4 compares the TCP/IP and OSI network models.

Do You Know?

The OSI model supports both connectionless and connection-oriented communication in the network layers..

The four layers of TCP/IP are:

1. Network Access Layer

TCP/IP design hides the function of this layer from users—its main objective is draw best route to push traffic across using mode of physical network (i.e., Ethernet, Optical, Token Ring, etc.). The functions performed at this level include encapsulating the IP datagram's into *frames* that are transmitted by the network. It also maps the IP addresses to the physical addresses used by the network. Thanks to TCP/IP addressing scheme it is possible to uniquely identify every computer on the network. This IP address is converted into whatever address is appropriate for the physical network over which the datagram is transmitted.

2. Internet Layer

The famous TCP/IP protocol at the Internet layer is the *Internet Protocol. IP* provides the basic packet delivery service for all TCP/IP networks. In addition to the physical node addresses used at the network access layer, the IP protocol implements a system of logical host addresses called IP addresses. IP addresses are used by the inter-network and higher layers to identify devices and to perform inter-network routing. The Address Resolution Protocol (ARP) is used to identify the physical address that matches a given IP address. IP is used by all protocols in the layers above and below it to deliver data. This implies all TCP/IP data flows through IP when it is sent and received, regardless of its final destination.

Internet Protocol (IP) is a *connectionless protocol.* This implies 'IP' does not exchange control information (called a *handshake*) to establish an end-to-end connection before transmitting data. In other hand, *connection-oriented protocol* exchanges control information with the remote computer to verify that it is ready to receive data before sending it. When the handshaking is successful, the computers are said to have established a *connection.* IP protocol relies on protocols in other layers to establish the connection in case connection-oriented services are required. IP also relies on protocols in another layer to provide error detection and error recovery. As it does not contain any error detection or recovery code it is sometimes called an *unreliable protocol.* Some of the functions performed at this layer are as follows:

1. Define the datagram, which is the basic unit of transmission in the Internet.
2. Define the Internet addressing scheme.
3. Move data between the Network Access Layer (NAT) and the host-to-host Transport Layer.
4. Route datagrams to remote hosts.
5. Fragment and reassemble datagrams.

3. Transport Layer (host-to-host layer)

The protocol layer just above the inter-network layer known as *host-to-host layer.* It is like *"referee"* in playground, i.e., layer is responsible for end-to-end data integrity. The two most important protocols employed at this layer are the

Transmission Control Protocol (TCP) and *User Datagram Protocol* (UDP). TCP provides reliable, full-duplex connections and reliable service by ensuring that data is resubmitted when transmission results in an error (end-to-end error detection and correction). TCP enables hosts to maintain multiple, simultaneous connections. UDP provides unreliable datagram service (connectionless) that enhances network throughput at the host-to-host transport layer. Both protocols deliver data between the *application layer* and the *inter-network layer*.

a. **User Datagram Protocol:** The *User Datagram Protocol* gives application programs direct access to a datagram delivery service, like the delivery service that IP provides. It is an unreliable, connectionless datagram protocol. "Unreliable" merely means that the protocol has no technique for verifying that the data reached the other end of the network correctly. Within your computer, UDP will deliver data correctly. When data to be transmitted in small, this protocol is ideal, moreover the overhead of creating connections and ensuring reliable delivery may be greater than the work of retransmitting the entire data set.

b. **Transmission Control Protocol:** Applications that require the host-to-host transport protocol to provide reliable data delivery use TCP as it verifies that the data is delivered across the network accurately and in the proper sequence. TCP is a *reliable, connection-oriented, byte-stream* protocol.

4. *Application Layer*

Widely known and implemented TCP/IP application layer protocols are FTP, HTTP, Telnet, and Simple Mail Transfer Protocol (SMTP). In addition to widely known protocols, the application layer includes the following protocols:

● **Domain Name Service (DNS):** Also called *name service*; this application maps IP addresses to the names assigned to network devices. Example: courtesy DNS service we do not have to memorze IP address of Websites!

● **Routing Information Protocol (RIP):** Routing is central to the way TCP/IP works. RIP is used by network devices to exchange routing information.

● **Simple Network Management Protocol (SNMP):** Its asset to any NMS (Network Management Station). Its protocol used to collect management information from network devices.

● **Network File System (NFS):** Working on Sun platform is not child's play, one need special skills to work on this platform. NFS is system developed by Sun Microsystems that enables computers to mount drives on remote hosts and operate them as if they were local drives.

1.2.6 Understanding HTTP

The most important protocol on Web is the **HyperText Transfer Protocol (HTTP)**. It is the application protocol that makes the Web work. Its application level protocol rides on top of the TCP layer in the protocol stack and is used by specific applications to talk to one another. In this case the applications are Web browsers and Web servers. These protocols are taken in detail in the discussions below.

Do not confuse HTTP with the HTML, as HTML is the scripting language used to create Web pages. Many times Web pages are called hypertext documents. Hypertext documents are the documents that contain links to connect them other documents or files. The user can activate these links (through a mouse button click, for example) and the target document will then be transferred on to the client machine and if it is a Web page, it would be displayed in the browser. These links can be placed on text, pictures, etc., in the hypertext document. A single Hypertext document can contain multiple hyperlinks. It is because of all this "linking" between the Web pages a virtual Web of connections is created.

Hypertext transfer protocol is a request response protocol. It is an application layer in TCP/IP protocol suite. It was originally developed to transfer files and data in distributed, collaborative, hypermedia information system. According to this protocol a process is run which create and store the resources like HTML image, files, etc. On request this process provides these resources and is called Web server. A Web server waits for request and response when required.

- Its main purpose is to transfer Web pages from one computer (Web server) to another computer (client server).
- It is useful to transfer Web pages containing links in an environment where there are rapid jumps among such hyperlink Web pages.
- It allows us to transfer a wide variety of data, such as text, image, audio, video or even the result of a query.
- It is used to access virtually all types of resources on Web.

Characteristics of HTTP

HTTP is a connectionless text-based protocol. Clients (Web browsers) send requests to Web servers for Web elements, such as Web pages and images. Please note, before an HTTP request can be made by a client, a new connection must be made to the server. After the request is serviced by a server, the connection between client and server across the Internet is disconnected. It is important to understand that a new connection is established between the client and the server each time when client makes a request.

> **Note:** Most protocols are connection-oriented, i.e., two computers communicating with each other keep the connection open over the Internet. HTTP does not however.

When you type a URL into a Web browser HTTP will work as follows:

1. In case URL contains a domain name (like www.yahoo.com) the browser will first connect to a domain name server and retrieves the corresponding IP address for the Web server. URL can be understood as the unique address of a file which can be accessed through Internet.

Note: URL has been taken in detail in a later sub-section.

2.   The Web browser connects to the Web server and sends an HTTP request for the desired Web page.

3.   The Web server receives the request and checks for the desired page. If the page exists, the Web server sends it. If the server cannot find the requested page, it will send an HTTP 404 error message. (404 means 'Page Not Found'). The Web browser receives the page back and the connection is closed. The browser then parses through the Webpage and looks for other page elements it needs to complete the Web page. These usually include images, applets, etc., for each element needed, the browser makes additional connections and HTTP requests to the server for each element. Once the browser has finished loading all images, applets, etc., the page will be displayed in the browser window.

Working of HTTP

● HTTP server process is created on a port which waits for clients to make a TCP connection.

● HTTP client initiates a TCP connection with HTTP server.

● HTTP server accepts the connection.

● Then HTTP client sends a request for a resource to the server.

● After receiving the request the server process the request and perform the desired task and sends a response back to the client.

● HTTP server closes the TCP connection.

● The HTTP client receives the response containing the information.

HTTP Message: There are two types of HTTP message.

(i)   Request Message: Message sent by the client.

(ii) Response Message: Message sent by the server.

Request Message: It consists of following parts:

Request Line
Header
Empty Line
Body(available for some message)

Request Line: It consists of three parts: Request type, URL and HTTP version. These three are separated by a space.

Request type: It indicates the type of request the client want to send. It is also known as methods. Some of the methods are following:

(i)   **Get-** It is specified when a client wants to retrieve a resource from server.

(ii) **Head-** It is used when the client wants to know header information about a resource but not the resource contain the response of the HEAD request contains only headers request and status line but not document content.

(iii) **Post:** It is used when a client wants to send some information to the server. The commonest form of the post method is to submit an HTML form to the server

(iv) **Put:** It is used to upload a new resource or replace an existing document.

(v) **Patch:** This is similar to the put method except that it specifies a list of difference that must be applied on the existing file.

(vi) **Copy:** This method is used to copy a file from one location to another.

(vii) **Move**: It is similar to copy method except that it deletes the source file.

(viii) **Delete:** This method is used to remove the document from the server.

(ix) **Link:** This is used to create a link or links from one document to another.

(x) **Options:** It is used to retrieve the set of method supported by the server. It usually checks whether a server is functioning properly before performing other task.

(xi) **Connect:** It is used to convert a request connection into the transparent TCP/IP tunnel.

(xii) **Trace:** It is used to instruct the Web server to echo the request back to client.

(xiii) **Unlink:** It is used to remove a link or links created by the Link method.

(xiv) **URL:** This is URL of the resource.

(xv) **HTTP Version:** This field specifies the version of the HTTP protocol being used. It can have the following values: HTTP/1.0 and HTTP/1.1.

Response Message: consists of following parts:

Status Line
Header
Empty Line
Body(available for some message)

o   **Status Line**: Status Line consists of three parts: HTTP Version, Status code and Status phrase. These three are separated by the space.

o   **HTTP Version**: This field specifies the version of the HTTP protocol being used. It can have the following values: HTTP/1.0 and HTTP/1.1.

o   **Status code:** It is a three digit code that indicates the status of the response. These are classified with respect to their functionality into five groups as discussed below.

1.   **1XX series (Informational):** It represents provisional responses. It is an informational resource. Some of its codes are:

Status code	Status phase	Description
100	Continue	The server receives the initial part and response back to client.
101	Switching	Server switches the protocol when receive the request from client.
102	Processing	Server receives the request which is currently under process.

2. **2XX series (Success):** It represents the clients request received, understood and accepted successfully.

Status code	Status phase	Description
200	Ok	This represents the request was valid and response depends on methods used.
201	Created	The request was successful and desired resource was created.
202	Accepted	The request was accepted for further processing.
203	Non-authoritative information	The server is not authoritative to information back.
204	No content	The body of response has no content.
205	Reset content	In this client needs to reset the document.
206	Partial content	Server sends partial content in response to the header.
207	Multi-status	Number of response codes depends on the number of request made.

3. **3XX (Redirectional):** this represents the additional actions must be taken by the client to complete the request.

Status code	Status phase	Description
300	Multiple choices	Client can follow multiple options for resource.
301	Moved permanently	Resource request no longer exists.
302	Found	Request is not found currently
303	See other	Method is possibly wrong.
304	Not modified	Request resource is not modified since last request.

4. **4XX Series (client error):** these codes are used to indicate the client request had an error and therefore it cannot be fulfilled.

Status code	Status phase	Description
400	Bad request	Request contains syntax error and cannot be fulfilled.
401	Unauthorized	The request has failed to be authorized.
403	Forbidden	Request was valid but server is refusing to respond to it.
404	Not found	Request resource was not found on the server.
405	Method not allowed	Method specified the request message is not supported by the resource.
406	Not acceptable	Requested resource can generate the content in the format mentioned.
408	Request time out	The server timed out waiting for the request.
409	Conflict	The request could not be processes due to conflict.
410	Gone	Requested resource is no longer available.
411	Length required	The length of the content which is required was not specified in the request message.
412	Precondition failed	Server fails to follow the preconditions of the request message.
413	Request entity too large	The request is too large for the server to process.
414	Request URI to long	Requested URI was too long for server to be processed.
415	Unsupported media type	Server does not support the media type specified.
416	Requested range is not satisfied	Server is unable to send the portion of the file is requested.
417	Expectation failed	Server fails to meet the values specified by the expect request header field.
422	Unprocessable entity	The request contains semantic errors and cannot be fulfilled.
423	Locked	The request resource is locked.
424	Failed dependency	The request fails due to the failure of previous request.

5. **5XX Series (Server Errors):** This code represents that the server encountered some problem and hence request cannot be satisfied at the given time.

Status code	Status phase	Description
500	Internal server error	A message indicating that a problem has occurred in the server.
501	Not implemented	The server fails to recognize the method specified.
502	Bad gateway	The server is gateway or proxy, has received and invalid response from the downstream server.
503	Service unavailable	The service is unavailable due to maintenance, shutting down overload.
504	Gateway time out	The server receives a timeout response from the downstream server.
505	HTTP Version not supported	Server fails to support the HTTP Version specified.

HTTP Headers

HTTP headers are very important part of both request message and response message. They mainly specify the characteristics of the resource requested and the data that are provided. For example, a client may want to accept image files only in some specified format. Similarly, the server may provide additional information about the resource being sent, such as the length of the message or the last modification date of the resource. Headers are separated by an empty line from the request and the message body. It consists of a single line or multiple lines. Each line is a single header of the following form:

Header-name: Header-value

The headers may be of two types:

- **HTTP Request header format:** The request header consists of three parts: General header, request header and entity header.

General Header
Request Header
Entity Header

- **HTTP Response header format:** The request header consists of three parts: General header, response header and entity header.

General Header
Response Header
Entity Header

General Header: HTTP general header provides information about the message themselves instead of what content they carry. They are mainly used to specify how the message is handled and processed.

Header Name	Description	Example
Cache-control	It shows whether the cache is used or not	Cache-control : max age = 10
Connection	It specifies whether the server should close the connection or not	Connection: close
Date	It shows the date and time when the message is originated	Date: Fri., 31jan 2014 08:12:31 GMT
MIME-version	MIME version used	MIME version: 1.0
Upgrade	Preferred communication protocol	Upgrade: HTTP/2.0
Transfer encoding	Type of transformation that has been used to transfer the message	Transfer-encoding: chunked
Warning	Specifies the status of message transfer	Warning: 199 Galaxy warning
Via	Intermediate host between the messages	Via: 1.0 fred 1.1 source .com

Request Header: It is only part of request message and contains the information about the client sending the request as well as data format that client expected.

Header Name	Description	Example
Accept-range	Range type of server support	Accept-range: bytes
Age	Age of the resource in the proxy	Age: 18
Public	List of methods	Public: head
Retry-after	Date after which the requested resource will be available	Retry-after: 60
Server	Name and version number of the server	Server: Apache/2.040

Entity Header: It is present in both request and response messages. It contains the information about the message body.

Header Name	Description	Example
Allow	List of valid methods	Allow: GET, HEAD, POST
Content-encoding	Type of encoding	Content-encoding: x-gzip
Content-language	Language of the content	Content-language: en
Content-length	Length of the response body in bytes	Content-length: 2453
Content-range	Location of the partial message	Content-range: bytes 10-15/25-35
Content-type	MIME type of content	Content-type: text/html
Etag	An identifier for the specific version	Etag: "678060c98se84 d83dd34e02d9"
Expires	Date and time the content will modified	Expires: Fri., 28 Feb. 2014 12:19:30 GMT
Last-modified	Last modification date of request resource	Last-modified: wed, 26 Feb. 2014 15:14:30 GMT

Do You Know?

The first GPS satellite was launched in 1978 and the full constellation of 24 became operational in 1995.

1.2.7 Noteworthy Statistics about Internet

Just have a look on the Figure 1. which provide insight to the way Internet is growing. Figure 1.5, 1.6 and 1.7 show the growing statistics of the Internet users in different parts of the world

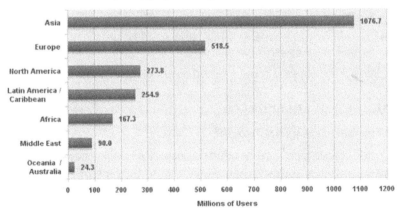

Figure 1.5: Internet Users

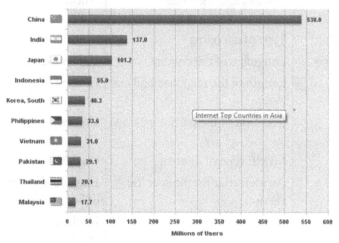

Figure 1.6 : Shows the growing rate of Internet users in Asia

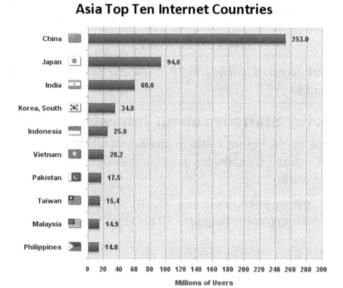

Figure 1.7 : Internet growth in different countries in Asia

1.2.8 Language of Internet

Does Internet have any language?

Internet World statistics presents its latest estimates for Internet users by language because of the importance of this research, and due to the lack of other sources. Internet World statistics publishes several tables and charts featuring analysis and details for the top ten languages and also for the top three languages in use by Internet users as shown in Figure 1.8.

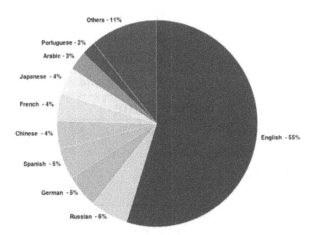

Figure 1.8 : Top 10 languages of Internet

1.2.9 Internet Management

Can you guess among biggies Bill Gates, Larry Page, and Jack Welch, who own Internet. Well none of them! There is no central control, management, or administration of the *Internet.* There are some noteworthy organizations that work day and night together in a relatively well-structured and roughly democratic environment to collectively participate in the development, research and management part of the Internet.

Internet management organizations are described, where the ASO, CCNSO, and GNSO are part of the ICANN.

- *ISOC* → *Internet Society*
- *IAB* → *Internet Architecture Board*
- *IETF* → *Internet Engineering Task Force*
- *IRTF* → *Internet Research Task Force*
- *ICANN* → *Internet Corporation for Assigned Names and Numbers*
- *IANA* → *Internet Assigned Numbers Authority*
- *NSI* → *Network Solutions*
- *Accredited Domain Name Registrars.*

Also couple of other organizations play a role in the management of the Internet is listed below.

Other Internet Organizations

- *W3C* → *World Wide Web Consortium*
- *Create A Usenet 8 newsgroup*
- *Create A Usenet Alt newsgroup*
- *Find IRC networks*
- *Find MUD servers*
- *Find mailing lists.*

Some other Internet (Commercial) Organizations

- *Google*
- *Linkedin*
- *eBay*

- *Amazon.com*
- *Twitter*
- *Wikipedia*

Review Time
1.   *What is the Internet?*
2.   *Discuss the growth of Internet.*
3.   *Who governs Internet?*
4.   *What is W3C?*

Do You Know?
Yahoo! derived its name from the word yahoo coined by Jonathan Swift in Gulliver's Travels, which means is a person who is repulsive in appearance and action, and is barely human.

1.3   Web Development Process and Strategies

There are numerous steps involve in the Website design and development process. For gathering initial information, to the formation of your Website, and lastly to maintenance to keep your Website up to date.

The main process will vary slightly from designer to designer:

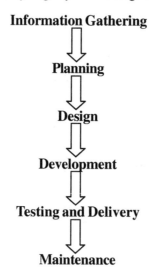

Information Gathering

Planning

Design

Development

Testing and Delivery

Maintenance

Let's discuss these phases in brief.

The first step in designing a booming Website is to gather information. Lots of things need to be taken into consideration when the look and feel for your site.

This first step is always the most important one. It involves a solid understanding of the company. It involves a good understanding of you what your business goals and dreams are, how the Internet can be utilized to help you achieve those goals.

It is more important that your Web designer starts by asking a lot of questions which help understand your business and your needs.

Certain things to be considered are:

- **Purpose:** What is the purpose of your site? Do you want to provide any information, promote any service, and sell any product?

- **Goals:** What do you hope to accomplish by building your Website? Two of the more common goals are either to share information or make money.

- **Target Audience:** Is there a specific group of people that will help you to reach your goals? It is helpful to picture the "ideal" person you want to visit your Website. You can also consider their age, sex or interests and this will later help determine the best design style for your site.

- **Content:** What kind of information will the target audience be looking for your Website? Are they looking for specific information, for particular product or service, and online ordering?

Phase Two: Planning

Using the information gathered from phase one. This is time to put together a plan for your Website. It is the point where a Website map is developed.

The Website map is a list of all main topic areas of the site and sub-topics. This serves used as a guide as to what content will be on the site. It is essential to developing a consistent, easy to understand navigational system. The end-user of the Website, i.e., your customer will be kept in mind when designing your site. A good user interface creates an easy to navigate Website.

During the planning phase your Web designer will also help you to decide what technologies should be implemented in your Website.

Phase Three: Design

Drawing from the information gathered up to this point. This is the time to determine the look and feel of your site. You mostly target audience is one of the key factors taken into consideration. The site aimed at teenagers, for example it will look much different than one meant for a financial institution. The part of the design phase is also important to incorporate elements, such as the company logo or colors to help strengthen the identity of your company.

Web designer creates one or more prototype designs for your Website. It is typically .jpg (or jpeg, an acronym for Joint Photographic Experts Group) image of what the final design will look like. After that you will be sent an e-mail with the mock-ups for your Website. Other designers take it a step further by giving you access to a secure area of their Website meant for customers to view work in progress.

Your designer should allow you to view your project throughout the design and development phases. The most important reason for this is that it gives you the opportunity to express your likes and dislikes on the Website design.

The communication between both you and your designer is crucial to ensure that the final Website will match your needs and taste. This is important that you work closely with your designer, exchanging ideas, until you arrive at the final design for your Website.

Phase Four: Development

Developmental stage is the point where the Website itself is created. Your Web designer will take all of the individual graphic elements from the prototype and use them to create the actual and functional Website.

This is typically done by first developing the home page then followed by a "shell" for the interior pages. This shell serves as a template for the content pages of your site, as it contains the main navigational structure for the Website. The shell has been created as your designer will take your content and distribute it throughout the site in the appropriate areas.

The elements, such as the Content Management System like Word Press is interactive contact forms or e-commerce shopping carts are implemented and made functional during this phase. This entire time your designer should continue to make your in-progress Website available to you for viewing. You can suggest any additional changes or corrections you would like to have done.

A successful Website requires an understanding of frontend Website development. It involves writing valid HTML / CSS code that complies with current Web standards, maximizing functionality, as well as accessibility for as large an audience as possible.

Phase Five: Testing and Delivery

Your Web designer will attend to the final details and test your Website. It will test things, such as the complete functionality of forms or other scripts. The last testing for last minute compatibility issues, i.e., viewing differences between different Web browsers. It ensures that your Website is optimized to be viewed properly in the most recent browser.

An efficient Web designer is one who is well-versed in current standards for Website design and development. Basic technologies currently used are HTML and CSS. As the part of testing, your designer should check to be sure that all of the code written for your Website validation. The Valid code means that your site meets the current Web development standards. It is helpful when checking for issues, such as cross-browser compatibility as mentioned above.

When your Web designer finally approved then it is time to deliver the Website. An FTP (File Transfer Protocol) is used to upload the Website files to your server. Some of the Web designers offer domain name registration and Web hosting services as well. Have recommendations as to where you can host your Website. Once these accounts have been setup then your Website uploaded to the server. Then Website should be put through one last run through. It is just precautionary to confirm that all files have been uploaded correctly.

Phase Six: Maintenance

The development of your Website is not necessarily over. One way to bring repeat visitors to your site is to offer new content/products on a regular basis. The Web designers will be more happy to continue working together with you, to update the information on your Website. Most designers offer maintenance packages at reduced rates. This is based on how often you anticipate making changes or additions to your Website.

It is totally up to you as far as how comfortable you feel with updating your Website. Most of the people prefer to have all the control so that they can make updates to their own Website the minute they decide to do. And the others prefer to hand off the Website entirely. As they have enough tasks on hand those are more important for them to handle directly.

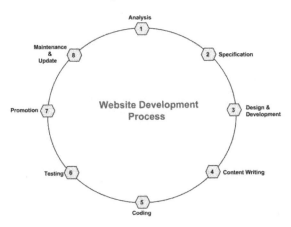

Figure 1.9 : Web Development Process

Figure 1.9 depict s Website development process which individual and corporate in deciding strategies to develop their Website.

1.3.1 Websites Development Strategies for Individual and Corporate

A Website is a set of related Web pages that have a common domain and are hosted on the same server. The computer on which these Web pages are hosted is called Web Server.

1.3.2 Discuss Web Applications, Web Project and Web Team

Projects can be implicit as the process to create a unique result with limited resources and time. To handle a project, proper project management is required in order to plan, control, execute and finally close the project.

Web Projects: Web Projects are defined as the projects which are particular for different types of Website. The Website can be B2B, B2C, and C2C. The needs and requirements of such Websites are different. The person having a technical skill can work on these projects but he/she has to work in coordination with the ultimate user of this project.

These are the steps to make a good Web project.

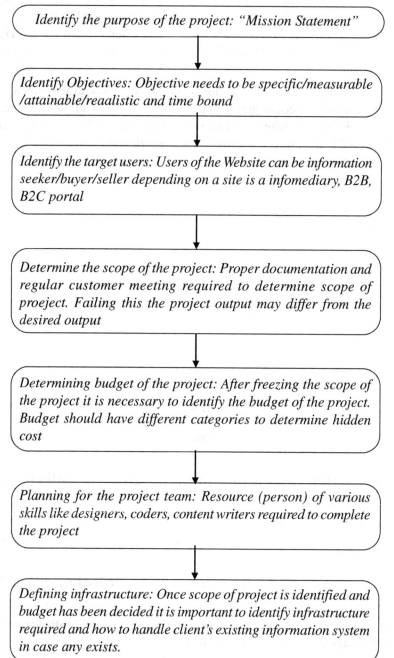

Identify the purpose of the project: "Mission Statement"

Identify Objectives: Objective needs to be specific/measurable /attainable/reaalistic and time bound

Identify the target users: Users of the Website can be information seeker/buyer/seller depending on a site is a infomediary, B2B, B2C portal

Determine the scope of the project: Proper documentation and regular customer meeting required to determine scope of proeject. Failing this the project output may differ from the desired output

Determining budget of the project: After freezing the scope of the project it is necessary to identify the budget of the project. Budget should have different categories to determine hidden cost

Planning for the project team: Resource (person) of various skills like designers, coders, content writers required to complete the project

Defining infrastructure: Once scope of project is identified and budget has been decided it is important to identify infrastructure required and how to handle client's existing information system in case any exists.

Difference Between Traditional and Web Projects

1. **Skill Set of a Project Manager:** Traditional project manager requires to be more focused on administrative details, such as resource availability and duration of tasks whereas the Web project manager's skill set needs to be dissimilar. He/she not only needs to have knowledge of primary discipline, such as Web best practices like information, architecture, and user experience. He/she also to be technically knowledgeable with a good background of descriptive statistics, probability, estimation, hypothesis testing.

2. **Vision:** In case of the traditional project priorities, requirements, current status you do not require constant management whereas in a Web project the Web project manger needs to continuously translate vision to project members. Several kinds of functional/technical requirements and constraint need to be translated into the business requirement.

3. **Schedule:** Incase of the traditional project schedule is well-structured and non-negotiable whereas in case of Web project the timeline is accelerated so that it is designed to meet various uncertain demands as Web is to be dynamic.

4. **Approach used:** In case of the traditional project the path is sequential like a waterfall model. It needs to complete one task before starting the next. As in case of Web project some tasks need to be done in parallel and also need order to accommodate evolving functional requirements.

5. **Price Structure:** The traditional projects have a well known price structure. As the Web projects can be prefabricated into different tiered price package.

Web Team

Web Team includes the Web masters who pay include persons having tasks ranging from coding the page to maintaining a Web server. Firstly it was the responsibility of one person who could write HTML script. Most of the times people who worked on the Website come from different department all over the company but as the Web environment has become competitive company keeps good budget for Website development and many times outsource the project to independent vendors. Several service companies like design shops and application development shops have developed that can increase interactivity of the Website. It provides a personalized experience to the user. E-Commerce and M-Commerce are gaining speed as Web team is expanding and can be divided into two categories client side and server side team. Client side Web teams are generally integral part of the company used to integrate the various pages of the Website where as Server side team is hired by the company to develop a Website.

As for any other business periodical review of Web team is required for long term gain. Some of the members of the Web team needs to be core and some are extended members who work on the value added services of the Website e.g. security guard who provides physical security to Web server.

1.3.3 Emerging technologies for Developing Websites

To be emerging technology must not yet be universally accepted by the Web community, its acceptance must be steadily increasing. The level of acceptance can be low, if it is steadily low and not increasing, it could not be considered emerging. The level of acceptance can also be high, if it is extremely high, if its popularity is steadily increasing. It would be considered an established technology and no longer emerging. That is why it is a good idea to keep updating the list of technologies that can be measured emerging.

1.   **HTML 5:** HTML5 aims to address the needs of the modern Web, by some extensive support for programmatic interaction between content and the local computer. HTML includes Application Programming Interfaces (APIs) to draw arbitrary graphics in the new canvas, your position on the globe, cache code and data. Offload compute-intensive tasks to keep the interactive portion of the browser responsive.

2.   **AJAX:** Asynchronous JavaScript and XML is a group of technologies used to create asynchronous Web applications.

3.   **API**: Application programming interface is a specification used to allow software components to communicate with each other.

4.   **Biometric Authentication**: Process of using unique physical / behavioral traits as a method to confirm the identity and determine the access profile of a person. As we take an example of face recognition through a Web camera can be used in place of a password to unlock a computer.

5.   **Microsoft Azure:** This is cloud services operating system by Microsoft. It supports ASP.NET, Java, PHP, Ruby and SOAP, ReST, and XML protocols.

6.   **RSS Feeds**: A new technology that allows the server-side is able to keep track of and deliver fresh content based on a client request.

1.3.4 Cyber Law

Cyber Law/Internet law is a term that encapsulates legal issues related to use of Internet. It is less a distinct field of law than intellectual property or contract law. It is a domain covering many areas of law and regulation. The leading topics include Internet access and usage freedom of expression, privacy and jurisdiction. There are intellectual properties in general, including rules on fair use, copyright and special rules on copy protection for digital media. The area of software patents is controversial and still evolving in Europe and elsewhere.

The related topics of end user license agreements, software licenses, free software licenses and open-source licenses can involve professional liability of individual developers, discussion of product liability warranties, trade secrets, contract law and intellectual property. In various countries areas of the computing and communication industries are regulated often strictly by government.

There are rules on the uses to which computers and computer networks may be put in particular there are rules on unauthorized access, the data privacy and spamming. There are limits on the use of encryption and of equipment which may be used to defeat copy protection schemes. Export of Hardware and Software between certain states is controlled.

There are some laws governing trade on the Internet, consumer protection, taxation and advertising. There are laws on rules on public access to government information, censorship versus freedom of expression and individual access to information held on them by private ones. There are laws on what data must be retained for law enforcement and what may not be gathered or retained for privacy reasons.

In some circumstances and jurisdictions computer communications may be used in evidence and to establish contracts. The new methods of tapping and surveillance made possible by computers have wildly differing rules on how they may be used by law enforcement bodies and as evidence in court.

The Computerized voting technology from polling machines to the Internet and mobile phone voting raise a host of legal issues.

1.4 Accessing Internet

Internet access joins individual computer terminals, mobile devices, and computer networks to the Internet enabling users to access Internet services, such as e-mail and the World Wide Web (WWW). The Internet Service Providers (ISPs) offer Internet access through various technologies that offer a wide range of data signaling rates.

Consumer use of the Internet first became popular through dial-up Internet access in the 1990s. The first decade of the 21st century many consumers used faster broadband Internet access technologies.

Do You Know?

The IEEE 802.11 Wi-Fi Wireless communication standard was invented for LANs.

1.4.1 Wireless Connectivity Options

a. Wi-Fi

Wi-Fi is a trade name for a Wireless Local Area network (WLAN) that uses one of the IEEE 802.11 standards. This is a trademark of the Wi-Fi Alliance. The individual homes and businesses often use Wi-Fi to connect laptops and smart phones to the Internet. The Wi-Fi Hotspots may be found in coffee shops and various other public establishments. The Wi-Fi is used to create campus-wide and city-wide wireless networks. The Wi-Fi networks are built using one or more wireless routers called access points. The **Ad hoc** computer to computer Wi-Fi networks are also possible. Wi-Fi network is connected to the larger Internet using DSL or cable modem and other Internet access technologies. The data rates range from 6 to 600 Mbit/s. The

Wi-Fi service range is fairly short typically 20 to 250 m or from 65 to 820 feet. Both data rate and range are quite variable depending on the location, Wi-Fi protocol, building construction frequency and interference from other devices. Directional antennas and with careful engineering Wi-Fi can be extended to operate over distances of up to several km. See Wireless ISP below.

b. Wireless ISP

Wireless Internet service providers typically employ low-cost IEEE 802.11 Wi-Fi radio systems can link up remote locations over great distances, i.e., long-range Wi-Fi. It may use other high-power radio communications systems as well. The Traditional 802.11b is an unlicensed omni-directional service designed to span between 100 and 150 m. By focusing the radio signal using a directional antenna 802.11b can operate reliably over a distance of many km. The technology's line-of-sight requirements hamper connectivity in areas with hilly or heavily foliated terrain. Compared to hard-wired connectivity there are security risks. Data rates are significantly slower 2 to 50 times slower. The network can be less stable due to interference from other wireless devices and networks weather, and line-of-sight problems. There are currently a number of companies that provide this service.

Motorola Canopy (a wireless networking system) and other proprietary technologies offer wireless access to rural and other markets that are hard to reach using Wi-Fi/WiMAX.

c. WiMAX

Worldwide Interoperability for Microwave Access (WIMAX) is a set of interoperable implementations of the IEEE 802.16 family of wireless-network standards certified by the WIMAX. It enables the delivery of last mile wireless broadband access as an alternative to cable and DSL. The original IEEE 802.16 standard now called **Fixed WiMAX.** It was published in 2001 and provided 30 to 40 megabit per second data rates. The Mobility support was added in 2005. The 2011 update provides data rates up to 1 Gbit/s for fixed stations. The WiMax offers a metropolitan area network with a signal radius of about 50 km far surpassing the 30-metre (100-foot) wireless range of a conventional Wi-Fi local area network. The WiMAX signals also penetrate building walls much more effectively than Wi-Fi.

d. Satellite Broadband

Satellite Internet service provides fixed or portable and mobile Internet access (See Figure 1.10). This is among the most expensive forms of broadband Internet access. The choice available in some remote areas. The data rates range from 2 kbit/s to 1 Gbit/s downstream and from 2 kbit/s to 10 Mbit/s upstream. The Satellite communication typically requires a clear line of sight. It will not work well through trees and other vegetation and is adversely affected by rain, moisture and snow known as rain fade and may require a fairly large carefully aimed directional antenna.

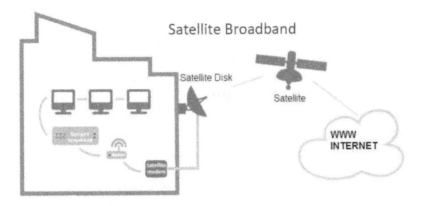

Figure 10 : Satellite broadband

e. *Mobile Broadband*

Mobile broadband is the marketing term for wireless Internet access delivered through mobile phone towers to computers, mobile phones called cell phones in North America and South Africa and other digital devices using portable modems. Mobile services allow more than one device to be connected to the Internet using a single cellular connection using a process called tethering. Modem may be built into laptop computers, mobile phones, tablets and other devices. Added to some devices using PC cards, USB modems, USB sticks or dongles, or separate wireless modems can be used.

1.4.2 Wireline Connectivity Options

a. *Dial-up Access*

Dial-up Internet access uses a modem and a phone call placed over the Public Switched Telephone Network (PSTN) to connect to a pool of modems operated by an ISP. Modem converts a computer's digital signal into an analog signal that travels over a phone line's local loop until it reaches a telephone company's switching facilities or central office where it is switched to another phone line that connects to another modem at the remote end of the connection.

Operating on a single channel a dial-up connection monopolizes the phone line and is one of the slowest methods of accessing the Internet. The dial-up is often the only form of Internet access available in rural areas as it requires no new infrastructure beyond the already existing telephone network to connect to the Internet. Dial-up connections do not exceed a speed of 56 kbit/s as they are primarily made using modems that operate at a maximum data rate of 56 kbit/s downstream (towards the end user) and 34 or 48 kbit/s upstream.

b.   *Local area Network*

The Local Area Networks (LANs) provide Internet access to computers and other devices in a limited area, such as school, home, computer laboratory or office building via an upstream link to an Internet service provider. The upstream links may be established by a variety of technologies, such as point-to-point protocol over Ethernet. LANs may provide high data rates that typically range from 10 to 1000 Mbit/s actual Internet access speed is limited by the upstream link. The LANs may be wired or wireless. The Ethernet over twisted pair cabling and Wi-Fi are the two most common technologies used to build LANs today but ARCNET Token Ring, FDDI, Local talk and other technologies were used in the past.

Mainly Internet access today is through a LAN. Often a very small LAN with just one or two devices attached. While LANs are an important form of Internet access this raises the question of how and at what data rate the LAN itself is connected to the rest of the global Internet. This technologies described below are used to make these connections.

Do You Know?
Ethernet over twisted pair cabling and Wi-Fi are the two most common transmission technologies in use for LANs.

c.   *Broadband access*

The Map in Figure 1.11 presents an overview of broadband affordability as the relationship between average yearly income per capita and the cost of a broadband subscription. The term broadband includes a broad range of technologies all of which provide higher data rate access to the Internet.

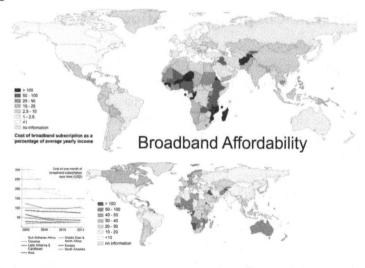

Figure 11 : Broadband Affordability in 2011

Source: *Information Geographies at the Oxford Internet Institute.*

d. Multilink dial-up

The multilink dial-up provides increased bandwidth by channel bonding multiple dial-up connections and accessing them as a single data channel. This requires two or more modems, phone lines and dial-up accounts. An ISP that supports multilinking and of course any line, and data charges are also doubled. This inverse multiplexing option was briefly popular with some high-end users before ISDN, DSL and other technologies became available. The Diamond and other vendors created special modems to support multilinking.

e. Integrated Services Digital Network

Integrated Services Digital Network (ISDN) is a switched telephone service capable of transporting voice and digital data is one of the oldest Internet access methods. It has been used for voice, video conferencing, and broadband data applications. It was very popular in Europe, but less common in North America. ISDN use peaked in the late 1990s before the availability of DSL and cable modem technologies.

Basic rate ISDN has two 64 kbit/s bearer or B channels. Channels can be used separately for voice or data calls or bonded together to provide a 128 kbit/s service. The Multiple ISDN lines can be bonded together to provide data rates above 128 kbit/s. The Primary rate ISDN known as ISDN-PRI has 23 bearer channels (64 kbit/s each) for a combined data rate of 1.5 Mbit/s (US standard). The ISDN E1 (European standard) line has 30 bearer channels and a combined data rate of 1.9 Mbit/s.

f. Leased lines

Leased lines are dedicated lines used primarily by ISPs and other large enterprises to connect LANs and campus networks to the Internet using the existing infrastructure of the public telephone network or other providers. Delivered using wire, optical fiber, leased lines are used to provide Internet access directly as well as the building blocks from which several other forms of Internet access are created.

g. Cable Internet access

Cable Internet access or cable modem access provides Internet access via hybrid fiber coaxial wiring originally developed to carry television signals. In a cable modem termination system all nodes for cable subscribers in a neighborhood connect to a cable company's central office, known as the head end. Cable company then connects to the Internet using a variety of means usually fiber optic cable or digital satellite and microwave transmissions. DSL, broadband cable provides a continuous connection with an ISP.

Downstream, i.e., the direction toward the user bit rates can be as much as 400 Mbits/s for business connections and 250 Mbit/s for residential service in some countries. Upstream traffic, i.e., originating at the user ranges from 384 kbit/s to more than 20 Mbit/s. Broadband cable subscribers share the same local line, communications may be intercepted by neighboring subscribers. The Cable networks regularly provide encryption schemes for data traveling to and from customers but these schemes may be thwarted.

h.   *Digital subscriber line (DSL, ADSL, SDSL, and VDSL)*

Digital Subscriber Line (DSL) service provides a connection to the Internet through the telephone network. DSL can operate using a single phone line without preventing normal use of the telephone line for voice phone calls. DSL uses the high frequencies while the low (audible) frequencies of the line are left free for regular telephone communication.

DSL originally stood for digital subscriber loop. The term digital subscriber line is widely understood to mean Asymmetric Digital Subscriber Line(ADSL) the most commonly installed variety of DSL. The data throughput of consumer DSL services typically ranges from 256 kbit/s to 20 Mbit/s in the direction to the customer (downstream) depending on DSL technology. The data throughput in the upstream direction, i.e., in the direction to the service provider is lowers than that in the downstream direction, i.e., to the customer hence the designation of asymmetric. With a Symmetric Digital Subscriber Line (SDSL), the downstream and upstream data rates are equal.

1.4.3 Internet Plan

Internet plans differ in terms of the following main aspects:
- Data download size
- Data download speed
- Costs
- Contract length

Key considerations when choosing the Internet plan are:
- Where you intend to use the Internet
    - o   At home (ADSL, cable or dial-up) or
    - o   Out and about (wireless)
- What you tend to use the Internet for:
    - o   General e-mail and Web surfing
    - o   Downloading large files such as music, video, playing games
- How often you use the Internet
- How many users at your home will be using the connection

1.4.4 Internet Cost

How much will my Internet cost?

Internet connection can include the following costs:
- **One-off hardware costs:** i.e., you may need to purchase a modem or wireless router.

- **One-off installation fees:** required to setup the connection at your home.

- **Ongoing monthly service fees**: a monthly fee covering your subscription.

- **Additional data fees**: some providers might charge you if you exceed your download limits, other providers respond to excessive downloads by slowing down the connection speed.

1.4.5 Internet Service Providers (ISPs)

The **Internet Service Provider** (**ISP**) is an organization that provides services for accessing, using, or participating in the Internet (See Figure 1.12). Internet service providers may be organized in various forms, such as commercial, community-owned, non-profit, or otherwise privately owned. Internet services typically provided by ISPs include Internet access, Internet transit, domain name registration, Web hosting, collocation.

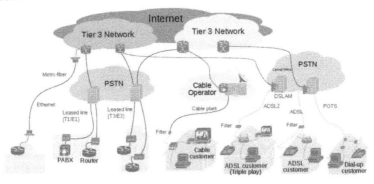

Figure 1.12: ISP

1.4.6 Internet IP address

An **Internet Protocol address** or **IP address** is a numerical label assigned to each device (e.g., computer, printer) participating in a computer network that uses the Internet Protocol for communication. An IP address serves two principal functions: host or network interface identification and location addressing. Its role has been characterized as follows:

"A name indicates what we seek. An address indicates where it is. A route indicates how to get there."

The designers of the Internet Protocol defined an IP address as a 32-bit number consisting of 4 octets and this system, known as Internet Protocol Version 4 (IPv4), is still in use today. However, due to the enormous growth of the Internet and the predicted depletion of available addresses, a new version of IP (IPv6), using 128 bits for the address, was developed in 1995. IPv6 was standardized as RFC 2460 in 1998, and its deployment has been ongoing since the mid-2000s.

IP addresses are binary numbers, but they are usually stored in text files and displayed in human-readable notations, such as 172.16.254.1 (for IPv4), and 2001:db8:0:1234:0:567:8:1 (for IPv6).

The Internet Assigned Numbers Authority (IANA) manages the IP address space allocations globally and delegates five Regional Internet Registries (RIRs) to allocate IP address blocks to local Internet registries (Internet service providers) and other entities.

Do You Know?
Tim Berners-Lee is known father of WWW.

1.5 Quality Assurance

Quality Assurance (QA) can be understood as the way of preventing mistakes or any kind of defects in manufactured products. This can help in avoiding problems when delivering solutions or services to customers. Quality Assurance can be applied to physical products in pre-production to verify whether it meets specifications and requirements. It can be used during manufacturing production runs by validating lot samples meet specified quality controls. **Quality Assurance** can also be applied to check whether software features and functionality meet business objectives. It also checks whether the code is relatively bug free prior to shipping or releasing new software products and versions.

1.5.1 Introduction of QA and Testing

Quality Assurance refers to administrative and procedural activities implemented in a quality system so that requirements and goals for a product, service or activity can be fulfilled accurately. It could be understood as the systematic measurement, comparison with a standard, monitoring of processes and an associated feedback loop that confers error prevention. This can be contrasted with quality control, which is focused on process output.

Two principles that are always included in Quality Assurance are:

1. **"Fit for purpose":** This implies that the product should be suitable for the intended purpose. Quality assurance includes management of the quality of raw materials, assemblies, products and components, services related to production, and management, production and inspection processes, etc.,

   It should be noted that suitable quality is determined by product users, clients or customers so they should always directly or indirectly be involved in quality testing. It should be understood that quality is not related to cost so descriptors, such as "high" and "poor" are not applicable. For example, a low priced product such as plastic glass may be viewed as a high quality product because it is disposable.

1.5.2 Types of Testing

Software testing could be understood as the process of evaluation a software item to detect differences between given input and expected output. It can be used to assess the feature of a software item. Testing helps to assess the quality of the product.

This process should be done during the development process. Software testing could also be understood as a verification and validation process.

Verification

Verification could be understood as the process to ensure that the product satisfies the conditions imposed at the start of the development phase. This helps to make sure that the product behaves the way we want it to behave.

Validation

Validation could be understood as the process that ensures that the product satisfies the specified requirements at the end of the development phase. Or we can say that ensures that the product is built as per customer requirements.

Basics of software testing

There are two basics of software testing: **Black box testing** and **White box testing.**

Blackbox Testing: Black box testing could be understood as a testing technique that ignores the internal mechanism of the system and just focuses on the output generated against any input and execution of the system. **Blackbox Testing** is also called functional testing.

Whitebox Testing : White box testing is a testing technique that takes into account the internal mechanism of a system. It is also called structural testing and glass box testing.

Black box testing is often used for validation and white box testing is often used for verification.

Do You Know?
The first computer mouse was wooden.

Types of testing

There are many types of testing like

1. Unit Testing
2. Integration Testing
3. Functional Testing
4. System Testing
5. Stress Testing
6. Performance Testing
7. Usability Testing
8. Acceptance Testing
9. Regression Testing
10. Beta Testing

1. Unit Testing

Unit testing can be understood as the testing of an individual unit or group of related units. It falls under the second class of testing, i.e., white box testing. It is often done by the programmer to test whether for given input the output is as per expectation or not.

2. Integration Testing

In case of Integration testing a group of components are combined to produce output. We can also test the interaction between software and hardware using integration testing if software and hardware components have any relation. It may fall under both white box testing and black box testing.

3. Functional Testing

Functional testing is the testing that is used to ensure that the specified functionality required in the system requirements works. It falls under the class of black box testing.

4. System Testing

System testing is the testing to ensure that software will work under different environments. System testing is done when system is fully implemented. It falls under the class of black box testing.

5. Stress Testing

Stress testing is the testing which evaluates the behavior of system under unfavorable conditions. This testing is conducted at beyond limits of the specifications. It falls under the category of black box testing.

6. Performance Testing

Performance testing is the testing which is used to assess the speed and effectiveness of the system, and to make sure it is generating results within a specified time as in performance requirements. It comes under the class of black box testing.

7. Usability Testing

Usability testing is used to determine the usability of the GUI which includes its looks and interactivity. How the GUI is user-friendly? How easily can the client learn? After learning how to use, how proficiently can the client perform? How pleasing is it to use its design? This falls under the category of black box testing.

8. Acceptance Testing

Acceptance testing is a type of testing often done by the customer to ensure that the delivered product meets the requirements and works as the customer expected. It falls under the category of black box testing.

9. Regression Testing

Regression testing could be understood as the testing after modification of a system or any of its components or related units. This is used to ensure that the modification is working correctly and is not damaging or imposing other modules to produce any unexpected results. It comes under the class of black box testing.

10. Beta Testing

Beta testing is a testing which is done by end users or any team outside development many times by publicly releasing full pre-version of the product. The aim of this kind of testing is to cover unexpected errors. It comes under the class of black box testing.

Do You Know?

Phillip Katz invented the ZIP file in 1986, and it was first implemented with the PKZip program for Katz's company, PKWare, Inc.

1.6 Frequent Terms in Web World

1.6.1 E-commerce

Electronic commerce is commonly known as **E-commerce** or **eCommerce.** It is a type of industry where the buying and selling of products or services which are conducted over electronic systems. Electronic commerce uses technologies, such as mobile commerce, electronic funds transfer, supply chain management, Internet marketing, online transaction processing, Electronic Data Interchange (EDI), inventory management systems, and automated data collection systems. E-Commerce today uses World Wide Web during transaction's life cycle and can be initiated through different media, such as e-mail, mobile devices, social media, and telephones, etc.,

1.6.2 Search Engine

A **Web search engine** could be understood as a software system that has been designed to search for information on the World Wide Web. The search results of Search Engine are generally presented in a line of results often called SERPS (Search Engine Results Pages). Some search engines can also be used to search data available in databases or open directories. Most of the Web directories are maintained only by human editors however search engines maintain real-time information by running an algorithm on a Web crawler.

1.6.3 Databases used in Web Application

A Web database could be understood as a system for storing information that can then be accessed via a Website. For example, An online community may have a database that stores details like username, password of all its members. You will find that the most commonly used database system for the Internet is MySQL as it can easily integrate with PHP which is one of the most widely used server side programming languages.

At its most simple level we can visualize a Web database as a set of one or more tables that contain data. Each table may include different fields for storing various type of information. These tables are then manipulated to make data useful and interesting. Most of the tables have a primary key which must be unique for each entry and will allow unambiguous selection of data.

Such Web database can be used for different purposes. Each field defined in a table needs to have a defined data type. For example, Numbers/Strings/Dates can all be inserted into a Web database. We need to choose a proper database design that involves choosing the correct data type for each field. This helps to reduce memory consumption and increase the speed of access. Unlike small databases big Web databases can grow to millions of entries and need to be well designed to work effectively.

Top 3 Web Databases

1. *MySQL Community Server*

This DBMS gets the number one nod mainly because the community version is free and is a great platform to begin. There are many commercial versions of MySQL for sale.

2. *Microsoft Access*

Microsoft Access have some key similarities to MySQL. It helps you design a table or task visually. Access has its on prons and cons. Access does not need two separate installations (one for the DBMS and one for the design tool) as all comes as a single application. Some of the limitations are: (1) It is nearly not flexible for different operating systems. (2) Number of concurrent connections Access can handle before performance degrades.

Do You Know?
9 out of every 1,000 computers are infected with spam.

3. *Oracle Express Edition*

Oracle Express has many tools and a separate server application. It also has many more operating system options as compared to Microsoft SQL Server Express.

1.6.4 Web browsers

When we want to drive a bike we need petrol similarly to access Internet we need tools like *Web browser.* Technically speaking Web browser could be understood as a software application which helps users to display and interact with text/images/videos/music/games and other information typically located on a Web page at a Website on the WWW cloud.

Web page includes hyperlinks to other Web pages at the same or different Website. It is a handy tool which allow user quickly and easily access information which is provided on many Web pages. You can find many Web browsers. Some of currently used browsers are Internet Explorer, Google Chrome, Mozilla Firefox, Safari, Opera, Bing, etc.

Web browsers can be understood as the most commonly used HTTP user agent.

They browsers are typically used to access the World Wide Web. We can also use them to access information provided by Web servers in private networks or content in file systems.

These Web browsers interact with Web servers primarily using HTTP to fetch Web page. This protocol allows Web browsers to submit information to Web servers as well as fetch Web pages from them. The most commonly used HTTP is HTTP/ 1.1, which is fully defined in RFC 2616.

Just like all of us Web pages also have address, i.e., Web pages are located by means of a URL (Uniform Resource Locator). This can be be treated as an address which begins with *http:* which implies HTTP access.

Most of the browsers support variety of other URL types, such as

1.   *gopher:* for Gopher (a hierarchical hyperlinking protocol)

2.   *ftp:* for FTP (File Transfer Protocol),

3.   *rtsp:* for RTSP (Real-Time Streaming Protocol),

4.   *https:* for HTTPS (an SSL encrypted version of HTTP).

Initially Web browsers supported only a very simple version of HTML. However as Internet grew robust development of proprietary Web browsers led to the development of non-standard dialects of HTML, leading to problems with Web interoperability. Now days, modern Web browsers support a combination of standards- and defacto-based HTML and XHTML, which should display in the same way across all browsers.

Many of the popular browsers now include additional stuff that can provide support to Usenet news/ IRC (Internet Relay Chat)/ e-mail. The protocols supported by browsers may include NNTP (Network News Transfer Protocol), POP (Post Office Protocol), IMAP (Internet Message Access Protocol), SMTP (Simple Mail Transfer Protocol). These type of browsers are often known as *Internet suites* rather than just simple Web browsers.

Browser Statistics

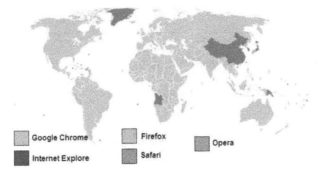

Figure 1.13: Browser Statistics for 2014

The figure 1.13 browser statistics for 2014. You can find

> # Do You Know?
>
> *TCP/IP — which allows computers to connect to one another and for applications to send data back and forth — was originally developed by Vint Cerf and Bob Kahn, while under contract at the US Department of Defense.*

1.6.5 Web Hosting

In order to have your Website available in the World Wide Web, you need a place where to host it. This place is provided by the Web hosting provider (See Figure 1.14). Storing the Web pages of a Website on a server is called Web hosting. While choosing a Web hosting service we need to choose a hosting service which is reliable, i.e., working 24 hours and secure. Whenever a Website project is started choosing a Web host should be the first step. The Web hosting as a service includes not only space where your Website files are stored but also a lot of extra services, such as firewall protection, e-mail services, technical assistance, FTP access, etc.,

Figure 1.14: Web Hosting using the Internet

Following steps are used for Web hosting service:

> Check the Web hosting service price some are free some are paid

> After comparing prices check for customer's feedback, you can google it and you can find the customer feedback and tech issue if any

> Availability of Technical Assistance : Technical assistance like How to get started? How to upload files? How to create an e-mail account? is always needed from the Web host so one should opt for host that provides good technical assistance

> Hosting features: Web space, bandwidth, CPU, etc., should be evaluated and compared before choosing a Web host. One can also check for facilities like E-mail, POP3, SMTP, IMAP, Autoresponders, E-mail forwarders

The PHP/MySQL capabilities are becoming more and more important for having a dynamic Website. Cron jobs may be needed for programs that you need to be run periodically (e.g. once a day).

Web Hosting service provider should provide Website tools like Blogs, CMS, galleries, forums, etc., Free Website creation tools can save money of Web designers and developer.

E-commerce option - Shopping cart, SSL (Secure Socket Layer) needs to be there so that Website owner can collect credit card information on his/her Website.

Availability of good control panel which is of great help for maintaining the Website

Do You Know?

Website address, such as http://www.ncert..nic.in is known by the term Uniform Resource Locater (URL).

1.6.6 URL

URL stands for Uniform Resource Locator. It implies that it is a **uniform** (same throughout the world) way to **locate** a **resource** (file or document) on the Internet. Each URL specifies the address of a file and every file on the Internet has a unique address. Browsers uses URL to retrieve a file from the computer on which it resides.

The actual URL is a set of four numbers separated by periods, for example 196.157.238.48. Such addresses are difficult to handle so alphanumeric form of addresses are used which are more descriptive and easy to remember. URL of site say e.g. 219.162.12.182 can also be written as www.abc.com.

1.6.7 Cyber Space

The word "cyberspace" was coined by science fiction novelist and seminal cyberpunk author William Gibson in his 1982 story "Burning Chrome".

Cyberspace can be understood as the global domain of electro-magnetic accessed through electronic technology and tapped through the modulation of electromagnetic energy to achieve a wide range of communication and control system capabilities. It is a term used to describe the space created through the concourse of electronic communications networks, such as the Internet which enables computer mediated communications between any numbers of people who may be geographically around the globe.

In pragmatic (useful) terms, Cyberspace is the interdependent network of Information Technology Infrastructures (ITI) including the Internet, computer systems, telecommunications networks, etc. A cyberspace is a virtual public space which individuals can access regardless of physical location (also irrespective type of connectivity to hookup) and can interact with. Typically they are places where individuals can meet and exchange their ideas. They can also share information, conduct online/offline and provide social support.

1.7. Web Servers

Web server is a program that, using the client/server model and the World Wide Web's HyperText Transfer Protocol (HTTP), serves the files that form Web pages to Web users. Every computer on the Internet that contains a Website must have a Web server program, two industry leaders are Apache and Microsoft's Internet Information Server (IIS).

Web servers often come as part of a larger package of Internet- and intranet-related programs for downloading requests for FTP files, serving e-mail and even for creating and publishing basic Web pages.

How a Web page is processed by a Web server?

You may want to get into a bit more detail on the process of getting a Web page onto your computer screen. Some of the basic steps that occur during processing of a Web page are:

1.   The browser splits the URL into three parts:
    o   The protocol ("http")
    o   The server name ("www.shrutikohli.com")
    o   The file name ("publications.html")
2.   The browser communicates with a name server to translate the server name "www.yahoo.com" into an **IP Address**, which it uses to connect to the server machine. The browser then forms a connection to the server at that IP address on port 80.
3.   Following the HTTP protocol, the browser will then send a GET request to the server, asking for the file "http://www.shrutikohli.com/publications.html".
4.   The server then sends the HTML text for the Web page to the browser.
5.   The browser then reads the HTML tags and presents the formatted page onto the screen.

How Web Servers Work?

1. Users visit a Website by either clicking on a hyperlink that brings them to that site or keying the site's URL directly into the address bar of a browser. E.g. suppose you want to visit 'gmail'. You need to type its URL into your Web browser (http://www.gmail.com).

2. Through an Internet connection browser will initiate a connection to the Web server that is storing the gmail files by first converting the domain name into an IP address (through a domain name service) and then locating the server that is storing the information for that IP address.

3. The Web server stores all of the files necessary to display gmail's pages on ther computer. Server will generally store all the individual pages that comprise the entirety of a Website, any images/graphic files and any scripts that make dynamic elements of the site function.

4. Once contact has been made, the browser requests the data from the Web server, and using HTTP, the server delivers the data back to your browser. The browser work is then to convert/format the page and display it on your screen.

5. A Web server can send the files to many client computers at the same time, allowing multiple clients to view the same page simultaneously.

6. Practically, **Web server** can be understood as follows: A computer program that is responsible for accepting HTTP requests from *clients* (user agents, such as Web browsers), and serving them HTTP responses along with optional data contents, which usually are Web pages, such as HTML documents and linked objects.

You can have a look at the Web server in the figure below:

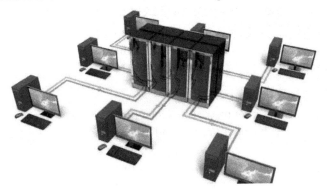

Figure 1.15: Web Server

Common features of Web Server

Although Web server programs differ in detail, they all share some **basic common features**.

a.   **HTTP:** Every Web server program operates by accepting HTTP requests (that's his job!) from the client, and providing an HTTP response to the client. The HTTP response usually consists of an HTML document, but can also be a raw file, an image, or some other type of document. In case error is found in client request or while trying to serve it, a Web server has to send an error response that may include some custom HTML or text messages to explain the problem to end users.

b.   **Logging:** Which helps security angle also, as most of the Web servers have the capability of logging some detailed information, about client requests and server responses, to log files. These log files allow the Web administrator to collect statistics by running log analyzers on log files.

Also, Web servers may implement following features for better functionality:

1.   **Authentication:** Authorization is an optional authorization request, which is very efficient for security/payment/critical information, related Websites (prompts for user name and password) before allowing access to some or all kind of resources.

2.   **HTTPS support:** To allow secure (encrypted) connections (all banking sites have same) to the server on the standard port 443 instead of usual port 80.

3.   **Content compression:** Success of any Website depends on visitors right, technology heroes use compression mechanism also, for example using gzip encoding, which may reduce the size of the responses (to lower bandwidth usage, etc.).

4.   **Virtual hosting:** Web server may work as virtual host to serve multiple Websites using one IP address. (Remember public IP has a cost!)

5.   **Large file support:** Web server may provide large file support to be able to serve files whose size is greater than 2 GB like AutoCAD / Corel drawing files.

6.   **Bandwidth throttling:** Another vital role, Web server should be able to limit the speed of responses in order to not saturate the network and to be able to serve more clients.

Load limits

Most of the Web server has defined load limits. When a Web server is near to or over its limits, it becomes overloaded and thus unresponsive, *Internet-worms hate that!* A Web server can handle only a limited number of concurrent client connections (usually between 2 and 60,000, by default between 500 and 1,000) per IP address (and TCP port) and it can serve only a certain maximum number of requests per second depending on following parameters:

I.   Its own settings

II.   The HTTP request type

III. Content origin (static or dynamic)

IV. The fact that the served content is or is not cached;

V. The hardware and software limits of the operating system where it is working.

1.7.1 Web Server Hardware

More robust architecture and technology better the performance and results are old saying in networking industry. Likewise, building a Web server is not child's play, it needs clear focus and dedicated attention because an Internet based business needs a server that's reliable and is able to run 24/7 for months without requiring any servicing. Reliability is another most important criteria for choosing any Web server. While designing Web server picking reliable components is key. Your analysis plays vital role here, i.e., performing a thorough analysis of what content you will be serving to your clients and after analyzing the scale of traffic that will be visiting the Website you will be able to properly define where possible bottlenecks might arise and accordingly pick the right components for the Web server. You need to make sure these bottlenecks are well understood, both in scale and frequency of occurrence and proper measures are in place to limit the effects on the performance of the server and more importantly the experience of the client.

The important factors to be taken care while deciding upon Web server hardware are:

o   **Hardware Analysis** content is database driven, you need to make sure that you do not create a bottleneck there. Databases usually require high-bandwidth throughout the system so it needs to be designed and size requirement accordingly.

o   **Storage, memory** and **processors speed** are all important factors here as a slow storage sub-system can slow down the fastest CPU, and similar for a high-speed storage sub-system that is slowed down by a underperforming CPU.

Do You Know?

The IBM Simon was the first phone with a touchscreen, released in 1992. It is referred to as the first "smartphone," though the term was not yet coined.

1.7.2 Web Server Software

Webserver Software: Check out the list of top Web server software vendors published in a Netcraft survey in September 2008. Table 1. summarizes the list of available Web server software.

Table 1: List of Available Web server Software

Vendor	Product	Web Sites Hosted	Percent
Apache	Apache	91,068,713	50.24%
Microsoft	IIS	62,364,634	34.4%
Google	GWS	10,072,687	5.56%
lighttpd	lighttpd	3,095,928	1.71%

nginx	nginx	2,562,554	1.41%
Oversee	Oversee	1,938,953	1.07%
Others	-	10,174,366	5.61%
Total	-	181,277,835	100.00%

Free Web Server Software

Web server software which are freely available:

- IIS (Internet Information Server) from Microsoft
- Communication Server from Netscape
- WebStar (Mac-based Web server)

Understanding Popular Web Servers

Internet Information Services (IIS): When we ask any fresher in Website building arena, first thing he/she will discuss would be IIS. Internet Information Server is a set of Internet-based services for servers created by Microsoft for use with Microsoft Windows. The servers currently include NNTP, FTP, HTTP/HTTPS services and SMTP. IIS 7.0 features a modular architecture. It has a core Web server engine, which makes it efficient. Modules offering specific functionality can be added to the engine to enable its features. The advantage of having this architecture is that only the features required can be enabled and that the functionalities can be extended by using custom modules. The following sets of modules are provided with the IIS 7.0 server:

1. HTTP Modules
2. Security Modules
3. Content Modules
4. Compression Modules
5. Caching Modules
6. Logging and Diagnostics Modules

1.7.3 Setting up a Web server

Brief Description

In order to manage own Web server one needs to follow basic steps for creating Web server which are listed below.

Step 1 - The computer: Web server requires a dedicated computer/server/laptop that is directly hooked on to Internet, by any media. Technical hardware of Web server will directly proportional to response one expects from Website/portal.

Step 2 - The operating system software: Operating systems that can support a Web server: Windows, Mac OS, UNIX, Linux, and Sun.

Step 3 - The networking software: Any device which intends to talk to Internet Cloud breaths on TCP/IP, and a Web server is no exception. Any kind of hardware (computer/laptop/server) should be directly connected to the Internet.

Step 4 - The Web server software: IIS (Internet Information Server) from Microsoft for windows is most famous of all. For Macintosh, a popular Web server is WebStar from StarNine. Apache is also available for variety of operating systems. One can download or purchase Web server software and install same on your computer.

Step 5 - Configuring your Web server: Once generic installation of Web server is done one will be prompted for basic settings like default directory or folder. Here one can define access rights for visitors to see the contents of a directory or folder, where to store the log file, etc. Now process and procedure for same will vary from Web software to software.

Step 6 - Managing your Web server: One of most important aspects of successful Web server is security and performance. As Web server is accessed by masses, one may need to monitor the log file (in consistent cum timely mode) to see which files people are reading, identify peak access times, and consider upgrading the computer. One may need more RAM and disk space/processor for his/her Web server computer to improve its performance. Also, one needs to track bottlenecks like running of TCP/IP software.

Do You Know?
Bluetooth was named for after Harald Blaatand (Bluetooth), a Viking king who unified Denmark and Norway.

1.8 Key Terms

The Web vs. the Internet: The Internet is a vast 'interconnection of computer networks'. It includes millions of computing devices that trade volumes of information. Today we can find that any desktop computers, mainframes, cell phones and video game consoles are connected to the Internet. The Internet contains many layers of information. These different layers are called 'protocols'. The most popular protocols are the WWW, FTP, Telnet, instant messaging, and e-mail.

http and https: http is a technical acronym that means 'hypertext transfer protocol'. It is also called a language of Web pages. When a Web page has this prefix, then your links, text, and pictures should work in your Web browser. **https** is 'hypertext transfer protocol Secured'. This implies that the Web page has a special layer of encryption. This layer is added to hide personal information and passwords. Whenever one logs into his online bank or his/her Web e-mail account, he/she should see https at the front of the page address.

Browser: A free software package that is used to view Web pages, graphics, and or any online content.

HTML and XML: HyperText Markup Language can be understood as programming language that are used create Web pages. HTML commands your Web browser to display text and graphics in orderly fashion. HTML uses commands called 'HTML tags' that look like as follows:

```
<title></title>
<a href="www.shrutikohli.com"></a>
<p></p>
```

XML is eXtensible Markup Language can be understood as brother of HTML.

URL: 'Uniform Resource Locators', are the Web browser addresses of the Internet pages and files.

IP Address: 'Internet Protocol address is a four-part or eight-part electronic serial number. An IP address can look something like '201.2.134.155'.

E-mail: E-mail implies is electronic mail (formerly spelled e-mail with a hyphen). It is like sending and receiving typed messages from one screen to another.

ISP: Internet Service Provider. That is the private company or government organization that plugs you into the vast Internet around the world.

Do You Know?
The URL was standardized in 1994 by Tim Berners-Lee.

1.9   Summary

The Internet is a worldwide collection of inter-connected computer networks that use TCP/IP protocol. TCP/IP provides flexibility to add up new services to the existing ones. WWW is one of the services provided by Internet. Other services provided by Internet are FTP, E-Mail, Telnet, Gopher etc. WWW uses hypertext transfer protocol to exchange information sound on Web pages. Many times Https is used for secure transfer of data. The Internet has gained popularity primarily due to the invent of WWW. The Internet addressing system needs to be understood in order to establish connectivity in Internet. There are many ways for establishing this connectivity. These ways can be broadly categorized as Wired and Wireless methods depending upon the medium used for communication. The Internet is really a rich resource of information and data. Its most important characteristic is that it is dynamic and is expanding at a massive rate.

1.10   Test Yourself

Section I: Short Answer Questions

A.   Fill in the blanks

1.   WWW stands for _____.

2.   TCP stands for _____.

3.   Protocol for WWW is _____.

4. Protocols for the Internet are _____ and _____.

5. Cyberspace is metaphor for_____.

B.   True/False

1. In Asia, India has highest number of Internet Users.

2. Top language used in the Internet is English.

3. TCP is protocol for WWW.

4. WWW is service of Internet.

5. 'www.yahoo.com' is an IP address.

C.   Answer the following:

1. Define WWW.

2. Expand HTTP.

3. Discuss the layers of TCP/IP.

4. Explain the function of HTTP.

5. Write the full form of TCP/IP?

6. Which continent has highest Internet Users in the world?

7. Define URL.

8. 209.62.20.192 is public or private IP address?

9. Find the domain type:

    com: commercial

    mil : military

    edu : education

    in :?

10. How many wireline and wireless modes of Internet access options available?

11. Which mode to access Internet was readily used?

12. Which Internet access has delay of 500-900 ms?

13. What is the speed of Wi-Fi?

14. Define Cyberspace.

15. What is DoD ?

16. Which browser is widely used in these days?

17. What is SMTP ?

18. Define Web Server.

19. What is IIS?

20. Define Web hosting.

Section II: Long Questions with Answers

1.   Discuss the difference of TCP/IP and OSI Reference Models.

Ans. Difference of TCP/IP and OSI has been summarized in table below:

OSI	TCP/IP
It has seven layers.	It has four layers.
It has horizontal approach.	It has vertical approach.
Its layers are:	Its layers are:
1. Application 2. Presentation 3. Session 4. Trasnport 5. Network 6. Datalink 7. Physical	1. Network access 2. Internet 3. Transport 4. Application

2.   Describe TCP/IP in detail.

Ans. TCP/IP have four layers as described below.

a.   Host to network Interface Layer:

- This layer defines the protocols hardware request to deliver data across physical network.

- The term network interface layer refers to the fact that it defines how to connect the host computer which is not a part of the network, to the network.

Ethernet is one example protocol at TCP/IP network layer. TCP/IP reference model does not really say much about what happens where, expect to point out that the host has to connect to the network using protocols so it can send up packets over it.

b.   Network/Internet Layer:

- This layer defines an official packet format and protocols called Internet Protocol(IP).

- The job of this layer is to deliver IP packets where they are supposed to go. Packet routing is clearly the major issue at this layer and avoiding congestion.

- For these reasons, it is reasonable to say that TCP/IP Internet layer is very similar in functionality to OSI network layer.

- This layer holds the whole architecture together. Its job is to permit host to inject packets into any network. This may even arrive in a different order than they were sent, in this case, it is the job of higher layer to rearrange them, if an order delivery is required.

- IP defines logical address called IP address that allows each TCP/IP speaking devices called IP host to communicate. It also defines routing that is the process of how a router should forward or route the packets of data. For example, Ordinary mail system.

c. Transport Layer:

- TCP is a connection-oriented protocol. Transport layer is designed to allow a wide stream originating on one machine to be delivered without error on another machine connected to Internet.
- The two end-to-end protocols have been defined here:
  1. TCP – reliable connection-oriented protocol
  2. UDP – unreliable connectionless protocol

d. Application Layer:

- This layer contains all the higher layer protocols. TCP/IP does not have a session and presentation layer. TCP/IP model has higher level protocols, such as Telnet. It allows users on one machine to login to a distant machine and work from there. NNTP (Network News Transfer Protocol) is used for moving news articles around and HTTP is used for patching pages on WWW.

3. What is the difference between TCP and UDP?

TCP: It is reliable connection-oriented protocol. It arranges the incoming widestream into discrete messages and passes each one to Internet layer. At the destination, the receiving TCP process reassembles the received messages into output stream. TCP also handles flow control to make sure a fast sender cannot flood a slow receiver with more messages that it can handle.

UDP: The second protocol of this layer is UDP. It is unreliable connectionless protocols that do not want TCP sequencing and flow control and wish to define their own. It is also widely used for one short client/server type request reply queries and application in which fast delivery is more important than accurate delivery, such as transmitting speech. UDP is a communication protocol that does not perform validity check on data. It is used in video conferencing.

Difference between TCP and UDP

TCP	UDP
Connection oriented.	Connectionless.
Reliability in delivery of messages.	No recovery is performed for any lost message.
Splitting messages into datagram.	No reassembly and synchronization.
Keep track of sequence.	No sequencing and in case of error, the whole message is retransmitted.

Use checksum for detecting errors and windows for acknowledgement.	No windows and acknowledgement mechanism.
Reliability is a must.	Server and client messages fit completely within a packet.
Overhead low but higher than UDP.	Overhead is very low.
Speed is high but not as high as of UDP.	Speed is very high. Example are:
Example are: FTP, SMTP, HTTP	SNMP, TFTP, DHCP

Section III: Unsolved Review Questions

1. What is a Web browser?
2. Is it possible to transfer a resource from the client computer to Web server? How you can do this? Illustrate with example.
3. Why is HTTP called a Stateless Protocol? What do you think about its advantages and disadvantages?
4. What is the difference between Internet and WWW?
5. What is the difference between GET and POST Methods of HTTP protocol?
6. In a URL say http://www.yahoo.com what do you understand by http?
7. What is a proxy server? How it is different from a server?
8. Is search engine a Website? Explain.
9. UDP works on which layer of TCP/IP?
10. What are the basic steps for designing a Website? Explain in detail.
11. Discuss the various methods available for connecting to the Internet.
12. What is the difference between client,server mode and peer-to-peer network?
13. What do you understand by Domain Name System?
14. How IP addressing is done? Discuss the various IP address classes in detail.
15. Discuss in detail how the system connects to a particular requested Web address.
16. Discuss briefly following terms:
    a. Internet Server   b. Internet Service Provider
    c. TCP   d. E-Mails
17. What is Web hosting?
18. What are the factors we need to keep in mind while designing Website for the client?
19. How does e-mail work?
20. Explain Cyber law in detail?

Section IV: Multiple Choice Questions

1. A piece of icon or image on a Web page associated with another Web page is called:

    a. URL

    b. Hyperlink

    c. Plug-in

    d. None of the mentioned

2. Dynamic Web page:

    a. Is same every time whenever it displays

    b. Generates on demand by a program or a request from browser

    c. Both (a) and (b)

    d. None of the mentioned

3. What is a Web browser?

    a. A program that can display a Web page

    b. A program used to view HTML documents

    c. It enables user to access the resources of the Internet

    d. All of the mentioned

4. Common gateway interface is used to:

    a. Generate executable files from Web content by Web server

    b. Generate Web pages

    c. Stream videos

    d. None of the mentioned

5. URL stands for:

    a. Unique Reference Label

    b. Uniform Reference Label

    c. Uniform Resource Locator

    d. Unique Resource Locator

6. A Web cookie is a small piece of data:

    a. Sent from a Website and stored in user's Web browser while a user is browsing a Website

    b. Sent from user and stored in the server while a user is browsing a Website

    c. Sent from root server to all servers

    d. None of the mentioned

7. Which one of the following is not used to generate dynamic Web pages?

    a. PHP

    b. ASP.NET

    c. JSP

    d. None of the mentioned

8. An alternative of JavaScript on windows platform is:

    a. VBScript

    b. ASP.NET

    c. JSP

    d. None of the mentioned

9. What is Document Object Model (DOM)?

    a. Convention for representing and interacting with objects in HTML documents

    b. Application programming interface

    c. Hierarchy of objects in ASP.NET

    d. None of the mentioned

10. AJAX stands for:

    a. Asynchronous JavaScript and XML

    b. Advanced JSP and XML

    c. Asynchronous JSP and XML

    d. Advanced JavaScript and XML

Section V: Previous Year Questions with Answers

Q. 1. **Discuss the most basic elements of good site design, including navigation considerations.** **[May 2008]**

Ans. Basic elements of good site design, including navigation considerations:

- Original Content: The hallmark of an excellent Website is content that clearly states your business in terms that are meaningful to your viewers. We spend a lot of time with our clients, learning how to capture the essence of their business "message" in their Web pages. Instead of presenting content in a format and language that follows your business organizational structure, we help you visualize your content the way someone "on the outside looking in" would want to view it.

- Well-organized and Easy to Read: Viewers equate "poor organization" with "poor design.' The most important information on any page should be "above the fold" as they say in the newspaper business. Your site should be easy to read ",. on the screen or printed. Viewers should easily find their way around your site,. and locate important information quickly.

- Viewers love to click! Hate to Stroll: Keep them moving with a site that has many short pages, thoughtfully linked to draw them through your Website. This is probably the most powerful, but often overlooked, advantage of using Websites to present information.

- Share your Knowledge: Every business has knowledge that their viewers might find useful. Use your Website to showcase that valuable asset! White papers, "how to" and "helpful hints" as well as publications you have shared in paper form all make good content, if they are organized and edited properly.

- Helpful Links to External Sites: While you may be concerned that this will take viewers away from your site, keep in mind that they will leave anyway if they don not find what they are looking for! If you provide a list of useful links, people will return to your site for reference. A well thought-out list of links adds credibility to your site, and in fact, will get your site listed higher in directories, such as Yahoo!

- Intelligent use of Graphics: A picture may say a thousand words, but if it takes too long to load, who will get the message? On the other hand, nobody wants to look at a site that is all text! We try to balance the graphic elements with the text so the viewer's interest is kept alive, and your message gets across.

- Be Interactive: We do our best to create a site that encourages viewer participation. Whether this is as simple as filling out a "Information page" Form or more complex database driven application.

- Keep it fresh: Updates are vital to keeping you site "alive" to your viewers. If you have detailed content that changes frequently, such as sale items or list of some kind, will make it easy for you to do the updating.

- The Important Web Page Title: The title is a very important element of your Web page, especially in telling search engines what your page is about.

- Corporate Slogan to Highlight Your Key Benefit: This element is at the top left of the header. Our Website templates let you easily insert the name of your site, or any corporate slogan that may highlight the key benefit your products or services deliver to your customers.

Q. 2. What do you mean by cyber crime? How can the cyber crimes be checked?   **[May 2008]**

Ans. Cyber Crime: *Cyber crime* is usually restricted to describing criminal activity in which the computer or network is an essential part of the crime, this term is also used to include traditional crimes in which computers or networks are used to enable the illicit activity. Examples of cyber crime which the computer or network is a tool of the criminal activity include spamming criminal copyright crimes, particularly those facilitated through peer-to-peer networks.

Examples of cyber crime in which the computer or network is a target of criminal activity include unauthorized access (i.e., defeating access controls), malicious code, and denial-of-service attacks.

Examples of cyber crime in which the computer or network is a place of criminal activity include theft of service (in particular, telecom fraud) and certain financial frauds. Additionally, certain other information crimes, including trade secret theft and industrial or economic espionage, are sometimes considered cyber crimes when computers or networks are involved,

Cyber Crime be checked: Cyber crime in the context of national security may involve hacktivism (online activity intended to influence policy), traditional espionage, or information warfare and related activities. Another way to define cyber crime is simply as criminal activity involving the information technology infrastructure, including illegal access (unauthorized access), illegal interception (by technical means of non-public transmissions of computer data to, from or within a computer system), data interference (unauthorized damaging, deletion, deterioration, alteration or suppression of computer_data), systems interference (interfering with the functioning of a computer system by inputting, transmitting, damaging, deleting, deteriorating, altering or suppressing computer data), misuse of devices, forgery (ID theft), and electronic fraud.

Q. 3. **What are the essential skills that must be identified while selecting the members of a Web project team? [May 2008]**

Ans. Essential skills for members of a Web project team:

Good administrative skills: Most of duties are directly related to strong administrative organizational skills. For example, bulk mail out procedures, identifying, collecting and organizing an extensive selection of Web-based resources and providing administrative assistance for training workshop. Some of other my duties are working as an office assistant included filing and sorting mail, preparing letters and answering phones etc.

Interpersonal skills: Leadership skills and extensive experience working in teams, may capable of communicating effectively with peers in a team, and also with individuals.

Well-developed communication skills (written and verbal): Being a member of Web project team, some of the required proficient communication skills you need to perform like providing support to people of different ages, backgrounds (with varying levels of English) or levels of technical or physical capabilities.

Organizational skills: In completing assessments for numerous tasks members of Web project team can work reliably in undertaking several tasks simultaneously.

Analytical skills: Analytical skill is the ability to visualize and solve the problems and make decisions based on information.

Good word processing, spreadsheet and Web-based skills: Web-based training is an effective way to train a good number of members of a Web project team in terms of providing Word processing technique, typing skills, Internet skills, Internet skills' and basic computer knowledge.

Chapter 2

An Introduction to Web Designing

HTML was developed by Tim Berners - Lee in 1980.

Key Topics

- *Introduction*
- *History of HTML*
- *HTML Document Format*
- *Elements of HTML Documents*
- *Lists*
- *Links and Anchors*
- *Images and Graphics*
- *Tables*
- *Frames*
- *Forms*
- *New Features of HTML5*

2.1 Introduction

HTML is an acronym for HyperText Markup Language. It is the primary language used to encode documents containing hyperlinks. It provides simple mechanisms for formulating text, creating links and lists inserting images, embedding audio and video, etc. Its first version was released in 1991 by Tim Berners-Lee, the founder of WWW. It is an application of Standard Generalized Markup Language (SGML), which is a standard that specifies a formal meta-language for markup documents. Any simple text editor, such as Notepad in Windows or simple Text in Macintosh can be used to create and edit HTML files.

- HTML documents are written using HTML "Tags".
- Tags are embedded in angular brackets (< >).
- HTML tags are case-insensitive.
- Tags are organized in hierarchical order.

- Documents are linked by special tag called anchor tags.
- Anchor tags are also called hyperlinks.
- HTML documents are viewed by software called 'browser'.

Elements, Attribute and Tags

An HTML document basically consists of HTML elements which in turn consists of tags and attributes.

HTML Tags

- HTML tags are used to markup HTML elements.
- HTML tags are surrounded by the two characters < and >.
- The surrounding characters are called angle brackets.
- HTML tags normally come in pairs like <b> and </b>.
- The first tag in a pair is the start tag, the second tag is the end tag.
- The text between the start and end tags is the element content.
- HTML tags are not case-sensitive, <b> means the same as <B>.

Tags are codes each of which marks up a certain region in an HTML document. A tag is written within angular brackets (< and >) and must be properly nested. The general format of a tag is as follows:

```
<tag> content </tag>
```

Where <tag> is the opening tag and </tag> is the closing tag.

There are two types of tags:

- **Embedded tags:** These tags have both opening and closing tags. For example, italic tag (<i>...</i>), Bold tag (<b>...</b>), etc.
- **Standalone tags:** These tags have only opening tags but they do not have their corresponding tags. For example, <hr> tag, used to draw horizontal line, etc.

Common HTML tags and their functionality:

Tag	Meaning
<html>...</html>	Root tag
<body>...</body>	Specifies the body of an HTML document
<head>...</head>	Specifies the header
<p>...</p>	New paragraph
 	Insert a line break
<b>...</b>	Make the text bold
<i>...</i>	Make the text italic
<tt>...</tt>	Make the text teletype face
<u>...</u>	Make the text underline
<center>...</center>	Align the text in center

`<hr>`	Insert a horizontal line
`<table>...</table>`	Insert a table
`<tr>...</tr>`	Create table row
`<img>`	Insert an image

Attribute

Attributes are the properties of the tags that can be optionally be assigned values to change the default behavior of these tags. These are placed within the starting tag. Even standalone tags may have attributes. Each tag has its own set of attributes.

Common attributes of body tag are discussed below:

Attribute	Meaning
`bgcolor`	It specifies background color of the document.
`background`	It specifies background image of the document.
`link`	It specifies the color of a not visited link yet.
`alink`	It represents the color of an active link.
`vlink`	It represents the color of a visited link.
`text`	It specifies the color of the enclosed text.

Test Your Progress

1. *What is HTML?*
2. *Whats are the types of tags in HTML? Discuss.*
3. *Whats are attributes in HTML?*

2.2 History of HTML

1989: Tim Berners-Lee invented the Web with HTML as its publishing language.

Through 1990: The time was ripe for Tim's invention.

September 1991: Open discussion about HTML across the Internet began.

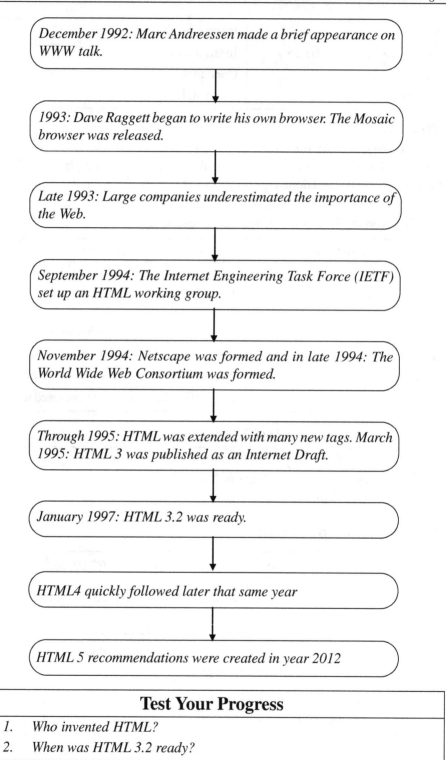

December 1992: Marc Andreessen made a brief appearance on WWW talk.

1993: Dave Raggett began to write his own browser. The Mosaic browser was released.

Late 1993: Large companies underestimated the importance of the Web.

September 1994: The Internet Engineering Task Force (IETF) set up an HTML working group.

November 1994: Netscape was formed and in late 1994: The World Wide Web Consortium was formed.

Through 1995: HTML was extended with many new tags. March 1995: HTML 3 was published as an Internet Draft.

January 1997: HTML 3.2 was ready.

HTML4 quickly followed later that same year

HTML 5 recommendations were created in year 2012

Test Your Progress

1.   *Who invented HTML?*
2.   *When was HTML 3.2 ready?*

2.3   HTML Document Format

Basic structure of HTML document

Every HTML document starts with <html> tag. This tells the browser that it is the beginning of an HTML document. This tag is embedded tag, and must have the corresponding </html> tag which inform the browser that it is the end of the HTML document.

An HTML page has basically two distinct logical sections: Head section specified by <head> and </head> tags and Body section specified by <body> and </body> tags. The structure of an HTML page looks like this:

```
< ! DOCTYPE html >   //The DOCTYPE declaration defines the
                            document type
< html >        //The text between <html> and </html> describes
                 the Web page
    < head >
            ......
    < /head >
    < body >   //The text between <body> and </body> is the
                 visible page content
        ......
    < /body >
< /html >
```

A simple HTML page

The first simple but complete HTML document that displays a simple text "Hello World" on the screen.

```
<html>
    <head>
    <title> my first HTML page </title>
    </head>
    <body>
        Hello World
    </body>
</html>
```

Test Your Progress
1. *Write a simple HTML docoument and run it in any browser.*
2. *Why is DOCTYPE used in HTML?*

2.4   Elements of HTML Document

These are the building block of a Web page. An element consists of a tag, its attributes and content. The content of a tag can be a simple text, or may be one or more tags or both. These are organized in tree-like structure. The root element of a HTML document is <html> which contains all the other elements.

HTML Comments

HTML comments start with < ! – and end with –>. Text written within these characters will be ignored by the browsers. It is used to explain the purpose the HTML tags used in the documents. It can be used anywhere in the document. Following is the general syntax:

```
<! – comment text –>
```

Basic Elements

1. **<head>**

   The <head> element could be understood as a container for all the head elements. It may include information like title of the Web page, scripts and style information. It may also include meta information about the Web page. The elements which could be used inside the <head> element are:

   - **<title>:** You need to specify title of the Web page using the title tag.

   - **<base>:** The <base> tag is used to specify the base URL/target for all relative URLs in a document. Please note that there can be maximum one <base> element in a document and it is always inside the <head> element

   - **<link>:** The <link> tag is used to define a link between a document and any external resource. Its major use is to link to external style sheets. You will learn about external style sheets in next Chapter.

   - **<meta>:** As we all know metadata is data (i.e., any kind of information) about data. This <meta> tag as name suggests provides information about the HTML document. Please note that the Metadata will never be displayed on the page. The metadata is extensively used by browsers (to determine how to display content or reload page), search engines (identifying keywords for indexing) and many other Web services. There are many meta elements used to specify page description, keywords, author of the document, last modified, and other information. Check out the example below for more information.

   - **<script>:** Used for including JavaScript in HTML document. It will be discussed in later Chapters.

   Example 1: Basic elements used in HTML document.

```
<html>
<head>
<title>My Web Page</title>
    <base href="http://www.shrutikohli.com/images/
    " target="_blank">
    <link rel="stylesheet" type="text/
```

```
css" href="shruti.css">
<meta charset="UTF-8">
<meta name="description" content="Education Portal">
<meta name="keywords" content="Web Technology,Operational
Research,Simulation and Modeling">
<meta name="author" content="Dr. Shruti Kohli">
<script>
document.getElementById("Name").innerHTML = "Hello Jian";
</script>
</head>
<body>
    Check out my experience and hobbies......
    <img src="passport.gif" width="30" height="20" alt="
    passportinfo">
    <a href="http://www.shrutikohli.com">My Web Portal</a>
</body>
</html>
```

2. **<body> tag**

    As the name suggests the <body> tag is used to define the document's body. It contains all the contents of an HTML document, for example text, hyperlinks, images, tables, lists, etc.

    Some attributes of <body> tag are:

Attribute	Value	Description
alink	Color	Specify the color of an active link in a document. For example, alink="#000000"
background	URL	Used to specify a background image for the document. For example, background="scene.gif"
bgcolor	Color	Used to specify the background color of a document. For example, bgcolor="#ffffff"
link	Color	Used to specify the color of unvisited links in a document. For example, link="#3499ff"
text	Color	Used to specify the color of the text in a document. For example, text="#000000"
vlink	Color	Used to specify the color of visited links in a document. For example, vlink="#9955ff"

Consider the following code:

```
<body bgcolor="#ffffff" background="scene.gif"
text="#000000" link="#3499ff" vlink="#9955ff"
alink="#000000">
```

Colors are here written in Hex code. Hex means Hexadecimal. Hex codes are always 3 groups of two numbers. These numbers signify the amount of Red, Green and Blue (RGB) in the color. These are the three primary colors of light. The range for each color is 0 to 9 and A to F. Here, 0 means none, for example #000000 implies pure black whereas f means (as implied in above code) full resulting in white. Using this range you can create 216 safe colors on Web. Please note that writing `background="white"` may work with some browsers and not with others so it is always better to express colours in Hex.

3.   **<h> Heading Element**

A Web page contains different heading with different sizes, colors and fonts. HTML provides different tags for such headings. There are 6 levels of headings h1 to h6, where h1 is the largest in size and h6 is the smallest.

```
<h1> heading 1 </h1>
<h2> heading 2 </h2>
<h3> heading 3 </h3>
<h4> heading 4 </h4>
<h5> heading 5 </h5>
<h6> heading 6 </h6>
```

4.   **<p> Paragraph Element**

HTML provides a <p> tag, which is used to start a new paragraph, escaping one line between new line and previous line. Following is the general syntax:

```
<p> this is a new paragraph </p>
```

5.   **<font> Font Style Element**

The <font> tag is used to specify the font face, font size, and color of text. Please note the tag has been deprecated in HTML 5 and can only be used in the older versions.

```
<font face="verdana" color="green" size="2">Check out!</
font>
```

Test Your Progress

1. *Define meta tag.*
2. *What is script tag?*
3. *How can you implement different heading elements?*

2.5 Lists in HTML

It is the collection of one or more items. There are three types of lists.

1. **Unordered Lists:** These are created using `<ul>` tag and each list item starts with the `<li>` tag. Some of the bullet options for `<ul>` tag are: "disc", "circle", "square".

    Example 2: unordered list Displaying.

    ```
    <ul>
    <li> item 1 </li>
    <li> item 2 </li>
    <li> item n </li>
    </ul>
    ```

2. **Ordered Lists:** These are created using `<ol>` tag and each list item starts with the `<li>` tag. Some of the numbering options for `<ol>` tag are: "1","A","I".

    Example 3: ordered list Displaying.

    ```
    <ol>
    <li> item 1 </li>
    <li> item 2 </li>
    <li> item n </li>
    </ol>
    ```

3. **Definition Lists:** It consists of two parts: a term and its definition. It is created using `<dl>` tag, term part by `<dt>` tag and definition part by `<dd>` tag.

    Example 4: Displaying definition list.

    ```
    <dl>
    <dt> 1st term </dt>
    <dd> 1st definition </dd>
    <dt>  nth term </dt>
    <dd> nth definition </dd>
    <dl>
    ```

Test Your Progress
1. *Define list in HTML.*
2. *Define ordered list.*
3. *Define unordered list.*

2.6 Links and Anchors used in HTML

Links and anchors are used in the same way in HTML. The tag used to link any URL with the text is `<a>...</a>`. This tag is same as anchor tag, as Web developers use it to anchor a URL with some text on the Web page. When users view the Web page, they mainly deal with the text part which is linked to some URL. As click on the text, it is redirected to the new page whose URL has been in the link.

Syntax:

```
<a href="http://www.google.com/" target="_blank">Google
Home</a>
```

Here, **target="_blank"** is used to open URL in new page in new browser window. The **target** attribute helps to define the style to open defined page when it may get clicked.

Target	Description
_blank	Open new page in a new browser window
_self	Load the new page in the current window
_parent	Load new page into a parent frame
_top	Load new page into the current browser window, cancelling all frames

HTML Link Types:

Global - href="http://gmail.com/"   It links to other domains outside your Website domain.

Local - href="../abc/mypage1.html"   It links to other pages within your Website domain.

Internal - href="#anchor_name"   It links to anchors embedded in the current Web page.

Test Your Progress
1.   *Why is use* **_blank** *used in anchor tag?*
2.   *Why is use _self used in anchor tag?*
3.   *Write the signification of internal anchor in HTML document.*

2.7   Images and Graphics in HTML

In HTML we use `<img>` tag to insert any images in our Web page. It you only use `<img>` tag, it means you just want to show empty image area. To display any image over the Web page you need to provide the source of the image file.

Syntax:

```
<img src=".../love.gif">
```

● **ALT attribute:** It helps to display the text belongs to the image attached.

Syntax

```
<img src="smiley.gif" alt="Smiley face">
```

● **Align attribute:** It helps for the alignment of image according to the surrounding objects. \

> **Note:** The `align` attribute of <img> tag is not used in HTML5. Use of CSS is beneficial.

Syntax:
```
<img align=" left | right | middle | top | bottom">
```

Value	Description
left	Align the image to the left
right	Align the image to the right
middle	Align the image in the middle
top	Align the image at the top
bottom	Align the image at the bottom

- **Setup Images Height and Width:** The height and width attributes are used to define the height and width of the image, respectively.

Syntax:
```
<img src="smiley.gif" alt="Smiley face" width="42"
height="42">
```

It is beneficial to add the height and width of the image as when page is loaded then the space required by the image is reserved. However, if it is not defined the layout of the page may get changed abruptly.

- **Image as a Link:** Images can also be used as the link. For this you have to use the `anchor` tag associated with the `image` tag.

Syntax:
```
<a href="default.html"><img src="smiley.gif" alt="HTML
tutorial" width="42" height="42"></a>
```

- **Borders in Image links:** The border tag is use to provide border to the image, it holds the width of the border around the image.

> **Note:** The `border` attribute of <img> tag is not used in HTML5. Use of CSS is beneficial.

Syntax:
```
<img border="pixels">
<img src="smiley.gif" alt="Smiley face" border="5">
```

Test Your Progress

1. *Define the use of* `Alt` *attribute?*
2. *How is* `border` *attribute is linked with* `image` *tag?*
3. *How is* `align` *attribute used in HTML document?*

2.8 Create Tables in HTML

A table is a two-dimensional matrix consisting of rows and columns. It is powerful tool for formatting the Web pages, which is created using three basic tags- `<table>...</table>`, `<tr>...</tr>`, `<td>...</td>`. All table related tags are included between the `<table>` and `</table>` tags. Each row of table is described between the `tr` tag, and each column is described in the `td` tag.

HTML table tags are as follows:

Tag	Meaning
trabel	Represents the whole table
tr	Represents a row
td	Represents a cell in a row
th	Column header
caption	Title of the table

The attributes of table tags are following:

align	Manage the horizontal alignments, which can be LEFT, CENTER, RIGHT
valign	Manage the horizontal alignments, which can be TOP,MIDDLE,BOTTOM
width	Sets the width of a specific no or pixels
border	It controls the border to be placed around the table
cellpadding	It controls the distance between the data in cell and the boundaries of the cell
cellspacing	Control the spacing between adjacent cell.
colspan	It is inserted inside a `<th>` or `<td>` tag, which instructs the browser to make the cell defined by the tag to take up more than one column.
rowspan	It works in same as the colspan except that it allows a cell to take up more than one row.

Captions and Headers in table

The `<caption>` tag is used to define the caption to the table. It is defined just after the `<table>` tag.

Note: You can define only one `<caption>` per table.

```
<table>
    <caption>Your Monthly Savings</caption>
    <tr>
    <th>Months</th>
```

```
<th>Savings</th>
</tr>
<tr>
<td>Jan</td>
<td>$175</td>
</tr>
<tr>
<td>Feb</td>
<td>$100</td>
</tr>
</table>
```

Output:

Your Monthly Savings	
Months	**Savings**
Jan	$175
Feb	$100

Test Your Progress

1. *What is the use of cellpadding in table?*
2. *What is the use of cellspacing in table?*
3. *Why we use colspan and rowspan in table?*

2.9   Frames in HTML

HTML provides a facility to divide a Web page into several blocks is known as frames. Each frame may display a separate Web page and HTML document window in a one browser. All browsers do not support the frames. The general use of frame is to have the menu in one frame and other frames contain the data. When user clicks on menu frame, data is displayed in corresponding frame.

Frame is started by using tags <frameset> and ends with </frameset>.

Basics of Frameset

The frameset tag requires two attributes in which the screen is divided into rows and columns.

Row: This attribute is used to divide page into multiple column or horizontally. Value of row indicates the height of frame. For example,

```
Rows="20%,"
Rows="30%, 40%, 30%"
```

Column: This attribute is used to divide page into multiple column or horizontally. Value of row indicates the height of frame. For example,

```
Cols="20%,"
Cols="25%, 25%, 50%"
```

Frame element

Attributes of the frame are as follows:

Tag name	Description
`name`	It gives the unique name of the frame.
`src`	It specifies the URL of the document to be loaded.
`noresize`	It disables the frame resizing property.
`marginwidth`	It specifies the amount of margin left along left or right side of the frame.
`marginheight`	It specifies the amount of margin left along top or bottom of the frame.
`scrolling`	Control the displaying of horizontal and vertical scroll bars in frame
`yes`	Scrollbar is always added
`no`	No scrollbar is provided
`auto`	Scrollbar will be added when it is required
`frameborder`	It indicates the border information about the frame
`1`	A border will be drawn
`o`	No border

Specifying target in frame

The `target` attribute is used to create links, such as `<a>`, `<link>`, `<area>`, `<form>`, etc., the value of these attributes refers to the frame where document is to be loaded.

Example 6: Specifying target attribute to create a link.

```
<html>
<head>
<title> target </title>
</head>
<body>
<a href=http://www.google.com target="right">google</a>
</body>
</html>
```

Test Your Progress

1. *Define frames in HTML.*
2. *What is frameset in HTML?*
3. *What are different frame elements in HTML?*

2.10   Forms in HTML

Form tag is important as it creates a section in the HTML document. It is used to collect the information from the user, it also contains special elements called controls. The forms are created using `<form>...</form>` tags.

Create Forms

Following is the syntax of form:

```
<form>
    Form elements, markups and other contents are specified
    here
</form>
```

Inputs elements in form application

Data in a form are collected using different types of control element. The control elements are created using <input> tag. There are ten input types.

- **Text field:** It is used to get single line textual data.
  ```
  <input type="text" value="n1">:Name
  ```

Output:

| U.K Roy | :Name

Use of Password field in form application

- **Password field:** It is similar to text field but the characters entered are represented by dots (.) or asterisks (*). It allows to hide information from others.
  ```
  <input type="password" value="p1">:Password
  ```

Output:

| ******** | :Password

- **Hidden field:** It is not displayed by the browser and users can never interact with it. The users can see the field by viewing the source code.
  ```
  <input type="hidden" name="userid"> value="U.K Roy">
  ```
- **Label:** It is used to add a label to a form field.
  ```
  <label for="Marriage">
  </label>
  ```

Output:

Marriage

Checkbox and Radio Buttons in form application

- **Checkbox:** It is like a toggled switch which is checked or unchecked. It allows user to select one option from a set of alternatives.

  Which of the following items do you have:

  ```
  <input type="checkbox" value="c1">Car   <br>
  ```

```
<input type="checkbox" value="c2"> COMPUTER <br>
<input type="checkbox" value="c3">CAMERA   <br>
```

Output:

Which of the following items do you have-

❏ Car

❏ COMPUTER

❏ CAMERA

● **Radio button**: It allows user to select one option from a set of alternatives.

Gender:

```
<input type="radio" name="r1">male<br>
<input type="radio" name="r1">female<br>
```

Output:

Gender:

   o Male

   o Female

● **Selection list**: It is a group of radio buttons or checkboxes which allows user to select one option from a set of alternatives.

Gender:

```
<select>
<option> male
<option> female
</select>
```

Multiple Lines text Input field in form application

● **Text area:** It is the extension of text field and used to enter large amount of text.

Comment:

```
<input type="textarea" rows="4" cols="10">
```

Enter your comment here...

Output:

Comment:

Enter your comment here...

Submit and Reset Buttons in form application

● **Button**

   ▪ Submit button-

```
<input type="submit" value="send">
```

- Reset button-
  ```
  <input type="reset" value="restore">
  ```
- Image button-
  ```
  <input type="image" src="a.jpg">
  ```

● **File upload:** It allows to upload more than one file. These files can be either image, text or other files.
```
<form action="upload.jsp" method="post">
</form>
```

Test Your Progress
1. *Define forms in HTML.*
2. *Define some of the input elements of form.*
3. *Implement multiple lines input field in form.*

2.11 Data Validation

Data validation is defined as the process of ensuring that a program operates on correct, clean and useful data. Data validation includes "validation constraints" or "validation rules" that check for the correctness, meaningfulness, and security of data. There are several benefits to add validation of data on the Web page itself. It means that we must put some validation on the client side. Most of the users are annoyed by forms, if we provide the validation of data while the users are filling it out, then the users can know immediately if they have made any type of mistake. This provides a good user interface and also saves the user time for the waiting of HTTP response. It helps your server from dealing with spam/bad form inputs.

Here we discussed the validation rules applied with HTML5 enabled documents and also with new browser capability. That is we validate a form using only the browser's built in validation.

Example 7: A simple booking form:
```
<form action="" method="post">
    <fieldset>
        <legent>Booking Details</legend>
        <div>
            <label for="name">Name (required):</label>
            <input type="text" id="name" name="name"
            value=" ">
        </div>
        <div>
            <label for="email">Email (required):</label>
            <input type="text" id="email" name="email"
            value=" ">
        </div>
        <div>
```

```
        <label for="num_Tickets"><abbr title="Number">
        No.</abbr> of Tickets (required):</label>
        <input type="text" id="num_Tickets"
        name="num_Tickets" value=" ">
    </div>
    <div class="submit">
        <input type="submit" id=" value=" ">
    </div>
  </fieldset>
</form)
```

Output:

Booking Details
Name (required): [   ]
Email (required): [   ]
No. of Tickets (required): [   ]
[Submit]

Notice that each input field is associated with a `<label>` tag. Under `<label>` `"for"` attribute is used to match it with the `id` attribute of the associated `input` tag. This help to keep the HTML semantics, with the use of labels provides the meaning to the input field. It also means that if you click the label then the associated input field receives the focused.

To validate any form, we will need to:

- Make sure that the required field must get filled.
- Make sure that whatever entered for Name must be like a Name.
- Make sure that the e-mail address entered must be in e-mail format.
- Make sure that a number has been entered into the No. of Tickets (required) field.

Test Your Progress
1.   *Define data validation in html.*
2.   *Why it is required to validate any form?*

2.12 Data Entry Validation

Required fields

To validate the required field we just have to add the "required" attribute to each of the `<input>` tag that must be completed. As here, we concerned about the Name Field.

Now Name field looks like:

```
<div>
    <label for="name">Name:</label>
    <input id="name" name="name" value=" " required>
</div>
```

If we try to submit the form without filling the Name field then it will prompt a message 'please fill out this field'.

Output:

2.13 Validation of Input Patterns in Forms

For the pattern validation in HTML all <input> tags can uses this attribute. This attribute use the case-sensitive regular expression as an input value. If the particular field is not empty and the input value does not match the desire pattern then it is an invalid input.

Code implementation:

```
<form>
    <label for="choose">Would you prefer a banana for
    cherry?</label>
    <input id="choose" name="i_like" pattern="banana|cherry"
    required>
    <button>Submit</button>
</form>
```

If we try to submit the form with invalid pattern input then it will show follows:

Output:

So you observed that the case-sensitive part plays a main role with this attribute.

Test Your Progress

1. *Define validation of input pattern.*
2. *How will you validate input pattern in HTML?*

2.14 Validation of Forms: Numeric, Email-Id and URL

Numeric

To validate the Numeric field we have define its type. Here in our example we need to validate the No. of Tickets field as a number type. For this we just have to specify the appropriate type, further validation is performed by the browser.

Code implementation:

```
<div>
    <label for="num_Tickets"><abbr title="Number">No.</abbr>
    of Tickets:</label>
    <input type="number" id="num_Tickets" name="num_Tickets"
    required>
</div>
```

If we try to submit the form with a character in numeric field then it will show as follows:

Output:

Similarly we can validate URLs and E-mail id fields. Go with the examples.

E-mail id

Code implementation:

```
<div>
    <label for="email">Email :</label>
    <input type="email" id="email" name="email" value=" "
    required>
</div>
```

If we try to submit the form without proper syntax of E-mail id in Email field then it will show as follows:

Output:

URL

Code implementation:

```
<div>
    <label>Website:</label>
    <input type="url" id="url" name="url">
</div>
```

If we try to submit the form without proper syntax of URL in Website field then it will show as follows:

Output:

Test Your Progress
1.   *How will you validate Numeric inputs in HTML?*
2.   *How will you validate Email inputs in HTML?*
3.   *How will you validate URL inputs in HTML?*

2.15 Validation of Date and Time Fields

For validating the Date and Time we have use the features of JavaScript to implement it.

Let's start with an example.

Example 8::

```
<form onsubmit="checkForm(this); return false;" action="/
javascript/validate-date/" method="POST">
<fieldset>
    <legend>Event Details</legend>
    <div>
        <label for="field_startdate">Start Date</label>
        <span>
            <input id="field_startdate" type="text"
            name="startdate" placeholder="dd/mm/yyyy"
            size="12">
            <small>(dd/mm/yyyy)</small>
        </span>
    </div>
    <div>
        <label for="field_starttime">Start Time</label>
        <span>
            <input id="field_starttime" type="text"
            name="starttime" size="12">
            <small>(eg. 20:19 or 8:19pm)</small>
        </span>
    </div>
    <div>
        <span>
            <input type="submit">
        </span>
    </div>
</fieldset>
</form>
```

The interface is shown as follows:

Output:

If we try to submit the form without proper syntax of Date format in Start Date field then it will show as follows:

Output:

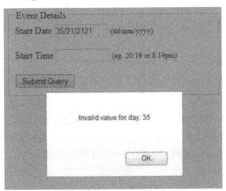 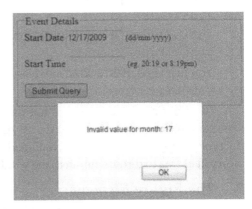

Similarly if invalid input is to time then it will show as follows:

Output:

 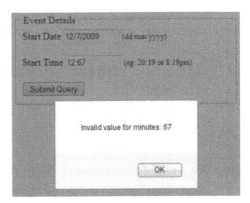

Test Your Progress
1.   *How will you validate date inputs in HTML?*
2.   *How will you validate time inputs in HTML?*

2.16 New Features of HTML5

Earlier versions of HTML (HTML 1.0 till HTML 4.0 and XHTML) include specifications for laying out text and images on a page. Later versions also provide some support to semantic data. HTML5 aims to be more of an application development platform. It not only includes features for laying out text and images, but also provides tags for playing video and audio, interactive 2d and 3d graphics, storing data in the application. It provides support for dealing with online and offline access to data. Some of the features of HTML 5 have been listed below:

1. New Doctype

There is no more need of lengthy declarations like:

```
<!DOCTYPE html PUBLIC "-//W3C//DTD XHTML 1.0 Transitional/
/EN"
"http://www.w3.org/TR/xhtml1/DTD/xhtml1-
transitional.dtd">
```

You just need to do a simple declaration.

```
<!DOCTYPE html>
```

Even giving a declaration is not mandatory. It is used for current, and older browsers that require a specified `doctype`. Browsers that do not understand this doctype will simply render the contained markup in standards mode. So, without worry, feel free to throw caution to the wind, and embrace the new HTML5 doctype.

2. *The Figure Element*

In the previous version of HTML markups for image were written as follows:

```
<img src="/image" alt="About image" /><p>Image Shri
Krishna </p>
```

By introducing `<figure>` and `<figcaption>` element in HTML5 we can now semantically associate captions with their image counterparts.

```
<figure>
    <img src="/image" alt="About image" />
    <figcaption>
        <p>Look at the marvelous image of Shri Krishna. </p>
    </figcaption>
</figure>
```

3. *No need for type attribute for Scripts and Links*

In previous version we added the type attribute to the link and script tags.

```
<link rel="stylesheet" href="/stylesheet.css" type="text/
css" /><script type="text/javascript" src="/code.js"></
script>
```

However, this is no longer required. You can rewrite these scripts as follows in HTML5:

```
<link rel="stylesheet" href="/stylesheet.css" />
<script src="/code.js"></script>
```

4. *To Quote or not to Quote*

Unlike XHTML in HTML5 you do not need to wrap the attributes in quotation marks and there is no need to close the elements. You may continue using them but that is not required.

```
<p class=first id=two> Let's accept the change
```

5. *Making the Content Editable*

The new version of HTML provides new attribute that can be applied to elements, called Content Editable. This allows the user to edit any of the text contained within the element, including its children. This feature could be used for a variety of purposes like use in app for making a simple to-do list. This takes advantage of local storage.

```
<!DOCTYPE html>
<html>
<body>
    <h2>The Shopping List </h2>
    <ul contenteditable="true">
    <li> Pulses </li>
    <li> Vegetables</li>
    <li> Milk</li>
    </ul>
</body>
</html>
```

6. Email Inputs

E-mail validation is a very important part of Website scripting. HTML5 provides a very easy to instruct the browser to yallows strings that conform to an e-mail address structure.

```
<!DOCTYPE html>
<html>
<head>
    <title>Try- new input validation </title>
</head>
<body>
    <form action="" method="get">
        <label for="email">User's Email:</label>
        <input id="email" name="email" type="email" />
        <button type="submit"> Click me</button>
    </form>
</body>
</html>
```

User's Email: anna ☒ Click me

You must enter a valid email address

7. Place holder

Till now JavaScript was being used to create placeholders for textboxes. However, now you can only initially set the value attribute. As soon as the user deletes that text and clicks away, the input will be left blank again. HTML 5 provides a solution.

```
<.input name="email" type="email"
placeholder="shruti@shrutikohli.com" />
```

It may still not work with some Web browsers. It will continue to improve with every new release.

8.   *The Semantic Header and Footer*

Early versions of HTML use <DIV> tag to add header and footer to a Web page. Code is somewhat like this:

```
<div id="header">
   ...
</div>
<div id="footer">
   ...
</div>
```

HTML 5 provies its own semantic header and footer as follows:

```
<header>
   ...
</header>
<footer>
   ...
</footer>
```

It is even possible to have multiple headers and footers in the Web page. These headers and footers are just container that could be used to provide meta information in the Web page.

9.   *Use of required Attribute*

Forms can now have a required attribute to specify the user whether a particular input is required. It could be declared in two ways as follows:

(i)   `<input type="text" name="subject" required>`

(ii) `<input        type="text"        name="subject" required="required">`

In case user leaves the input field blank and submits the form the textbox will be highlighted.

```
<form method="post" action="">
   <label for="subject"> Your Name: </label>
   <input type="text" id=" subject" name=" subject"
   placeholder="Web Technology" required>
   <button type="submit">Go</button>
</form>
```

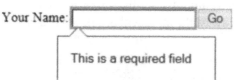

10. *Autofocus Attribute*

With HTML5 there is no need for JavaScript solutions for implementing "autofocus" in form. In case a particular input should be "selected," or focused, by default, we can just use the the "autofocus" attribute.

```
<input type="text" name="subject" placeholder="Web
Technology" autofocus>
```

11. *Audio Support*

While using earlier versions of HTML third party plug-ins were required to render audio. However, with HTML5 the <audio> element. This supports for the time being which is offered only by the recent browsers of HTML5 audio. So, you need to provide some form of backward compatibility.

```
<audio autoplay="autoplay" controls="controls">
    <source src="rehman.mp3" />
    <a>Listen to this music</a>
</audio>
```

However, the support may vary in different browsers.

12. *Video Support*

As <audio> similarly HTML5 provides video support. Even YouTube has announced a new HTML5 video embed for their videos. However, HTML5 specifications do not specify any specific codec for video so it is left to the browsers to decide. For example, Safari, and Internet Explorer 9 may support video in the H.264 format. This format Flash players can play. However, Firefox and Opera are using the open source Theora and Vorbis formats. So, when displaying HTML5 video, you need to offer both formats.

```
<video controls preload>
    <source src="jian.ogv" type="video/ogg;
    codecs='vorbis, theora'" />
    <source src="rehman.mp4" type="video/mp4;
    `codecs='avc1.42E01E, mp4a.40.2'" />
    <p> You may be using an old browser versio <a
    href="rehman.mp4">Download here d.</a> </p>
</video>
```

Few key points to remember:

1. It is not technically required to set the type attribute. However, in case we do not do then browser has to identify the type itself.
2. All browsers do not understand HTML5 video. So, it is always better to offer a download link, or embed a Flash version of the video instead.

13. *Preload Videos*

The preload attribute could be used in case if the browser preloads the video.

Suppose a visitor accesses a page which is only meant for displaying a video then you should definitely preload the video and save the waiting time of the visitor.

Videos can be preloaded by setting `preload="preload"` or by simply adding preload.

```
<video preload>
```

14. *Display Controls*

In case if you want that the video appears with controls add controls then to the code. For example,

```
<video preload controls>
```

15. *Regular Expressions*

Using the `pattern` attribute it is easy to verify the content of a particular textbox. This helps to insert a regular expression directly into the markup.

```
<form action="a.php" method="post">
    <label for="Name">Enter the name:</label>
    <input type="text"
    name="name"
    id="name"
    placeholder="5 <> 11"
    pattern="[A-Za-    z]{5,11}"
    autofocus
    required>
    <button type="submit">Click me
</button></form>
```

Here, pattern: `[A-Za-z]{5,11}` implies that the textbox can only accept only uppercase and lowercase letters. Further, this string must also have a minimum of five and a maximum of eleven characters.

2.17 Key Terms

- **Attributes:** Parts of tags that control the behavior and appearance of elements on a page.

- **Body element:** An element that contains all the content that is displayed on the Web page.

- **Closing tag:** The tag that is on the right side of a two-sided tag.

- **Comments:** Comments are used to explain and clarify code or to prevent code from being recognized by the browser. Comments start with " *<!—" and end with " —>".

- **Definition list:** Definition list could be defined as a list style that could be used to format a list of terms, followed by definitions.

- **DOCTYPE:** DOCTYPE tells the browser which type of HTML is used on a Web page. In turn, the browsers use DOCTYPE to determine how to render a page.

- **Head element:** Head is an element of HTML that contains information about the document.

- **HTML:** HTML stands for HyperText Markup Language. It is a simple but a dominant markup language for creating Websites and other Web browser applications.

- **HTML elements and tags:** HTML elements are needed to perform communication with the browser for rendering the text. When surrounded by angular brackets <> they form HTML tags. For the most part, tags come in pairs and surround text.

- **Hyperlinks:** Hyperlinks are HTML elements used in a hypertext document to jump from one location in the document to another.

- **Hypertext:** Hypertext could be understood as a method of organizing information that gives the readers freedom to read the information as per their desire.

- **Markup language:** A language that describes a document's structure and content.

- **Ordered list:** Ordered list as name suggests is the list of items that must appear in a sequential order.

- **Semantic HTML:** Semantic HTML is a coding style where the tags embody what the text is meant to convey. While using Semantic HTML, tags like `<b></b>` for bold, and `<i></i>` for italic should not be used as they just represent formatting without giving any indication of meaning or structure. While using semantic HTML you should use `<strong></strong>` and `<em></em>`. These tags will have the same bold and italic effects, while demonstrating meaning and structure (emphasis in this case).

- **SGML (Standard Generalized Markup Language):** SGML is a language used to create other languages. Also known as metalanguage.

- **Web browser:** Application or a client software that retrieves a Web page and displays it.

- **Web server:** Web server is a computer that stores a Web page and makes it ●vailable to other computers on a network or the Internet.

- **Website:** A collection of linked hypertext documents.

- **World Wide Web:** A system of interconnected hypertext documents accessible over the Internet.

- **World Wide Web Consortium (W3C):** A group of Web developers, programmers and authors who set standards for browsers to follow.

2.18 Summary

HTML is the primary language used to encode documents containing hyperlinks. It provides simple mechanisms for formulating text, creating links and lists inserting images, embedding audio and video, etc. An HTML document basically consists of

HTML elements which in turn consists of tags and attributes. Tags are the code which marks up a certain region in an HTML document. A tag is written within angular brackets < and > and must be properly nested. Embedded tags and Standalone tags are two types of tags used in HTML document. Attributes are the properties of the tags that can be optionally be assigned values to change the default behavior of these tags. These are placed within the starting tag. Even Standalone tags may have attributes. Each tag has its own set of attributes. Basic Elements of HTML are head, meta, link, body, base, style, script, h, p and font. Unordered Lists, Ordered Lists and Definition Lists are the three types of list in HTML. Links and anchor are used as a same in HTML. This tag is name as anchor tag, as Web developers use it to anchor a URL with some text on the Web page. A table is a two dimensional matrix consisting of rows and columns. It is powerful tool for formatting the Web pages. It is created using three basic tags-<table>, <tr> and <td>. All table related tags are included between the <table> and </table> tags. Form tag is important as it creates a section in the html document. It is used to collect the information from used and it also contains special elements called controls. Data validation is defined as the process of ensuring that a program operates on correct, clean and useful data.

2.19 Test Yourself

Section I: Review with Ease

1. What is the W3C and what does it do?
2. What is HTML validation? Do you ever validate your HTML? Why?
3. What are the factors we need to keep in mind while designing Website for the client?
4. What is HTML? How is HTML interpreted?
5. Develop HTML code for the following :
   a. How do I add MIDI music to my Web page?
   b. How do I make a picture as a background on my Web pages?
   c. How do I make it so that someone can mail me by just clicking on text?
   d. How do I add floating text to my page?
   e. How to add multiple color text to a Web page?
   f. How to make a hyperlink on a picture?
   g. How can I make my link which does not have border?
   h. How to align pictures on a Web page?
   i. How to make a link to another Web page?
   j. How to create links to sections on the same page in HTML?
   k. Opening new Web page window when clicking on a link.
   l. Creating a new window in HTML for a single image.

m. How do I create multicolor links in HTML?

n. How to create a fixed background image on a Web page/

o. Creating a Web page with a single background image not a tiled background. Can HTML document be a long line of tags and still be valid.

p. Can HTML tag-pairs be nested inside each other? Explain with example.

q. Demonstrate a link from one page to specific point in another page.

6. How to generate image map in HTML? What is its use?

7. Demonstrate a succession of links that reuse the same additional window.

8. How will you develop a scrolling option in a frame? Also show the script for allowing the user to resize the frame.

9. Why we use data validation?

10. Implement different types of data validation in your form.

Section II: Exercise

1. Design a HTML page for the following:

    a. Set an image as a link.

    b. Open a link in a new browser window.

    c. Jump to another part of a document (on the same page).

    d. How to link to a mail message with CC. BCC, and Subject entries.

    e. Redirect a user to another URL after 5 seconds.

2. Design a Web page, insert an image on to the Web page such that image is of height 300 and width 300 pixels. The image should have an ALT text in it.

3. Develop a Sports portal

    ● Site Design: Good designing is recommended.

    ● Site Content: Your site should have at least five pages and each page should have content. Make sure your pages do not look empty. Use HTML5 for incorporating validation checks in the Website

4. Develop a Music portal

    ● Site Design: Good designing is recommended.

    ● Site Content: Your site should have at least five pages and each page should have good audio, videos embedded on the Web page.

5. Create a Website with at least three pages that include all the formatting tags discussed in the Chapter. Your site must use at least three different font styles, sizes, colors, and include other characteristics, such as bold,/italic/underline. Use at least two list and two tables in your site.

Section III: Short Questions with Answers Exercise

Q. 1. **Write the number of HTML tags to be used for designing the most simple Web pages.**

Ans. 4 pairs of tags. For example,

```
<HTML>
<HEAD>
<TITLE>My Web page</TITLE>
</HEAD>
<BODY> Check out my hobbies
</BODY>
</HTML>
```

Q. 2. **Explain the difference between linking to an image, a Website, and an e-mail address?**

Ans. For linking an image, use `<img>` tag. The `src` attribute is used to define the source of the image. For example,

```
<img src="HTMLrocks.jpg"></img>
```

For hyperlinking, you need to use the `anchor` tag, `<a>`. Its `href` attribute is used to link to the Website/source to be linked. For example,

```
<a href="www.shrutikohli.com">My Website</a>
```

For linking to an e-mail, the `href` specification will be "`mailto:send@shrutikohli.com.`"

For example,

```
<a href="shruti@shrutikohli.com">Email Author</a>
```

Q. 3. **How to create bulleted list and numbered list in a HTML Web page?**

Ans. For creating a bulleted list or unordered list you need to use `<ul>` tag. For creating a numbered list or ordered list you need to use `<ol>` tag.

Q. 4. **Explain difference between <div> and <frame>.**

Ans. `<div>` tag could be understood as a generic container element for grouping and styling. `<frame>` tag is used for creating divisions within a Web page and is always used within the `<frameset>` tag. The `<frame>` tag has been eliminated in HTML5.

Q. 5. **How to add scrolling text to a Web page?**

Ans 5. Using a `<marqee>` tag

For example,

```
<marquee> LET THE CELEBRATION BEGIN </marquee>
```

Q. 6. **Name some HTML5 markup elements.**

Ans. There are several: `<article>`, `<aside>`, `<bdi>`, `<command>`, `<details>`, `<figure>`, `<figcaption>`, `<summary>`, `<header>`, `<footer>`, `<hgroup>`, `<mark>`, `<section>`, `<time>` etc..

Q. 7. What are the elements that have been eliminated in HTML5?

Ans. `<frame>` and `<frameset>` have been eliminated. Other elements that are no longer supported include: `<noframe>`, `<applet>`, `<bigcenter>` and `<basefront>`.

Q. 8. What are the new media-related elements in HTML5?

Ans. HTML5 has strong support for media. There are now special `<audio>` and `<video>` tags to support audio/video.

Q. 9. What are the new image elements in HTML5?

Ans. Canvas and WebGL. `<Canvas>` is a new element that acts as a container for graphical elements like images and graphics. Coupled with JavaScript, it supports 2D graphics. WebGL stands for Web Graphics Language, a free cross-platform API that is used for generating 3D graphics in Web browsers.

Q. 10. What is difference between HTML5 and its earlier versions?

Ans. Earlier versions of HTML (HTML 1.0 till HTML 4.0 and XHTML) include specifications for laying out text and images on a page. Later versions also provide some support to semantic data. HTML5 aims to be more of an application development platform. It not only includes features for laying out text and images, but also provides tags for playing video and audio, interactive 2D and 3D graphics, storing data in the application. It provides support for dealing with online and offline access to data.

Previous Year Questions with Answers

Q. 1. What are the technologies used in Web design? What is the role of plug-in and cookies? Explain. [May 2008]

Ans. Technologies Used in Web Design:

1. **HTML:** HyperText Markup Language or HTML provides the basis for creation of Web pages. It creates text files which are readable by Web browsers. HTML files are very versatile as they permit delivering of image files, content and form fields to online users. HTML can be created either by directing the code directly in Notepad or with the help of HTML editors which are used extensively by Web designers. Some of the most popular HTML editors are Dreamweaver and FrontPage. Most Websites use HTML and you can determine this by seeing the file extension which would be HTML.

2. **Photoshop:** Photoshop is software which is used for image editing. Most images posted online are edited with the help of Photoshop. Photoshop provides tools to manipulate the images of a Website and sometimes designers may even create the basic Website layout in Photoshop and on approval from the customer go ahead and convert it to HTML.

3. **Flash:** Interactive Web pages which have an interesting presentation form are created with the help of Flash. Flash files tend to be slightly heavier than the

regular HTML files due to the code it contains for interactive elements and thus is resource hungry. However, the impact of a Flash Website is a lot more than HTML Website and is used to create a lasting impression on online users.

4. **AJAX:** AJAX is a very new entrant in the user interface technology space and some of the leading Websites, such as Google has started using it to provide users a better level of interactivity and customization of the display options. AJAX provides the users an ability to mould the interface and have only those items on display which they need.

5. **CSS:** Though CSS or Cascading Style Sheet is not a separate technology, it is worth a mention since it helps creates uniformity across the entire Web site. CSS allows Web designers to create the rules of display in a central lite which is then implemented throughout the Website. A Website can have more than one CSS. Some of the things which a CSS files helps in maintaining are font styles and colors, navigation bar, footer and sometimes even some of the graphics on the Website.

6. **JavaScript:** Javascript provides certain user interface controls which can make a Website more interesting as well as also supports user friendly features on the Website. Mouse roll avers, navigation drop-downs and validation of Web forms are some of the most practical uses of JavaScript.

There are many other user interface technologies which can be put to use by designers.

Role of Plug-in and Cookies: Plug-in interacts with a host application to provide a certain, usually very specific, function "on demand". Applications support plug-ins for many reasons. Some of the main reasons include: enabling third-party developers to create capabilities to extend an application, to support features yet unforeseen, reducing the size of an application, and separating source code from an application because of incompatible software licenses.

The main purpose of cookies is to identify users and possibly prepare customized Web pages for them. When you enter a Web site using cookies, you *may be* asked to fill out a form providing such information as your name and interests. This information is packaged into a cookie and sent to your Web browser which stores it for later use. The next time you go to the same Web site, your browser will send the cookie to the Web server. The server can use this information to present you with custom *Web* pages. So, for example, instead of seeing just a generic welcome page you might see a welcome page with your name on it.

Q. 2.   Why planning is must before developing a Website? What are advantages of early planning?   [May 2008]

Ans. Planning before developing a Website: When you begin thinking about creating a Website, you should follow a series of planning steps to make sure your site is successful. Even if you are just creating a personal home page that only friends and family will see, it can still be to your advantage to plan the site carefully in order to make sure everyone will be able to use it easily.

- Creating goals for your site
- Organizing the site structure
- Creating your design look
- Designing the navigation scheme
- Planning and gathering your assets

  Advantages of early Planning:
- Your Website will be easier to use.
- Your Website will be easier to maintain.

Q. 3. What are the application areas for forms? [June 2003]

Ans: The application areas for the forms on WWW are forever evolving. Some typical areas where they can be seen today are:

a. Education Sites: For collecting names, addresses, telephone numbers, e-mails and other information by the Website to register users for a service or event.

b. Online purchase order: Gathering information from the e-commerce Websites. For example, Amazon, eBay, etc.

c. Collection feedback about a Website: Most Website that offers a service encourages users to send feedback with making any kind of relation.

d. Provide the interface for a chat: It is like providing an interface or users are required to fill out a form if they want to participate in a chat session or a discussion group.

Chapter 3
DHTML

Key Topics

- *Introduction*
- *DHTML CSS*
- *DHTML DOM*
- *DHTML Events*
- *JSSS*
- *Layers*
- *CSSP*

3.1 Introduction

In this Chapter, you will study about Dynamic HTML. Dynamic HTML popularly called DHTML can be defined as an emerging technology that has evolved to develop attractively and mind catching Websites. It is important to understand that DHTML is not a language, but a combination of technologies that can be used together to develop attractively, animated Web pages.

3.1.1 DHTML: An Overview

As per World Wide Web Consortium (W3C), DHTML can be defined as follows:

"Dynamic HTML is a term used by some vendors which describes the combination of HTML, style sheets and scripts that allow documents to be animated. "

> **Note:** World Wide Consortium is an international organization where member organizations and the public together work with full-time staff, to develop Web standards.

DHTML includes following technologies:

1. **JavaScript:** JavaScript is the scripting standard for HTML. DHTML is used with JavaScript, and also used manipulate HTML elements and to control access.

2. **HTML Document Object Model (DOM):** includes a standard set of objects for HTML. Also, includes the way to access and manipulate them. DOM is used by DHTML to access and manipulate HTML elements.

3. **HTML Events:** DHTML is used to create Web pages that react to (user) events.

4. **Cascading Style Sheets (CSS):** It is the standard style and layout model for HTML. It is used by the Web developers to control style and layout of Web pages.

Thus, DHTML combines HTML with the Cascading Style Sheets (CSS) and Scripting languages. HTML can be used to specify element of Web page, such as table, frame, paragraph, bulleted list, etc. , whereas cascading style sheet determines a number of other features of an element, such as size, color, and position. Together with scripting languages like JavaScript DHTML can be used to manipulate Web page's element and styles assigned to them can change in the response to user's input.

3.2   DHTML CSS

As discussed, DHTML is a combination of style sheets and scripting languages. This Section explains about style sheets that are popularly being used for making presentable Web pages. You will also be discussing various HTML elements which play an important role in developing style sheets.

Cascading Style Sheets (CSS)

Style sheets are the powerful mechanism for adding styles (e.g. fonts, color) to a Web page. Adding style means defining how to display a HTML element. The purpose of Style sheet is to create a presentation for a specific element or set of elements like style for <h1> tags in the document. A browser reads a style sheet and it formats the document according to the specification given in the stylesheet, and they are not replacement for HTML. A style sheet needs to be binding to a HTML element to introduce style in the document. By the use of Style sheets, text and the image formatting properties, can be predefined in a single list.

> **Note:** A Style sheet is called cascade (Cascading Style Sheet) when they combine to specify the appearance of a Web page. Multiple style definitions may cascade into one to determine the display of whole Web page.

Advantage of using CSS

1. **Making a presentable Document:** HTML tags are used to define the content of a document. It cannot clearly define the presentation layout. To solve this problem, W3C created styles in addition to HTML 4. 0. CSS is equipped to control display of various HTML elements and is supported by all major browsers.

2. **Style Sheets saves a lot of Work:** With CSS the style and layout of multiple Web pages can be controlled all at once. For each HTML element, you can define a style and apply it to as many Web pages as you want. The advantage of the style sheet is that it is able to make global changes to all documents from a single location. Styles can be stored in an 'External style sheet'. You can make a global change by making change in this external style sheet. All Web pages formatted according to this style sheet will be updated automatically.

3.   **Multiple Styles will cascade into One:** While using the stylesheet, you can specify style information in many ways. You can specify style inside a single HTML element, inside the <head> element or in an external CSS file. You can even refer multiple external style sheets from a single HTML document.

Using <Style> Tag

<Style> tag is used for the style assignment process. CSS includes a set of tags and selectors that are used to create and use styles in a Web page. While defining a style you need to determine the HTML element (like <h1>, <p>) which need to be formatted and accordingly develop style for the element. The <style> tag is used to surround the style rules developed for various elements of the document. The <style>...</style> tags are written within the <head>.... </head> tags of the document.

Syntax:

```
<style type="text/css">
selector {property: value; propertyN; valueN}
```

The type attribute of a style tag defines the type of scripting language being used in creating a stylesheet. In the above case type="text/css" implies CSS is being used for creating a style sheet.

You can find out the CSS syntax consists of the components: a selector, a property, and a value. Selector is a tag that needs to be styled. It is normally the HTML element/tag you wish to define. You wish to change the attribute property. Each property can take a value. Property and value are both separated by colon (:) and surrounded by curly braces ({}).

body {color: black}

> **Note:** In cases value is multiple words you need to put values around the quotes like this: **p {font-family: "sans serif"}**

In case you need to specify more than one property, you need to separate them with a semicolon (;). defining a center aligned paragraph, with a red text color:

p {text-align: center; color: red}

On each line you can describe one property. This will improve readability of the style definitions.

> **Note:** No space should be between the property value and the units.

For example, you should write "text-align: center" rather than writing "text-align: center" as it may not work with some browsers.

For example, developing style rule for the <p> tag in a Web page

```
P
{
    text-align: center;
    color: black;
```

```
        font-family: arial
}
```

> **Note:** Style tags are written in the Head tag. Type= "text/css" indicates the style sheet conforms CSS syntax.

Grouping Selectors: The selectors are grouped together in case they need to be styled in the same way and have same attributes. For example, you may wish that content of all header tags in document(h1, h2, h3…) are displayed in blue color. This can be done by grouping the selectors separating each of them with a comma.

For example, grouping the header elements so that all the header elements of the Web page are displayed in blue text color:

h1, h2, h3, h4, h5, h6{ color: blue }

Using id Selector: 'id' selector is used to definingstyle for few html elements. e.g. you may need to apply some style to one of the <h1> tag or to a set of <h1> tags. You can define such styles using the id selector. 'id' selector is defined with a '#'. You can make a 'id' rule by starting with # followed by a name that can then be referred with HTML elements that need to be styled according to this rule.

The given below ID selector matches the H1 element having ID value "chap1":

H1#chap1 {text-align: left}

For example, using ID attribute for styling <p> tag

```
<style>
p#para1
{
    text-align: center;
    color: red
}
</style>
```

In the above example, the style rule will match the element <p> that has an id value "para1".

In the next example, the style rule will only match an h1 element having id value "mine". This rule will not match the <p> element and will not be applied there. Check this example.

```
<html>
    <head>
        <title>Styling header element</title>
            <style type="text/css">
                h1#mine {text-align:left}
            </style>
    </head>
    <body>
        <p id=mine>The style rule will not be applicable for
```

```
            this paragraph. <h1> tag having id mine. </p>
      </body>
</html>
```

CSS Comments

You can use comments to explain the code. This will help you to edit the source code at a later date. Comment in the CSS begins with "/*" and ends with "*/" or it can be simple HTML comment like '///' (double slash).

> **Note:** Browser ignores comments.

For example, adding comments in a style sheet

```
, p
{
      text-align: center;
      /* Paragraph text needs to be aligned centrally on a
      web page*/
      color: black;
      font-family: arial
}
```

> **Note:** Comments cannot be nested.

<STYLE> Attributes

Attributes defined in <STYLE> tag are:

1.   Font Attributes
2.   Style Color
3.   Background Attributes
4.   Text Attributes
5.   Margin Attributes
6.   List Attributes

A.   *Font Attributes*

Attributes	Values
font-family	A comma-delimited sequence of font family names like arial, sans-serif.
font-style	Used to determine style of the font like Normal, Italic or Oblique
font-weight	Normal, bold, bolder, lighter or one of nine numerical values (100, 200, 300, 400, 500, 600, 700, 800, 900)
font-size	Used to determine the absolute size (xx-small, x-small, small, medium, large, x-large, xx-large), relative size (larger, smaller). It can also be stated in pixels or percentage (of the parent element's size).

Example 1: Use of Font Attributes

```
<html>
<head>
<title>This is my first Web page</title>
<style type="text/css"><!- shows you are using CSS for
developing
          stylesheet ->
   h1{font-family:arial, verdana}<!-for writing h1 content
   use this style rule
      ->
   p{font-size:10pt; font-style:italic}<!-for writing <p>
   use this style rule->
</style>
</head>
<body>
<h1>This is my first Web page</h1>
<p> I am applying style sheet</p>
</body>
</html>
```

> **Note:** First font-family choice is 'arial' in case it is not available 'verdana' can be chosen. In this way you can give alternative choices for various attributes.

B. Color and Background Attributes

Attributes	Values
color	Used to set element's text color. It can be a color name or color code. For example, h1{color:#23238e} or h1{color: red}
background-color	Specifies color in element's background. It can be a color name or color code. For example, P{background-color: red}
background-image	Used to set the back ground image. For example, h1 { background-image:url(images/a. gif)}
background-repeat	This sets up how the image repeats through out the page. Repeat-x(repeats horizontally), repeat- y (repeats vertically)

Example 2: Styling backgrounds

```
<html>
<head>
<style type="text/css">
   body {background-color: red}
```

```
   h1 {background-color: #00ff00} /*color has been depicted
   in hexadecimal notation */
   h2 {background-color: transparent}
   p {background-color: red}
</style>
</head>
<body>
   <h1>Welcome to this tutorial</h1>
   <h2>JavaScript Basics</h2>
   <p>JavaScript is an Interpreted Language</p>
</body>
</html>
E. g. Putting Image in background of a Web page
<html>
<head>
<style type="text/css">
   body{background-image:url('bg. jpg')}
</style>
</head>
<body>
 In this example you have displayed image 'bg. jpg' as
   background of the document.
</body>
</html>
```

Example 3: Defining various background attributes for <body> tag.

```
<html>
<head>
<style type="text/css">
   body
   {
       background-image: url('snow. gif');
       background-repeat: no-repeat;
       background-attachment:fixed;
       background-position: 50px 100px;
   }
</style>
</head>
<body>
   <p><b>Check this image</b></p>
</body>
</html>
```

Example 4: Image will not scroll in the background

```
<html>
```

```
<head>
<style type="text/css">
    body
    {
        background-image: url('snow. gif');
        background-repeat:no-repeat;
        background-attachment: fixed
    }
</style>
</head>
<body>
    <p>You will find that this image will not scroll with
    rest of the Web page</p>
</body>
</html>
```

> **Note:** You should use the shorthand property when you want to set all of the background properties using only one declaration.

```
<html>
<head>
<style type="text/css">
    body
    {
        background: #00aa00 url('snow. gif'), no-repeat, fixed
        center;
    }
</style>
</head>
<body>
    <p>Check out the style </p>
</body>
</html>
```

C. *Text Attributes*

Attributes	Values
text-decoration	Used to add decoration to an element's text. It can take values like None, Underline, overline, blink.
vertical-align	Used to identify element's vertical position. It can take values like baseline, sub, super, top, middle, bottom also percentage of element's height.
text-align	Aligns text with in an element. It can be left, right center, justify.

`text-indent`	Used to indent first line of text. It is percentage of element's width or a length.
`text-transform`	Used to apply transformation like uppercase, lowercase or none on the text.

Note: There are two basic kind of length unit:relative/absolute. The various unit of measurement are discussed in Table below.

Unit Name	Explanation	Can be used in relative positioning
Point (pt)	1/72 of an inch	No
Pixel (px)	One dot on the screen	Yes
Millimeter (mm)	Printing unit	No
Centimeter (cm)	Printing unit	No
Inch (In)	Printing unit	No

Example 5: Styling font using Text attributes

```
<html>
<head><title> Concept of Global Warming</title>
<style type="text/css">
    h1{ font-family:arial;font-size:25pt;color:yellow}
    p{font-size:10pt;font-style:normal;font-
    weight:bold;color:yellow}
</style>
</head>
<body>
    <h1> Global Warming </h1>
    <p><b>Global warming</b>occurs due to the in the rise in
    the average temperature of the Earth's near-surface air
    and oceans.
</p>
</body>
</html>
```

D. Use of Border Attributes

Attributes	Values
`border-style`	Solid, double, groove, ridge, inset, outset
`border-color`	A color name or color code
`border-width`	Thin, medium, thick or length
`border-top-width`	Thin, medium, thick or length
`border-bottom-width`	Thin, medium, thick or length
`border-left-width`	Thin, medium, thick or length

border-right-width	Thin, medium, thick or length
border-top	Specifies width, color, and style
border-bottom	Specifies width, color, and style
border-left	Specifies width, color, and style
border-right	Specifies width, color, and style
Border	Sets all the properties at once

Example 6: Customizing border for a <p> tag using 'Border' attributes

```
<html>
<head>
<title>Using the border attributes</title>
<style type="text/css">
    h1{font-family:arial, verdana;font-size:30pt;color:blue}
    h2{font-family:arial, verdana;font-size:30pt;color:red}
    p{font-size:11pt;font-style:italic;color:#24248e;border-
    color:red;border-
    style:double;border-width:thick}
</style>
</head>
<body>
    <h1> Global Warming </h1>
    <h2> Definition</h2>
    <p><strong>Global warming</strong>occurs due to the rise
    in average temperature of the Earth's near-surface air
    and oceans. </p>
</body>
</html>
```

E. *Margin Related Attributes*

Attributes	Values
margin-top	Percent, length or auto
margin-bottom	Percent, length or auto
margin-left	Percent, length or auto
margin-right	Percent, length or auto
Margin	Percent, length or auto

Example 7: Customizing margins of a paragraph

```
<html>
<head><title> Introduction to Global Warming</title>
<Style type="text/css">
    h1{ font-family:arial;font-size:20pt;color;red}
    p{font-size:10pt;font-style:normal;font-
```

```
    weight:bold;color;yellow;margin-
    left:12%;. margin-right:12%}
</style>
</head>
<body>
<h1> Global Warming </h1>
<p><strong>Global warming</strong>occurs due to the rise in
average temperature of the Earth's near-surface air and
oceans. </p>
</body>
</html>
```

F. List Attributes

Attributes	Values
`list-style`	Disc, square, circle, decimal, lower-roman, upper-roman, lower-alpha, upper-alpha, none

Example 8:. Formatting unordered list on a Web page

```
<html>
<head><title>
<html>
<head><title> Environmental Hazards</title>
<Style type="text/css">
    h1{ font-family:arial;font-size:20pt;color;red}
    ul{list-style:disc}
</style>
</head>
<body>
    <h1> Environmental Hazards </h1>
    <ul>
        <li> Global Warming
        <li> Water Pollution
        <li> Air Pollution
        <li> Noise Pollution
    </ul>
</body>
</html>
```

Defining Class in CSS

Style sheet provides exciting control over the HTML elements but it is possible that some style need to apply to a particular HTML tag rather than a complete set of these tags on the Web page. You can increase the granularity of control over elements style sheet supports classes. A 'class' can be defined to change the style in the specific way for any element it is applied to. Class can help to identify logical set of style change that might be different for different HTML elements. Such style change can be applied directly to any HTML element or part of the Web page by using <span>tag discussed in the next sub-section.

Suppose two paragraphs in a document need different alignments. One is right-aligned whereas the other one is center-aligned paragraph. This can be done creating class right and center for the <p> tag.

This can be done as follows:

```
p. right{text-align: right}
p. center{text-align: center}
```

Using the `class` attribute to align paragraphs

```
<p class="right"><!- Styling the paragraph as right-aligned.
->
    Cost of Computer is Rs 20, 000
</p>
<p class="center"> /* Styling the paragraph as center aligned.
*/
    Tips for studying computers.
</p>
```

> **Note:** In case you need to apply more than one classes for given element the syntax is:

```
<p class="left italic">
    This is a paragraph. <!- Here left and italic are
    classes created for paragraph
     Tag - >
</p>
```

This paragraph will be styled according to the class "left" and "italic".

Defining a Style that can be used by all HTML elements

With CSS it is possible to develop a style, which can be applied to any HTML element. If the tag name is ommited in the selector you will be able to define a style, that will be used for all HTML elements using a particular class. In the example given below, all HTML elements with

`class="left"` will be center-aligned:

. left{text-align: left}

Code given below h1 element and the pelement have `class="center"`, that means both elements will be following the rules in the ". center" selector:

Example 9: Styling using ` . ` operator

```
<h1 class="left">
```

This heading will be left-aligned

```
   </h1>
   <p class="left">
```

This paragraph will also be left-aligned.
```
   </p>
```

Suppose you need to design a FAQ (Frequently Asked Questions) on a Web page. It will include two type of paragraphs one that will include question and the other paragraph will include answers. Style the two different type of paragraphs using style sheet.

```
<html>
<head><title> FAQ </title>
<style type="text/css">
    p{font-size:10pt;font-weight:bold;text-
    align:justify;margin-
    left:15%;margin-right:15%}
    . questions{color:red; font-style:italic}
    . answers{color:blue}
</style>
<body>
    < p class="questions">1. What is a style sheet? /*
    styling will be done according to style developed for
    'questions' class*/ </p>
    <p class="answers">Solution: Style sheet is the document
    that creates style rule for formatting Web pages. /*
    styling will be done according to style developed for
    'questions' class*/ </p>
    <p> Comment: You should discuss the advantages of style
    sheet if it is a 4 marks question /* styling will be
    done according to the style rule developed for paragraph
    tag*?
    </p>
</body>
</html>
```

Different ways of inserting style sheet in a Web document

Inserting a style sheet:

1. External Style Sheet

An external style sheet can be used when you need to apply a style to many pages. By using the external style sheet you can easily change the look of an entire Website by changing only one file. It is needed to link each page to the style sheet using the <link> tag. The <link> tag is to be used in the head section as follows:

```
<head>
<link rel="stylesheet" type="text/css" href="new.
```

```
css" />
</head>
```

Here '**new. css**' is the style sheet which has been linked with the Web page. Before displaying the Web page the browser will read the style definitions from the file '**new. css**', and format the document according to it. Any text editor can be used to write an external style sheet. You should note that style sheet file does not contain any html tags. You need to save the file using . css extension.

Check out the following style sheet file:

```
hr {color: yellow}
p {margin-left: 25px}
body {background-image: url("image/a. gif")}
```

Example 10: The HTML file given below links to an external style sheet with the<link>tag

```
<html>
<head>
    <link rel="stylesheet" type="text/css" href="sampl1. css"
    />
</head>
<body>
    <h1>DHTML</h1>
    <h2>DHTML Technologies</h2>
    <p>You need to understand various technologies that
    make up an attractive Website</p>
</body>
</html>
```

sample1. css

```
body {background-color: yellow}
h1 {font-size: 36pt}
h2 {color: blue}
p {margin-left: 50px}
E. g. The given below HTML file links to an external style
sheet with the tag<link>
<html>
<head>
    <link rel="stylesheet" type="text/css"href="sample2. css"
    />
</head>
<body>
    <h2>Sample CSS illustration</h2>
    <p>Style sheet has formated the text</p>
    <p><a href="http://www. w3sabc. com"target="_blank">
    This is a link</a></p>
```

```
</body>
</html>
```

sample2. css

```
body {background-color: red}
 h1{color:blue}
 hr{color:blue}
 p{font-size:10pt; margin-left: 25px}
 a:link{color:yellow}
a:visited{color:red}
a:hover{color:blue}
a:active{color:black}
```

> **Note:** Many Web pages can be styled through single CSS file by linking them
> with the stylesheet. For example with sample1. css you can style many
> Web pages by linking them to this file through the link tag.

2.   *Internal Style Sheet*

You can use an internal style sheet when you want the document to have a unique style. Internal styles can be defined in the head section by using the <style> tag. This can be done as follows:

```
<head>
<style type="text/css">
    h1 {color:red}
    p {margin-left:25px}
    body {background-image: url("images/a. gif")}
</style>
```

This way you can define the style for different elements in the document. The browser will read these style definitions and will format the various elements of the document accordingly.

> **Note:** You should note that browser ignores unknown tags. It is possible that any
> old browser which donot support styles will ignore the <style> tag. It
> will display the content of the <style> tag on the page. You can prevent
> an old browser from displaying such content by hiding it using HTML
> comments. Check out the following example:

```
<head>
<style type="text/css">
<!-
    h1{color:red}
    p {margin-left: 25px}
    body {background-image: url("images/a. gif")}
->
```

```
</style>
</head>
```

3. *Inline Styles*

When a style is to be applied to the single occurrence of an element. For using inline styles you can use the `style` attribute with the tag to be formatted. Since inline style mixes content to be displayed with its presentation it is recommended that this method should be used at its minimum.

For example, change the color and the margin of a paragraph using Inline Styles

```
<p style="color: red; margin-left: 25px">
```

This is a paragraph

```
</p>
```

4. *Using Multiple Style Sheets*

It is possible that the same document has been formatted using different style sheets. Also, you case use different methods of inserting style sheets as discussed above. It may have set some properties for the same selector in different style sheets, for example style rule for <h1> tag have been defined in external style sheet as well as in internal style sheet. In such cases the style values will be taken from the more specific style sheet.

Consider multiple style rules developed for the <h1> selector

External style sheet has following properties for the h1 selector:

```
h1
{
    color: red;
    text-align: left;
    font-size: 8pt
}
```

The internal style sheet may have following properties for h1 selector:

```
h1
{
    text-align: right;
    font-size: 20pt
}
```

In case the page with an internal style sheet is linked to an external style sheet the properties for h1 will be defined as follows:

```
    color: red;
    text-align: right;
    font-size:20pt
```

You can see that `color` has been taken from the external style sheet. Text alignment and font size has been defined using the internal style sheet.

In short, above mentioned styles will cascade into a virtual style sheet. This is done on basis of following rules:

1.   Default browser
2.   External style sheet
3.   Internal style sheet (inside the `<head>` tag)
4.   Inline style (inside an HTML element)

> **Note:** Rule (4) has the highest priority.

According to the priority list inline style has the highest priority. This implies that it will override any other style declared for the element.

Using `<DIV>....  </DIV>` Tag

While using the style sheets, you will find that application of some elements of HTML are indispensable. `<div>` and `<span>` are two such elements. `<div>` is a logical block of the tag what is used for structuring HTML documents. A Web page can be divided into segments or division using `<DIV>` tag. Each segment is started and ended with a `DIV` tag. The `<div>` tag precisely defines a division or a section in an HTML document. It is often used to group block elements to format them with styles. Using the position attribute of `DIV` tag one can set absolute or relative position of the segment with respect to left or top edge of the browser window. Relative position can be set relative to the other elements on the Web page Under tradition HTML `<div>` tag was mostly used to align sections of content by setting its align attribute. While developing a style sheet it is possible to apply a style to the particular section/division of a document using `<div>` tag. For example:

```
<div style="background-color: red; font-weight: bold;
color: blue">
<p>
```
> Style sheets play a key role in improving structure of a document from its presentation. Separating layout and presentations can have many benefits and helps to develop attractive Websites.
```
</p>
</div>
```

Primary attributes of the `<div>` tag are:

Attributes	Description
ID	This is a unique identification tag used for the `div` element. Using this tag you can apply many controls to the `div` block. This attribute helps to identify a `div` tag in case when there can be more than one `div` tag on the Web page.

align	This attribute indicates that the tag text needs to be horizontally aligned on the Web page. Its default value is left.
class	Determines class of the element. It is used to specify a class in the styles heet.
width	Used to determine the width of the block.
style	Used to give an inline style definition.
left	This can be used to specify the horizontal position of the div tag. For example Left:80 implies the div block is located 80 pixels from the left border of the page.
height	It tells the height of the div block.
border	It can be used to add border to a div tag, and specify color size and style of the border.
position	It can be used to specify whether the div element is taking the position relative to its actual position (or position without any value specified).

Example 11: Defining a segment in a Web page

```
<html>
<head><title> Working with div tag</title>
</head>
<body>
    <div id="index" style="position: relative; right: 0px;
    top: 10px; background-
    color: #cccc33; width: 16px; color: yellow; border:
    2px; "> Using DIV tag
</div>
</body>
</html>
```

Example 12: Divides a Web page into four segments and each containing an image

```
<html>
<head><title> Working with DIV tag </title></head>
<body>
    <div id=image1 style='background-color:red;
    position:absolute; left:200; top:200 ;
    width:200">
    <img src=image_catalog/im1. gif>
    </div>
    <div id=image2 style='background-color:yellow;
    position:absolute; left:200;
    top:200; width:200">
    <img src=image_catalog/im2. gif>
```

```
    </div>
    <div id=image3 style='background-color: blue; position:
    absolute; left: 200;
    top:200; width:200">
    <img src=image_catalog/im3. gif>
    </div>
    <div id=image4 style='background-color: blue; position:
    absolute; left:200;
    top:200; width:200">
    <img src=image_catalog/im4. gif></div>
</body>
</html>
```

In the above example, images are put in four different segments. DIV tag together with JavaScript can be used to create dynamic features in the Web page like making all other images invisible when mouse is on the first image. Such features will be discussed in Chapter 4 when you will be studying about JavaScript.

Using <SPAN> Tag

<SPAN> is an HTML tag which plays a prominent role in style sheets. It is used to group inline text, and the scripting or style rules can be applied to the content. It can be understood as the very important inline element for associating style and script with the content.

Example 13: Using span tag

```
<html>
<head><title>Using SPAN tag </title></head>
<style type="text/css">
    p{font-size:10pt;font-weight:bold}
    .questions{color:blue;font-style:bold}
    .answers{color:yellow}
    .large{font-size;8pt;text-decoration:underline;text-
    transform:uppercase;color:yellow}
</style>
</head>
<body>
    <p class="questions"> How <span class="large"> Global
    Warming
    occurs?</span>Explain?</p>
    <p class="answers"> The <span class="large">Global warming
    </span> is
    caused due to increase in the average temperature of the
    Earth's near-surface air.
    It is caused due to pollution. </p>
</body>
</html>
```

Test Your Progress

1. *What are the advantages of using CSS?*
2. *How do you use a class in CSS?*
3. *What are the different ways of incorporating styles in a Web page?*
4. *When a style sheet is called cascading style sheet?*
5. *How* `<span>` *tag can be used to develop a style sheet?*

3.3   Document Object Model

The HTML Document Object Model (DOM) includes the objects, and properties of all the HTML elementsand the **methods** (interface) to access them. The HTML DOM includes a standard for how to get, add, change, or delete HTML elements.

The HTML/DHTML DOM can be defined as:

1. A standard object model for HTML
2. A standard programming interface for HTML
3. Platform- and language-independent model, supported by W3C.

The DOM presents HTML as a tree-structure (a node tree), with elements, attributes, and text as shown in Figure 3.1.

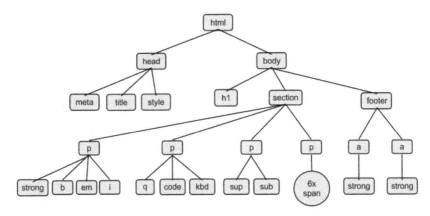

Figure 3.1: A Tree-Structure DOM

Exanoke 14: Using the HTML DOM to change an HTML element

```
<html>
<body>
    <h2 id="header2">Styling Header</h2>
    <script type="text/JavaScript">
    document. getElementById("header2"). innerHTML="You have
    changed the content";
    </script>
</body>
</html>
```

In the above example, the HTML document contains a header with id="header". The DOM gets the element with id="header" and JavaScript is used to change the HTML content (innerHTML). This will be discussed in detail in Chapter 4.

Defining Nodes in a DHTML DOM

According to the document object model everything, in an HTML document is a node. Every HTML tag can be interpreted as an element node, text in the HTML elements as text nodes, HTML attribute as an attribute node and the comments as comment nodes.

Example 15: Understanding DOM

```
<html>
<head>
    <title>Introduction to Document Object Model</title>
</head>
<body>
    <h1>Understanding DOM</h1>
    <h2> Finding the
    <p>HTML is the root element</p>
</body>
</html>
```

In above example the root node is <html>. You can see that all other nodes in the document are contained within <html>. The <html> node further has two child nodes namely <head> and <body>. The <head> node will hold the <title> node and the <body> node will holds <h1>, <h2> and <p>node.

Note: The text of an element node is always stored in a text node. Many times an element node is expected to contain text. This is a common error in DOM processing to expect.

For example,

<title>Understanding DOM Tutorial</title>: It is the element node <title> that holds a text having value "Understanding DOM".

Properties and methods of DOM

According to DOM, HTML is just a set of node objects. These nodes can easily be accessed with JavaScript or other programming languages. This part will be taken in detail in Chapter 5. In this Section, you will see the various properties and methods of DOM that provide a good programming interface.

Properties: Properties can be defined as an attribute of a node (for example, name of the node).

Typical DOM properties are:

1.   a.innerHTML - The inner text value of a (It is an HTML element).

2.   `a.nodeName` - The name of a

3.   `a.nodeValue` - The value of a

4.   `aparentNode` - The parent node of a

5.   `a.childNodes` - The child nodes of a

6.   `a.attributes` - The attributes nodes of a

Note: Here a is node object. (It is an HTML element).

Methods: Methods can be referred to as something that can be done with nodes (e.g. deleting any node).

Example 16: Using the HTML DOM to change an HTML attribute

```
<html>
<body>
    <img id="i1" src="hill. gif">
    <script type="text/JavaScript">
    document. getElementById("i1e"). src="plain. gif";
    </script>
</body>
</html>
```

In the above example the HTML document loads with an image with `id="image"`. The DOM gets the element with `id="i1"`. In this example JavaScript has been used to changes the `src` attribute from `hill. gif` to `plain. gif`. JavaScript will be discussed in detail in Chapter 5.

Test Your Progress

1.   *What is document object model? Discuss with examples.*

2.   *What are the various methods available with DOM?*

3.   *Discuss briefly how you define nodes in an HTML document.*

4.   *Discuss the DOM with respect to the following HTML script:*

```
<html>
<head>
<title>DOM Tutorial</title>
</head>
<body>
    <h1>DOM Lesson one</h1>
    <p>Hello world!</p>
</body>
</html>
```

3.4   DHTML Events

Before you study about DHTML events and their handling it is important to understand what exactly is an event. Events can be defined as user action, such as clicking a button, pressing a key, moving a window or simply moving a mouse around the screen. An event can also refer to external actions like page loading HTML events trigger actions like starting a JavaScript function as user clicks on a button on the Web page. With an event handler you can execute code when corresponding event occurs.

List of Event Handlers

Event	Event Description	List of Some HTML Elements that support this event
onabort	Occurs when a user aborts any event like page loading	
onblur	Occurs when a user leaves an object	`<A>`, `<Area>`, `<button>`, `<input>`, `<select>`
onchange	A user changes the value of an object	`<input>`, `<select>`, `<textarea>`
onclick	Indicates user has clicked on an object	Most elements
ondblclick	A user double-clicks on an object	Most elements
onfocus	Occurs when a user makes focus on an object in form control	`<A>`, `<Area>`, `<button>`, `<input>`, `<select>`
onkeydown	Indicates a key has been pressed.	Most elements
onkeypress	Indicates a key is being pressed and released.	Most elements
onkeyup	Indicates a released key has been	Most elements
onload	Indicates when a window or frame finishes loading an element	`<body>`, `<frameset>`
onmousedown	Indicates user has pressed a mouse button	Most elements
onmousemove	Indicates user has moved an object	Most elements
onmouseover	Indicates user has moved mouse over an element	Most elements
onmouseout	Indicates mouse has moved away from an element	Most elements
onmouseup	Indicates user has released a mouse-button	Most elements

onreset	Indicates that a form is being reset possibly by clicking on reset button.	<form>
onselect	Indicates selection of a text by the user	<input>,<textarea>
onsubmit	Indicates a user submits a form by clicking the submit button	<form>
onunload	Indicates browser is leaving the current document. It is unloading it from the window or frame.	<body>, <frameset>

Example 17: Using Event Handlers for creating dynamic Web pages.

```
<html>
<head><title> Studying the use of Event Handlers </title></
head>
    <body onload='alert(" You need to Understand Event
    Handling")'>
    onunload='alert("I hope Event Handling Concept are clear
    to you)'>
    <h1 align="center"> DHTML EVENT HANDLERS </h1>
    <form onreset='alert("You are resetting the form
    information will be lost")'
    onsubmit='alert("You are submitting the information
    entered in the form");return false;'>
    <ul>
    <li> onblur: <input type="text" value="On leaving the
    field you will get a message" size="50" onblur='alert
    "Lost Focus")'><br><br>
    <li> onclick: <input type="button" value="You will get
    a message on clicking in this field" size="50"
    onblur='alert("You clicked on this field")'><br><br>
    <li> onchange: <input type="text" value="You will get a
    message on changing content of this field" size="50"
    onchange='alert("Content of this field have been
    changed")'><br><br>
    <li> ondblclick: <input type="button" value="You will
    get a message on double clicking on this field" size="50"
    ondblclick='alert("You just double clicked on this
    field")'><br><br>
    <li> onfocus: <input type="text" value="You will get a
    message on focusing on this field" size="50"
    onfocus='alert("You want to enter data in this
    field")'><br><br>
```

```
<li> onkeypress: <input type="text" value="You will get
a message on pressing key in this field" size="50"
onkeypress='alert("You just pressed a keyboard
key")'><br><br>
</ul>
</form>
</body>
</html>
```

> **Note:** Most of the event handlers discussed above are supported by almost all major browsers but the extent to which the events can be used in various elements may vary from browser to browser.

For example, a header changes when the user clicks it:
```
<h1 onclick="this.innerHTML='Text is changed'">Just
click me</h1>
```

A script can also be added in the head section of the page. You can call the function from the body section. Check out the following example:

Example 18: Adding script in the head section

```
<html>
<head>
<script type="text/JavaScript">
function changetext(id)
{
    id.innerHTML="Text is changed!";
}
</script>
</head>
<body>
    <h1 onclick="changetext(this)">Just click me</h1>
</body>
</html>
```

> **Note:** JavaScript together with event handlers can be used to develop attractive dynamic Web pages. JavaScript and event handling with JavaScript will be discussed in detail in Chapter 5.

Test Your Progress

1. *Discuss the various mouse events that are available in DHTML.*
2. *What do you understand by the `keypress` event?*
3. *Give an example of using a mouse event with <h1> tag?*
4. *Why is `onblur` event used?*

3. 5 JSSS(JavaScript Style Sheet)

JavaScript Style Sheets is an alternative to the Cascading Style Sheets (CSS) technology. JSSS supports the style provided by CSS, and has advantage of making these styles available as JavaScript properties. Since JavaScript is a powerful programming language JSSS can do things, that ordinary style sheet languages can not do. For instance, the functions and assigned values may be used to make expression of the style information easier for the style sheet creator. In addition, complex calculations and querying of external properties reflected into JavaScript scope may be used to calculate the property values in new and unique ways.

As JSSS uses JavaScript code as a stylesheet it styles individual element by modifying properties of the document tags. In the Example 19 `<style>...</style>` tags are surrounding tags. They surround four JavaScript statements that assign color values to different sub properties of the `document.tags` property. The `<style>` tag uses the `type` attribute determine the type of style sheet is being used. Value of text/JavaScript imply that JSSS is being used for developing style sheet. This is similar to text/css value which is used when CSS is being used.

Example 19: Using JSSS for creating styles in a document

```
<html>
<head><title> Using JSSS for creating Styles</title>
<style type="text/javascript">
    document.tags.BODY.backgroundColor='red'
    document.tags.H1.Color='yellow'
    document.tags.H2.Color='blue'
    document.tags.P.Color='green'
</style>
</head>
<body>
    <br><br>
    <Center></h1> Studying JSSS</h1><h2> Developing Styles
    with JSSS</h2>
    <P> JSSS are used to develop style sheets and develop
    interesting Web pages</p>
</body>
</html>
```

Same code is written in CSS Example 20.

Example 20: Creating styles in a document using CSS

```
<html><head><title> Working with Cascading Style Sheet</title>
<style type="text/css">
    body{background-color:'red'}
    h1{color:'red'}
    h2{color:'blue'}
```

```
    p{color:'green'}
</style></head>
<body>
    <br><br>
    <center><h1> Studying JSSS</h1></center>
    <h2> Developing Styles with JSSS</h2>
    <p> JSSS are used to develop style sheets and develop
    interesting Web pages</p>
</body>
</html>
```

You can see that JSSS is in some ways more powerful and in some way less powerful than CSS. Actually it lacks various CSS selector features as supports only a simple tag name selector. However, it is written using a complete programming language so JSSS can easily include highly complex dynamic calculations and conditional processing.

This can be achieved with CSS by using JavaScript to modify the style sheets applicable to the document at runtime. Being written in JavaScript many times JSSS seems less friendly than CSS. Specially to users having no programming background. You will find that designing simple style sheets with JSSS is easy. For this you just need to know little HTML and some simple JavaScript assignment statements. Example, seting the text color of 'H2' elements to blue just write the following statement:

```
document.tags.h2.color = "blue"
```

In Example 20, JavaScript is used to set the `color` property of all `h2` tags to `"blue"`. Since "document" is implicitly scoped. Therefore, the above statement could be written as:

```
tags.h2.color = "blue"
```

Consider another example. Suppose you have an `h2` element with a bold element inside:

```
<h2>Studying is important!</h2>
```

In case no color has been assigned to <b> element, it will inherit the color of the parent element. In this case the color of content in <h1> tag is red. Other style properties are likewise inherited. You should know that the inheritance starts from the oldest ancestor which is the top-level element. In an HTML <html> element is parent followed by the <body> element. To set the default style for the whole Web page style can be built for the <body> element as follows:

```
with(tags.body) {
    color = "blue";
    bgColor = "red";
}
```

> **Note:** Some style properties of the parent element may not be inherited by its child element.

As in case of CSS, JSS can be combined with HTML in following three ways:

1. Using `link` element for linking an external style sheet: The `link` element is used to refer to alternative style sheets while imported style sheets can be automatically merged with the rest of the style sheet.

2. Using `style` element inside the `head` element:

```
<style type="text/javascript">
    tags.h2.color = "red"
</style>
```

3. Using `style` attribute on an element which is inside the `body` element. This option mixes style with content so should be used at minimum.

```
<p style="color = 'red'">color of the flower is red.
</p>
```

Example 21: Combining JSS with HTML

```
<html>
<head>
<title>Learning JSSS</title>
    <link rel=stylesheet type="text/javascript" href="http:/
    /your_style.com/new"
    title="Lesson">
    <style type="text/javascript">
        tags.h1.color = "red"
    </style>
</head>
<body>
    <h1>headline is red</h1>
    <p style="color = 'blue'">let the color be blue.
</body>
</html>
```

Some Important Features of JSSS

1. **Assigning Style-Evaluating Functions:** While using JSSS it is possible to create a style function and assign it to any tag by using "`apply`" property. Function assigned to "`apply`" property will be run each time the tag is encountered:

```
<style type=text/javascript>
evaluate_style() {
    if (color == "blue"){
        color = "red";
    }   else if (color == "red"){
        color = "green";
```

```
    }   else if (color == "green") {
        color = "red";
    }
}
tag.OL.color = "green";
tag.UL.apply = evaluate_style();
</style>
```

2. **Evaluating Expressions for Property Values:** Since JSSS uses JavaScript property of any tag can be assigned, and as a result of a JavaScript expression. Check out following example:

```
tags.img.width = (50 * 2/3) * .3;
tags.img.width = .35 * document.width;
if(img.width >3) {
    body.bgColor = "yellow";
    body.color = "red";
}
else {
    body.bgColor = "red";
    body.color = "yellow";
}
```

> **Note:** You can use expressions to customize the document according to the user's need.

3. **Simplifying Assignment Using Methods:**In JSSS you can use method to simplify the assignment of some values. For example, the assignment of margins can be made easier as follows:

```
// Assigning values
with(tags.p)
{
    topMargin = 40;
    bottomMargin = 40;
    rightMargin = 40;
    leftMargin = 40;
}
// assignment using method in JSSS
tags. P. margins(40, 40, 40, 40);
```

4. **Setting Text Properties:** Using JSSS it is possible to set text properties. Some of properties that can be customized are:

Text Property	Description	Example
`wordSpacing`	Used to set word-spacing between each word in any HTML element like '**H1**' element.	`tags.H1.` `wordSpacing = 4`

`text-`
`decoration`
	This property describes decorations that are added to the text of an element. Text can be decorated as `underline	overline	line-through	blink`.	`tags.BLOCKQUOTE.`
					`textDecoration =`
					`"underline"`

'`width`'	This property used to determine width of an image.	`ids.imag.width =` `100;`
'`height`'	This property used to determine the height of an image.	`ids.imag.height =` `100;`

Test Your Progress

1.   *What does JSSS stand for?*
2.   *Discuss the advantage of using JSSS for styling Web pages.*
3.   *How does JSSS differ from CSS?*
4.   *What are the various attributes available for styling text in JSSS?*

3.6   Layers

Layer tag can be used in DHTML to segment a Web page. Netscape introduced 'layers' in Navigator 4 to add on the dynamic functionality of the Web page. The tag can be positioned anywhere on the Web page (without any relation to the other content), moved around, and the content inside updated on demand. By using layers one thing can be placed on the top of other and give it position on the page. Layers (Positioned Element) has been observed to have a powerful built-in feature: the layers can load and display external HTML files.

3.6.1   Creating a Layer

To create a layer you need to use the <layer> tag. The <layer> tag is a content tag, in which content can be added as done in <table> tag. Between the tag and its closure, one can put HTML code, and this becomes a layer which can be positioned anywhere on the Web page. The layer once created can then be freely moved over or under the other layers that make up the document. It is a paired tag.

Example 22: Creating a layer using <layer> tag

```
<layer left="100" top="100" name="picture">
<img src="hill.jpg">
</layer>
```

This script will create a layer with name "picture". The content of the layer picture will be the image in the <img> tag. This layer will be located 100 pixels from the top of the browser window and 100 pixels from left of the browser window, which is the exact position of the layer on the page. You need to adjust the pixel positions to place the layer on the desired location in a Web page. The layer will then sit right on top of anything in its way, i.e., the text or other images. In case you want to place some text over this image you can create one more layer on top of the image layer. Let the name of the layer be "super".

```
<layer left="100" top="400" name="super">
<img src="hill.jpg" width="100" height="100">
</layer>
<layer left="100" top="400" name="high">
<font color="yellow">Using Layers.</font>
</layer>
```

With this code line of text will start right over your image. The position in the "top" attribute has been changed so that layers would show up in the correct spot on this page. Then the second layer is positioned just on top of the first one.

> **Note:** When you create layers, the first will be on the bottom, next one on its top and so on. You can put content, image in the layer as required.

3.6.2 Layer Transparency

Layers are transparent by default. In case you want a layer to be opaque you need to specify a bgcolor in the layer tag. This will hide all layers behind this layer. To specify the background *image* for a layer - just write background="img.gif" where img.gif is any image to be displayed in the background. Visibility of a layer can also be controlled by using the *visibility attribute* inside the layer tag. Attributes of the layer tag have been briefly discussed in Section 3.6.5.

3.6.3 Positioning a Layer

Apart from moving the layer you can also specify its starting position. You can do so by specifying the top and left coordinates of the layer.

3.6.4 Limiting the Layer

Layer's extent can be limited in following ways:

1. Defining width of the layer (in pixels or as a percent of screen width)

   width="30%";

2. Defining *clipping rectangle*. This takes four arguments thus:

   clip="20, 50, 150, 100"

This code will display a layer and then clip 20 pixels off left margin, 50 off on the top, 150 off on the right and 100 off bottom margins. In case top and left margins need not to be clipped format is :

```
clip="150, 100"
```

By including two numbers, it is assumed that they specify right, bottom clipping margins. Left and the top margins are set to the zero. The object *clip* has 6 properties: clip.top, clip.bottom, clip.left, clip.right as well as clip.width and clip.height.

3.6.5 Layer Attributes

Layers support attributes which allow its positioning using the -, - coordinates-system. You can make it a background, clip it (make only the certain area of layer visible), hide it from view, and so on. The most important layer attributes have been listed below.

Attribute	Function	Example
id/name	The name of the layer, used to identify it in your script.	id="first"
bgColor	Used to set background color of the layer. Similar is *background*, that is used to set the background image.	bgColor= "#FFFFFF"
clip	It is the viewable area of a layer.	clip="20, 50, 150, 100"
left	The position of layer in the relationship to X-coordinates. Offset of layer can be set in pixels or percentage.	left="25" or left ="2%"
top	The position of the layer in relationship to the Y-coordinates	top="20" or top="2%"
width	The width of the layer set in px or %.	width="20%"
height	The height of layer, in px or %.	height="400"
visibility	Used to control visibility of a layer. Its options are visible, hide or inherit.	visibility= "show"
z-index, above, below	This helps to determine stacking order of a layer. z-index is a positive integer which tells about the frame which is in front. Similarly *above* and *below* identify the frame objects above and below the current one. Frames with bigger z-indices are in front of the smaller ones.	z-index="1"
src	Path name of a file that contains external content.	src="new. html"

Layer Methods

Method	Functions
moveAbove(layer)	To move the layer above the specified layer.
moveBelow	To move the layer below the specified layer.
moveTo(x, y)	To move the layer to the specified position determined by -, - coordintaes.
moveBy(x, y)	To move the layer by the specified x and y pixel increments.
captureEvents()	Allows the layer to capture all events of the specified type.
load()	Loads the given URL into the layer.
releaseEvents()	Used to end the capturing of specified event type.
handleEvent()	Invokes the event handler for the specified event.

Event Handler	Description
onMouseOver	Event handler when mouse enters a layer.
onMouseOut	Event handler when mouse leaves a layer.
onBlur	Event handler when a layer loses focus.
Onfocus	Event handler when a layer receives focus.
onLoad	Event handler when a layer is loaded for the first time.

Note: Layers only work with Netscape Navigator 4.

Example 23: Creating layers to format various HTML elements

```
<html>
<head><title> Using layers</title></head>
<body>
    <layer id="pic1" width=80px height=80px></layer>
    <img src="pollution. gif" height=50 width=50>Discussing
    Pollution</layer>
    <layer id="pic2" width=80px height=80px></layer>
    <img src="pollution2.gif" height=50 width=50>more about
    pollution</layer>
    <!- text written below does not belong to the second
    layer->
    <p>Global Warming has occurred due to pollution</p>
</body>
</html>
```

> **Note:** In example 23, you can order the stacking of layers on one above the other using z-index attribute. Higher the value of z-index higher the layer will be stacked.

Example 24: Stacking of layers using z-index attributes

```
<layer name="second" left=25 top=35 z-index=2>
    <font size=9color="red">Second</font>
</layer>
<layer name="first" left=25 top=25 z-index=1>
    <font size=6 color="#ffff00">First</font>
</layer>
<layer name="third" left=55 top=55 z-index=3>
    <font size=5 color = "yellow" > Third</font>
</layer>
```

In this case layer third will be stacked higher then layer second which will be stacked higher than layer first.

Inflow Layers `<ilayer>`

You can use the `<ilayer>` tag to offset content from the original place in the page. Natural position implies the position, where the content would normally be in case it is not positioned. By using this tag you can position content relative to its natural position. This relatively positioned can be inflow as it occupies space in the document flow and also inline as it shares line space with other HTML elements.

Syntax:

```
<ilayer id="layer_name" left="pixelposition"
top="pixelposition" pagex ="pagex" pagey"="pagey" src="file"
z-index="n" above="layername" below="layername" width="width"
height="height" clip="n, n, n, n" visibility="visibility"
bgcolor="color" background="imageurl" onmouseover="jscode"
onmouseout="jscode" onfocus="jscode" onblur="jscode"
onload="jscode">....</ilayer>
```

Using `<ilayer>` tag

```
<ilayer id="layer2" left="100" top="100" src="a. gif"
z-index="1" above="layer3" below="layer1" >....</ilayer>
```

Test Your Progress
1. *Layer visibility can be controlled using _____ attribute.*
2. *Tags used to create in flow layer are _____.*
3. *Discuss the attributes of layer in detail.*
4. *How can you change the position of a layer in Web page?*
5. *Discuss the event handlers that can be used with a layer tag.*

3.7 CSSP

CSS Positioning can be defined as an extension of the CSS style script standard that you can use to provide specific position of various elements of your Web page. When it is decided to move the element or change its position you need to access the CSSP elements slightly differently. CSSP has many advantages. It enables you to precisely position elements on the page even without interfering with the markup. A page can be created, that look completely different in CSS-compatible browsers and can be viewed in a non-graphical or incompatible browser. CSSP is some what similar to regular CSS properties. A new class can be created to specify a position for an element, and class attribute can be added to a particular element or use the elements `<span>` or `<div>` to assign the position class to number of elements. Some of the CSS properties that are useful for positioning an element on a Web page have been listed in below.

Property	Possible Values	Example	Description
`posi tion`	absolute, relative, static	`position: absolute`	Static value used when it is a HTML element without any particular CSSP markup.
`left`	number and units	`left:100px`	To define position from left
`top`	number and units	`top:50px`	To define a position from the top
`width`	number and units	`width:250px`	To determine width of the element
`height`	Number and units	`height:5in`	To determine the height of the element
`clip`	rect (top, bottom, right, left)	`rect (100px, 50px, 50px, 100px)`	To determine the small portion of a division which needs to be positioned

These properties make you able to work with the individual element, division, or span as a single box. Specific size box can be defined, and then begin at a specific place on page, which is either relative where it would have appeared on page without the styling (the relative position), or relative to top-left corner of the page itself (the absolute position). The clip property is used for the part of a particular division visible. It works similar to cropping an image in an image-editing application, by hiding part of the element that is not enclosed within a rectangle, that is created by the property.

Example 25: Using CSSP position properties to style positions for a class

```
.text_board {
    position: absolute;
    left: 25px;
```

```
    top: 80px;
    width: 210px;
    clip: rect(10px, 200px, 500px, 10px);
}
```

Example 26: Positioning a Headline and News Story via CSSP

```
<html>
<head>
<title>CSSP Usage</title>
</head>
<style type="text/css">
.headline {
    position: absolute;
    left: 35px;
    top: 30px;
    width: 100px;
    height: 60px;
}
.text_board {
    position: absolute;
    left: 25px;
    top: 80px;
    width: 210px;
}
</style>
<body>
    <h1 class="headline">Global Warming</h1>
    <div class="text_board">
    <p><b>Greenhouse effect</b>has occurred due to pollution</
    p>
    </div>
</body>
</html>
```

Overlapping Elements and z-index

CSSP gives you the flexibility to layout boxes and elements on your page with exact specifications. Sometimes element may get overlapped due to change in positioning. For example, By changing positioning of text board class it is possible that it may overlap with another element that have been provided same positions. You can prioritize which element should be on the top by giving higher z-index value to that selector.

Example 27: Using z-index to determine an element to be placed at the top

```
<html>
<head>
```

```
<title>Overlap Text and Images</title>
</head>
<style type="text/css">
.image1{
    position: absolute;
    left: 25px;
    top: 20px;
    width: 300px;
    height: 225px;
    z-index: 0;
}
.textual{
    position: absolute;
    left: 125px;
    top: 200px;
    width: 210px;
    z-index: 1;
    font-face: courier;
    font-weight: bold;
    color: white;
}
</style>
<body>
    <img src="house. jpg" class="image1">
    <p class="textual">This is my house</p>
</body>
</html>
```

The text positioned in this example over the image makes it appear that it is a part of the image. It is possible to specify which element will appear on top another elements. By default, later elements are piled over the top of the previous elements. In this case text that appears after an image in the Web document, will appear on top of that image. By using the property z-index of CSSP, the order can be changed by giving each element or class a number. The number will be closer to the top of the pile that element as it goes higher.

Nesting CSSP Elements

It is also possible for you to nest various CSSP elements.

Example 28: Nesting position elements in a Web page

```
<!DOCTYPE html PUBLIC "-//W3C//DTD XHTML 1.0 Transitional/
/EN"
"http://www. w3.org/TR/xhtml1/DTD/xhtml1-transitional. dtd">
<html xmlns="http://www. w3.org/1999/xhtml">
<head>
    <title>Try to nest CSSP examples</title>
```

```
</head>
<style type="text/css">
.header1 {
    position: absolute;
    left: 25px;
    top: 20px;
    width: 200px;
    height: 50px;
}
.textual {
    position: absolute;
    left: 25px;
    top: 80px;
    width: 210px;
}
</style>
<body>
    <div class="header1">
    <h1>Evolution of DHTML</h1>
    <div class="textual">
    <p>Talk about emergence of HTML and various other
    technologies. </p>
    </div>
    </div>
</body>
</html>
```

In the above Examples, the classes have been assigned to two different <div> containers where the first one is contains the second one.

Relative Positioning

You can provide relative positioning rather than providing absolute one in a Web page.

Suppose for some element you want to provide exact width and position from left and top however for some element you just want to write its relative position with respect to the parent element.

Example 29: Using relative positioning for 'textual class'

```
.textual{
    position: relative;
    top: 10px;
}
```

In Example 28, this class has been defined as a child of the first <div> this class will still bound to the coordinates specified by <div class="header1">. It just needs to be positioned 10 pixels below where it normally would be.

Test Your Progress

1. *Discuss advantages of CSSP.*
2. *Discuss the HTML elements that are used with CSSP for providing specific positions in a Web page.*
3. *Discuss with examples how can you provide relative positioning in a Web page using CSSP.*
4. *<div> and <span> can be used for positioning in style sheet. Explain?*

3.8 Case Study

1. *Well Behaved DHTML*

Source: http://www. sitepoint. com/article/behaved-dhtml-case-study/

It is not secret that over last few years DHTML has been used exclusively for evil purposes. The technology is associated by users with intrusive advertisements and error-prone pages, and it is associated by developers with browser detection and hideous hacks. This assumption is unfortunate. Browser technology has made the advancements over the last couple years. When it is done right, DHTML can improve the users' experience of many Web pages, and hacks used is to be required to make it all work are now practically non-existent. Many DHTML scripts rely too heavily on a browser features, and throw the errors or degrade improperly when those requirements are not met. They do not work well with other scripts on same page, and they sometimes create dependencies upon other technologies. Such scripts can be called badly behaved. They have potential to be good; all the tools are there. They are not doing what they should.

There is a need of well-behaved DHTML. You can always sell a client on fact, that script will either work or it will gracefully not work in any browser. They do not always appreciate obvious generalizations like practically everyone has DHTML enabled these days code, that degrades gracefully in situations where it is not supported. While developing such kind of DHTML you may follow five-step process discussed below. Check out the following example of using the process to create a basic DHTML script. Once its principles you understand, apply this process to DHTML effects with repeatedly impressive results.

The Labels Script

A most popular use of the DHTML on the Web is to create a Dynamic Label. A Dynamic Label is used to label a form field. However, the text for label is rendered inside form field, instead of adjacent to it (which would be more usual). If the form field receives attention, the label disappears so that the user may type. If user does not type anything, the label is restored as soon as the user clicks or tabs away from the field. Dynamic label saves space, look sharp and feel slick. A dveloper might implement a dynamic label script like this:

```
<input type="text" name="name" value="name" onfocus="if
```

```
(this.value == 'name') this.value = '';" onblur="if (this.value
== '') this. value = 'name';" />
```

It is a valid first step, but that's all. DHTML like this, is an example of badly designed scripts, and should never make it into any production Website.

Now we look the problems.

1. **Relies on JavaScript:** The effect does not work, if JavaScript is disabled. In this case, the label will still show up as it was hard coded into the `value` attribute of the field. However, when user focuses the form nothing happens. The user experience is badly broken probably worse than if it would be there simply been a normal textual label beside the field.

2. **Couples to code that processes the form:** The term coupling is in the programming circles to indicate, when two components implementations are tied tightly together. Coupling means, that when one component's code changes, the other component's code might also have to change. In the above code, the JavaScript that creates an effect is tightly coupled to the server code that processes the forms. The server code must be aware of what the labels are for each form field and should be able to take them out of the form submission. This is because the label's text has been put in the `value` attribute of each field. If the user does not type anything into one of these fields, the label will be submitted instead.

3. **Exclusively binds to event handlers:** A hitch among novice DHTML scripts is that, they set the values of elements' event properties directly. This can be done through attributes of an element, or in JavaScript with properties. Directly setting JavaScript events is not a good idea as only one block of code can use each event. If more than one script on a page are run, the various scripts' event handlers can overwrite each other. This type of DHTML is difficult to maintain, and can result in errors, which are difficult to debug. In modern browsers, and event listeners can be bind to more than one function to a specific event. Avoid the old style of the event handling except when it is absolutely required.

4. **Non-modular design:** This script is not modularly designed. In case you decide to implement another Dynamic Label you have no choice but to copy and paste the current code into that box's event handlers, and change the different places the label text shows up. If a bug is find in the script, or want to make a change, do not forget to make the changes for each label. If you decide to change the label text, change is required at three places. It is difficult to maintain non-modularly designed programs and develop because they are so error prone. It is easy to make errors but hard to debug them.

After analyzing the problems in first Dynamic Labels script you must have got a good idea of what your goals for improving this script. In short, you need to develop a Dynamic Label script that:

● Does not rely on JavaScript

● Does not couple with any other component

- Does not exclusively bind to any events
- Is modularly designed

5. **Steps to writing well behaved DHTML:** The goals of the production Dynamic Label script are not unlike the goals for most DHTML enhancements to Web pages. In fact, almost all scripts will share these same goals. There is a simple process that can be followed for almost any DHTML effect to ensure that these goals are met:

    1. Identify underlying logical structure of the effect.
    2. Creating the full working example of the effect.
    3. Identify all user agent requirements.
    4. Write code to transform logical structure when the agent requirements are met.
    5. Thoroughly test each target platform.

Step 1: Identify the underlying logical structure of thee ffect

One of the primary goals should be to avoid any reliance on JavaScript. A popular, but ultimately flawed approach to this problem is, try to detect "supported" browsers on the server. If the browser is supported, it is sent the dynamic version of the code. Otherwise, it is sent a simpler version. The problem is, that it is practicallyimpossible to unambiguously detect browser type and version on the server. Even if you are able, you will not be able to detect whether JavaScript was actually enabled for a particular user. Browsers simply do not send the server enough information to reliably identify themselves or their configuration. The best way to avoid JavaScript reliance is to build DHTML effects on the top of a simple, logical document structure which does not require it. The effect will become enabled dynamically on the client if it is supported. If not, user will see the basic document.

The logical structure of the dynamic label will be created should nicely work as the label element structurally links a form element to its textual label. In most of the visual browsers, the only difference between using the label element, and any other element (or no element at all) is that clicking the label focuses the form on the field with which that label is associated. However, at this point you may be interested in building the most logical underlying structure for this effect, so you will use the label element.

Check out example below.

The logical structure of Dynamic Label script is pretty simple. It consists of the following code:

```
<form>
    <label for="username">Username</label>
```

```
        <input type="text" id="username" name="username" />
    </form>
```

Step 2: *Create a full working example of the effect in a best-case environment*

The next thing to do, once you got the logical structure in place, is to update it, to create a full working example of the effect. It is not required to worry, how the script will degrade at this point, make it work with the assumption that each feature you require will be available and turned on. From the work done in Step 1 it is easy to see the high-level tasks to accomplish for each dynamic label to display our effect:

1. Hide the regular HTML label element.

2. Attach JavaScript functions to `onfocus` and `onblur` events of the associated field, which show and hide the label at the right times.

The easy way to complete first task is with a CSS rule like so:

```
<style type="text/css">
label {
    display:none;
}
</style>
```

The problem with CSS rule like this is that, it will turn off display of every label on the page. You have to modify the rule, when want to use it at page that has label elements you want displayed in the regular way, without the effect. This would not be a very modular design at all. The solution, is to give a special class to the labels you want to behave dynamically.

```
<style type="text/css">
label.dynamic
{
    display:none;
}
</style>
```

The second task essentially requires that you loop over all label elements on the page and check to see whether they have correct class, and if they add event handlers to their associated field. Save a copy of label text in a property of field for easy access, and initialize the label display. Code given below can be use to perform this task. It uses `getElementsByTagName` and `getElementById` methods, as well as the className property, which are defined in the DOM Level 1 – HTML. The event addEventListener method from DOM Level 2 is also used by the code.

```
n setupLabels() {
    // it get all of the labels on entire of the page
    var objLabels = document. getElementsByTagName("LABEL");
    var objField;
```

```
for (var i = 0; i < objLabels. length; i++) {
    // it is if the label is supposed to be the dynamic...
    if ("dynamicLabel" == objLabels[i].className) {
        // get the field associated with it
        objField =
        document.getElementById(objLabels[i].htmlFor);
        //it add event handler to the onfocus and onblur
        events
        objField. addEventListener("focus",
        focusDynamicLabel, false);
        objField.addEventListener("blur",
        blurDynamicLabel, false);
        // save a copy of the label text
        objField._labelText =
        objLabels[i].firstChild. nodeValue;
        // initialize the display of the label
        objField. value = objField._labelText;
    }
  }
}
```

Step 3: Identify all user-agent requirements

This step is easy: now go through to the code from the Step 2 and find out the objects, features and other browser requirements you used. This information will be be used to create a function of JavaScript, which weeds out all the browsers that do not meet these requirements. Labels script, use many different DOM technologies, but you really need to test for three only:

- document.getElementById
- window.attachEvent or
- window.addEventListener

This function you can use:

```
function supportsDynamicLabels() {
    //it returns true if the browser supports getElementById
    and a method to
    // create event listeners
    return document.getElementById &&
    (window.attachEvent || window.addEventListener);
}
```

You do not need to test for more properties is because all the DOM functions used by you are are either from DOM Level 1 HTML or DOM Level 2 Events. Once you see that one of the methods from each recommendation is supported by the current browser, it can be assumed that it implements the remainder of that recommendation.

You are only using a small subset of each recommendation, so it is not needed to go into more detail in the testing. Some browsers support only certain recommendations, and as the scripts grow more complex, it is required that more specific features to be tested.

The W3C recommendations proposes the way to browser indicating which levels of the DOM it supports.

The DHTML will include partially and wrongly implemented specifications. Developer has to decide whether to required features they test properly or not.

Step 4: When the agent requirements are met, transform the logical structure

Next step is to write the code, which will actually transform the structure from the logical code, which is written in Step 1 to the dynamic code in Step 2. Wherever transformation is to be made , it is required to check whether the current browser is supported. The effect will be either be completely implemented, or it will not be implemented at all. The two main places where you made changes to the logical structure of the document were some addition of the style rule to turn off display of the HTML labels, and the setup function that runs in the window's onload event. If the browser is not supported, it is required to prevent those transformations from occurring. For the style rule, you will change the code so that JavaScript is used to actually write the rule out to the document. This is a solution that I often use because it is so reliable. The best way to ensure the document structure is only changed, when JavaScript is present is to be use only JavaScript to change the document structure.

Step 5: Thoroughly test on all the targetpl atforms

The importance of careful testing for DHTML effects cannot be understated. The fact is that if you are going to write DHTML, you need to be able to test it personally on the majority of the platforms on which it is intended torun. For example, a Google search will find that Windows IE 5+, Gecko, and Safari all seem to implement the features youneed. However, if you were to run Example E on Safari 1. 0, you'd notice a big problem: the effect runs only once!, first time you click in the textbox, the label disappears correctly. But upon blur, nothing happens. The textbox stays blank, and you can never get the label back again. It turns out that Safari has a bug — it does not fire onblur for a textbox until the next textbox is focused. Most importantly, the five-step process used to get to the point can easily be applied to any other DHTML effect for a modern Website. DHTML can be used to supplement the UI of many Web pages, and it can be done so that its support is not required. This style of DHTML coding should not be viewed in the same light as the badly behaved scripts of the past, but should be considered another worthy tool in the professional Web developer's arsenal.

2. Search Engine Optimization and DHTML Menu Case Study
Source: http://www. milonic. com/

Once you are well verse with DHTML you may use DHTML menu because you liked the way it looks and works across different Web browsers. Now you are ready to adapt his menu for your Website, it is time to consider another important question would using DHTML menu have impact on how a search engines index and rank your Website?

Using any technology might have some positive implications, while others negative. So, let us look at how Andy used his own DHTML menu and search engine optimization techniques to ensure that Milonic. com is on the top position of the search engines, when searched for DHTML menu.

How did you run across the DHTML menu?

If you are like me, you went to the Google home page or the Google toolbar on your Internet Explorer, and ran a search for "DHTML menu". The search result page most likely showed on the Milonic Website its first position.

Before you begin, some terminology:

"Search Engine Optimization" (SEO) refers to the act of altering your site so that it may rank well for particular terms, especially with crawler-based search engines. This article deals with SEO and how it relates to sites using DHTML menus. "Search engine submission" refers to the act of getting your Website listed with search engines. Getting list does not mean that you will necessarily rank well for particular terms. It simply means that the search engine knows your pages exist. This article does not deal with search engine submission. For more information on this subject, visit the WebSage Search Engine pages. Let us also clarify that there are two types of search engines:

1. **Directory-based search engines (Yahoo, LookSmart and The Open Directory)**

    Directories are search engines powered by human beings. Human editors compile all the listings that directories have.

2.   **Crawler-based search engines (Google, Inktomi, FAST, Teoma and AltaVista)**

Crawler-based search engines automatically visit Web pages to compile their listings. By taking care in how you build your pages, you might rank well in crawler-produced results.

Whether you want your Website found via a directory-based or crawler-based search engine, you want it to be attractive and intuitive to use. This, in fact, is most likely the reason you chose to use Andy Woolley's code – because it is free, it works across multiple browsers and versions, it is cool, and can pack a ton of information in very little screen space. This takes care of rule number one of Web design – thinking about your users and how your users would navigate the site in order to find information. However, there is another rule, and it states that if no one can find your Website, it does not matter how attractive or user friendly your Website is.

Do Search Engines Matter?

A Website can be found by following a link from another Website, or by going directly to the site's URL advertised either by word-of-mouth or by expensive branding campaigns. In addition, a Website can receive a lot of traffic through the search engines if properly optimized for both their Web crawlers and Web viewers. The power of search engine optimization should not be underestimated. According to a press release by WebSideStory, one of the Web analytics market leaders:

"As of Thursday, March 6, 2003, search sites accounted for more than 13.4 percent of global referrals, up from 7.1 percent the previous year, according to WebSideStory's StatMarket division (www. statmarket. com), a leading source of data on global Internet user trends. "

Global Internet Usage (data from StatMarket):

Referral Type	As of Thurs. 3/06/03	As of Thurs. 3/07/02
Direct Navigation	65.48%	50.21%
Web links	21.04%	42.60%
Search Engines	13.46%	7.18%

What this means for us all is that while nothing will replace a comprehensive online branding campaign, more and more people use the search engines to find the information they are looking for. Search engines should be even more important to small and medium size businesses, which cannot afford expensive branding campaigns.

Site navigation and content

To rank highly on a search engine's result pages your Website needs to be optimized and indexed. As you prepare to launch your newly redesigned Website you should keep in mind two important points:

- Make it easy for the search engine crawler to index your Website
- Make sure your content is optimized for high rankings

Every search engine's crawler is different as are the algorithms which the search engines use to rank their results. What is the same, is that every search engine's crawler automatically and periodically crawls the URLs of different Websites and then inserts them into the search engine's index.

DHTML, JavaScript and search engines crawlers

Web crawlers essentially behave as archaic pre-1995/6 Web browsers – they do not read JavaScript and cannot see layers (<div> tags). For those of you who do not remember (or know about) the childhood of the World Wide Web, JavaScript originally as LiveScript, in order to enable client-side interactivity in the Netscape Web browser.

Since the DHTML, is built exclusively on JavaScript and hidden layers, the Web crawlers are unable to crawl the links placed in the menu. You can use the Search Engine Spider Simulator, which, as its name suggests, emulates what a Web spider would see.

Just put your URL in the form and pay close attention to the links listed there. You will notice that if there were any links listed at all, they would be the ones placed in the content or the footer of the Web page and not the ones placed in the menu itself. Why? Because the Web crawler is unable to follow the links composed by JavaScript statements all it can follow are plain HTML links, i. e., `<a href="mypage.html">My page</a>`.

Tip One: Do not depend on the DHTML menu alone

As you can see already, while using a DHTML menu can be a very attractive idea from a human-visitor point of view, it is a very poor navigational approach for a Web crawler. In order to enable to Web crawler to follow the links to the rest of your site, make sure there are regular HTML links throughout the body of your page and at the footer or side/top navigation.

Search Engines   13.46%   7.18%

What this means for us all is that while nothing will replace a comprehensive online branding campaign, more and more people use the search engines to find the information they are looking for. Search engines should be even more important to small and medium size businesses, which cannot afford expensive branding campaigns.

Site navigation and content

To rank highly on a search engine's result pages your Website needs to be optimized and indexed. As you prepare to launch your newly redesigned Website you should keep in mind two important points:

- Make it easy for the search engine crawler to index your Website.
- Make sure your content is optimized for high rankings.

Every search engine's crawler is different as are the algorithms which the search engines use to rank their results. What is the same, is that every search engine's crawler automatically and periodically crawls the URLs of different Websites and then inserts them into the search engine's index.

Tip One: Do not depend on the DHTML menu alone

As you can see already, while using a DHTML menu can be a very attractive idea from a human-visitor point of view, it is a very poor navigational approach for a Web crawler. In order to enable to Web crawler to follow the links to the rest of your site, make sure there are regular HTML links throughout the body of your page and at the footer or side/top navigation.

Tip Five: The keyword placement

Andy has placed his chosen key phrase in all the critical places:

- At the page title tag;
- Throughout the content;
- At the text of Web link pointing to relevant Web pages;
- At the description meta tag so that the search engine results will show a friendly and helpful summary of what the page is about.

Search Engine Spider Simulator Results	
Status	200 (return error code 0)
Spider url	http://www.milonic.com
User Agent	Mozilla/4.0 (compatible; MSIE 5.0, Windows NT 5.0) 170.97.67.115
Referrer	http://www.searchengineworld.com/cgi-bin/sim_spider.cgi
Spider title	DHTML Cross Browser Javascript Menu, DHTML Menus & Web Site Navigation Menus. Popup Menus Sample Demos, JavaScript WebSite Menu, DHTML Help & Dynamic HTML Source Code
Spider meta desc	Free JavaScript Menu DHTML Menu Dynamic HTML Menu Cross Browser DHTML Menu Website Menu Works on all Browsers, Microsoft Internet Explorer, Netscape Navigator, Netscape Communicator, Mozilla, Konqueror & Opera. The Menu uses Cascading Style Sheets, Divs, Layers, HTML, DHTML and JavaScript
Spider meta keywords	free javascript dhtml menu javascript menu javascript website menu popup navigation menu bar cross browser javascript menu DHTML pop up menu code builder cascading css netscape navigator communicator microsoft internet explorer computer pop-up popup dynamic DHTML HTML javascript menu programming script samples tool stylesheet jscript internet intranet java js library php mysql sql database demo design designer drop down development editor example fade fader filter generator horizontal popup sample slide software transition tutorial vbscript vertical webmaster wizard asp active server cold fusion

To see the Web page through the eyes of a Web crawler, go to the Search Engine Spider Simulator. You will see that the selected keyword phrase appears throughout all the critical places mentioned above.

Tip Six: The keyword density

While different search engines have different algorithms for ranking Web pages, one of the general rules is the importance of frequent appearance of the key phrases throughout the content of the page. Of course, simply stacking keywords could backfire unless their presence is purposeful and aims to inform the readers. Again, follow the rule of "whatever is good for the reader should be good for the search".

Andy's key phrase of choice "DHTML menu" appears 18 times throughout the content of the home page. Different combinations of "JavaScript dhtml menu" appear multiple times as well. With such keyword density, no wonder the page shows high on the search engine result pages.

Using keyword density analysis tool will help you see your pages through the eyes of a Web spider. It will help you understand if indeed the keyword phrases of your choice appear throughout the page title, meta tags, and page content consistently and often enough to convince the search engines that this page is relevant, has substantial content, and is worth high ranking.

Conclusion

In summary, what this article has covered are some of the best practices for search engine optimization as applied to Websites using a DHTML menu like the one developed by Andy Woolley for Milonic. com:

- Do not depend on the DHTML menu alone for navigation – provide additional links throughout the body of the page;

- Build a list of links to the most important sections of your site in the `<noscript>` tags which both the archaic browsers and the search engine crawlers will be able to see and follow;

- Build an informative sitemap to enable access to the most important sections of the site; in addition, provide links to these sections from the footer of every page;

- Select several two-three word keyword phrases and place them within the page title, the meta tags, and most importantly, throughout the body of the page;

- Whatever you do, do it to make the page readable and usable for the people who will find your Website via a search engine – do not do it just for the search engine positioning. After all, if you are number one on Google but nobody stays at your Website to read or purchase from it, your search engine optimization has been a waste of time and energy;

- Be patient – the search engines take their time to crawl and index the newly discovered pages. Do not expect improved results within the first 3-4 weeks; sometimes this can take several months. If even after several months your Website's position on the search engines result pages has not improved, you might want to consider the services of a professional search engine optimization expert, such as WebSage.

3.9   Key Terms

- **CSS:** CSS stands for Cascading Style Sheet. A style sheet is said to be cascading when multiple style definitions may cascade into one to determine the display of whole Web page.

- **CSSP:** CSS Positioning can be defined as an extension of the CSS style script standard that you can use to provide specific position of various elements of your Web page. It enables you to precisely position elements on the page even without interfering with the markup.

- **DHTML:** Dynamic HTML is used to develop attractive and dynamic Web pages. It includes scripting languages like JavaScript that are used together with style sheets to develop dynamic Web pages.

- **DHTML Events:** DHTML Events can be defined as user action, such as clicking a button, pressing a key, moving a window or simply moving a mouse around the screen. An event can also refer to external actions like page loading HTML events can trigger actions in the browser, like starting a JavaScript when a user clicks on an element.

- **DOM:** DOM implies document object model.

- **JSSS:** JavaScript Style Sheets is a stylesheet language technology developed by Netscape. As JSSS uses JavaScript you can use functions and assigned values to make the expression of style information.

- **Layers:** Layer tag can be used in DHTML to segment a Web page. Layers allow one to place one thing on top of another and give it an exact position on the page. It is a dynamic tag as to be positioned anywhere on a Web page (without relation to other content), moved around, its content inside updated on demand, and more.

- **Style Sheet:** Style sheets are the files containing style rules for a Web page. The style sheets can be written in CSS or JSSS and can be externally linked to a Web page or embedded with in the Web page itself.

- **W3C:** W3C (WWW Consortium) is an international organization dedicated in developing Web standards and guidelines.

3.10 Summary

Tim Berners-Lee, invented, WWW Consortium (W3C) which is dedicated in developing Web standards and guidelines. The W3C is the main international standards organization for the World Wide Web. With a mission to develop well-formatted, attractive dynamic Websites DHTML has been introduced. DHTML includes a set of technologies that can work together to produce dynamic Web pages. The technologies used are Cascading Style Sheets, Document Object Model, DHTML events and scripting language like JavaScript. Style sheets are powerful mechanism for adding styles like fonts, color to a Web page. Layer tag can also be used to segment a Web page and then style each segment. Layer can be imagined as a sheet of paper that resides on top of the rest of the page, and does not take up space within the flow of the document. With CSS it is possible to specify exact position of elements on Web page using CSS's positioning elements. Apart from CSS JSSS can be used to style Web page document. It works using JavaScript syntax and is less popular then CSS. DHTML document object model and DHTML events have been introduced in this Chapter.

3.11 Exercises

A.   Fill in the blanks:

1.   _____ are powerful mechanism for adding styles (e.g. fonts, colors, spacing, etc.) to Web documents.

2.   The advantage of style sheets include the ability to make _____ changes to all documents from single location.

3.   The Style assignment process can be accomplished with the _____ and _____ tags.

4.   The `<style>` tag should be within _____ and _____ element.

5.   _____ attribute is used to set the color of the border.

6.   The layer's visibility can be controlled using the _____attribute.

B.   True or False

1.   `BACKGROUND-REPEAT:repeat-x` will repeat the image specified vertically.

2.   `Text-indent` is used to indent the first line of text encountered.

3.   `<DIV>….. </DIV>` are used to divide a Web page into segments which can be positioned anywhere on the page.

C.   Short Answer Questions

1.   How to display a background image only one time?

2.   How to style headers in a Web page using style sheet?

3.   How to set the background color of a part of the text?

4.   How to specify space between characters?

5.   How to specify space between lines?

6.   Develop a style sheet and position an image on page using `background` attribute of `style` tag.

7.   Develop a style sheet illustrating use of CSSP.

D.   Long Answer Questions

1.   Design a Web page for DHTML DATA Inc using style sheet with following specification:

    a.   Define a style class 'MAJOR' with the following attributes:

       `{font-size:125%; color:'green'; font-weight:bold; font-family:sans-serif}`

       Use the defined Style class wherever the text "DHTML DATA" appears on the document.

    b.   Use unordered list giving advantage and disadvantage of DHTML.

    c.   Define 4 segments using `<DIV>…. </DIV>` tags with background colors blue, green, red, yellow.

3.12 Solutions to Selected Questions

A. Fill in the blanks:

1. Style sheets
2. Global
3. `<style>….</style>`
4. `<head>......</head>`
5. `color`
6. Visibility

B. True or False

1. False
2. True
3. True

C. Short Answer Questions

1.
```
<html>
<head>
<style type="text/css">
body
{
    background-image: url('bgdesert.jpg');
    background-repeat: no-repeat
}
</style>
</head>
<body>
</body>
</html>
```
2.
```
<html>
<head>
<style type="text/css">
h1 {color:red}
h2 {color: #dda0dd}
p {color:yellow}
</style>
</head>
<body>
    <h1>This is header 1</h1>
    <h2>This is header 2</h2>
    <p>This is a paragraph</p>
</body>
</html>
```

```
3.   <html>
     <head>
     <style type="text/css">
     span.change
     {
         background-color:red}
     </style>
     </head>
     <body>
         <p>
         <span class="change">Let us change the style</
         span>Change style<span class="change">You can see
         change in style. </span>
         </p>
     </body>
     </html>
4.   <html>
     <head>
     <style type="text/css">
         h1 {letter-spacing: 1px}
         h4 {letter-spacing: 0.5cm}
     </style>
     </head>
     <body>
         <h1>This is header 1</h1>
         <h4>This is header 4</h4>
     </body>
     </html>
5.   <html>
     <head>
     <style type="text/css">
         p.small {line-height: 90%}
         p.big {line-height: 200%}
     </style>
     </head>
     <body>
         <p>
         You will see a paragraph with a standard line-height.
         </p>
         <p class="small">
         You will see a paragraph with a smaller line-height.
         </p>
         <p class="big">
         You will see a paragraph with a bigger line-height.
         </p>
```

```
    </body>
    </html>
6.  <html>
    <head>
    <style type="text/css">
        body
        {background-position: 60% 80%}
    </style>
    </head>
    <body>
        <p><b>Note:</b> background-attachment property must
        be set to
        "fixed".</p>
    </body>
    </html>
7.  <html>
    <head>
    <title>CSSP in detail</title>
    </head>
    <style type="text/css">
    .story1 {
        position: absolute;
        left: 25px;
        top: 20px;
        width: 200px;
        height: 50px;
    }
    .story2 {
        position: absolute;
        left: 25px;
        top: 80px;
        width: 210px;
    }
    </style>
    <body>
        <h1 class="story1">Green House Effect</h1>
        <div class="story2">
        <p><strong>Greenhouse effect</strong>It causes of
        the recent warming are an active field of research.
        </p>
        </p>
    </div>
    </body>
    </html>
```

Previous Year Questions with Answers

Q. 1.   What are different types of selectors used in CSS? [June 2006]

Ans: The Different types of selectors are:

a.   Simple Selectors

b.   HTML Selectors

c.   Class Selectors

d.   ID Selectors

e.   Contextual Selectors

Q. 2.   What is CSS? What are its advantages? [June 2005]

Ans: Cascading Style Sheet (CSS): CS are the powerful mechanism for adding styles (e.g. fonts, color) to a Web page. Adding style means defining how to display a HTML element. The purpose of style sheet is to create a presentation for a specific element or set of elements like style for <h1> tags in the document. A browser reads a style sheet and it formats the document according to the specification given in the stylesheet, and they are not replacement for HTML. A style sheet needs to be binding to a HTML element to introduce style in the document.

Advantage of using CSS

● Making a presentable document

● Style sheets save a lot of work

● Multiple styles will cascade into one

Q. 3.   What do understand by DHTML? [May 2007]

Ans: As per World Wide Web Consortium (W3C) DHTML can be defined as follows:

"Dynamic HTML is a term used by some vendors to describe the combination of HTML, style sheets and scripts that allow documents to be animated. "

DHTML combines HTML with the Cascading Style Sheets (CSS) and Scripting languages. Together with scripting languages like JavaScript DHTML can be used to manipulate Web page's element and styles assigned to them can change in the response to user's input.

Chapter 4

XML

4.1 Introduction

As you all know HTML is the most popular markup language which has been designed to display data whereas XML has been designed to describe and structure data. XML itself is not used to describe the way of displaying the data. This markup language is competent to structure the data in a standard manner. This structured data can then be easily read and used by other systems. In short we can say that we can use XML to provide an 'interoperable file format''. This file can then be interpreted using other languages. Most popular language used to transform and interpret XML is XSL (Extensible Stylesheet Language).

XML stands for 'Extensible Markup Language'. XML can be seen as a general-purpose specification used for creating custom markup languages. It is classified as an extensible language as it allows its users to define their element and, it enables to create custom tags that suit their requirement. XML has been primarily developed to information systems to share their structured data online. It can be used to encode documents as well as to serialize data so that it can be efficiently used. Some of the features of XML have been summarized below.

1. XML is freely available and can be seen as an extensible language.

2. XML tags are user made tags. They are not predefined tags. In case of the HTML, predefined tags are used (like <p>, <h1>, etc.). While working with

XML author can define his/her tags and develop own document structure.

3.   XML is a complement to the HTML

4.   XML is not a replacement of the HTML. Both the scripting languages have their own purpose. As a Web is developing, XML is being popularly used to describe the data and HTML will be used to format and display the same data.

5.   XML has been inherited from SGML

SGML stands for *Standard Generalized Markup Language.* It is an ISO standard that defines an extremely powerful markup language. Publishing industry and manufacturing companies are popularly using it. It can be understood as the *metalanguage* that can be used to create other markup languages, such as HTML. It marks the origin of XML.

XML is a markup language like the HyperText Markup Language (HTML) which is commonly used for scripting Web page. XML is specifically designed to describe data so that it can be effectively stored online. Web these days contains huge amount of information. XML enables structuring of data so that it can then be mined to get suitable information. In the case of XML unlike HTML there are no predefined tags. XML can also be called as self-descriptive markup language as users need to define their on tags.

For better understanding check out the example below.

Suppose you are storing information about a set of books. You may store the information in HTML.

Example 1: Creating HTML and XML files for choosing a song

Song.html

```
<html>
<head><title>Choosing a song</title>
<body>
    <p>Michael Jackson</p><br>
    <p>Mikka Singh</p>
</body>
</html>
```

Song.XML

```
<catalog>
<album>
    <title>Song Album<title>
    <singer>Annu Malik</singer>
</album>
<album>
    <title>Marketing Research<title>
    <singer>Lata Mangeshkarr</singer>
</album>
</catalog>
```

Just check out this example now you can define the data in an XML file very easily. It shows that there is a catalog containing songs, each of which contains title and album detail of the songs. You will find that XML file size is more than the other file size. However, XML makes this loss by speeding up the processing of XML file. Interpretation of XML file is different from HTML file. HTMLl file is dependent on the pre-defined tags however XML file tags are user defined and represent the information in a hierarchical manner. This kind of data is also described as metadata. This kind of data supports great strength to the XML because own specifications can be created, and data can be structured the way asone want it to be interpreted by other system.

4.1.1 Differences between HTML and XML

XML cannot be used to replace HTML. The XML and the HTML both have been different goals, and are summarized as follows:

- XML is used to describe the data whereas HTML is used to display the data.

- XML focuses on defining data with its attributes. It tells about data. HTML focuses on presentation of data, and it is used to customize looks of data.

- In case of HTML, document tags are used, and the document's structure is predefined. Tags that are that are defined in the HTML standard can only be used. XML allows to define your own tags and you can also develop your document structure.

- An .XML extension is used to save XML document, whereas .HTML extension is used to save an HTML document.

Example 2: Creating a file in which an e-mail from Ram to Shyam is stored as XML

```
<email>
<to>Kanchi</to>
<from>Gauri</from>
<subject>Lets go for a movie</subject>
<content>Hi Di!!!!!!!!!! Lets go for a movie tomorrow</content>
</email>
```

In this example, XML is used to store e-mail. It can be seen that own tags have been created for storing names of the sender and the receiver. Different tags have been created to store subject and the content of the Web page.

Test Your Progress
1. *What is XML?*
2. *How HTML it different from XML?*
3. *Is XML complement to HTML?*

Do You Know?
XML was invented by Charles F. Goldfarb, Ed Mosher, and Ray Lone at IBM in 1970.

4.2   Learning Scripting in XML

The language XML is a generic language, which is used to describe another markup languages. XML makes distinction between the markup and the content of the Web page. Markup hereapplies the tags and the attributes which are the XML document used, and the content refers to the information presented in document.

```
<b>Hi!!! Check out difference between XML and HTML</b>
```

In this example .... refers to the markup which is used in the document. The text written within these tags refers to the document's content.

Markup is used to describing the content's presentation and which uses standard tags and attributes available in HTML. The XML markup is used to describe the content of the document and, which is not related with the appearance of the document.

```
<exam ans="Rectangle">What is shape of a TV</exam>
```

In this example the tag <exam> is used to describe the content type and the answer for this question is specified by attribute answer.

To start using XML effectively, it is required to know the terminology used in XML and to understand the structure of a XML file. Consider the following Example 3.

Example 3: Scripting in XML

```
<Collection_books>
<books>
    <title>Web Technology</title>
    <author>Dr. Shruti Kohli</author>
</books>
</Collection_books>
```

XML files's structure is hierarchical and each tag defines an element. The elements required to have an opening and a closing tag. For example, <library> has opening as well as a tag closing. Some of the elements are self contained, and it is not required to enclose any information within them. The tags can be considered as a empty element and can be made self closing by adding " / > " at the end of opening tag. The hierarchical structure makes easy parsing of the document.

XML Syntax

Now considering the example given below.

```
Line 1: <?XML version="1.0" ?>
Line 2: <library>
Line 3: <subjects type="Science" year="2014">
Line 4: <subject1>Physics</subject1>
Line 5: <subject2>Chemistry</subject2>
Line 6: <subject3>Biology</subject3>
Line 7: </subjects>
Line 8: </library>
```

The processing Instruction is given in the first Line, and it defines the XML version for the document. The document shows the 1.0 specification of XML:

```
<?XML version="1.0"?>
```

The first element of the document is defined by Line 2, which is the root element:

```
<library>
```

Child elements of the root, i.e., subjects which further has child elements (subject1, subject2, subject3) are defined in the next lines.

An XML documents use self-describing and simple syntax. Before you read further XML scripting, you need to know the main components of theee XML documents. XML markup document can be broadly classified into a set of components, which describe the XML document. The components are defined as given below:

Element Tag

An element is a piece of information, which corresponds to a XML document's tag or a set of tags. The element can be seen as a logical piece of markup, which is represented as a tag in a XML document. E.g. In the above given example 'quiz' is an element and, that has been used as tag <exam></exam> in the document. An element need to have the starting and the ending tags like <exam>...</exam>, ... or a empty tag, such as <img/>. Whereas coding in HTML empty tag <br> do not required an end tag. However, XML need every tag to be closed.

Processing Instruction

Apart from markup and content, processing instructions written in a XML document, is the first statement in document. A processing instruction can be seen as a special command passed to the program and, that will process the document. Processing instructions are written with in <?.....?>.

```
<?XML version="1.0"?>
```

This processing instruction is a XML document's first statement. The processing instruction is just like to a tag. It includes name and the attribute/value pair. The processing instruction describes that the document adheres to the standard of the XML version 1.0.

XML Comments

Comments in a XML document can be written using the syntax given below:

```
<!—The document makes you learn about XML —>
```

Note: Comments in **XML** are writen like HTML.

Document type declaration

Document Type Declaration (DTD) describes structure of an XML document. It identifies the external DTD, which defines structure of an XML document. 'Document Type declaration' is always placed at the top of the XML document and just below the processing instruction. It is used to perform following three basic tasks:

● Identifies the root element of the document. XML document has a root element and the other elements are children of the element root.

● Identifies the external DTD of the file. According to the document structure, an XML file is defined in the DTD.

For example 4: Describe the audio/video collection

```
<? XML version="1.0"?>
<!DOCTYPE entertainment SYSTEM entertainment.dtd>
<Collection>
<Audio_tracks>
    <track1>Song</track1>
    <track2>RockOn</track2>
</Audio_tracks>
<Movie>
    <Hindi>Welcome</Hindi>
    <English>Ocean11</English>
</Movie>
</Collection>
```

The above given example includes first line, a processing instruction and it shows that the document should be according to the XML version 1.0 standards. The second line < ! DOCTYPE...> is the document type declaration and, which states that for this XML file, the root element is `entertainment`. Further, it identifies that according to the external DTD namely "entertainment.dtd", the document required to be verified. The browser needs to look for "entertainment.dtd" while processing this file and then validate the document structure according to this file.

4.2.1 XML Elements in detail

As you learnt, an XML element is defined as anything that is included in the start and end tags in an XML document. Since XML follows a hierarchical structure, an element can further include another element. Precisely an element can contain element content, mixed content, simple content or nothing at all. An element can also have attributes. An element is said to have element content when it contains other elements. An element is said to have mixed content when it contains both text and other elements. Similarly, an element contains simple content (or text content) when it only contains text. It is possible that an element contains empty content. In such case element carries no information.

Example 5: Arranging XML elements in detail

```
<Text_books>
<title>Computers</title>
    <Pub id="3004" hard_copy="no"></Pub>
    <Index>
    <Chapter1>Introduction to Advantages of XML</Chapter1>
    <Chapter2>Disadvantage of XML</Chapter2>
</title>
<title> Physics</title>
    <Pub id="20001" hard_copy="yes"></Pub>
    <Index>
    <Chapter1>Introduction to Force</Chapter1>
    <Chapter2>Usage of Force</Chapter2>
</title>
</Text_books>
```

In above Example 5, `Text_books` is the root element. `Title, Pub, Index` are child elements of `Text_books`. `'title'` is the parent element of `Pub, Index`. `Pub, Index` are sister elements or siblings as they have the same parent. Element `'pub'` has attributes `'id'` and `'hard_copy"`. The attribute named `'id'` has the value `'3004'` and the attribute named hard_copy has the value `'no'` indicating it is an e-book. While using the element you need to be careful as every element should have the closing tag and each element needs to be properly nested. While creating XML elements you can use any name. However, you need to be careful while inventing name for the elements. You cannot use reserve words. It would be better if you chose descriptive names, which describe the use of an element. `" : "` should not be used while inventing element names as it is reserved to be used for namespaces (discussed in later sub-section). Avoid using `' - '` and `' . '`. Descriptive names, with an underscore separator like `<Text_book>`, `<hard_copy>`, `<soft_copy>` are popularly used. You can have long element names but short and simples ones are encouraged. Example suppose you are storing book data. Creating a tag `<author>` is better the tags like `<author_of_the_book>`. It is important to know that XML documents may have a corresponding database where fields exist corresponding to each XML elements exist. A good practice to follow the naming rules of your database for inventing names in a XML documents. Some of the rules for naming XML elements have been stated below.

- Element names may contain letters, numbers, and other characters.
- Element name may not start with a number or punctuation character.

- Element name must not start with the letters XML.
- Names cannot contain spaces.

4.2.2 XML Attributes

While scripting in HTML, you will used pre-defined attributes like `src` attribute of an `<img>` tag.

```
<img src="mill.gif">
```

In this example 'src' attribute provides path from where image need to be retrieved. Thus, it is providing some additional information about the `img` element.

Attributes often provide information which is not the part of data or content. In the example below track type is irrelevant to the data, but can be important for the software that will run this track.

```
<song lang="hindi">Song</song>
```

Similarly, you can create attributed for elements in a XML document. These attributes generally provide some kind of extended information about the element or describe some kind of characteristics of the element.

`<child gender="female">`

In the above example, the `gender` attribute defines the sex of the child and can take value male/female.

> **Note:** Attribute values need to be always enclosed in quotes. The quote style can be either single or double like **"female"** or **'female'.** In case attribute value itself contains double quotes then it is necessary for you to use single quotes.

`<captain sports="badminton" name='Jin Ju jain>`

4.2.3 Elements with Attributes

While designing, a XML document you need to visualize which data needs to store in a XML element and which data need to be stored as XML attribute. Any data can be stored in child elements or in attributes.

Illustration 1

Example 6: Use of Element without attributes

```
<child gender="female">
    <first_name>Gauri</first_name>
    <last_name>Kohli</last_name>
</child>
```

Illustration 2

Example 7: Use of Element with attributes

```
<child>
    <gender>female</gender>
    <first_name>Veena</first_name>
```

```
        <last_name>Sondhi</last_name>
</child>
```

Check out the Examples 6 and 7. In the first case gender of the child is stored as an attribute of a child element whereas in second case it is stored as a separate element. Both Examples 6 and 7 thus provide the same information about the child. You should understand that there are no rules for using attributes or child elements. While using attributes, some problems may be faced.

- Attributes cannot contain multiple values whereas child elements can contain multiple values.

- Attributes cannot be easily expanded to incorporate future changes however with child you can do this. It is possible to make further child elements for any element and to add more attributes to the elements. In other words you can say that elements are more flexile than attributes.

- With attributes, it is not possible to describe structures whereas with child elements you can easily do it.

- It is more difficult to manipulate attributes using program code.

- Attribute values cannot be easily tested against a Document Type Definition (DTD). It has been discussed in detail in later Sections.

- Above stated problems with attributes and advantages of using child attribute may provide you with some insight of choosing a child element or an attribute while making a XML document. It is advised to use child elements for storing information. In case you use attributes as containers for data it is possible that you generate a document, which is difficult to read and maintain. Attributes can be used to provide information that is not relevant to the data.

```
        <notice day="31" month="7" year="2014" to="delegates"
        from="Convener" subject="library notice"
        data="Information about conference">
        </notice>
```

You can use ID references to elements by storing them as attributes. These ID references can be further used to identify and access various XML elements.

Example 8: Identifying and referencing XML elements using ID reference

```
<Notice_board>
<notice id="10">
    <for>Delegates</for>
    <from>Convener</from>
    <Agenda>Conference Opening Ceremony</Agenda>
    <Info>Conference will start on 7th July 2014 at 2:00 PM</
    Info>
</notice>

<notice id="11">
```

```
<for>Delegates</for>
<from>Convener</from>
<Agenda>Conference Closing Ceremony</Agenda>
<Info>Conference will end on 10th July 2014 at 5:00 PM</
Info>
</notice>
</Notice_board>
```

Check out the Example 8. Here `id` attribute helps to identify different notices uniquely, which are posted on the notice board. You can store data about data (metadata) as attributes and data itself as elements in a XML document.

4.2.4 Rules for XML Document

Always remember:

● *XML documents must have a root element*

```
<child>
    <gender>female</gender>
    <first_name>Veena</first_name>
    <last_name>Sondhi</last_name>
</child>
```

Here **child** is the root element.

● *All XML elements need to have a closing tag.*

Just check out the previous Examples all tags are closed. Some elements in HTML do not have to have a closing tag. The following code is legal in HTML:

```
<b> Bold is beautiful </b>
<b>Be bold </b>
```

All the elements in XMLmust have a closing tag, like this:

```
<book_rack>
<books>
    <title>Operational Research </title>
    <author>Kanto Swaroop</author>
</books>
</book_rack>
```

Consider above the example an XML document has been created to store a book collection. You can find that all the XML elements like <book_rack>, <books>, <title>... have been properly closed.

> **Note:** You might have noticed that the XML declaration does not have a closing tag. This is not an error as declaration is not the part of a XML document itself. It is not considered as an XML element and so this rule does not apply to the declaration.

● *XML tags are case sensitive*

As you need to take care of variable names while writing any program code similarly, you need to be careful while naming and using names of XML elements. For example, <BOOK> and <book> will be treated as different XML elements.

> **Note:** Be careful while using XML elements. Opening and closing tags need to be written with the same case. For example,
>
> Incorrect : <name>RAM</Name>
>
> Correct: <name>RAM</name>

● *XML Elements needs to be properly nested*

You need to know that improper nesting of tags will not make any sense to XML.

In HTML even though some elements are improperly nested document may get displayed by the browser. For example,

```
<i><b>You need to make a text italic or bold to make it
impressive</i></b>
```

In above example <b> tag opened inside <i> tag but is closed outside <b> tag. Such improper nesting may some times give abrupt result but will work.

In case of XML all elements needs to be properly nested like this:

Wrong way	Correct Way
<book_rack>	<book_rack>
<book1>	<book1>
<title>Introduction to Computers </title>	<title>Introduction to Computers</title>
<author>S.C Chand</author>	<author>S.Kumar</author>
</book_rack>	</book1>
</book1>	</book_rack>

In above example <book> tag opened with in <book_rack> tag so it needs to be closed before closing the <book_rack> tag. In above case <book1> tag is closed outside the <book_rack> tag. This may generate errors while executing the document.

● *All XML documents contains a single tag pair to define the root element.*

All the elements should be within the root element. Further the elements can have subelements (child elements) and, subelements should be nested correctly within their parent element:

```
<root>
<child>
```

```
<subchild>.....</subchild>
</child>
</root>
```

● ***XML attribute values is to be quoted***

Omitting quotation marks around attribute values is illegal with XML. Like in HTML, XML elements can have attributes in name/value pairs. The XML attribute value must always be quoted. Study the XML documents given below. The first is the incorrect and, the second is the correct.

```
<?XML version="1.0"?>
<notice date=12/10/2008>
    <to>Ram</to>
    <from>Shyam</from>
</notice>

<?XML version="1.0"?>
<notice date="12/10/2008">
    <to>Ram</to>
    <from>Shyam</from>
</notice>
```

The first document has the error, that the attribute date in the note element is not quoted. This is correct: `date="12/10/2008"`. This is incorrect: date=12/10/2008.

● ***With XML, Whitespace is preserved***

> **Note:** With XML, the whitespace in your document is not truncated. This is unlike HTML. HTML decreases multiple consecutive whitespace characters to a single whitespace.

4.2.5 Correctness of XML Document

One of the finest characteristics of XML is the ability to determine the correctness of a XML document. An XML document can have two levels of correctness:

● **Well Formed Document**: First level of correctness is to check whether the document meets strict requirements of XML language. To verify whether a document is 'well formed' or not one needs to check its XML markup against the stand XML rules.

● **Valid XML document:** At the second level of correctness a document is said to be a "valid 'XML' document if its structure is at par the one defines in the external DTD file. In such case the document markup is checked against the standard defined in the external DTD file. XML document can be validated by checking whether it adheres to XML rules or not.

> **Note:** Any valid document is a well-formed document but the reverse may not always be true.

4.2.6 Writing first XML Document

Once you have scripted your XML document you must be curious to know:

- Who will process your XML document?
- How exactly will the document look like?

Write the following script in the Notepad and save the file with extension XML say try.XML.

Example 9: A sample of XML document

```
<?XML version="1.0"?>
<Notice_board>
<notice id="01">
    <for>Students</for>
    <from>Librarian</from>
    <subject>Library Notice</subject>
    <content> Library will be closed on Monday </content>
</notice>

<notice id="02">
    <for>Faculty</for>
    <from>Librarian</from>
    <subject>Change in library timings</subject>
    <content> Faculty tie for library has been extended
    from 9:00 to 5:00
    PM</content>
</notice>
</notice_board>
```

You will get errors as shown below.

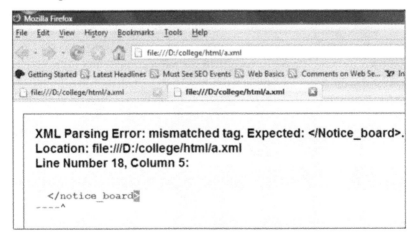

In the case of HTML browser displays whatever it interprets from an XML document. However, while interpreting XML document browser identifies the error and displays them to the user. For example, in above case `<Notice_board>` and `</notice_board>` are not the same. Just correct the closing tag as `</notice_board>` and run the file on the browser you will find a screen as follows:

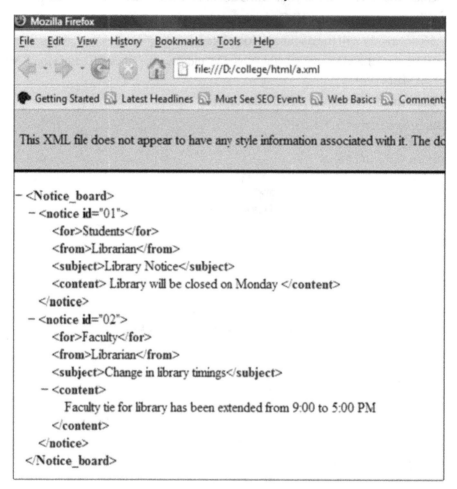

You will find that the XMLdocument does not contain any information about the way information will be displayed in the browser and the browser neither tries to interpret the elements of the XML document. Instead it focuses on the highlighting different parts of the document. Just check the above screen shot a hyphen (-) on the left hand side of some elements shows that these elements have further child elements. On clicking on these hyphens you will find that the sign changes to a (+) sign and these elements are closed, i.e., child elements are hidden and no more visible.

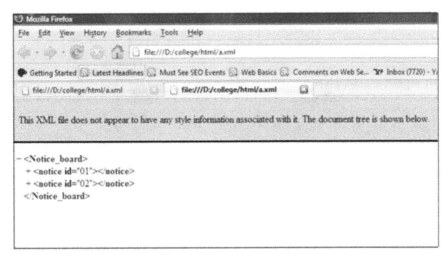

In the above screen shot notice element has been closed thus hiding is child elements. Such kind of layout is very helpful in understanding the structure of a large document.

> **Note:** You can find that Firefox has displayed a message on top of the XML document. This message states that there is no style associated with this document. In this XML file structure of the document has been displayed as there is no style information or HTML code for presenting information. For styling the XML document and extracting information from them XSL (Extensible style sheets) are popularly used. You will learn about these in later sub Sections. All browser may not display such kind of message and may just display the XML document as it is.

4.2.7 What is the need of a Namespace?

There may be a conflict in the meaning that arises from a XML file. Consider the following XML files, both the files describe the same data:

```
Movie.XML
    <movie-type>Humour</movie-type>
    <movie-type>Action</movie-type>
</movie-types>
```

```
Movie.XML
<movie-types>
    movie-type>Normal</movie-type>
    movie-type>Color</movie-type>
</movie-types>
```

The first file specifies different types of movies whereas second specifies different color schemes in which movie can be seen. But it is difficult through elements determine the difference between contents of the two files. This can be done using

Namespaces.The XML namespace qualifies an element in the same way as telephone area code can be used to identify any phone number. In case of a XML file the "area code" for XML namespaces is the URI (Uniform Resource Identifier), which is associated with a prefix for the namespace. Namespace is defined using an XML and declaration followed by the prefix which is actually the URI uniquely identifies the namespace:

```
XMLns:movie="http://www.abc.com/movie">
```

By adding the namespace definition as an attribute to a tag, one can use prefix movie in the tag and any tags it contains, to fully qualify our elements:'

```
<movie:movie-types XMLns:movie="http://www.sitepoint.com/
movies">
    <movie:movie-type>Action</movie:movie-type>
    <movie:movie-type>Adventure</movie:movie-type>
</movie:movie-types>
```

The second file can have namespace "color":

```
<color:movie-types XMLns:color="http://www.sitepoint.com/
color">
    <color:movie-type>B&W </color:movie-type>
    <color:movie-type>colour</color:movie-type>
```

XML Parsers can now easily recognize the meanings of the film types and handle them accordingly.

Test Your Progress
1.   *What is element?*
2.   *What are the rules for making a XML document?*
3.   *What is the need of namespace?*

4.3   Using XML

- **Using XML for separating data from HTML:**

  When you use XML data is stored without using HTML. In an HTML document HTML tags are used to display data so in that case data is stored inside HTML. Using XML you can arrange data in separate files. This can help you to concentrate on using HTML for just presentation data. Any modification in the underlying data will not bring changes in the data layout you designed with HTML.

- **Using XML for Data Exchange**

  By using XML it is possible for you to exchange data between incompatible systems. In most of the computer systems and databases data have been stored in incompatible formats. Exchanging data between computer systems over the Internet has been one of the most time-consuming challenges for developers.

By converting such data into XMLit is possible to greatly reduce such complexity. It can be used for the generation of data and, that can be read by many different types of applications.

● **XML can be helpful for B2B models:**

B2B integration on the Internet is now being done using XML with simple protocols like HTTP and FTP.XML has become popular for B2B integration because of its inherent capabilities like simplicity, extensibility and ease of processing. Using XML it is possible to easily exchange financial information over the Internet. XML is emerging as the popular language to exchange financial information between businesses over the Internet.

● **XML can be used to share data:**

By using XML it is possible to store data in plain text files. Simple text editor like Notepad can be used to store data and share it with other applications. Thus, XML provides a software/Hardware independent way of sharing data.

XMLcan make data more useful for diversified applications. XML is independent of the hardware, software and application the data can be easily accessed by various users by using simple browsers. It is possible for clients and applications to access XML files as data sources. It is similar to accessing databases for using data.

● **New Languages can be created using XML:**

XML is the mother of WAP and WML (Wireless Markup Language). The WML, being popularly used as markup for accessing Internet applications from devices, such as mobile phones, is written in XML.

Test Your Progress
1. What is the use of XML?
2. What is WML?
3. How can XMLmake data useful for different applications?

4.4   Introduction to XHTML

XHTML means 'Extensible HyperText Markup Language'. It can be interpreted as 'the stricter and cleaner version of HTML'. It is a W3C recommended XML application and is almost identical to HTML 4.01. You can understand it as the combination of HTML and XML which consist of elements of HTML 4.01 defined by the syntax of XML.

Many Websites, which are there on Web, are coded in "bad" HTML. Interesting thing about HTML is that its code is going to work fine even if it does not strictly follow the HTML rules. For example,

```
<html>
<head>
<title>You should learn XHTML</title>
```

```
<body>
    <b>It is an easy language</b>
     possible to work with HTML even when you do not follow
    its rules strictly.
    <p>Just have a look on its code </p>
</body>
```

With advancement of technology there are many browsers available in market. Some browsers run Internet on computers whereas some are run on mobile phones or other small devices. Some browsers like one working on mobile phones may not be able to interpret incomplete HTML or in other words we an say "bad" HTML. By combining HTML and XML their strengths have been used to develop a markup language (xhtml) that will work with all the browsers.

4.4.1 XHTML Components

An XHTML document can be divided into following components:

- The DOCTYPE declaration
- The <head> section
- The <body> section

The basic document structure is:

```
<!DOCTYPE ...>
<html>
<head>
    <title>... </title>
</head>
<body> ... </body>
</html>
```

Note: The DOCTYPE declaration is always the first line in an XHTML document!

Illustrative example

```
<!DOCTYPE html
PUBLIC "-//W3C//DTD XHTML 1.0 Transitional//EN"
"http://www.w3.org/TR/xhtml1/DTD/xhtml1transitional.dtd">
<html>
<head>
    <title>Introduction to XHTML</title>
</head>
<body>
    <b>Check out this XML document</b>
</body>
</html>
```

4.4.2 Characteristics of XHTML

● *XHTML Elements need to be always closed*

As discussed in HTML incomplete code may work however when making a page according to XHTML standard it is important to check that all XHTML elements are closed. For example, check out this code written as incomplete html.

```
<html>
<body>
<b>Be bold
```

Although this code may work in HTML, it will not work with XHTML. According to XHTML rules code needs to be written as follows:

```
<html>
<body>
<b>Be bold</b>
```

● *Every 'Empty Element' must be closed*

HTML tag can be broadly divided in two categories:

Paired Tag	Singular Tag/ Empty tag
<html>...</html>	
<body>...</body>	<hr>
<style>...</style>	<img>
<p>...</p>	

According to XHTML rules empty elements must have either an end tag or the start tag must end with />.

```
<br> needs to be written as <br/>
<hr> needs to be written as <hr/>
```

Check out this code in HTML

You need to close this tag <br>.

Tag for horizontal rule also needs to be closed <hr>.

Tag for displaying image is singular tag but it needs to be closed in XHTML, like

```
<img src="a.jpg">
```

Writing the same code in XHTML

You need to close this tag <br/>. Tag for horizontal rule also needs to be closed <hr/>. Tag for displaying image is singular tag but it needs to be closed in XHTML

```
<img src="a.jpg"/>
```

- ## *In XHTML elements must be properly nested, must be in lower case*

    HTML is not case sensitive, i.e., `<html>`, `<Html>`, `<HTML>` all will work. However according to XHTML specification the tag names and attributes need to be lower case.

- ## *XHTML Documents must have one root element*

    In case of XHTML all elements must be nested within the `<html>` root element.

    All other elements in XHTML are sub-element or children of the root element. Other elements can further have sub-elements. You need to be careful as sub-elements needs to be paired and correctly nested within their parent element.

    For any XHTML document basic structure is:

```
<html>
    <head> ... </head>
    <body> ... </body>
</html>
```

Here you can see that `<html>` is the root element and it has children

```
<head> ... </head>,
<body>...</body>.
```

These tags can further have children. For example, `<p>...</p>` tag in `<body>` tag is the children of `<body>` tag.

Now let us define XHTML attributes:

a. You should always write attribute name in the lower case.

    For example, incorrect way of writing XHTML:

```
<table HEIGHT="20 %">
```

Correct XHTML:

```
<table height="20 %">
```

here *height* is an attribute of table and needs to be written in lower case.

b. You should write attribute values always in quotes.

Incorrect	Correct
`<table height=20%>`	`<table height="20%">`

Note here you are assigning value to attribute *height* so need to put it in quotes.

c. Try to minimize attributes.

Incorrect	Correct
`<input disabled>`	`<input disabled="disabled" />`
`<frame noresize>`	`<option selected="selected" />`
`<option selected>`	`<frame noresize="noresize" />`

There is a list of the HTML minimized attributes and, how to write them in XHTML:

HTML	XHTML
Compact	compact="compact"
Checked	checked="checked"
Nohref	nohref="nohref"
Noshade	noshade="noshade"
Nowrap	nowrap="nowrap"
Multiple	multiple="multiple"
Noresize	noresize="noresize"

d. Use XHTML DTD to define mandatory elements: XHTML DTD has been discussed in later sub-sections.

Important XHTML elements

All XHTML documents must have a DOCTYPE declaration. The html, head and body elements must be present, and the title must be present inside the head element.

This is a minimum XHTML document template:

```
<!DOCTYPE......................>
<html XMLns="http://www.w3.org/1999/xhtml">
<head>
    <title>Here we need to write the title</title>
</head>
<body>
</body>
</html>
```

> **Note:** The DOCTYPE declaration is not a part of the XHTML document itself. It is not an XHTML element, and it should not have a closing tag.

Need of XHTML DTD

The DOCTYPE declaration is required to determine the document type. In SGML **Document Type Definitions (DTD)** specifies the syntax of a Web page. It is used by SGML applications like HTML, to specify rules for documents of a particular type, including a set of elements and entity declarations. An XHTML DTD describes in precise, computer-readable language, the allowed syntax of XHTML markup.

There are three XHTML DTDs:

● Strict
● Transitional

- Frameset

  Let us discuss each of them in brief.

- **XHTML 1.0 Strict:** You can use STRICT DOCTYPE whenever want really clean markup, free of presentational clutter. It is used with CSS.

  ```
  <!DOCTYPE html
  PUBLIC "-//W3C//DTD XHTML 1.0 Strict//EN"
  "http://www.w3.org/TR/xhtml1/DTD/xhtml1-strict.dtd">
  ```

- **XHTML 1.0 Transitional:** You can use the transitional DOCTYPE when you want to use HTML's presentational features.

- **XHTML 1.0 Frameset:** Use the frameset DOCTYPE to use HTML Frames to split the Web page into two or more frames.

  ```
  <!DOCTYPE html
  PUBLIC "-//W3C//DTD XHTML 1.0 Frameset//EN"
  "http://www.w3.org/TR/xhtml1/DTD/xhtml1-
  frameset.dtd">
  ```

Note: 1. The most common DTD is XHTML Transitional.

2. `<!DOCTYPE>` is mandatory.

Steps to Convert HTML to XHTML

1. **Add DOCTYPE Definition was added**

   The given below DOCTYPE declaration was added as the first line of every page:

   ```
   <!DOCTYPE html PUBLIC
   "-//W3C//DTD XHTML 1.0 Transitional//EN"
   "http://www.w3.org/TR/xhtml1/DTD/xhtml1
   transitional.dtd">
   ```

   In case of using Strict or Frameset DTD use appropriate declaration.'

Note: You need to have a DOCTYPE declaration on the Web page for validating the XHTML.

2. **Lower case tags and attribute names**

   As you know XHTML is case-sensitive, and only accept lower case tags and attributes. You need to "find-and-replace" all upper case with lower case if any found in tags and attributes.

3. **All attribute values need to be quoted**

   According to the XHTML 1.0 recommendation all attribute values must be quoted.

4. **Replacing empty tags.**

   Empty tags like `<hr>`, `<br>` and `<img>` are not allowed in XHTML. You need to replace `<hr>` and `<br>` tags with `<hr/>` and `<br/>`.

> **Note:** There are many online tools available that you can use for validating XHTML. The official tool is available at W3C Website called W3C DTD Validator. There are other free tools available like Dave Raggett's HTML TIDY which is a free tool and can be used for cleaning up HTML code. Such kind of tools works very well for the hard-to-read markup, and it can help to identify where you need to pay further attention on making your pages more accessible to people with disabilities.

Using id attribute in XHTML

In HTML you can use name attribute with elements like `<a>`, `<frame>`, `<img>` etc., for assigning name to the element however in case of XHTML such attribute has been deprecated. `id` can be used instead of `name` attribute.

Incorrect way of writing XHTML:

```
<img src="a.jpg" name="Saree" />
```

Correct way of writing XHTML:

```
<img src="a.jpg" name="Saree" id="picture1" />
```

Another important attribute is "`lang`" Attribute

This attribute can be applied to almost every XHTML element. Here "Lang" attribute specifies the language of the content of an element.

To use `lang` attribute you need to add the `XML:lang` attribute. Check out the following example:

```
<div lang="no" XML:lang="no">Heia Norge!</div>
```

Test Your Progress
1. How is XML different from HTML?
2. Can you convert a HTML document into XHTML document?
3. What is use of `lang` attribute of XHTML?

4.5 Understanding DTD

Document Type Definition (DTD) could be understood as legal building blocks of an XML document. You need to define the document structure with a list of legal elements and attributes. The purpose of a DTD is to define the legal building blocks for an XML document, and defines the structure of the document with a list of legal elements. It appears on the top of the document just before the XML processing instructions and identifies the root element of the document and document type definition.

Usage of DTD?

Before you continue reading about DTD you need to understand the usage of DTD. By using a DTD an XML files can carry a description of its format. You can use a standard DTD for verifying whether the data you received for your XML is valid or not. Precisely by using a DTD it is possible for you to verify your own data.

Components of a DTD

Like a **XML** document a DTD can be considered as a collection of a set of components. These components can be identified as follows:

1. **Elements:** Elements can be understood as the main building blocks for the XML and HTML documents. The elements of a XML document can be declared in the DTD. As HTML have elements "body" and "table" whereas examples of XML elements could be "subject" and "content".The elements can have text, other elements, or be empty. Examples of empty HTML element are "hr", "br" and "img". For example:

    ```
    <subject>some text</subject>
    <content>some text</content>
    ```

2. **Attributes:** Extra information about about element is provided by attributes. Attributes are always placed within the opening tag of an element. Attributes come in name/value pairs. The "img"element given below has additional information about a source file:

    ```
    <img src="comp.gif" />
    ```

    In the above given example the name of theelement html is "img". "src" is the name of the attribute. The value of the attribute is "comp.gif". Here the element is an empty elementso need to be closed by a "/".

3. **Entities:** In XML, there are some characters, that have special meaning, such as less than sign (<) that defines the start of an XML tag. The HTML entity: " ". This "no-breaking-space" entity is used in HTML to insert an extra space in the document. Entities can be expanded when a document is parsed by an XML parser.

    Entities can be defined as variables that are used to define shortcuts for standard text/special characters.

*   Entity references are references to entities.
*   Entities can be declared internal or external.

An Internal Entity Declaration

Syntax: `<!ENTITY entity-name "entity-value">`

For example, `<!ENTITY name "Elizabeth">`

`<!ENTITY book_written "Thinking for World">`

Usage in XML:

```
<author>&name;&book_written;</author>
```

In the example given above, the entity has three component: an ampersand (&), an entity name, and a semicolon (;).

You can also declare entities externally using following declaration:

Syntax: `<!ENTITY entity-name SYSTEM "URI/URL">`

For example, `<!ENTITY   name   SYSTEM   "http://` `www.elizabeth.com/entities.dtd">`

```
<!ENTITY book SYSTEM "http://www.elizabeth.com/
entities.dtd">
```

Usage in XML:

```
<author>&writer;&copyright;</author>&DTD Validation
```

Pre-Defined Entities of a XML document

The following entities are predefined in XML:

PCDATA: PCDATA implies parsed character data. It is the text that will be parsed by a parser. The parser examines the text for entities and markup. Tags within the text will be treated as markup and expands the entities. However, parsed character data should not contain any &, <, or > characters; these need to be represented by the & < and > entities, respectively.

CDATA: CDATA denotes character data. It implies the text that is found within the start and the end tags of an XML element. This data refers to the text that will not be parsed by a parser. Thus the tags inside the text will not be treated as any markup and entities will not be expanded.

Defining attributes in a DTD

In a DTD, attributes are declared using an ATTLIST declaration. ATTLIST is a declaration that is used to define elements that can have attributes. It provides the name of attribute, its type and default value (if any).

An attribute declaration has the following syntax:

```
<!ATTLIST element-name attribute-name attribute-type
default-value>
```

For example, `<!ATTLIST fabrictype CDATA "cotton">`

Declared element can be used in XML as follows:

```
<fabric type="cotton" />
```

The attribute- type can be one of the given below.

Assigning Default-values

You can assign default values to the elements. Check out the following example:

```
<!ELEMENT filler EMPTY>
<!ATTLIST fillerspace CDATA "0">
```

Declared element can be used in XML as follows:

```
<filler width="100" />
```

In the above example 'filler' element is defined as an empty element. It has an attribute 'space' of type CDATA. In case no value specified for the 'space' attribute it will take default value that is declared to be '0'.

Using specific keywords for defining values

It is possible to define the values that can be given to a specific attribute. Check out the following keyword usage:

1. **#REQUIRED:** Use the keyword #REQUIRED if you don not have an option for a default value, but still want to force the attribute to be present.

    Syntax : `<!ATTLIST element-name attribute-name attribute-type #REQUIRED>`

    For example, `<!ATTLIST telephone number CDATA #REQUIRED>`

    Valid XML: `<telephone number="01123456" />`

    Invalid XML: `<telephone />`

    This will be considered as invalid XML as attribute value is required as per the declaration of the element in DTD.

2. **#IMPLIED:** `#IMPLIED` keyword can be used in cases when you do not want any author to include an attribute and you cannot define a default value for the attribute.

    Syntax: `<!ATTLIST element-name attribute-name attribute-type #IMPLIED>`

    For example, `<!ATTLIST calltelephone CDATA #IMPLIED>`

    Valid XML: `<contact telephone="011-2234656" />`

    Invalid XML: `<contact />`

3. **#FIXED:** Use the keyword #FIXED if you want an attribute to have a fixed value without allowing the author to change it. If an author includes another value, the XML parser will return an error.

    Syntax: `<!ATTLIST element-name attribute-name attribute-type #FIXED "value">`

    For example, `<!ATTLIST interview company CDATA #FIXED "Birla Soft">`

    Usage in XML:

    > **Valid:** `<interview company="Birla Soft"/>`

    > **Invalid:** `<interview company="Microsoft" />`

4. **Enumerated Attribute Values:** Use enumerated attribute values if the attribute value to be one of a fixed set of legal values.

    Syntax: `<!ATTLIST element-name attribute-name (en1|en2|..) default-value>`

    For example, `<!ATTLIST fabric type (cotton|silk) "cotton">`

    Usage in XML: `<fabric type="cotton" />` or `<fabric type="silk" />`

Declaring Elements in a DTD

In a DTD, XML elements are declared with an element declaration with the syntax given below.

```
<!ELEMENT element-name category>
```

or

```
<!ELEMENT element-name (element-content)>
```

Some specific ways of declaration are:

1. **Declaring Empty Elements**

    Empty elements can be declared using the category keyword EMPTY:

    ```
    <!ELEMENT element-name EMPTY>
    ```

    For example, `<!ELEMENT hr EMPTY>`

    Element can be used in XML as follows:

    ```
    <hr />
    ```

2. **Declaring elements with Parsed Character Data**

    #PCDATA is used to declare elements which contain parsed character data.

    ```
    <!ELEMENT element-name (#PCDATA)>
    ```

    For example, `<!ELEMENT from (#PCDATA)>`

3. **Declaring elements with Contents**

    Such elements are declared with the category keyword 'ANY' and can contain any combination of parsable data:

    ```
    <!ELEMENT element-name ANY>
    ```

    For example, `<!ELEMENT note ANY>`

4. **Declaring Elements with Children (sequences)**

    Elements having children are declared with the name of the children elements inside parentheses. This can be done using following syntax:

    ```
    <!ELEMENT element-name (child)>
    ```

    In case element have multiple child elements you can use following syntax:

    ```
    <!ELEMENT element-name (child1, child2, ...)>
    ```

    For example,

    ```
    <!ELEMENT notice_board (for, from, subject, content)>
    ```

Notes: 1. The order of children in the XML document should be same as they are declared in the DTD and separated by commas. The children must appear in the same sequence in the document as they are declared.

2. In case of a full declaration children must be declared. Children may also have children so full declaration is required.

```
<!ELEMENT note (to, from, heading, body)>
<!ELEMENT to (#PCDATA)>
<!ELEMENT from (#PCDATA)>
<!ELEMENT heading (#PCDATA)>
<!ELEMENT body (#PCDATA)>
```

5. **Declaring Only One Occurrence of an Element**

    For cases where there is only one occurrence following declaration can be used:

    ```
    <!ELEMENT element-name (child-name)>
    ```

    For example,

    ```
    <!ELEMENT notice_board(notice)>
    ```

    According to this example the child element "notice" must occur only once inside the 'notice_board' element.

6. **Declaring Zero or More Occurrences of an Element**

    For declaring Zero or More Occurrences of an Element you need to use following declaration:

    ```
    <!ELEMENT element-name (child-name*)>
    ```

    For example, `<!ELEMENT notice_board(notice*)>`

    In this example '*' sign shows that the child element "notice" can occur zero or more times inside the "notice_board" element.

7. **Declaring Minimum One Occurrence of an Element**

    For declaring minimum one occurrence of an element you need to use following declaration:

    ```
    <!ELEMENT element_name (child_name+)>
    ```

    For example, `<!ELEMENT notice_board(notice+)>`

    In the above example '+' sign shows that the child element "notice" must occur one or more times inside the "notice_board" element.

8. **Declaring Zero or One Occurrences of an Element**

    ```
    <!ELEMENT element_name (child_name?)>
    ```

    For example, `<!ELEMENT notice_board(notice?)>`

    In the above example '?' sign declares that the child element "notice" can occur zero or one time inside the "notice_board" element.

9. **Declaring element which may or not have a child element**

    You can declare element which may have child element at some instances and may not have child element at other instances. In such cases following declaration syntax can be used:

    For example,

    ```
    <!ELEMENT notice_board(for, from, subject,
    (content|message))>
    ```

In the above example 'notice_board' element has been declared. It states that 'notice_board' must contain a 'for', 'from', 'subject' and either a 'content' or 'message' element.

10. **Declaring Mixed Content**

In case you need to declare an element which may contain or further chid element you need to use following declaration syntax:

For example <!ELEMENT note (#PCDATA|to|from|header| message)*>

In the above example a notice_board can have zero or more occurrences of parsed character data, "for", "from", "subject", or "content" elements.

Declaration of a DTD

DTD can be declared in two ways:

1. Declaring DTD inside an XML document.
2. Declaring DTD as an external reference.

Internal DTD Declaration

DTD can be declared inside the XML file. In such cases it should be wrapped in a DOCTYPE definition using the following syntax:

<!DOCTYPE root-element [element-declarations]>

Example XML document with an internal DTD:

```
?XML version="1.0"?>
<!DOCTYPE mails [
<!ELEMENT e-mail (to, from, subject, content)>
<!ELEMENT to (#PCDATA)>
<!ELEMENT from (#PCDATA)>
<!ELEMENT subject (#PCDATA)>
<!ELEMENT content (#PCDATA)>
]>
```

The DTD above is interpreted like this:

!DOCTYPE mails: This defines that the root element of this document is 'mails'.

!ELEMENT e-mail: defines that the element note contains four elements: "to, from, heading, body".

!ELEMENT to defines the to element to be of the type "#PCDATA".

!ELEMENT from defines the from element to be of the type "#PCDATA".

!ELEMENT heading defines the eleeement heading to be of the type "#PCDATA".

!ELEMENT body defines the element body to be of the type "#PCDATA".

External DTD Declaration

If the DTD is declared in an external file, it should be wrapped in a DOCTYPE definition with the syntax given below:

```
<!DOCTYPE root-element SYSTEM "filename">
```

This is the same XML document as given above, but with an external DTD (Open it, and select view source):

```
<?XML version="1.0"?>
<!DOCTYPE note SYSTEM "note.dtd">
<note>
    <to>Tove</to>
    <from>Rani</from>
    <heading>Remember</heading>
    <body>Do not forget the date!</body>
</note>
```

And this is the file "notice.dtd" which contains the DTD:

```
<!ELEMENT notice_board(for, from, subject, content)>
<!ELEMENT for (#PCDATA)>
<!ELEMENT from (#PCDATA)>
<!ELEMENT subject (#PCDATA)>
<!ELEMENT subject (#PCDATA)>
```

DTD Example: Create a DTD for FM Schedule

```
<!ATTLIST TITLE RATING CDATA #IMPLIED>
<!ATTLIST TITLE LANGUAGE CDATA #IMPLIED>
```

Consider the following example:

Step 1: `<!ELEMENT music_collection (songs +>`

Step 2: `<!ELEMENT music (title, singer +, track +, comments ?)>`

Step 3: `<!ATTLIST music`

```
    Type (rock | pop | classical)
    "rock"
    review (3 | 4 | 5) "3"
    year <CADTA# IMPLIED>
<!ELEMENT title (#PCDATA)>
<!ELEMENT artist (#PCDATA)>
<!ELEMENT track (#PCDATA)>
<!ELEMENT comments (#PCDATA)>>
```

The music element in Step 1 shows that music is a child of music_collection. The + sign next to music shows that there can be multiple music elements in an music_collection tag.

Step 4: You need to write attributes of an element in parenthesis. The + sign after the singer shows that you can have multiple instances of the singer.

> **Note:** The ' ? ' sign in the above DTD shows that it is optional and can only be used for comments.

CDATA – Used for character value.

PCDATA – Used for test value.

An Overview of XML Schemas

Apart from DTD, XSD can be used for specifying XML schema. XSD stands for XML Schema Definition. It is a newer standard developed to provide good control for XML validation and is gaining wide popularity. It is possible that an XML file conforms to the XML specification but is notvalid. With XML schema you can easily verify whether certain elements are present and have been assigned correct values. The first line of a schema generally looks like:

```
<xs:schema XMLns:xs="http://www.w3.org/2001/
XMLSchema">
```

This code identifies the file as a schema and defines the XML Schema namespace (xs prefix stands for XML schema) that will be used to validate elements of a XML. Through this validation you can easily check whether elements are of the correct type or not. This can be used for validating data type like you do not want any character value for an element. You only want integer value for the same. Such checks can be applied as follows:

```
<xs:element name="telephone" type="xs:integer"/>
```

The above code implies that any elements named telephone can only integral values. Thus according to this declaration following code is valid:

```
<telephone>9810283939310</telephone>
```

and following code will be invalid:

```
<telephone>This is some text</telephone>
```

Check out another example:

Suppose you want an element to only take Boolean values, i.e., "0" or "1". This can be done using following syntax:

```
<xs:element name="switch">
<xs:simpleType>
<xs:restriction base="xs:integer">
    <xs:enumeration value="0"/>
    <xs:enumeration value="1"/>
</xs:restriction>
</xs:simpleType>
</xs:element>
```

Check out the above code. The '**restriction element**' is used to provide base type. Here values has been restricted to be integer. In the next line **'enumeration'** element is used to denote values that can be taken by the element.

```
<xs:element name="author">
    <xs:attribute name="gender" type="xs:string"/>
</xs:element>
```

It is possible that for an attribute value is optional. This can be defined as follows:

```
<xs:attribute name="author" type="xs:string"
use="optional"/>
```

Similarly complex elements can be easily defined in the schema.

> **Note:** Complex elements are the one which contains other elements.

```
<book>
    <Title> Programming</title>
    <author> A Bajaj</author>
</book>
```

In this example `<book>` is a complex element as it further contains other elements `<title>`, `<author>`. So while creating the schema you need to make sure that book element contains these two elements. This can be done as follows:

```
<xs:element name="book">
<xs:complexType>
<xs:sequence>
    <xs:element name="title" type="xs:string"/>
    <xs:element name="author" type="xs:string"/>
</xs:sequence>
</xs:complexType>
</xs:element>
```

Test Your Progress

1. *What is the meaning of DTD?*
2. *How can you give a data type declaration?*
3. *What is PCDATA?*
4. *What is CDATA?*

4.6   Understanding XSL

The previous Section covers how to create XML and get it displayed in the browser. As discussed when you will display a XML file in the browser, it will show you a hierarchical structure of the document. In order to retrieve information from the XML file, you need to transform XML. To retrieve information from XML, you can use XSL. XSL is an acronym for Extensible Stylesheet Language. XSL can be understood as XML-based style sheet language. As CSS is used to style HTML elements similarly XSL can be used to style XML elements. In other words, the style sheet is a well-formed XML document which describes the tree of the source and the resulting document. It also includes the process to transform the source into resultant document.

The top level element/root element of the XSL document is:

```
<xsl:stylesheet XMLns:xsl="http://www.w3.org/1999/
XSL/Transform/"
XMLns="http://www.w3.org/TR/REC-html40">
```

Since stylesheet includes elements from different documents name spaces needs to be used to organize these elements. For the XSL vocabulary, xsl namespace is used. Its URI is:

http://www.w3.org/1999/XSL/Transform/1.0.

Note: The resulting document has another namespace, default namespace is attached to the HTML 4.0.

XSL can be further divided as follows:

1. **XSLT** - XSLT is a language that isfor transforming XML documents into XHTML documents or to the other XML documents.

2. **XPath**- a language for navigating in the XML documents.

3. **SL-FO** - a language for formatting XML documents

Figure 4.1 illustrates how an XML document is transformed in XSL document.

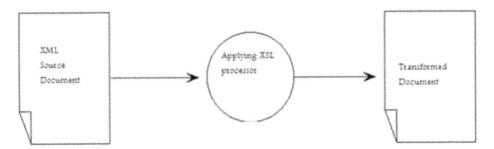

Figure 4.1: Transforming an XML Document Using XSL

XSLT: XSLT implies XSL Transformations. It is the component of XSL used for transforming an XML document into anoother type of document, and that is recognized by the browser, like HTML and XHTML.This is done by transforming each XML element into an HTML/XHTML element. XSLT uses XPath for navigation in XML documents. XML paths always begin from the root of the document and list the elements along the way. The "/" character are used to separate the elements. The"/" is the root of the document. The root node, sits before the top level element. It represents the document as a whole. With XSLT one can add/remove elements and attributes to or from the output file that will be displayed to the user. With this it becomes easy for you to customize the display of the information. It is possible to rearrange and sort elements, perform tests with them and make decisions about the elements that need to be hided or displayed. Apart from styling XSLT has many applications like adding elements specifically for viewing, for example logo or some message, creating new content from the original one, creating table of contents, presenting information according to the viewer like using a style sheet for presenting high-level information for managers and different style sheet for providing information to workers. It can also be used to convert DTDs, for example converting a particular company specific DTD according to the industry standard.

4.6.1 Working with XSL

Work of XSLTis to transforms XML source-tree into XML result-tree. While doing this, you can use XPath to find information in an XML document. XPath is used for navigation through elements and attributes in XML documents. XSLT uses XPath, in the transformation process, to define parts of the source document, which need to match one or more predefined templates. On finding a match XSLT transforms the part, that is matching of the source document into the result document.

> **Note:** Nearly all major browsers have support for XML and XSLT.

4.6.2 Declaring XSL

Like an XML document XSL document needs to have a root element. The root element can be `<xsl:stylesheet>` or `<xsl:transform>`.

> **Note:** You can use either of `<xsl:stylesheet>` and `<xsl:transform>`.
> These are just synonymous to each other.

4.6.3 Declaring Namespace

In order to get access to the XSLT elements, its attributes and features you need to declare XSLT namespace and, declared at the top of the document as follows:

```
<xsl:stylesheet version="1.0" XMLns:xsl =http://
www.w3.org/1999/XSL/Transform>
```

or

```
<xsl:stylesheet version="1.0" XMLns:xsl =http://
www.w3.org/1999/XSL/Transform>
```

XSL Style Sheet

Just look at the example of XSL below. In the second line, XSL namespace has been declared. You will be well-versed with the XSL coding after reading this section.

Example 10: Declaring XSL namespace

```
<?XML version="1.0"?>
<xsl:stylesheet
```

```
XMLns:xsl="http://www.w3.org/1999/XSL/Transform"
XMLns="http://www.w3.org/TR/REC-html40">
<xsl:output method="html"/>
<xsl:template match="/">
<html>
<head>
    <title>Article</title>
</head>
<body>
    <xsl:apply-templates/>
</body>
</html>
</xsl:template>
<xsl:template match="title">
    <P><B><xsl:apply-templates/></B></P>
</xsl:template>
<xsl:template match="p">
    <P><xsl:apply-templates/></P>
</xsl:template>
</xsl:stylesheet>
```

4.6.4 Transforming XML document

1. Create an XSL Stylesheet.
2. The XSL Style Sheet is to be linked with the XML Document.
3. Add the XSL style sheet reference to your XML document. You need to add this statement in the second line in a XML document.

    ```
    <?XML-stylesheet type="text/xsl" href="style.xsl"?>
    ```

    Here `style.xsl` refers to the xsl file to be used for formatting XML.

4.6.5 Creating an XSL Style Sheet

An XSL style sheet consists of set of rules that is known as emplates. A template containing rules are applied when a specified node is matched. An XSL style sheet is an XML document itself and, begins with the XML declaration: `<?XML version="1.0"?>`. The next element is `<xsl:stylesheet>` which defines that the document is an XSLT style sheet document. This element includes the version number and XSLT namespace attributes).

4.6.6 XSL Elements

For making a XSL there are set of elements that needs to used:

1. **`<xsl:template>` Element:** The `<xsl:template>` element is used to build templates. One will find that the bulk of the style sheet is a list of templates. It has a match attribute that needs to be used to associate template with an XML element. It has a match attribute that can be used to define a template for

the entire XML document. The value of match attribute isset as an XPath expression. For example `match="/"` implies the whole document). The template consists of two parts:

1. **Match parameter:** First part is the match parameter which defines path to the element on which template needs to be applied.

2. **Content of the template:** The content of the template includes the elements that need to be inserting in the resulting output.

```
<xsl:template match="section/title">
<P><I><xsl:apply-templates/></I></P>
</xsl:template>
<P><I>Styling</I></P>
```

2. **Using `<xsl:value-of>` element:** The element `<xsl:value-of>` is to extract the value of an XML element and, add it to the output stream of the transformation:

Example 11: Extracting XML element to add to the output stream of transformation

```
<?XML version="1.0"?>
<xsl:stylesheet version="1.0"
XMLns:xsl="http://www.w3.org/1999/XSL/Transform">
<xsl:template match="/">
<html>
<body>
<h2>MCA Text Books Collection</h2>
<table border="2">
<tr bgcolor="blue">
    <th>Semester</th>
    <th>Publication</th>
</tr>
<tr>
    <td><xsl:value-of select="catalog/book/semester"/></td>
    <td><xsl:value-of select="catalog/book/publication"/></
    td>
</tr>
</table>
</body>
</html>
</xsl:template>
</xsl:stylesheet>
```

Note: The value of the attribute `select` is an XPath expression. An XPath expression works like navigating a file system; where a forward slash (/) selects subdirectories.

3. **The <xsl:for-each> Element:** The element <xsl:for-each> allows to do looping in XSLT. The XSL element <xsl:for-each> is used to select every XML element of the specified node-set:

    Example 12: Looping in XSLT

```
<?XML version="1.0"?>
<xsl:stylesheet version="1.0"
XMLns:xsl="http://www.w3.org/1999/XSL/Transform">
<xsl:template match="/">
<html>
<body>
<h1>BCA Book Collection</h1>
<table border="2">
<tr bgcolor="red">
    <th>Title</th>
    <th>Author</th>
</tr>
<xsl:for-each select="catalog/book">
<tr>
    <td><xsl:value-of select="title"/></td>
    <td><xsl:value-of select="author"/></td>
</tr>
</xsl:for-each>
</table>
</body>
</html>
</xsl:template>
</xsl:stylesheet>
```

> **Note:** The value of the attribute select is an XPath expression. The expression XPath, works like navigating a file system; and a (/)forward slash selects subdirectories.

The transformation result given above will look like as given below.

Output:

BCA Book Collection

Title	Author
Linear Programming	A.S.Bajaj
Operational Research	M. L Khanna
Marketing Research	Kotler
Mathematical Programming	I.P.Roy

4. **The element <xsl:sort> is used to sort the output.**

To sort the output, simply add an element <xsl:sort> within the element <xsl:for-each> in the XSL file:

Example 13: Sorting the output using <xsl:sort> element

```
<?XML version="1.0"?>
<xsl:stylesheet version="1.0"
XMLns:xsl="http://www.w3.org/1999/XSL/Transform">
<xsl:template match="/">
<html>
<body>
<h1>MCA Text BooksCollection</h1>
<table border="2">
<tr bgcolor="red">
    <th>Title</th>
    <th>Author</th>
</tr>
<xsl:for-each select="catalog/book">
<xsl:sort select="author"/>
<tr>
    <td><xsl:value-of select="title"/></td>
    <td><xsl:value-of select="author"/></td>
</tr>
</xsl:for-each>
</table>
</body>
</html>
</xsl:template>
</xsl:stylesheet>
```

Note: The attribute select indicates what XML element sorts the values.

---

5. **<xsl:if> Element:** The element <xsl:if> is used to put a conditional test against the content of the XML file. To put a conditional if test against the content of the XML file, add an <xsl:if> element to the XSL document.

Syntax:

```
<xsl:if test="expression">
    . . .
    ...some output if the expression is true...
    ....
</xsl:if>
```

To add a conditional test, add the <xsl:if> element inside the <xsl:for-each> element in the XSL file.

Example 14: Adding a conditional test

```
<?XML version="1.0"?>
<xsl:stylesheet version="1.0"
XMLns:xsl="http://www.w3.org/1999/XSL/Transform">
<xsl:template match="/">
<html>
<body>
<h2>MCA Text Books Collection</h2>
<table border="2">
<tr bgcolor="red">
    <th>Title</th>
    <th>Author</th>
</tr>
<xsl:for-each select="catalog/cd">
<xsl:if test="price &gt; 200">
<tr>
    <td><xsl:value-of select="title"/></td>
    <td><xsl:value-of select="author"/></td>
</tr>
</xsl:if>
</xsl:for-each>
</table>
</body>
</html>
</xsl:template>
</xsl:stylesheet>
```

> **Note:** The value of the required attribute `test` contains the expression to be
> evaluated. The code above will only output the title and author elements of
> the Books that has a price that is higher than 200. The result of the
> transformation of above will be:

Output:

MCA Text Books Collection

Title	Artist
Linear Programming	A.S.Bajaj
Operational Research	M. L Khanna
Marketing Research	Kotler

6. **<xsl:choose> Element:** The element <xsl:choose> is used in
    conjunction with <xsl:when> and <xsl:otherwise> to express multiple
    conditional tests. To insert a multiple conditional test against the XML file, add
    the <xsl:choose>, <xsl:when> and <xsl:otherwise> elements
    to the XSL file:

Syntax:

```
<xsl:choose>
<xsl:when test="expression">
    ... some output ...
</xsl:when>
<xsl:otherwise>
    ... some output ....
</xsl:otherwise>
</xsl:choose>
```

Example 15: Inserting multiple conditional test

```
<?XML version="1.0"?>
<xsl:stylesheet version="1.0"
XMLns:xsl="http://www.w3.org/1999/XSL/Transform">
<xsl:template match="/">
<html>
<body>
<h1>BCA Book Collection</h1>
<table border="2">
<tr>
    <th>Title</th>
    <th>Author</th>
</tr>
<xsl:for-each select="catalog/book">
<tr>
<td><xsl:value-of select="title"/></td>
<xsl:choose>
<xsl:when test="price &gt; 200">
<td>
<xsl:value-of select="author"/></td>
</xsl:when>
<xsl:otherwise>
<td><xsl:value-of select="author"/></td>
</xsl:otherwise>
</xsl:choose>
<xsl:when test="price &gt; 200">
<td>
<xsl:value-of select="author"/></td>
</xsl:when>
<xsl:otherwise>
<td><xsl:value-of select="author"/></td>
</xsl:otherwise>
</xsl:choose>
</tr>
</xsl:for-each>
```

```
</table>
</body>
</html>
</xsl:template>
</xsl:stylesheet>
```

Output:

BCA Book Collection

Title	Artist
Linear Programming	A.S.Bajaj
Operational Research	M. L Khanna
Marketing Research	Kotler

XSL Element Description

`xsl:element`	Creates element with a computed name
`xsl:attribute`	Creates attribute with a computed value
`xsl:attribute-set`	Conveniently combines several `xsl:attributet` element
`xsl:text`	Creates a text node
`xsl:processing-instruction`	Creates a processing instruction
`xsl:comment`	Creates a comment
`xsl:copy`	Copies the current node
`xsl:value-of`	
`xsl:if`	Instantiates its content if the expression is true
`xsl:choose alternatives`	Selects elements to instantiate among possible
`xsl:number`	Creates formatted number

Making trial.XML

Example 16: Creating and linking .XML and .xsl files (trial.XML and trial.xsl)

```
<?XML version="1.0"?>
<catalog>
    <book>
        <title>Linear Programming</title>
        <author>A.S.Bajaj</author>
        <price>210</price>
        <year>1985</year>
    </book>
```

```
<book>
    <title>Operational Research</title>
    <author>M.L.Khana</author>
    <price>420</price>
    <year>1997</year>
</book>

<book>
    <title>Marketing Research</title>
    <author>Kotler</author>
    <price>200</price>
    <year>1994</year>
</book>

<book>
    <title>Mathematical Programming</title>
    <author>I.P.Roy</author>
    <price>160</price>
    <year>1998</year>
</book>
```
</catalog>

Opening trial.XML in browser:

The XML file does not appear to have any style information associated with it. The document tree is shown below.

```
-<catalog>
    -<book>
        <title>Linear Programming<title>
        (author>A.S. Bajaj</author>
        <price>210</price>
        <year>1985</year>
    </book>
    -<book>
        <title>Operational Research<title>
        <author>M.L. Khana</author>
        <price>420</price>
        <year>1997</year>
    </book>
</catalog>
```

Making trial.xsl file

```
<?XML version="1.0" encoding="ISO-8859-1"?>
<xsl:stylesheet version="1.0"
XMLns:xsl="http://www.w3.org/1999/XSL/Transform">
<xsl:template match="/">
```

```
<html>
<body>
<h2>My Book Collection</h2>
<table border="1">
<tr bgcolor="#9acd32">
    <th align="left">Title</th>
    <th align="left">Author</th>
</tr>
<xsl:for-each select="catalog/book">
<tr>
    <td><xsl:value-of select="title"/></td>
    <td><xsl:value-of select="author"/></td>
</tr>
</xsl:for-each>
</table>
</body>
</html>
</xsl:template>
</xsl:stylesheet>
```

On opening the trial.xsl file in the browser you will get:

```
-<xsl:stylesheet version="1.0">
-<xsl:template match="/">
-<html>
-<body>
    <h1>BCA BOOK Collection</h1>
    -<table border="2">
        -<tr bgcolor="black">
            <th>Title</th>
        </tr>
        -<tr>
            <td>new</td>
            <td>...</td>
        </tr>
    </table>
</body>
</html>
<xsl:template>
</xsl:stylesheet>
```

To link XSL file with the XML element.

Linking XSL file with XML file to apply style to trial.XML. To do this you need to add xsl reference in the XML file as follows:

```
<?XML version="1.0"?>
<?XML-stylesheet type="text/xsl" href="trial.xsl">
```

After linking the XSL file to XML again open the XML file in browser. After opening the trial.XML file browser will display it as follows:

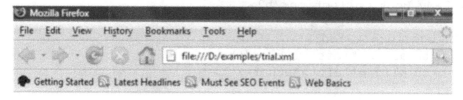

My Book Collection

Title	Author
Linear Programming	A.S.Bajaj
Operational Research	M.L.Khana
Marketing Research	Kotler
Mathematical Programming	I.P.Roy

Illustrative Example: Develop a Mathquiz using XML. Create its DTD, XMLSchema, display information using CSS and extract various type of information using XSL. The rules for developing XML are:

- Root element should be `<math_quiz>`.
- `<math_quiz>` should contain a `<title>` and an `<items>` element.
- `<sets>` contains one or more `<set>` element.
- `<ques_sets>` contains one `<ques>`, at least 2 `<ans>` and no more than 4 `<ans>` tags.
- One of the `<ans>` tag must have an attribute correct with value "yes". This denotes a correct answer.

  Create different XSLs file which meets following requirements:

1. **Requirement 1**: Display title, question and answer. Ignore all other elements.
2. **Requirement 2:** Use table and Bullets to display quiz.
3. **Requirement 3:** Show correct answer in different color.

Math Quiz XML

Example 17: Displaying Match quiz

```
<?XML version="1.0"?>
<math_quiz>
<title>Math Quiz</title>
<ques_sets>
<set>
    <ques>What is 2+4=?</ques>
    <anscorrect="yes">6</ans>
```

```
    <ans>3</ans>
    <ans>4</ans>
    <ans>7</ans>
</ques>
</set>
<set>
    <ques> How many points are on a triangle?</ques>
    <ans>1</ans>
    <ans correct="y">3</ans>
    <ans>2</ans>
    <ans>4</ans>
</set>
<set>
    <ques>How many points are on a hexagon?</ques>
    <ans>5</ans>
    <ans>6</ans>
    <ans>7</ans>
    <ans correct="y">8</ans>
</set>
</ques_sets>
</math_quiz>
```

DTD Declaration

```
<!ELEMENT math_quiz (title, ques_sets)>
<!ELEMENT title (#PCDATA)>
<!ELEMENT ques_sets (set)+>
<!ELEMENT set(ques, ans, ans+)>
<!ELEMENT ques (#PCDATA)>
<!ELEMENT ans (#PCDATA)>
<!ATTLIST ans correct (yes) #IMPLIED>
```

To limit the number of <ans> tags to 4. You can use following declaration in the DTD:

```
<!ELEMENT set(ques, ((ans, ans)|(ans, ans, ans)|(ans,
ans, ans, ans)))>
```

Using XML Schema

Example 18: Program shows how to use XML schema

```
<?XML version="1.0"?>
<xsd:schema XMLns:xsd="http://www.w3.org/2001/XMLSchema">
<xsd:element name="title" type="xsd:string"/>
<xsd:element name="ques" type="xsd:string"/>
<xsd:simpleType name="correctType">
<xsd:restriction base="xsd:string">
    <xsd:enumeration value="yes"/>
```

```
</xsd:restriction>
</xsd:simpleType>

<xsd:element name="ans">
<xsd:complexType>
<xsd:simpleContent>
<xsd:extension base="xsd:string">
<xsd:attribute name="correct" type="correctType"/>
</xsd:extension>
</xsd:simpleContent>
</xsd:complexType>
</xsd:element>

<xsd:element name="set">
<xsd:complexType>
<xsd:choice>
<xsd:sequence>
<xsd:element ref="ques"/>
<xsd:element ref="ans" minOccurs="2" maxOccurs="4"/>
</xsd:sequence>
<xsd:sequence>
<xsd:element ref="ans" minOccurs="2" maxOccurs="4"/>
<xsd:element ref="ques"/>
</xsd:sequence>
</xsd:choice>
</xsd:complexType>
</xsd:element>

<xsd:element name="ques_sets">
<xsd:complexType>
<xsd:sequence>
<xsd:element ref="ques" minOccurs="1" maxOccurs="unbounded"/
>
</xsd:sequence>
</xsd:complexType>
</xsd:element>

<xsd:element name="math_quiz">
<xsd:complexType>
<xsd:sequence>
<xsd:element ref="title" minOccurs="1" maxOccurs="1"/>
<xsd:element ref="ques_sets" minOccurs="1" maxOccurs="1"/>
</xsd:sequence>
</xsd:complexType>
</xsd:element>
</xsd:schema>
```

Displaying the XML data using cascading style sheet

Example 19: Displaying XML data using CSS

```
title
{
    font-family:arial;font-size: 20px;display:block;
    color:blue;
}

ques_sets
{
    display: block;font-family:arial;font-size: 20px;color:
    red;
}

set
{
    display: block;border:2px solid gray;margin: 4mm;font-
    family:arial;
    font-size: 10px;color: blue;
}

ques
{
    display: block;font-family:arial;font-size: 12px;font-
    weight: bold;color: red;
}

ans
{
    display: block;font-family:arial;font-size: 12px;color:
    blue;
}
```

Displaying Data Using XSL.

1.   Making XSL according to Requirement 1.

```
<?XML version="1.0"?>
<math_quiz:stylesheet
XMLns:math_quiz="http://www.w3.org/1999/XSL/Transform"
version="1.0">
<math_quiz:template match="/">

<html>
<head><title>MathQuiz </title></head>
<body>
    <math_quiz:apply-templates />
</body>
</html>
```

```
</math_quiz:template>
<math_quiz:template match="title">

    <h1><math_quiz:value-of select="."/></h1>
</math_quiz:template>
<math_quiz:template match="ans">
</math_quiz:template>
<math_quiz:template match="ques">
    <b><math_quiz:value-of select="."/></b><br/>
</math_quiz:template>
</math_quiz:stylesheet>
```

2.   Making XSL according to Requirement 2

```
<?XML version="1.0"?>
<math_quiz:stylesheet
XMLns:math_quiz="http://www.w3.org/1999/XSL/Transform"
version="1.0">

<math_quiz:template match="/">
<html>
<head><title>Quiz formatted according to requirement 2</title></head>
<body>
    <table border="1" bgcolor="red">
    <math_quiz:apply-templates/>
    </table>
</body>
</html>
</math_quiz:template>

< math_quiz:template match="title">
    <tr><td><H1>< math_quiz:value-of select="."/></H1></td></tr>
</ math_quiz:template>

< math_quiz:template match="ques_sets">
<tr><td><ol>< math_quiz:apply-templates/></ol></td></tr>
</ math_quiz:template>

< math_quiz:template match="set">
<LI><b><font size="6" color="00FFFF">

< math_quiz:value-of select="ques"/></font></b></LI><br/>
<!-- this code will loop between answers and apply bullet for
each answer-->
<UL>
    < math_quiz:for-each select="ans">
    <LI>< math_quiz:value-of select="."/></LI>
    </ math_quiz:for-each>
```

```
</UL>
</ math_quiz:template>
</ math_quiz:stylesheet>
```

3. XSL according to Requirement 3.

```
<?XML version="1.0"?>
<math_quiz:stylesheet
XMLns: math_quiz="http://www.w3.org/1999/XSL/Transfor m"
version="1.0">

< math_quiz:template match="/">
<html>
<head><title>MATH Quiz</title></head>
<body><table border="2" bgcolor="#EEEEFF">
    < math_quiz:apply-templates/></table>
</body>
</html>
</ math_quiz:template>

< math_quiz:template match="title">
<tr><td><H1>< math_quiz:value-of select="."/></H1></td></
tr>
</ math_quiz:template>

< math_quiz:template match="ques_sets">
<tr><td><ol>< math_quiz:apply-templates/></ol></td></tr>
</ math_quiz:template>

< math_quiz:template match="set">
<LI><b><font size="6" color="00EEFF">
< math_quiz:value-of select="ques"/></font></b></LI><br/>

<!—looping between answers and applying bullet for each
answer—>
<UL>
    < math_quiz:for-each select="ans">
    < math_quiz:choose>
    < math_quiz:when test="@correct='y'">
    <font color="red"><LI>< math_quiz:value-of select="."/
></LI></font>
    </ math_quiz:when>
    < math_quiz:otherwise>
    <math_quiz:apply-templates select="." />
    </math_quiz:otherwise>
    </ math_quiz:choose>
    </ math_quiz:for-each>
</UL>
</ math_quiz:template>
```

```
< math_quiz:template match="answer">
<li>< math_quiz:value-of select="."/></li>
</ math_quiz:template>
</ math_quiz:stylesheet>
```

Test Your Progress
1. *What is XSL style sheet?*
2. *How can you display data using XSL?*
3. *What is the relation between XML and XSL?*

4.7   Using WAP with XML

WAP stands for Wireless Application Protocol. It is an application communication protocol used to access services and information. It has been inherited from Internet standards and is used in handheld devices, such as mobile phones. It can be understood as a protocol designed for Micro Browsers. It helps to create Web applications for mobile devices. It uses WML (not HTML) as markup language which is an XML 1.0 application WAP uses a Micro Browser to display Web applications in mobile phones. A Micro Browser can be understood as a small piece of software which makes minimal demands on hardware, memory and CPU. Such browser displays information which are written in a restricted mark-up language called WML. It is also capable to interpret a reduced version of JavaScript called WMLScript. It is a markup language which has been inherited from HTML. WML is based on XML and, it is much stricter than HTML. It isused to create pages that can be displayed in a WAP browser. Such pages are called decks as they are constructed as a set of cards. WML uses WMLScript to run code on the client. WMLScript can be understood as a light JavaScript language. However, unlike JavaScript WMLscripts are not embedded in the WML pages. These pages contain references to script URLs. WML scripts need to be compiled into byte code on a server before they can run in a WAP browser.

4.7.1 Uses of WAP

WAP can been used for diversified applications. Some are listed as follows:

- Checking train (arrival/departure) table information
- Ticket purchase
- Flight check-in
- Viewing traffic information
- Checking weather conditions
- Looking up stock values
- Looking up phone numbers
- Looking up addresses
- Looking up sport results

4.7.2 Use of WMLScript

- To validate user input WMLScript is used.
- To view error messages and confirmations faster, WMLScript is used for generating message boxes and dialog boxes locally.
- To access facilities of the user agent, WMLScript is used.

4.7.3 Calling WML Script

As you have learnt WML scripts are not actually embedded in WML pages. The WML pages just contain references to script URLs. Check out the illustrative example as follows:

```
<?XML version="1.0"?>
<!DOCTYPE wml PUBLIC "-//WAPFORUM//DTD WML 1.1//EN"
"http://www.wapforum.org/DTD/wml_1.1.XML">
<wml>
    <card id="no1" title="Go to URL">
        <do type="options" label="Go">
            <go href="use.wmls#try_url('abcSchools')"/>
        </do>
    </card>
</wml>
```

In the above example Document type declaration in the second line is referring to external DTD of WAP. The go label directs the script to http://www.abcSchools.com/wap.wml. It refers to script file called 'use.wmls' available on this url.

'use.wmls' may include WMLscript code like follows:

```
extern function try_url(the_url)
{
    if (the_url=="abcSchools")
    {
        WMLBrowser.go("http://www.abcSchools.com/wap.wml")
    }
}
```

In the above script function is using the `extern` keyword as it can be called by other functions or WML events outside the wmls file.

4.7.4 Understanding WML Script

WMLScript also uses Dialogs Library Functions which are similar to JavaScript dialog functions. Some of the functions used are:

1. **WMLScript Float Library Functions:** The `Float` library can be used only when the clients that support floating-point numbers. In case floating-point numbers are not supported functions should return *invalid*.

2. **WMLScript Lang Library:** This library include functions used for data type manipulation, random number generation, etc.

3. **WMLScript Lang Library Functions:** This library is like a `Math` library andfunctions, which are related closely to the core of the WMLScript engine.

4. **WML Script WMLBrowser Library:** This library contains functions used for accessing browser variables.

Test Your Progress
1. *What is WAP?*
2. *What is WML?*
3. *What are basic characteristics of WML?*

4.8   Using XML with .NET

In this Section a brief about application of XML in .NET has been given to familiarize you with their basic syntax and relationships. .NET organizes its XML classes under the `System.XML` namespace. In this Section a brief about application of XML in .NET has been given to familiarize you with their basic syntax and relationships.

.NET organizes its XML classes under the system.XML namespace. For this you need to understand some classes that are frequently used. `XMLTextReader class` is just one of the methodsthat can be used for reading XML files. This classs reads the XML file in a way similar to a `DataReader`. The document is read element by element and the whole document is parsed. Similar to `'XMLTextReader'` there is an `'XMLTextReader'` class that can be used for writing XML files line-by-line. `'XMLValidatingReader'` class can be used to validate an XML file against a schema file. Theses classes have been discussed briefly below.

1. **Reading XML in .NET:** `XMLTextReader` is based upon the `XML Reader`class.It has been specially designed to read byte streams and make it suitable for XML files that are to be located on disk/network/stream.

2. **Create a new instance for XML Reader:**The constructor takes the location of the XML file that it will read. It can be done using one of the following ways:

```
//  Inserting  XML  file  that  needs  to  be  read
XMLTextReader  reader1  =  new  XMLTextReader
("hello.XML");

//  Identifying  URL  where  the  file  is  available
XMLTextReader  reader1  =  new  XMLTextReader("http://
www.abc  point.com/hello.XML");
```

3. **The file can be read using 'Read' method as follows:**

```
while (reader.Read())
{
```

```
    //reading the file
}
```

The above loop will continue until you EOF (End of File) file is reached or when there is a break in the loop.

Suppose book.XML contains following data:

```
<?XML version="1.0"?>
<catalog>
    <book>
        <title>Linear Programming</title>
        <author gender="male">A.S.Bajaj</author>
        <price>210</price>
        <year>1985</year>
    </book>
</catalog>
```

XML file data is read in form nodes. This is done in the order elements are displayed in the XML file. For example, XMLReader will read following element as three different nodes:

```
<title>Linear Programming</title>

<title>{starting tag}:XMLNodeType.Element node.
    Linear Programming {text}:XMLNodeType.Text node
</title>{closing tag}:XMLNodeType.EndElement node.
```

The code below shows how you can output the XML tag through the `reader` object that has been created.

```
while (reader1.Read())
{
    switch (reader1.NodeType)
    {
        case XMLNodeType.Element:
            Console.Write("<"+reader1.Name+">");
            break;
        case XMLNodeType.Text:
            Console.Write(reader1.Value);
            break;
        case XMLNodeType.EndElement:
            Console.Write("</"+reader1.Name+">");
            break;
    }
}
```

In case an element has set of attributes. You can iterate through attributes using XML Text `Reader.MoveToNextAttribute`.

```
case XMLNodeType.Element:
Console.Write("<"+reader.Name);
while (reader.MoveToNextAttribute())
{
    Console.WriteLine(reader.Name+" = "+reader.Value);
}
break;
```

4.8.1 Validating XML in .NET

Using the XMLValidatingReader class you can easily validate an XML file against a schema file. For this there are a set of classes that you need to use. You can point XMLValidatingReader object towards related schema files by filling an XMLSchemaCollection as follows:

```
XMLSchemaCollection Collection = new
XMLSchemaCollection(); Collection.Add ("schemafile",
"pattern.xsd");
```

In the above examples chema file pattern.xsd has been used. The actual XMLValidatingReader class takes an XMLReader in its constructor so you need to create and fill an XMLTextReader with the XML file you need to validate:

```
XMLTextReader reader;
XMLValidatingReader validatingReader;
reader = new XMLTextReader("book.XML");
validatingReader = new XMLValidatingReader(reader);
```

You can add your schemaCollection to the schemas you wish the validation reader to use:

```
validatingReader.Schemas.Add(xsdCollection);
```

4.9   Wrting XML in .NET

Once you have learnt to read and validate an XML file you need to write XML. Writing XML can be done using 'XMLTextReader' class. You can build XML files from different node types as follows:

1.   *Creating an instance of the class*

```
XMLTextWriter writer = new XMLTextWriter("hello.XML",
null);
```

In the above declaration the second parameteris set to null to for producing standard UTF-8 encoded XML file. The encoding attribute can be set in the document.

2.   *Writing the XML using 'WriteStartElement' method*

Suppose you are creating following XML:

```
<catalog>
<book>
    <title>Linear Programming</title>
```

```
         <author gender="Male">A.S. bajaj</author>
</book>
</catalog>
```

The first line is the element `catalog` and can be written as follows:

```
writer.WriteStartElement("catalog");
```

Other elements can be written as follows:

```
     writer.WriteStartElement("book");
```

In the next line in the **XML** file 'title' element has some content. In this case writing method will be little different. You will write the start element and the value needs to be specified. For this you need to use 'WriteElementString method' as follows:

```
     writer.WriteElementString("title", "Linear Programming");
```

For writing attribute value you need to use `WriteAttributeString` method as follows:

```
     writer.WriteElementString("author", "A.S. Bajaj");
     writer.WriteAttributeString("gender", "male");
     writer.WriteEndElement();
```

In the above example `author` element has been specified using 'WriteElementString' method. Its attribute 'gender' has been written using 'WriteAttributeString' method. This method takes two values the name of the attribute and its value. In above example the attribute 'gender' of element 'author' takes the value 'male'.

Once the elements have been written you need to close all elements in that order. For this you need to use `WriteStartElement` method. This is done as follows:

```
     writer.WriteStartElement("track");
```

```
     writer.WriteEndElement();
     writer.WriteEndElement();
```

Once all opened elements are closed you need to "Flush" the writer i.e., output the information and `close` the writer in order to free file and resources. This can be done as follows:

```
     writer.Flush()
     writer.Close()
```

Test Your Progress
1.   *How to read XML file in .NET?*
2.   *What is the use of* `XMLTextWriter` *class?*

4.10 XML-based Web Services

With XML many other technologies have been developed like Xquery which is used for querying any XML data, Xlink is used for creating hyperlinks in any XML documents, Xpointer allows hyperlinks created by Xlink to point to more specific parts in the XML document, Xforms are used to define form data in a XML document. Some technologies can be exclusively used with many applications like SMIL (Synchronized Multimedia Integration Language) is popularly used for describing audio-visual presentations, SVG (Scalable Vector Graphics) is used to define graphics in any XML document. Apart from these there are many technologies that help in Web based applications. Some of the technologies have been listed below.

1.   **SOAP:** SOAP stands for Simple Object Access Protocol. It is an XML-based protocol which allows applications to exchange information over HTTP. SOAP can form the foundation layer of a Web services protocol stack, providing a basic messaging framework upon which Web services can be built. A SOAP message could be sent to a Web service enabled Web-site, for example, a house price database, with the parameters needed for a search. The site will return an XML-formatted document with the resulting data (prices, location, features, etc). As the data is returned in a standardized machine-parse able format, it may be integrated directly into a third-party site.

2.   **WSDL:** WSDL stands for Web Services Description Language. It is an XML-based language used for describing Web services.

3.   **RDF**: RDF refers to Resource Description Framework. It is an XML-based language for describing Web resources.

4.   **RSS:** RSS refers to 'Really Simple Syndication'. It provides a format for syndicating news and content of other news like Websites. RSS is a format used for syndicating news and the content of news sites, news-oriented community sites and personal Web logs. However it may not be limited to news. Anything which can be broken down into discrete items can be syndicated using RSS like recent changes in any Website can be tracked using RSS. Once the information is in RSS format an RSS-aware program like news aggregators which are popular in the Web logging community can be used to check the feed for changes and reacts to such changes in an appropriate way. Many Web logs make their content available in RSS. A news aggregator can be used to be update with the changes in favourite Websites by checking their RSS feeds and displaying new items from each of them.

5.   **WAP:** WAP implies Wireless Application Protocol. It can be understood as an XML based language for displaying content on wireless clients, like mobile phones.

4.10.1 Overview of SOAP

SOAP stands for Simple Object Access Protocol. It is a W3C recommended communication protocol used for SOAP is for communication between applications. It can be understood as format for sending messages. It is platform, language independent and uses Internet for communication. Best part is that it is simple and extensible and allows you to get around firewalls. It is important for application development to allow Internet communication between programs.

4.10.2 Uses of SOAP

SOAP defines a set of rules that allow HTTP and XML to be used to access services, objects and servers in a platform-independent manner. SOAP is popular as it is able to link all operating systems, languages and component models. SOAP defines a message format in XML that allows objects to communicate. Such messages can be remotely created and invocated. SOAP has another advantage over other distributed application communication protocols. It can easily traverse firewalls. You can use any of the standard HTTP ports for making a SOAP connection. By this your connections can pass quickly through a pre-configured firewall. In case you want to make a secure connection you can use HTTPS. This implies SOAP can be used to implement secure e-commerce solutions as HTTPS ensures that the sensitive information is transferred confidentially. SOAP can also be used to trigger a response in a billing system, or use it to monitor events in a distributed control system.

4.10.3 Functioning of SOAP

A SOAP message is an ordinary **XML** document containing the following elements:

1. An Envelope element that identifies the XML document as a SOAP message. The required SOAP Envelope element is the root element of a SOAP message. This element defines the XML document as a SOAP message. For example,

```
<?XML version="1.0"?>
<soap:Envelope
XMLns:soap="http://www.w3.org/2001/12/soap-envelope"
soap:encodingStyle="http://www.w3.org/2001/12/soap-
encoding">
```

Write down the message information here

```
        </soap:Envelope>
```

2. **A Header element:** Header element contains header information. It is an optional element and contains application-specific information (like authentication, payment, etc) about the SOAP message. In case you use the Header element it should be the first child element of the Envelope element. The immediate child elements of the Header element need to be namespace-qualified.

```
<?XML version="1.0"?>
<soap:Envelope
    XMLns:soap="http://www.w3.org/2001/12/soap-envelope"
    soap:encodingStyle="http://www.w3.org/2001/12/soap-
    encoding">
    <soap:Header>
    ....
    ...... .
</soap:Header>
. . . . . .

</soap:Envelope>
```

3. **Body element**: Body element contains all call and response information. It needs to contain the actual SOAP message. The Immediate child elements of the Body element needs to be namespace-qualified. For example,

```
<?XML version="1.0"?>
<soap:Envelope
XMLns:soap="http://www.w3.org/2001/12/soap-envelope"
soap:encodingStyle="http://www.w3.org/2001/12/soap-
encoding">
<soap:Body>

</soap:Body>
</soap:Envelope>
```

4. **Fault element**: Fault element contains errors and status information. It is an optional SOAP element used to indicate error messages. In case you use Fault element it must appear as a child element of the Body element.

> **Note:** Fault element can only appear once in a SOAP message.

As you do in XML all the elements need to be declared in the default namespace for the SOAP envelope which is:

    http://www.w3.org/2001/12/soap-envelope

Similarly the default namespace for SOAP encoding and data types is:

    http://www.w3.org/2001/12/soap-encoding

Let us consider a program to creat a SOAP message.

```
<?XML version="1.0"?>
<soap:Envelope
XMLns:soap="http://www.w3.org/2001/12/soap-envelope"
soap:encodingStyle="http://www.w3.org/2001/12/soap-
encoding">
<soap:Header>
    . . .
    . . .
```

```
</soap:Header>
<soap:Body>

    . . .

    . . .
<soap:Fault>

    . . .

    . . .
</soap:Fault>
</soap:Body>
</soap:Envelope>
```

4.10.4 Learning RSS

Really Simple Syndication (RSS) is a lightweight XML language designed for sharing headlines and other Web content. It was originated by UserLand in 1997 and has evolved into a popular means of sharing content between sites like BBC, CNET, CNN, `Disney`, and more. Most of the popular Web browsers, readers like Google Reader and Bloglines can read RSS. It has emerged as a powerful tool for Web developers who want to improve visibility of their Websites on the Web. RSS defines an XML grammar for sharing news and information. Each RSS text file contains both static information about the Website as well as dynamic information about new updates/stories surrounded by matching start and end tags. RSS can be understood as a mini database that contains headlines and descriptions and provides information about updates in the Website. It not only displays news on other Websites and headline viewers but also causes data to flow into other products and services like PDAs, cell phones, e-mail ticklers, etc. E-mail newsletters can easily be automated with RSS. As a joint contribution affiliate networks and partners of like-minded sites can harvest each other's RSS feeds, and automatically display the new stories from the other sites in the network, driving more traffic throughout. This will no doubt contribute to the popularity of the Websites.

Some tools required by RSS are:

1. **Text Editor:** For creating RSS you can can use almost any editor that will generate plain ASCII text. You can use HTML editors like Dreamweaver or BBEdit or use editors like jEdit which checks for XML as well.

2. **RSS Validator:** RSS validator is required to validate feed against errors,

4.10.5 Elements of RSS

1. RSS must be well-formed XML document and include DTD, and all elements must be closed.

2. The first element of RSS document needs to be an `<rss>` element. This includes a mandatory version attribute.

3. The next element you need to use is the `<channel>` element. This element is called the main container for all RSS data.Each of this channel can contain up

to 15 items and is easily parsed using PERL or other open source software.

4.   Another element is the `<title>` element. It depicts title of either entire site (in case used at the top) or title of the current item (in case used within an `<item>` tag).

5.   The `<item>` element contains all the headlines (`<title>`), URLs (`<link>`) and descriptions that will be in the feed of the Website.

6.   The `<link>` element denotes URL of the Web page that corresponds to the RSS feed. In case it is within an `<item>` indicates URL to that item.

7.   The `<description>` element describes the RSS feed or any item of the feed.

Note: Each of the story is defined by an `<item>` tag which contains a headline title, URL, description tags described above.

Let us consider the complete below.

```
<item>
    <title>RSS News</title>
    <link>http://www.Webreference.com/authoring/languages/
    XML/rss/</link>
    <description>RSS resources provide tools, tips and
    tutorials for your ease</description>
</item>
```

4.10.6 Steps to create RSS Feed

This RSS 2.0 document has one item in the feed along with the feed information. This is the minimum you need to have a valid and usable RSS feed.

1.   **XML Declaration:** The first line in your rss feed must be the XML declaration.

```
<?XML version="1.0"?>
```

This is required as RSS 2.0 must validate as XML,

2.   **Developing RSS Channel:** In this step you need to open up the `rss` tag and the `Channel` tag. These tags are required as all the feed content goes inside these tags.

```
<rss version="2.0">
<channel>
```

3.   **Including RSS Feed Information:** Now you can place information RSS feed like its title, the description, and a link to the site.

```
<title>The title of my RSS 2.0 Feed</title>
<link>http://www.example.com/</link>
<description>This is my rss 2 feed description</
description>
<lastBuildDate>Mon, 12 Sep 200518:37:00 GMT</
lastBuildDate>
<language>en-us</language>
```

The lastBuildDate should be the date and time that the feed was last changed. Dates in RSS feeds should comply to RFC 822. In CFML the DateFormat mask would be ddd, dd mmm yyyy and the TimeFormat would be HH:mm:ss. Dates should be offset to GMT. The lastBuildDate tag is not required but is highly recommended.

4. **RSS Items:** Next we enumerate over each RSS item, each item has a title, link, and description, publication date, and guide.

```
<item>
    <title>Title of an item</title>
    <link>http://example.com/item/123</link>
    <guid>http://example.com/item/123</guid>
    <pubDate>Mon, 12 Sep 200518:37:00 GMT</pubDate>
    <description>[CDATA[ This is the description. ]]</
    description>
</item>
<!- put more items here ->
```

5. **Close channel and rss tags**

```
    </channel>
    </rss>
```

6. **Validate your feed**

Validate your feed using FeedValidator.org.

Once you have created and validated the RSS text file you need to register it at the various aggregators. Any site can now grab and display the feed regularly. There are a number of RSS news aggregators out there that collect content from content providers and present the news in a variety of ways (for example my.netscape.com, my.userland.com, XMLtree.com, moreover.com). Many make it easy to drop an RSS feed into your site. This will drive traffic to your Website. As you will update your RSS file all the external sites that have subscribed to the RSS feed will be automatically updated.

Test Your Progress
1. *Explain WAP.*
2. *What is RSS?*

4.11 Key Terms

● **RDF:** Resource Description Framework. It is an XML-based language for describing Web resources.

● **RSS:** RSS refers to 'Really Simple Syndication'. It provides a format for syndicating news and content of other news like Websites.

● **SOAP:** Simple Object Access Protocol. It is an XML based protocol which allows applications to exchange information over HTTP.

- **WAP:** Wireless Application Protocol. It can be understood as an XML based language for displaying content on wireless clients, like mobile phones.
- **WML:** Wireless Markup Language.
- **WSDL:** Web Services Description Language. It is an XML-based language used for describing Web services.
- **XML:** 'Extensible Markup Language'.
- **XSL:** XML-based Style Sheet Language.

4.12 Summary

In this Chapter, the structure of an XML document has been discussed in detail. There is nothing special about XML. It is just plain text with the addition of some XML tags enclosed in angle brackets. Software that can handle plain text can also handle XML. In a simple text editor, the XML tags will be visible and will not be handled specially. In an XML-aware application however, the XML tags can be handled specially. The tags may or may not be visible, or have a functional meaning, depending on the nature of the application. XML Elements are extensible and they have relationships.

XML is a cross-platform, software and hardware independent tool for transmitting information. XML can be used to store data inside HTML documents. XML can be used as a format to exchange information. You have also learnt how to use a DTD for defining the legal elements of an XML document, and how a DTD can be declared inside your XML document, or as an external reference. You have also learnt how to declare the elements, attributes, entities, and CDATA sections for XML documents. You have also learnt how to validate an XML document against a DTD.

XHTML is the extensible markup language that is at par XML standards. XHTML have syntax rules like attribute names must be in lower case, attribute values must be quoted, attribute minimization is forbidden, the id attribute replaces the name attribute. XHTML DTD defines mandatory elements.

4.13 Test Yourself

Section I: Review with Ease

Q. 1.   What does XML stands for?

Ans 1. XML stands for Extensible Mark up language. It uses DTD to describe the data.

Q. 2.   What does XSL stands for?

Ans 2. XSL stands for eXtensible Style sheet Language.

Q. 3.   Develop a XML file which includes lunch food menu?

Ans 3.

```
<?XML version="1.0"?>
```

```
<?XML-stylesheet type="text/xsl" href="menu.xsl"?>
<lunch_menu>
<food>
    <name>Shahi-Paneer</name>
    <price>Rs45.95</price>
    <description>
        Paneer Soaked in Cheese</description>
    <calories>250</calories>
</food>
</lunch_menu>
```

Q. 4. Discuss steps for converting HTML document to XHTML document?

Ans 4. Steps for convert HTML to XHTML are:

a.   Add DOCTYPE definition was added

The following DOCTYPE declaration was added as the first line of every page:

```
<!DOCTYPE html PUBLIC
"-//W3C//DTD XHTML 1.0 Transitional//EN"
"http://www.w3.org/TR/xhtml1/DTD/xhtml1-
transitional.dtd">
```

In case of using Strict or Frameset DTD use appropriate declaration.'

b.   Lower case tags and attribute names

As you know XHTML is case-sensitive, and only accept lower case tags and attributes. You need to "find-and-replace" all uppercase with lowercase if any found in tags and attributes.

c.   All attribute values need to be quoted

According to the XHTML 1.0 recommendation all attribute values must be quoted.

d.   Replacing empty tags.

Empty tags like <hr>, <br> and <img> are not allowed in XHTML. You need to replace <hr> and <br> tags with <hr/> and <br/>.

Section II: Exercises

1.   Create a new XML document to store information about your Stamp collection. It should be reasonably comprehensive and include all important information about the Stamps. Populate your XML document with at least 5 Stamp instances. Create corresponding XSL to extract Stamp name and detail of its use.

2.   Convert the following relational table named Students into an XML document:

StudentID	Name	Class	SkillId
12345	Kanchi	MBA	Table Tennis
12346	Sanjana	MBA	Skating
12347	Gauri	Btech	Dancing
12348	Alisha	Btech	Gymnastics
12349	Prisha	MBBS	Music
12350	Krish	MBBS	Cricket

Generate a XSL to extract Student ID, Name and skills of all the students.

3.   You are to write an XML file on "Restaurant Menu". Here are the minimum requirements for that file
   •   Obviously it should have a root element.
   •   The child of the root should have at least 4 children.
   •   Each child should have at least two child properties.
   •   There should be an attribute that has a default value.

Write an XSL to retrieve Vegetarian Food.

5.   Create a XML for Toyata Showroom. It should contain information about all types of cars available in showroom for purchase. Showroom can contain used cars also. It should be reasonably comprehensive and include all important information about the cars. Populate your XML document with at least 5 Car instances. Create corresponding XSL to extract data about brand new models (in tabular format) and about used cars (in tabular format).

Previous Year Questions with Answers

Q. 1.   Write an XML document to store the details of employees. Also design a Web page to get the input of employee id and retrieve the full details from the Web, document. [May 2008]

Ans. Write program:

Input his or her name so that you can display it on your page.

Let's look at the script:

```
<HTML>
<HEAD><TITLE>Welcome users by their name</TITLE>
</H EAD>
<body bgcolor=ffffff>
<SCRIPT>
    var temp="Input your name";
    varuser_name=prompt(temp,"web surfer");
    if (user_name)
    docurnent.write("<h2>Hello "+ user_name +"! Thanks
```

```
    forvisiting!</h2>");
    else
    document.write("<h2>Hello and thanks for visiting! /
    h2>");
<JSCRIPT>
</BODY>
<THTML>
```

In our next example, we show you how to submit a user feedback form to an e-mail account.

```
<HTML>
<HEAD>
<TITLE>Submitting a form Via Email</TITLE>
</HEAD>
<BODY BCCOLOR="ffffff" TEXT-"000000"><H2><u>Submitting a form
Via Ernail</u></H2>
    <form METHOD="POST" ENCTYPE="text/plain"
    action='mailto:shruti@gmail.com>
    <input type="hidden" name="Type of Form" value="Feedback
    on google.com">
    <b>Your Name</b><BR>
    <input type="text" name="Name" SIZE="50"
    MAXLENGTH="50"><BR>
    <b>Your Email</b><BR>
    <input type="text" name="Email" SIZE="50"
    MAXLENGTH="50"><BR>
    <b> Your Comment:</b><BR>
    <textarea name="Comment" wrap=physical rows=7 cols=43></
    textarea><BR>
    <input type="submit" VALUE="Send Form"><input
    type="reset" Value="Reset Form"></FORM>
</BODY>
</HTML>
```

Let's see an example:

```
<HTML>
<HEAD>
<TITLE>Form Validation<TTITLE>
<SCRIPT LANGUAGE-"JavaScript>
    functionvalidate_textl(form)
    {
        varinput_str=document.forms[0].user_name.value;
        varinput_lenl=input_str.length;
        if(input_lenl== 0){
        alert("Input your name!"); return false;
```

```
        }
        else {
            for (var j = 0; j < input_len1; j++) {
                var ch2 = input_str.substring(j, j + 1);
                if (((ch2 < "a") || (ch2 > "z")) &&
                ((ch2 < "A") || (ch2 > "Z" )))
                alert("Input a valid name!");
                return false;
            }
        }return true;
}
// end function validate_text1
function validate_text2(form)
varinput_str=document.forms[0].text2.value;
var input_len2=input_str.length; if(input_len2== 0)
{
    alert("Input your age!");
    return false;
}
else{
    for (vari =0; i< input_len2; i++) 1
    varch =input_str.substring(i, i + 1);
    if ((ch< "0" )||( ch> "9" ))
        {
            alert("Input number only for your age!"); return
            false;
        }
    }
    if (input_str>150 || input_str<1)
    {
        alert("Please input a valid age (you must be between
        1-150 years of age)!");
        return false;
    }
}
return true;
}
// end function validate_text2
function validate_text3(form)
{
    varinput_str=document.forms[0].text3.value; var
    input_len3=input_str.length;
    if (input_len3==0 || input str.indexOf ('@', 0)== -1)
    {
        alert ("Please input a valid e-mail!");
```

```
        return false;
    }
    return true;
}// end function validate_text3
functionreturnSelection(radioButton)
{
    var selection=null;
    for(var    i=0; i<radioButton.length; i++)
    {
        if(radio.Button1[i].checked)
        {   selection=radioButton[i]value;
            return selection;}
    }
    return selection;
}// end function returnSelection
functionvalidate_radio(form)
{
    if (returnSelection(document.forms[0].contact)== null)
    {
        alert("Please select if want to be contacted!");
        return false;
    }
    else return true;
} // function validate radio
functionsubmitme(form)
{
    if(validate_text1 (form)&& validate text2(forrn) &&
    validate_text3(form) &&validate_radio(form)) {alert("All
    Inputs are Ok.");
    /*Add the following lines to submit the form via e-mail:
    document.forms[0].action="mailto:username@ gmail.com";
    document.forms[0].submit();
    Add the following lines to submit the form via cgi:
    document.forms[0].action="mail-bin/ mail.p1";
    document.forms[0].submit0;
*/ }
}
// end function submitme
</SCRIPT>
</HEAD>
<BODY  BCCOLOR="ffffff"  TEXT="000000"  ><H2><u>Input
Validation</u></H2>
    <form METHOD="POST" ENICTYPE="text/ plain"
    onSubmit='submitme(this.form);>
    <b>Your name (Input Only Text):<BR></b><input type="text'
```

```
        name="user_name" SIZE-"5O MAXLENGTH="50"><BR>
        <b>Your Age (Input Only Numbers):</b><BR><input
        type="text" name="text2" SIZE="50" MAXLENGTH="50"><BR>
        <b>Input Email</b><BR>
        <input type="text" name="text3" S1ZE="50"
        MAXLENGTH="50"><BR>
        <b>Do you want us to contact you? </b><BR><input
        type="radio" name="contact" VALUE ="1">Yes
        <input type="radio" name="contact" VALUE="0">No
        <p>
        <input type="submit" VALUE="Send Form"><input
        type="reset" Value="Reset Form"></FORM>
</BODY>
</HTML>
```

First we create the main frame page that holds the frames together.

```
<HTML><HEAD>
<TITLE>Frames and JavaScript <TITLE></ HEAD>
<FRAMESET  FRAMEBORDER="0"  border="0"  FRAMESPACING="0"
ROWS="72", "">
        <FRAME MARGINWIDTH="0" MARGINHEIGHT="0" SRC=" top.htm"
        NAME="top"
        NORES1ZE SCROLLING="auto">
        <FRAMESET FRAMEBORDER="0" border="0" FRAMESPACING="0"
        COLS="15%,7 0%,15%"><FRAME MARGINWIDTH="2"
        MARGINHEIGHT="0"   SRC="left.htm"
        NAME="left"
        NORESIZE SCROLLING="no">
        <FRAME MARGINWIDTH="10"
        MARGINHEIGHT="5"   SRC="Center.htm"
        NAME="Center " scrolling=AUTO>
        <FRAME MARGINWIDTH="10"
        MARGINHEIGHT"5" SRC-"right.htm"
        NAME="right" scrolling=no>
</FRAMESET></FRAMESET>
<NOFRAME>
You need Netscape 3.0 to visit this site... </NOFRAME>
</HTML>
```

Q. 2. Explain the role of SAX and DOM in XML document verification.

[May 2008]

Ans. Role of SAX and DOM in XML document verification: Simple API for XML (SAX): SAX is a lexical, event-driven interface in which a document is read serially and its contents are reported as "callbacks" to various methods on a handler object of the user's design. SAX is fast and efficient to implement, but difficult to use for extracting information at random from the XML, since it tends to burden the application author with keeping track of what part of the document is being processed. It is better suited to situations in which certain types of information are always handled the same way, no matter where they occur in the document.

DOM: DOM is an interface-oriented Application Programming Interface that allows for navigation of the entire document as if it were a tree of "Node" objects representing the document's contents. A DOM document can be created by a parser, or can be generated manually by users (with limitations). Data types in DOM Nodes are abstract; implementations provide their own programming language-specific bindings. DOM implementations tend to be memory intensive, as they generally require the entire document to be loaded into memory and constructed as a tree of objects before access is allowed. DOM is supported in Java by several packages that usually come with the standard libraries. As the DOM specification is regulated by the World Wide Web Consortium, the main interfaces (Node, Document, etc.) are in the package `org.w3c.dom.*`, as well as some of the events and interfaces for other capabilities like serialization (output). The package `com.sun.org.apache.xml.internal.serialize.*` provides the serialization (output capacities) by implementing the appropriate interfaces, while the `javax.xml.parsers.*` package parses data to create DOM XML documents for manipulation. Though each parser implementation will differ in their exact class diagram, they should each implement the functionality shown.

Chapter 5
JavaScript

Key Topics
- *Introduction to JavaScript*
- *Understanding JavaScript*
- *JavaScript Basics*
- *JavaScript Programming Constructs*
- *Function in JavaScript*
- *JavaScript Objects*
- *String Object*
- *Array Object*
- *Date Object*
- *Math Object*
- *JavaScript Events*
- *Relating JavaScript to DHTML*

5.1 Introduction

With popularity of the Web, it is needed that users should be allowed to interact with the Website.

Websites required to be intelligent enough to accept request/feedback of the user, and dynamically change content of Web page on the basis of user input. Some of the changes, such as changing background when content get changed or show the content on basis of the input entered by the user and attract users. JavaScript has been developed for improving the design, validating form entries, detecting browsers and manipulating the object, and to create cookies, etc. It has emerged as a popular scripting language on the Internet.

JavaScript is a scripting language, which includes interactivity to the HTML pages. It is embedded into HTML pages and, it is an interpreted language. Topics, that to be covered in the Chapter are:

1. Write simple programming constructs on a Web page.
2. Take inputs from user and provide desired output.
3. Add interactivity to HTML Web page.

4. Use Objects and manipulate their properties.

5. Use event handling in Web page

6. Use **JavaScript** with the DHML for dynamically changing content and style of a Web page.

5.1.1 Evolution of JavaScript

Brendan Eich introduced first scripting language in 1996. He was the member of Netscape 2 group which was responsible for providing interactivity to Web page. First version called LiveScript in initial development phase could process HTML forms. It was called LiveScript as browser could itself interpret it without the use of a compiler. On release, it was renamed as JavaScript. Because of similarity in names JavaScript is many times confused with Java however both of them are different languages and they serve entirely different purpose. JavaScript was capable to refer links, forms, anchors as children of document object as well as form elements. In 1997 initial ECMA Script was developed by ECMA (European Computer manufacturers Association). This standard specified core JavaScript syntax. Later Netscape 3 released JavaScript 1.1 following ECMA standard. In 1998 Netscape introduced JavaScript 1.3. In the 1999, Microsoft introduced an updated version of JScript. It supports event handling, adding, modifying HTML elements and their attributes and styles even after loading the page.

5.2   Understanding JavaScript

JavaScript syntax can be embedded in the HTML file. The way browser reads and interprets a HTML file, in the same way **JavaScript** engine is used by browser for its inbuilt to interpret code in **JavaScript**. Thus, **JavaScript** code required to be include as an integral part of a HTML document. The question arises from this discussion is, how the browser recognizes **JavaScript** code. Browser gets information about **JavaScript** code through tag `<script>`. Whenever you need to insert a **JavaScript** code in a HTML document you need to write the code with in a script `<script>` tag. The script tag notifies browser that everything within the `script` needs to be interpreted.

Example 1: Writing the JavaScript Code

```
<html>
<body>
<script language="Javascript">
    .../* Write the Javscript code here*/
</script>
</body>
</html>
```

The optional attribute language is sometimes used to specify the language for scripting. There are many scripting languages like VBScript, JavaScript so it is important to instruct the browser which interpreter is required to interpret the code.

Check out the following given below **JavaScript** code embedded in a HTML document.

```
<html>
<body>
<script language="Javascript">
   document.write("Let's learn Javascript!");
</script>
</body>
</html>
```

In the above given example the `document.write` is a standard **JavaScript** command , which is used for writing output to a page. It is through the `document.write` command written between the `<script>`and `</script>` tags browser will recognize, and it is **JavaScript** command, and will write Let's learn **JavaScript**! on Web page as given below:

Output:

Let's learn Javascript!

What will happen if, you write the **JavaScript** code and do not write any HTML tag. Then browser will treat document.write ("Let's learn **JavaScript**') command as pure text, and it will write the entire line on the page.

Example 2: Code entered in the Web page

```
<html>
<body>
   +document.write("Let's learn Javascript!");
</body>
</html>
```

On running script in the browser, you will get the following output:

Output:

document.write("Let's learn Javascript!");

> **Note: Editing JavaScript**
> You can use simple editor like Notepad for writing the Web page and you need to save the Web page as a HTML file (e.g. trial.html).

5.2.1 Advantages of Using JavaScript

Before we study JavaScript further let's discuss the advantages of JavaScript.

1. **Embedded with in HTML:** JavaScript is embedded in a HTML document. You do not need any other separate editor for the programs to be written / edited/compiled. Similar to HTML, JavaScript can be written in the editor, such as Notepad.

2. **Improved Performance:** JavaScript is written with HTML tags and is interpreted by the browser. This minimizes requirement of storage on the Web server and download time for the client.

3. **Designed for Simple Programs:** Small programs can be written and implemented using JavaScript. Such programs can be integrated in a Web page.

4. **Minimal Syntax:** JavaScript has simple rules for the syntax. Its applications can be built quickly.

5. **An Interpreted Language:** JavaScript is an interpreter based language. The syntaxs are interpreted by the browser just as it interprets HTML tags.

6. **Good programming constructs:** Like any other programming languages, JavaScript supports facilities, such as looping, branching, condition checking, etc.

7. **JavaScript can react to events** - JavaScript can be set for execution when something happens, such as when the page has finished loading, or when a user clicks on the HTML element.

8. **Easy Debugging:** Since JavaScript is an interpreter-based language, and easily debug it line-by-line. Also the errors are listed as they are encountered.

9. **Platform Independence:** JavaScript is independent of hardware being used. It needs a proper installation of browser for its functioning.

10. **JavaScript gives HTML designers the programming tool:** HTML authors are not programmers, JavaScript is a scripting language with simple syntax! Almost everybody can put small "snippets" of code into the HTML pages.

11. **With JavaScript you can put the dynamic text into an HTML page:** JavaScript statement, such as : `document.write("<h1>" + name + "</h1>")` can write a variable text into an HTML page.

12. **JavaScript can read and write the HTML elements:** JavaScript can read and modify content of the HTML element.

13. **JavaScript can be used for validating the data:** JavaScript can be used to validate form data before submitting to the server, that saves server for processing more.

14. **JavaScript detects the visitor's browser:** A JavaScript detects the visitor's browser, and, depending on the browser load another page, that is specifically designed for that browser.

15. **JavaScript can be used for creating cookies:** JavaScript can be used for storage and retrieval of information on the visitor's computer.

5.2.2 Is Java and JavaScript Similar?

Java and JavaScript are confusing due to in their names similarity. While, Java and the JavaScript are two different languages, in concept and the design. Java is a language developed by Sun Microsystems and is as complex as C or C++.

5.2.3 Browser Support

A browser may not support the JavaScript, in that case JavaScript, would be displayed as the content of Web page as describe. To prevent them from doing this, and as a part of the JavaScript standard, use HTML comment tag to hide the JavaScript. For this you need to add an HTML comment tag < ! − before first JavaScript statement, and a −> (end of comment) after the last JavaScript statement.

Example 3: Using HTML comment tag

```
<html>
<body>
<script language="Javascript">
<!-
    document.write("Learning HTML");
//-->
</script>
</body>
</html>
```

> **Note: Commenting JavaScript**
>
> In the above Example the two forward slashes at the end of comment line (/ /) are the JavaScript comment symbol. This prevents JavaScript from executing the −> tag. In case browser does not support JavaScript, the JavaScript code will not be displayed in the Web page as it is written inside the HTML comment tag.

Output:

Learning HTML

5.3 JavaScript and HTML

As you JavaScript can be easily embedded in HTML document. Whenever JavaScript code need to be written, use `<script>` tag. Thus the `<script>` tag can be used any number of times in a Web page. You can also write HTML tag with JavaScript code. Check out the following:

Example 4: Using HTML tags with JavaScript code

```
<html>
<body>
<script language="Javascript">
    document.write("<h1>We can use HTML tag with javascript
    </h1>");
    document.write("<h2>Just try it yourself</h2>");
</script>
</body>
</html>
```

Output:

We can use HTML tag with javascript

Just try it yourself

In the above given example it can been seen that text, which is to be written by the JavaScript code, is formatted with the header tags `<h1>` and `<h2>`.

Before learning the syntax of JavaScript, it is needed to know where the JavaScript code can be written. JavaScript code can be inserted within the head tag as well as in HTML document. You only require using `<script>` tag for writing the JavaScript code. This tag will tell the browser about the language being used for writing the script inside this tag. JavaScript in a page executes immediately as the page loads into the browser but it may be needed to execute a script as the page is called or when a page loads, and other times when a user triggers an event.

5.3.1 Writing JavaScript in Head section of HTML

When you write the scripts in the head section they are executed as when they are called or when an event is triggered. Writing the code in the head section will display the Web page as the code will be executed as the page is called from the client machine. Placing the script in the head section ensures that script is loaded before anyone uses it. Head Section is an ideal place for creating JavaScript and variables as head of the HTML document is always processed before the body section of the document. By placing the JavaScript variables, constants, user defined functions, etc., in the head section they will be defined by the JavaScript interpreter before their use in the document.

Note: Calling JavaScript Variable

Any attempt to call a variable or any other JavaScript object before it is defined results in an error

---

You can place the script in `head` section like this:

```
<html>
<head>
<script language="Javascript">
    ....
</script>
<body>
    ..
    ..
</body>
</html>
```

5.3.2 Writing JavaScript in Body section of HTML

Scripts to be executed, when you placed at the `body` section, and the content of the page is generated.

```
<html>
<head>
</head>
<body>
<script language="Javascript">
    ....
</script>
</body>
</html>
```

Note: Number of JavaScripts in a HTML document

Any number of JavaScripts can be placed in both the `body` and the `head` sections of the document.

```
<html>
<head>
<script language="JavaScript">
    ....
</script>
</head>
<body>
<script language="JavaScript">
```

```
    . . . .
</script>
</body>
```

In the above given code JavaScript is present in the `head` and in the `body` sections of the document.

5.3.3 Linking a Web page to an External JavaScript

JavaScript may be run in several pages without writing the same script again and again, and which can be done by making an external JavaScript file and linking it with Web page. The external JavaScript file is to be saved with file extention a .js. For using external script, link the external .js file by specifying the file path in the "src" atribute of the `<script>` tag:

Example 5: Linking a Web page using external script

```
<html>
<head>
    <script src="Intro.js"></script>
</head>
<body>
</body>
</html>
```

In the Example 5, using the `'src'` attribute of the script tag, Web page is linked to an external JavaScript code. At the time of executing the document browser will look for the 'trial.js' file to execute its code. The .js file does not include the `<script>` tag. The tag needs to be placed in the HTML document at the appropriate place where JavaScript is to be executed.

Test Your Progress
1. *How many JavaScripts we can write in a HTML document?*
2. *What is difference between wrting JavaScript in Head and Body sections?*
3. *How can you link a HTML document with an external JavaScript file?*

5.4 JavaScript in Detail

JavaScript has programming features similar to the most other programming languages, such as variables, data types, constants, programming constructs, user defined functions, etc.

5.4.1 Basic Characterstics

1. **JavaScript Case-Sensitive:** JavaScript is a case-sensitive, while HTML is not. While writing JavaScript statements, creating or calling variables, objects and functions one need to take care.

2. **JavaScript Statements:** JavaScript contains a sequence of statements, which are to be executed by browser and tells the browser what needs to do. The

JavaScript statement given below tells the browser to write "Welcome" on the Web page:

```
document.write("Welcome");
```

A semicolon (;) needs to be added at the end of each and every executable statement. Browser interprets the end of the line as the end of the statement. Use of semicolons, makes it possible to write multiple statements on one line. It is also a good programming practice.

3.   **JavaScript code:** JavaScript code is sequence of the JavaScript statements. Every statement is executed by the browser in the sequence they are written. The code given below will write a header and a paragraph on the Web page.

```
<script language="Javascript">
    document.write("<h1>Let's learn Javascript</h1>");
    document.write("<p>Good Luck</p>");
</script>
```

4.   **JavaScript Blocks:** JavaScript statements can be group in blocks. The blocks begin with the left curly bracket ' { ', and ends with a right curly bracket ' } '. The purpose of the block is to execute the sequence of statements together. The code given below will write a header and paragraphs to a Web page.

```
<script language="Javascript">
{
    document.write("<h1>Learning Javascript</h1>");
    document.write("<p>It is easy</p>");
}
</script>
```

5.4.1.1 JavaScript Keywords

JavaScript keywords as in any other programming language are reserved, which cannot be used as variable or function names. Some of JavaScript keywords are listed below:

break	case	default	function	if	switch	typeof
continue	catch	finally	for	instanceof	this	var
delete	do	else	new	return	throw	while

5.4.2 Variables in JavaScript

Variables could be understood as "containers" for storing information. A variable can have a short name, such as x, or a descriptive name, such as empname. Rules for the variable names in JavaScript:

● Variable names are case-sensitive, such as a and A are different two variables.

● Variable name must start with either with a letter or the underscore character (_).

JavaScript variables are different from others as they are un-typed. "Un-typed" means no type keyword is used during the declaration of the variable. This implies type of variable is determined by its content only. The variable may change from time to time as the content of the variable changes.

> **Note:** *JavaScript is case-sensitive*
> Since JavaScript is case-sensitive, variable names are case-sensitive.

A value of variable can be changed during the execution of a script. A variable can be reffered by its name to display or change its value.

5.4.2.1 Creating Variables

The `var` statement is used to create variables in JavaScript [It is most often referred to as declaration of variables].

Declaration of Variables

```
var s;
var address;
```

In the above given examples the variables s and the `address` have been declared.

> **Note:** The variables s and `address` are empty, since value is not allocated.

```
var s=2;
var address="C40";
```

In the example s has been assigned value 2 and `address` has assigned string `"C40"`. After execution of the statements above the variable s will hold the value 2, and `address` will hold the value C40.

> **Note:** *Usage of Quotes*
> While assigning text value to a variable, use quotes around the value.

JavaScript does not need to explicitly declare a variable, that can be done by initializing a variable with some value. However, good programming style it is recommended to declare a variable in the JavaScript. Variable declaration in JavaScript tells JavaScript interpreter that variable exists, which can be referenced through out the document. Declaration of the variable is done to make certain, that the program is well organized and helps to keep track of the scope of the variables in the program.

5.4.3 Assigning Values

In JavaScript, assignment of values to the variables is also possible that have not been declared. Variables will automatically be declared, in that case. Check out the above example once again. The statements:

```
s=2;
name="Gauri";
```

have the same effect as:

```
var s=2;
var name="Gauri";
```

5.4.4 Redeclaring Variables in JavaScript

If variables are redeclared in JavaScript, it will not loose its original value.

Redeclaring Variables

```
var t=2;
var t;
```

In the above given example t has been redeclared however, value of it will be 2. The t is not reset (or cleared) due to re-declaration.

5.4.5 Data Types

The peculiar thing about JavaScript data type is that same variable may hold different type of data at different times as the JavaScript code is executed. While writing a JavaScript code it is not needed to declare the variable before using it in a Web page. JavaScript supports four primitive types of data types:

- Number
- Boolean
- String
- Null

Apart from these basic data types there are complex types like Array and Objects. Literals can also be used at different parts of the program for providing fixed values.

Number: Number data types include integer and floating point numbers. It also contains a special value called NaN which implies 'not a number'. Integral literals can be represented in decimal/hexadecimal/octal form in a JavaScript. The hexadecimal and octal integers are first converted in the decimal form before they are used or displayed on a Web page. For example,

```
20, 1.1, -36, 4F7, 0x6A
```

Boolean: Boolean variables contain logical values, i.e., true or false. Logical operators can be used in a boolean expression.

String: String data types include the string values enclosed in the single or double quotes. A string is enclosed in single (') or double (") quotes. The string that begins with a double quote needs to close with a double quote. Similarly, the string that begins with a double quote needs to close with a double quote. For example,

```
'Richa',"Jai",'12 Ashok Vihar.
```

Null: Null data type consists of single value, i.e., Null. Null value is common to all data types. Generally this value is used to initialize a variable. This helps in reducing errors that result from un-initialized variables. Null value gets automatically converted to other default values as other data types are used in an expression.

5.4.6 Type Casting in JavaScript

As you have seen in JavaScript variables are loosely casted. Variables are generally implicitly defined through the value that is assigned to them. For example,

```
e=9;
```

This statement shows that 'e' is a variable of type number which has been assigned an integral value, i.e., 9.

Variable can change data type depending on the value assigned to it. For example,

```
e='GAURI';
```

You can assign value 'GAURI' to 'e' in the same document. Now the data type of variable 'e' will be string. Let's check another example.

```
e='GAURI';
e=e+ 9;
```

In the above example variable 'e' contains a string 'GAURI' on adding 9, the two gets concatenated to form one string, i.e., 'GAURI9'.

On other hand in case variable 'i' has numeric values, for example

```
i=9;
i=i+8;
```

variable 'i' will have a numeric value 17.

5.4.7 Comments using in the JavaScript

JavaScript comments are used for the code to make more readable. JavaScript comments can be included to explain the JavaScript, or making it more readable.

A single line comment as well as comments with multiple lines can be used:

JavaScript single line comment: Single line comment begins with the '//'.

Check out the following example with single lime comment:

```
<script language="Javascript">
    // This statement used to write script in JavaScript
    document.write("<B>Learning JavaScript</B>");
</script>
```

JavaScript Multiline Comments: Multiline comments begin with /*, and also end with */. The example given below uses a multiline comment to explain the code.

```
<script language="Javascript">
/* Use this code for practicing Javascript*/

    document.write("<h1>learning Javascript</h1>");
    document.write("<p> it is needed need to use some HTML
    before using Javascript</p>");
</script>
```

5.5   Operators in JavaScript

JavaScript has a set of operators, which are used for data manipulation. An operator transforms value into the resultant value. Operend is the value to which operator is applied. Operands and operators are combined to form an expression. Expressions can be used to evaluate and determine value of the expression. The operators have been discussed as given below.

5.5.1 Arithmetic Operators

Arithmetic operators are the operators, which are used for common arithmetic calculations. Arithmetic operators supported by JavaScript are given below.

Operator	Description	Expression	Evaluating expression for v=4
+	Addition	u=v+5	u=7
−	Subtraction	u=v-2	u=2
*	Multiplication	u=v*7	u=13
/	Division	u=v/4	u=2
%	Modulus	u=v%4	u=1
++	Increment	u=++v	u=5
−	Decrement	u=−v	u=1

The operator = is used for assigning values, operator + is used for adding values, assignment operator = is used for assigning values to the JavaScript variables and to add values together, the arithmetic operator + is used. For example,

Adding numbers using arithmetic operators

```
vara=2;
var b=3;
c=a+b;
document.write (c);
```

The output will be 5.

An operator using only one operand is called the unary operator, which requires more than one operator is called the binary operator. The arithmetic operators, such as +, −, *,/, in the above given Table are the binary operators. Both the operators, increment and the decrement presented in the above given Table are the unary operators.

5.5.2 Increment/Decrement Operators in JavaScript

The operator increment (++) and decrement (−) can be used in the two different ways. Operators can be used before the operand, and after the operand but result will be different. When the operator is placed before an operand, such as ++u then the value of the operand will be incremented by 1. Check out the Examples given below:

Using increment operator before the operand

```
x=6;
y=++x;
document.write(y);
```

Output: 76

Using decrement operator before the operand

```
x=5;
y=--x;
document.write(y);
```

Output: 4

```
u=5;
v=++u;
w=--u;
document.write(v);
document.write(w);
```

Output: 6 4

Placing operator after operand returns value of the variable, and before incrementing or decrementing its value. Check out the example given below:

```
u=5;
v=u++;
w=u--;
document.write(v);
document.write(w);
```

Output: 5 6

In the above given example v is assigned the value of u (v=5) before u gets incremented by 1. w is then assigned the value of u (w=6) and then u gets decremented by 1.

5.5.3 Assignment Operators

Assignment operators can be used for assigning values to JavaScript variables. Some of the assignment operators can be used to manipulate and assign values at the same time. For example, u=u+v can also be performed as u+=v. The operators that are supported in **JavaScript** are given below.

Operator	Explanation	Expression	Evaluating for u=6, v=4
=	Set variables on the left of operator to value of the expression placed on right	u=v	u=4

+=	Incrementing variable on the left of the += operator by value of the expression on its right. If the value is string of right appended to the value of variable on the left hand side.	u+=v	u=10
-=	Decrement the variable on left side by the value of expression on right	u−=v	u=4
*=	Multiply variable on the left side by value of the expression on right	u*=v	u=24
/=	Divide variable on the left side by value of the expression on right	u/=v	u=1
%=	Take modulus of variable on the left side by value of the expression on right	u%=v	u=2

Assignment operators work for the job which can be done only by using multiple operators. This has been summarized in the Table as shown below.

Operator	Expression providing similar results
+=	u=u+v
−=	u=u−v
*=	u=u*v
/=	u=u/v
%=	u=u%v

5.5.4 Logical Operators

Logical operators can be used to perform boolean operations, such as and, or, not. They determine the logic between variables or values. The JavaScript supports following logical operators:

Operator	Description	Expression	Evaluating Expression for a=2, b=5
&&	and	(a <4 && b > 2)	True
||	or	(a==3 || b==3)	False
!	not	!(a==b)	False

5.5.5 Comparison Operators

Comparison operators are used for logical statements, which determine the equality or difference between the variables or the values. Comparison and logical operators are used to test for the value true or false. Comparison operators, which are supported by JavaScript are given below.

Operator	Description	Expression	Evaluating Expression for u=9
==	is equal to	u==9	False
===	is exactly equal to (value and type)	U===8 u==="8"	u===9 is True u==="7" is False
!=	is not equal	u!=5	True
>	is greater than	u>8	False
<	is less than	u<8	True
>=	is greater than or equal to	u>=8	False
<=	is less than or equal to	U<=8	True

The operators equal (==) and not equal (!=) are used for the type conversion before testing for the equality. For example, "5"==5 evaluates will be 'true', as string "5" is converted to an integral value 5. While any type conversion is not performed by equal (= = =), and strictly not equal (!===) before testing for equality. For example, "5"===5 will return false as data types are different.

> **Note:** The comparison operators used in conditional statements for comparing the values and take action depending on the result.

```
if (age<18) document.write
("Not eligible for vote");
```

5.5.6 Conditional Operators

Conditional expression operators are supported by JavaScript are ' ? ' and ' : '. These operators are called ternary operators, as they use three operands, a condition to be evaluated and the alternatives, which need to be returned. The return value is based on condition, and value can be either true or false.

Syntax:

```
variablename=(condition)?value1:value2
```

Let us consider the following example:

```
result=(percentage==60)?"pass":"fail";
```

In the above given example, if the variable percentage has the value 60, then the value "pass" will be assigned to the variable result else it will be assigned the value "fail".

5.5.7 Using + Pperator

The + operator can be used for adding string variables or text values together. If operands are number, operator + performs addition. If operands are strings it is used to concatenate them. For example,

Concatenating of the two Strings

```
x1="Hello";
x2="India";
x3=x1+x2;
```

After execution of the statements given above, the variable x3 will contain the string "Hello India".

With the operator +, it is possible to concatenate two or more strings. A space can be inserted and concatenate a string with a number. For example,

To add a space betweentwo strings, space can beinserted into one of the strings:

```
x1="Hello";
x2="India";
x3=x1+" " + x2;
```

After execution of the statements given above, the variable x3 contains string "Hello India".

Note: If you add a number and a string, the result will be a string.

Test Your Progress

1. *What do you understand by block of code?*
2. *Name three data types in JavaScript?*
3. *What will be the output of the following code:*

```
s=3;
w=++s;
z= w++;
document.write(s)
document.write(w)
document.write(z)
```

5.6   Programming Constructs in JavaScript

Most of the programming languages contain a common set of programming constructs. JavaScript also have a complete range of basic programming constructs. As any other programming language uses conditional statements, JavaScript also used to perform various actions based on the conditions.While writing a code it is needed to perform various actions for different decisions. For this JavaScript has the conditional statements as given below.

5.6.1 `if` Statement

`if` statement is used to execute some code when a condition specified is true.

Syntax:

```
if (condition)
{
    /* ifthe specified condition is true only then code
    will be executed */
}
```

Use of **if** statement

```
<script language="Javascript">
//Using Date object to wish "Good morning"
var a=new Date();
var time=a.getHours();

if (time<12)
{
    document.write("<b>How are you?</b>");
}
</script>
```

Example

```
<script language="JavaScript">
//Use Date object for wishing Good Morning
var d=new Date();
var time=d.getHours();
if (time==12)
{
    document.write("<i>Good Morning!</i>");
}
</script>
```

> **Note:** i f is written in the lower case letters, but if statement is used uppercase letters (IF), it will generate a **JavaScript** error!

5.6.2 if..else Statement

This statement is used when some code need to be executed, when condition specified is true and the code specified in else part is executed if the condition is false.

Syntax:

```
if (condition)
{
    //This code will beexecuted when the specified
    condition is true
}
```

```
else
{
    //This code will be executed when the condition
    specified is not true
}
```

Displaying greeting with the use of `if else` construct

```
<script language="JavaScript">
//Use Date object to display greeting message.
var c = new Date();
var greeting_time = c.getHours();

if (greeting_time < 12)
{
    document.write("<i> Good morning </i>");
}
else
{
    document.write("<i> Good Afternoon</i>");
}
</script>
```

5.6.3 `if... elseif .... else` Statement

Syntax:

```
if (conditionk)
{
    //code to be executed if condition k is true
}
else if (conditionj)
{
    // The code will be executed if the condition j is true
}
else
{
    / / The code will be executed if condition k and
    condition j are not true
}
```

E.g. `if ... elseif .... else` statement

```
<script language="Javascript">
var d = new Date()
var time = d.getHours()
if (time<12)
{
```

```
    document.write("<i>Good morning</i>");
}
else if (time>12 && time<14)
{
    document.write("<i>Good Afternoon</i>");
}
else
{
    document.write("<i>Good Day</i>");
}
</script>
```

> **Note:** When compare variables, use two equals signs next to each other (==). The code will be only be executed if the specified condition is true.

5.6.4 `switch` Statement

`switch` statement selects one of the blocks of code that is to be executed. The `switch` statement is used to select from a number of alternatives.

Syntax:

```
switch(value)
{
    Case 1:
        //Executed if first alternative is chosen
        break;
    Case 2;
        //Executed if second alternative is chosen
        break;
        default://executed when default action is to be taken
}
```

> **Note:** *Usage of* **Break**
> You need to use `break` to come out of the `switch` statement once selected case code is executed.

Test Your Progress

1. *What are different programming constructs in JavaScript?*
2. *What are different form of '`if`' constructs ?*
3. *How `switch` statement is used?*

5.7 JavaScript Loops

Very often, the same block of code need to be run over and over again. For performing such type of tasks the programming language have loop constructs. Loops in the JavaScript, execute same block of the code number of times specified or while a specified condition is true. Loops are of two types in the JavaScript:

5.7.1 `for` Loop

The loop executes a block of code for specified number of times, `for` loop is used. The `for` loop is used when number of times script to be executed is known in advance.

Syntax:

```
for(var = startvalue; var <= end value; var = var+increment)
{
    //The code which is to be executed
}
```

The Example 6 defines a loop, which begins with the value of `j=1`. It will be continued until `j` is less than, or equal to `4`. `j` will be increased by 1 each time the loop runs.

Example 6: Defining `for` loop

```
<html>
<body>
<script language="Javascript">
    var j=1;
    for (j=1;j<=4;j++)
    {
        document.write("Now the token no. is" + j);
        document.write("<br />");
    }
</script>
</body>
</html>
```

> **Note:** Increment parameter can be negative as well, and the `<=` could be any comparing statement.

Output:

```
Now the token no. is 1
Now the token no. is 2
Now the token no. is 3
Now the token no. is 4
```

5.7.2 `while` Loop

The `while` loop is to be used, when the loop to be executed and continue executing while a specified condition is true.

Syntax:

```
while (var<=endvalue)
{
    // Enter the code, which is to be executed
}
```

Note: The <= could be any comparing statement

Example 7: Displaying 5 numbers using `for` loop

```
<html>
<body>
<script language="Javascript">
var j=1;
document.write("Now calling");
document.write("<br />");
while (j<=5)
{
    document.write("<br />");
    document.write("roll no." + j);
    document.write("<br />");
    j=j+1;
}
</script>
</body>
</html>
```

Output:

Now calling

roll no.1

roll no.2

roll no.3

roll no.4

roll no.5

5.7.3 `do...while` loop

The loop `do...while`, is a variant of the `while` loop. In such a loop the block of the code is executed at least once. The loop gets repeated as long as the condition specified is true.

Syntax:

```
do
{
    // Enter the code which you want to be executed
}
while (var<=endvalue);
```

Example 8: Display numbers using do...while loop

```
<html>
<body>
<script language="Javascript">
var j=0;
do
{
    document.write("Number: " + j);
    document.write("<br />");
    j=j+1;
}
while (j<5)
</script>
</body>
</html>
```

Output:

Number: 0
Number: 1
Number: 2
Number: 3
Number: 4

Note: About do...while

This loop will always be executed at least once, even if the condition is false, because the code is executed before the condition is tested.

5.7.4 **break and continue**

JavaScript has two statements, which can be used inside loops:

a.   **break:** Thecommand break will break the loop, and the continue executing the code that follows after the loop (if any).

Example 9: To come out from for loop using the break statement

```
<html>
<body>
```

```
<script language="Javascript">
var j=0;
for (j=0;j<=10;j++)
{
    if (j==2)
    {
        break;
    }
    document.write("<br />");
}
</script>
</body>
</html>
```

Output:

The number is 0

The number is 1

b. **continue:**The command continue is used when it is needed to break the current loop and continue with the next one.

Example 10: To break the current loop and continue with the next one using `continue` command

```
<html>
<body>
<script language="Javascript">
var j=0
for (j=0;j<=5;j++)
{
    if (j==2)
    {
        continue;
    }
    document.write("Number:" + j);
    document.write("<br />");
}
</script>
</body>
</html>
```

Output:

Number:0

Number:1

Number:3

Number:4

Number:5

5.8 JavaScript Popup Boxes

JavaScript has the feature to pickup the user input, or display small amount of the text to the user using dialog boxes. Various kinds of popup boxes are available: Alert box, Confirm box, and Prompt box. The dialog box appears as separate windows, and the content depend on the information which has been input by the user.

> **Note:** The dialog box's contents are independent of text in the HTML page and they do not effect content of the Web page in any way.

The three types of dialog boxes are:

5.8.1 Prompt Box

Prompt box can be used to input a value before entering a page. When a prompt box pops up, after entering an input value, the user is required to click either OK or Cancel to proceed. If user clicks OK button prompt box returns the input value, whereas if the user clicks Cancel the box will return null value.

Syntax:

prompt("text message ","default value");

Example 11: Prompt the user for answering a question using prompt box

```
<html>
<body>
<script language="Javascript">
document.write("<h1>Testing Prompt Box</h1>");
var question="Evaluate 10*10";
var answer=10;
var response=prompt(ques,"0");
if(response!=answer)
    alert("Your answer is wrong");
else
alert("Your answer is correct");</script>
</body>
</html>
```

Output:

Testing Prompt Box

If the user enters wrong answer, i.e., user enters 25, a message is displayed as 'your answer is wrong' in the browser.

Testing Prompt Box

5.8.2 Alert Box

Alert box is used to make sure information comes through to the user. It is a way to output small amount of the textual information to browser's window. The JavaScript method `alert()` takes a string argument and displays an alert dialog box at the window of the browser, when this is invoked by some code in JavaScript. The alert box will display the string passed to the method `alert()` and the OK button. User cannot proceed until clicks on the alert button.

Syntax:

alert("text message ");

Example 12: Displaying Alert Box to message user

```
<html>
<body>
<script language="Javascript">
document.write("<h1>using html tag with Javascript</h1>");
document.write("<h2>Just try it yourself</h2>");
alert("Welcome to the world of Javascript");
</script>
</body>
</html>
```

Output: **using html tag with javascript**

Just try it your self

5.8.3 Confirm box

JavaScript has a feature of confirm box to prompt the user, for verification or confirmation before continuing further with execution of the JavaScript. When a confirm box pops up, user has the options either to click on OK or Cancel button to proceed.If user clicks at the OK, the box returns value true and if the user clicks Cancel, the box returns false.

Syntax: confirm("text message");

Let's check out an example.

Example 13: Displaying confirm box

```
<html>
<body>
<form name=form>
<input type=button value="Let's try confirm box"
onClick="if(confirm('Do you want to restart your system?'))
alert('You have invited virus');
else alert('You just escaped disaster!')">
</form>
</body>
</html>
```

The output given below will be generated, as the browser finds confirm box.

Output:

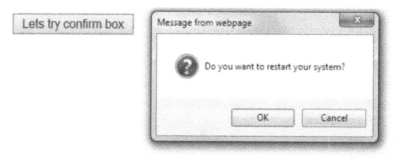

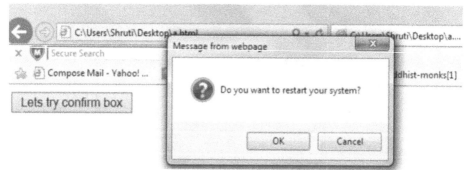

Test Your Progress
1. *What is use of Alert Box?*
2. *How is Prompt box different from Confirm box?*

5.9 Functions in JavaScript

The function is a block of codes , that performs specific task and often returns a value. Any function can be seen as a reusable code block that will be executed by an event, or when the function is called. A JavaScript function may return parameter zero or more. Parameters can be seen as the standard technique of passing control to a function. JavaScript functions can be of two types:

5.9.1 Built-in functions

JavaScript contains a set of in built-in functions, that perform specific functions. Some of them are `eval()`, `parseInt()`, `parseFloat()`.

a. **`eval()`:**The function `eval()` is used to convert in a string expression to a numeric value. For example

Evaluating a expression using `eval()`

```
var a=eval("5*5+6");
```

The function `eval()`, evaluates the expression and 31 is assigns to the variable `a`.

> **Note:** If a string value is passed as a parameter to `eval()`, expression will not be generated. You need to convert the data type. This can be done using `parseInt()`, which is discussed below.

b. **`parseInt()`:**`parseInt()` function converts a string value to an integer. This returns the first integer contained in the string. The function will return avalue 0, is the string that does not begin with an integer. For example,

```
var a=parseInt("889Hi");
```

In the above example `parseInt()` will return the integer value, i.e., `a=889`. For example,

```
var a=("889hi");
var a1=parseInt(a);
```

In the above given example `parseInt()` returns integer value of the string stored in variable a.

c. **`parseFloat()`:**`parseFloat()` converts a string value to float value.

Example 14: Applying functions

```
<html>
<body>
<script language ="Javascript">
document.write("<h1>Let's try Javascript built in functions</h1>");
```

```
a=eval("20*20");
document.write("Output is"+ a);
document.write("<br>");
a=parseInt("9Racecourse");
document.write("Separating integer from string we get"+
a);
document.write("<br>");
var b="99.5hello";
c=parseFloat("99.5Racecourse");
document.write("Separating float from string we get" +
c);
document.write("<br>");
</script>
</body>
</html>
```

Output:

Let's try javascript built in functions

Output is400
Seperating integer from string we get9
Seperating float from string we get99.5

5.9.2 User-defined Functions

Functions offer the ability to group together code to form a block which can be repeatedly used in the JavaScript program. A user-defined function needs to be declared and coded. Once this is done function can be invoked by calling it with the name it is declared. Function can accept information in the form of arguments and can return results. You need to use appropriate syntax to declare functions, invoke them, pass those values and accept their return values. A function consists of the code that will be executed by the event or by a call to that function. A function can be called from any where with in page (or even from other pages, if function is embedded in an external .js file).

5.9.2.1 Defining Functions in JavaScript

Function can be defined in JavaScript using following syntax:

```
function functionname(var1,var2,...,varN)
{
    //enter the code to be executed
}
```

here `var1`, `var2`,..., `varN`, etc., are variables or values passed into the function. The ' { ' and the ' } ' define the start and end of the function, respectively.

> **Note:** In case a function does not have any parameters it must include the parentheses ( ) after the function name.

function_name()

```
{
    //enter the code to be executed
}
```

> **Note:** The word function needs to be written in the lowercase letters, otherwise a JavaScript error occurs. Alsoyou must call a function with the same capitals as in the function name.

5.9.2.2 *Passing Parameters to a Function*

Values can be passed to a function by including them in the parentheses, which is followed by the function name. Multiple values can be passed by separating them by commas. Multiple values can be accepted only if function has been coded to accept multiple parameters. During the declaration, function needs to mention about number of values that will be passed. You should understand that both built-in and user-defined function can accept parameters, process them and return their values. During such declaration function need to be informed about number of value that need to be passed. Let us consider an example.

Declaring a function 'printing' that accepts a parameter which is name to be printed.

```
function printing(name1)
{
    document.write("<h1>Name of the visitor</h1>");
    document.write(name1);
}
```

In the above example the parameter called `name1` is passed a value at the time of invoking of the function. Within the function reference to parameter name refers to the value which has been passed to the function.

Calling function

Function can be called from any point in the body part of the document. For example,

Calling a function by passing a static value

```
<body>
<script language="Javascript">
    print("john");
```

```
</script>
</body>
```

In above example function has been called with the parameter value `'john'`. Let us discuss one more example.

Calling a function by passing a variable

```
<body>
<script language="Javascript">
    var a="john"
    print(a);
</script>
</body>
```

In above example function has been called with the parameter value stored in variable a.

Consider the following example: Calling a function without passing any value

```
<body>
<script language="Javascript">
    print();
</script>
</body>
```

> **Note: About the variables**
>
> It is possible to pass both variables and literals as arguments when calling a function. In case a variable is passed to the function changing the value of variable within the function will not change the variable passed to the function. Always remember that parameters exist only for the life of the function.

In this example function has only been called without passing any parameter value. So function needs to be efficient enough to perform a job without any input.

The return statment

The return statement is used to specify value that is returned from the function. In case function needs to return a value it must contain the return statement. The value will be returned to the statement from where function has been invoked. Let us discuss an example.

Creating a function to return the sum of two numbers (a and y)

```
function product(a,b)
{
    c=a*b;
    return c;
}
```

In above example a function `product` takes two values a and b as arguments and return the value of variable c. When this function is called the two argument value a, b need to be passed along the two parameters:

```
res=product(7,4);
```

The returned value from the above function will be 2s which will be stored in the variable called `res`.

Example 15: Creating a function `display1()`

```html
<html>
<head>
<script language="Javascript">
function display1()
{
    alert("You just used built-in function");
}
</script>
</head>
<body>
<form>
<input type="button" value="Try it!"
onClick="display1()" >
</form>
</body>
</html>
```

Output:

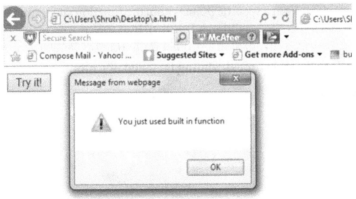

Note: In Example 15 if the `alert`(*"You just used* `built-in function"`) had not been put within a function this function would have been executed as soon as the line was loaded. On executing this code you will find that the code is invoked as soon as user hits the button labelled "`Try it!`". The `onClick` event is added on the button which executes the function `display1()` as soon as the button is clicked.

5.9.2.3 *Places of Declaration*

Function can be placed anywhere within an HTML page. It can be defined both in the <head> as well as <body> section of a document. By putting the function in the <head> you can ensure that all functions will be parsed before they are invoked or called by other parts of the document. The term parse implies the process by which the JavaScript interpreter evaluates each line of code and converts it to pseudo-compiled byte code before attempting to execute it. By putting code in the <head> you can keep browser from executing a script when the page loads.

> **Note:** If the function is called before it is declared and parsed it will result in an error condition as function has not been evaluated and browser does not know whether it exists or not.

5.9.2.4 *Lifetime of JavaScript variable*

It is needed to understand the scope of a variable with in a function. In case variable is declared within a function it will be accessed within that function. As you exit the function the variable will be destroyed. Such variables which have a scope within the function are called local variables. Local variables can be declared with the same name in the different functions, because each is recognized only by function in which it is declared. In case you declare a variable outside a function, all functions on your page can access it. Such variables are called Global Variables. The lifetime of these variables will start when the variables are declared, and end when the page is closed.

Recursive Functions

Recursive functions are functions which call themselves. Such function males a call to themselves from a specific point within the function and terminate or return value only when a specific condition is fulfilled. In JavaScript recursive function are handled in same way as handled in any other programming language. For example,

Recursive Function for calculating factorial of a number

```
function fact(x)
{
    if (x>1)
    {
        return x*fact(x-1);
    }
    else
    return x;
}
```

The above function receives a argument x, applies the formula of a factorial of a number. The function calls itself until the value of x is 1. This is the terminating condition of the recursive function.

Test Your Progress
1. What are the different type of functions available in JavaScript?

Test Your Progress
1.   What are the different type of functions available in JavaScript?
2.   What is a recursive function?
3.   What is difference between local and global variable?
4.   Discuss lifetime of a JavaScript variable.

5.10 Objects in JavaScript

JavaScript is an Object Oriented Programming language, which allows to define own objects and make your own variable types. Built-in JavaScript objects are available and you can as well create your own objects. Objects can be defined as the named collection of data that has properties and can be accessed through methods. Property provides some information about the object and methods are used to read or modify data contained in object's property. The objects are called by combining the object name with the method name;

```
Object-name.Method-name
```

Check out the following example. The length property of the String object has been used to determine number of characters in a string:

```
<script language="JavaScript">
    var w="Let's learn Javascript";
    document.write(w.length);
</script>
```

In the above example, the length opf given string is displayed.

In the following example toUpperCase() method of the string object is used for displaying a text in uppercase letters:

```
<script language="Javascript">
    var s="Learning Javascript";
    document.write(s.toUpperCase());
</script>
```

Learning JavaScript:

> **Note:** The document object of a JavaScript has a method which is used for placing text in the browser. This method is called write(). This method accepts the string and places it in the browser window.

```
document.write("hello delhi");
```

5.10.1 String Object

In JavaScript string is declared as an object.The String object can be used to manipulate a stored piece of data. You can declare a string as follows:

```
var name=new String(string);
```

A simple assignment of string to a variable also creates a String.

var a="Hello"

String "Hello" is a string so you can use String object properties and methods with variable a.

Some of the string object properties and methods supported by JavaScript are:

Property	Usage
constructor	It is a reference to the function that creates the object.
Length	It returns number of the characters in a string.

Example 16: Using String Object property

```html
<html>
<body>
<script type="text/Javascript">
    var s="Hello";
    document.write(s.length);
</script>
</body>
</html>
```

Output: 5

Method	Usage
charAt()	It returns the character at a specified position.
concat()	It joins two or more strings.
indexOf()	It returns position of the first occurrence for a specified string value in a string.
italics()	It displays a string in italic.
lastIndexOf()	It returns position of last occurrence of a specified string value. It searches backwards from the specified position in a string.
replace()	It is used to replace some characters with some other characters in a string.
search()	It searches a string for a specified value.
split()	It splits a string into an array of strings.
substr()	It extracts a specified number of characters in a string, from a start index.
toLowerCase()	It displays a string in lowercase letters.
toUpperCase()	It displays a string in uppercase letters.

Example 17: Using `indexOf()` method to find position of a string.

```html
<html>
<body>
<script type="text/Javascript">
    var s="Hello Every One! How are you?";
    document.write(s.indexOf("Hello"));
</script>
</body>
</html>
```

Output: 0

5.10.2 Array

JavaScript arrays are implemented as objects. The Array object is used to store multiple values in a single variable. JavaScript Array objects are capable of storing a sequence of values. These values are stored in the indexed locations in an array. The length of the array is measured as the number of elements in the array. You need to declare an array before using this. Syntax is as follows:

Syntax:

```
arrayName = new Array(Array length)
{
    Used to declare an array having a finite length}
    arrayame = new Array()
    {
        Used to declare an array having no finite length
}
```

The individual elements can be accessed by using array name followed by its indexed value. For example,

```
order = new Array( )
order[50]="1"
```

In the above example an array of name order has been declared.

The 51st item of the array is assigned value 1.

Array position starts from 0 so the `order[50]` refers to 51st location.

> **Note:** You can always extend the size of an array. In case of fixed length array this can be done by referencing elements that are outside the array's size.

There are two ways to add values to an array.

1. Assinging values using the subscript

```
var order=new Array();
order[0]="paste";
order[1]="brush";
```

```
order[2]="comb";
```

2. *Intializing array with the values*

```
var order=new Array("paste","brush","comb");
```

> **Note:** In case you specify numbers or value true/false inside the array then the type of variables will be numeric/Boolean instead of string.

5.10.2.1 *Elements of an Array*

The array can be accessed using the array subscript. The values to the elements of the array can be assigned during the declaration of the array or using the assignment operator.

```
name = new Array("Ram","Shyam","Jai");
name[0]="Ram";
name[1]="Shyam";
```

Two – dimensional level array can be created as follows:

```
num1 = name[4][7];
num2= name[2][3];
```

An array can also be assigned as an element of another array. For example,

```
array_name = new Array("Ram",new Array(3));
```

5.10.2.2 *Accessing Array*

You can access a particular element in an array by referring by the name of the array and the index number.

> **Note:** The index number starts at 0.

Accessing an element of array order

```
document.write(name[0]);
```

Output:

Ram

5.10.2.3 *Changing Values in an Array*

To modify value of an existing array for adding a new value to array with a specified index number:

```
order[0]="cream";
```

Now, the following code:

```
document.write(order[0]);
```

The output will be displayed as given below.

```
cream
```

5.10.2.4 *Properties of an Array*

The popular property of an array is length of an array. Length of the array implies number of elements in the array. For example,

```
a = name.length;
```

In the above example variable 'a' captures the length of the array 'name'.

Look at following example:

```
marks= new Array(1,2,3,4,5);
a = marks.length;
```

In above example value of 'a' will be 5.

Since the arrays are JavaScript object they have several methods associated with it them. These can be used to manipulate array content.

5.10.2.5 *Methods associated with an Array*

1. **join():** join() returns all elements of the array joined together as a single string. It takes one argument, a string to be used as a separator between each element of the array in the final string.

2. **reverse():** It is used to reverse the order of elements in the array.

Example 18: Input elements in a array

```
<html>
<head><title> Inputting elements in an array</title></head>
<body>
<script language="JavaScript">
<!-Declare an array ->
stud = new Array(5);
var  stud={"Gauri","Krish","Alisha","Prisha","Kanchi",
"Sanjana"}
stud[0]="Gauri"
stud[1]='Krish"
stud[2]="Alisha"
stud[3]="Kanchi"
stud[4]="Sanjana"
stud[5]="Prisha"
for(j=1;j<=4;j++)
{
    document.write(stud[j];
    j++;
}
</script>
</body>
</html>
```

> **Note: Regarding Array Elements**
>
> In an array element count starts from 0. In case array elements range from 0 to *n* its length will be *n+1*

5.10.2.6 Array Objects Supported by JavaScript

Method	Description
`concat()`	This joins two or more arrays and returns the result.
`join()`	This puts all elements of an array into a string. Eelements are separated by a specified delimiter.
`pop()`	It removes and returns last element of an array.
`push()`	It adds elements to the end of an array, and returns the new length.
`reverse()`	This reverses order of elements in an array.
`shift()`	It removes, and returns first element of an array.
`sort()`	Sorts the elements of an array.

5.11   Data Object

The Date object is used to work with dates and times. It provides capability to retrieve, manipulate and display date and time.

5.11.1 Creating Date Objects

Let's creating a date object called new_Date:

```
var new_Date =new Date();
```

> **Note:** The JavaScript Date object automatically holds current date and time as its initial value.

5.11.2 Setting Dates Using Date Objects

You can easily manipulate the date by using the methods available for the Date object. Check out the following examples:

Setting Date object to a specific date (26th January 2009)

```
var new_Date=new Date();
new_Date.setFullYear(2014,0,24);
```

Now let's set Date object for 10 days in future:

```
var fut_Date=new Date();
fut_Date.setDate(fut_Date.getDate()+10);
```

> **Note:** While adding seven days it is possible there is shift in the month or year. Such changes are handled automatically by the Date object itself.

5.11.2 Comparing Two Dates

Let's compare two dates using JavaScript Date object.

Example 19: Comparing today's date with the 26th January 2010

```
var c_Date=new Date();
c_Date.setFullYear(2010,0,26);
var c = new Date();
if (c_Date>c)
{
    alert("Today's date comes before 6th July 2014");
}
else
{
    alert("Today's date comes after 6th July 2014");
```

5.11.3 Date Objects supported by JavaScript

Method	Description
Date()	Returns today's date and time.
getHours()	Returns hour of a Date object (from 0-23).
getMilliseconds	Returns milliseconds of a Date object (from 0-999).
getDate()	Returns day of the month from a Date object (from 1-31).
getDay()	Returns returns the day of the week from a Date object (from 0-6).
getFullYear()	Returns year, as a four digit number, from a Date object.
getMinutes()	Returns minutes of a Date object (from 0-59).
getMonth()	Return month from a Date object (from 0-11).
getSeconds()	This method returns the seconds of a Date object (from 0-59).
getTime()	Returns number of milliseconds between midnight of January 1, 1970 and the specified date.
getYear()	Returns the year, as a two-digit or a three/four-digit number, depending on the browser. Use getFullYear() instead.
setDate()	It sets day of the month in a Date object (from 1-31).
setFullYear()	It sets year in a Date object (four digits).
setHours()	It sets hour in a Date object (from 0-23).
setMinutes()	Sets the milliseconds in a Date object (from 0-999).
setMinutes()	The method is used to set the minutes in a Date object (from 0-59).
setMonth()	Sets month in a Date object (from 0-11).
setSeconds()	Sets the seconds in a Date object (from 0-59).
setTime()	Calculates a date and time by adding or subtracting a specified number of milliseconds to/from midnight January 1, 1970.
toString()	Converts a Date object to a string.

5.12   Maths Objects in JavaScript

JavaScript Math object allows you to perform mathematical tasks. It includes several mathematical constants and methods.

Syntax:

Mathematical Constants
Math.PI
Math.SQRT2
Math.SQRT1_2
Math.LN2
Math.LN10
Math.LOG2E
Math.LOG10E
Math.E

5.13 Mathematical Methods

In addition to the mathematical constants there are also several methods available with the math object. Some of the mathematical methods supported by JavaScript are summarized below

Method	Use
abs(x)	Returns absolute value of a number.
ceil(x)	Returns value of a number rounded upwards to the nearest integer.
cos(x)	It returns the cosine of a number.
exp(x)	It returns the value of E^x.
floor(x)	It returns value of a number rounded downwards to the nearest integer.
log(y)	It returns natural logarithm (base E) of a number.
max(x,y)	It returns the number with the highest value of x and y.
min(x,y)	It returns the number with the lowest value of x and y.
pow(x,y)	It returns the value of x to the power of y.
random()	It returns a random number between 0 and 1.
round(x)	It rounds a number to the nearest integer.
sqrt(y)	It returns the square root of a number.

Using the round() method to round a number to the nearest integer

```
document.write(Math.round(4.6));
```
Output:4

Using the `random()` method to return a random number between 0 and 1

```
document.write(Math.random() ) ;
```

The above given code can result in the following output:

0.24567443234

Test Your Progress
1. *What are the different event objects supported by JavaScript?*
2. *How array is created in JavaScript?*
3. *How can you declare Date object in JavaScript?*
4. *Discuss use of Math object with a suitable example?*

5.14 Events in JavaScript

Events can be defined as actions. In JavaScript you can detect these actions. By using **JavaScript** you have the ability to create dynamic Web pages. Each element on a Web page has certain events from which **JavaScript** functions can be triggered. These functions can then be used to perform a specific task. E.g. You can use the onClick event of a button element to trigger a **JavaScript** function. The function will run as the user clicks on the button. These events are defined using the HTML tags. The events can be associated with the action of mouse cursor or on loading of a Web page.

JavaScript handles the event using a multi-step process this has been represented in the diagram below:

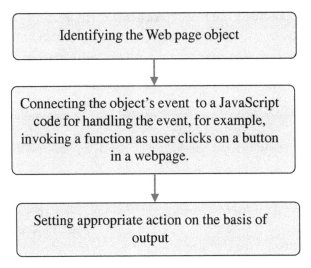

Figure 5.1: Event Handling using multi-step process

5.14.1 Events Handlers in JavaScript

JavaScript event handlers can be broadly divided in two types:

1. **Interactive Event Handlers:** Interactive Event handlers depend on user interaction with the Web page. `onMouseClick` event is an interactive event handler as it requires the user to click on a Web page object like button on a Web page. Some of the popular interactive event handlers have been explained below:

   a. **onFocus, onBlur and onChange:** The `onFocus`, `onBlur` and `onChange` events are used in combination for validating fields of a form.

   Executing a event as content of a text box change

   ```
   <input type="text" id="Result"
   onChange="post_Result()">
   ```

   In the above example `onChange` event is being used to trigger event `post_Result()` has content of a text box change.

   b. **onSubmit:** The `onSubmit` event is to validate all the form fields as the user clicks on the submit button.

   Triggering a event as user clicks on Submit button

   ```
   <form method="post" action="result.html"
   onSubmit="return Score_card()">
   ```

   In the above example `onSubmit` event has been used. The `verify()` function will be called when user clicks the submit button in the form. In case form field values are not accepted, the submit should be cancelled. The function `verify()` will return either true or false. In case return value true the form will be submitted, otherwise submit will be cancelled.

   c. **onMouseOver and onMouseOut:** The `onMouseOver` and the `onMouseOut` are used to capture mouse movement over a button.

   E.g. As mouse moves over an image, an alert box appears on the browser window. When an onMouseOver event is detected:

   ```
   <a href="result.html"
   onmouseover="alert('Check your exam result
   here');return false">
   <img src="score_card.gif" width="250" height="150">
   </a>
   ```

2. **Non-Interactive Event Handlers:** Non-Interactive Event Handlers are the one which do not need user interaction, for example clicking of `onLoad` event. The onLoad event handler will trigger as soon as page is loaded on the browser. Non-Interactive Event Handlers like `onLoad`, `onUnload` are triggered when user enters or leaves the page. The onUnload event is often used to determine visitor's browser type,version in order to load proper version of the Web page based on the information. You can also use these events to deal with cookies you need to set when a user enters or leaves a page.

   Popular events supported by JavaScript have been summarized below:

Event	Description
onabort	Occurs on loading of an image is interrupted.
onblur	Occurs when an element loses focus.
onchange	Occurs when user changes the content of a field.
onclick	Occurs when mouse clicks an object.
ondblclick	Occurs when mouse double-clicks an object.
onerror	Occurs when an error occurs when loading a document or an image.
onfocus	Occurs when an element gets focus.
onkeydown	Occurs when a keyboard key is pressed.
onkeypress	Occurs when a keyboard key is pressed or held down.
onkeyup	Occurs when keyboard key is released.
onload	Occurs when a page or an image is finished loading.
onmousedown	Occurs when a mouse button is pressed.
onmousemove	Occurs when mouse is moved.
onmouseout	Occurs when the mouse is moved off an element.
onmouseover	Occurs when the mouse is moved over an element.
onmouseup	Occurs when a mouse button is released.
onreset	Occurs when the reset button is clicked.
onresize	Occurs when a window or frame is resized.
onselect	Occurs when a text is selected.
onsubmit	Occurs when the submit button is clicked.
onunload	Occurs when from the page user exits.

Note: Events are used in combination with functions. These function will not be executed before the event occurs!

Example 20: Using `onclick` Event to copy content of one box into the another

```
<html>
<body>
Name: <input type="text" id=" " value="Enter student's name">
<br />
copied_Name: <input type="text" id="text2">
<br /><br />
Clicking the button below will copy of first box in the other.
<br />
<button onclick="document.getElementById(' text2').value=
document.getElementById(' text1').value">Copy it</button>
</body>
</html>
```

Output:

Test Your Progress
1.   *What do you understand by event?*
2.   *What are different types of event handlers?*
3.   *How can you code event handlers in JavaScript?*
4.   *Discuss the use of* `onClick`*,* `onReset` *event handles.*

5.15 JavaScript DOM

JavaScript can be used with DHTML to modify content style layout. With HTML 4, JavaScript, and HTML DOM can be used to change style any HTML element.

Before you read more about dynamically changing content style, layout using JavaScript, DHTML you need to know about JavaScript DOM. The HTML DOM defines standard set of objects ,way to access and manipulate them in HTML documents. All the HTML elements, along with their containing the text and attributes, can be accessed through the DOM. Contents can be updated or deleted, and new elements can be created. Some of the HTML DOM objects are discussed below.

Object	Description
Window	Window is the top level object in the JavaScript hierarchy. It represents a browser window. This object is created automatically with every instance of a `<body>` or `<frameset>` tag. It has properties to retrieve information about the browser and methods to manipulate such information.
Navigator	Navigator object contains information about the client's browser.
Screen	Screen object contains information about the client's display screen.
History	History object contains the visited URLs in the browser.
Location	Location object contains information about the current URL.

The Document object is very often used to access document elements and manipulate them. Document object further include objects like anchor[], forms[], images[], links[] to store corresponding information about the Web page.

5.15.1 JavaScript Object Properties

Property	Description
body	It provides direct access to the \<body> element.
lastModified	It returns the date and time a document was last modified.
referrer	It returns the URL of the document that loaded the current document.
title	It returns the title of the current document.
URLL*	It returns the URL of the current document.

5.15.2 JavaScript Object Methods

Method	Description
getElementById()	This method returns a reference to the first object with the specified id entity (ID).
getElementByName()	This method returns a collection of objects with the specified name.
open()	It opens a stream to collect the output from document.write() or document.writeln() methods.
write()	This method is used to writes HTML expressions or JavaScript code to a document.
writeln()	It is just identical to the write() method except that it adds a new line character after each expression.
close()	This method closes an output stream opened with the document.open() method, and displays the collected data.

Document Object method getElementById() is often used to access a particular element of the Web page through its ID and then manipulate it dynamically.

Example 21: Using Document Object Method to access a particular element of the Web page

```
<html>
<body>
<h1 onclick="document.getElementById('para1').
style.visibility='hidden'">
    Click me to see magic!</h1>
<p id="para1">As you click the header content will go
invisible</p>
```

```
</body>
</html>
```

Output: Following page loads on the browser window:

Click me to see magic!

As you click the header content will go invisible

In the above example <p> tag has been identified by its id 'para1' using the element getElementById() method. The element visibility has been set to hidden by using the style object which has been discussed below.

Click me I will get invisible!

5.15.3 Using Style Object in JavaScript

The Style object is used to represent an individual style statement in a document. It can be accessed from the document or from elements to which that style is applied.

Syntax:

```
document.getElementById("id").style.property="value"
```

Some of the style object properties are:

Attribute
Background
List
Positioning
Border and margin
Layout
Table
Text

Each of the property can be manipulated using set of attributes discussed in DHTML section. Some of the background properties and layout properties have been summarized below:

Property	Usage
backgroundAttachment	Determine whether a background-image is fixed or scrolling with the page.
backgroundPositionX	Used to set the X-coordinates of the background Position property.
backgroundPositionY	Used to set the Y-coordinates of the backgroundPosition property.
backgroundPosition	Used to set the starting position of a background-image.
backgroundColor	Used to set the background-color of an element.
backgroundImage	Used to set the background-image of an element.
backgroundRepeat	It sets if/how a background-image will be repeated.

5.15.4 Layout Properties in JavaScript

Property	Usage
maxHeight	It sets maximum height of an element.
maxWidth	Used to set the maximum width of an element.
minHeight	Used to set the minimum height of an element.
minWidth	Used to set the minimum width of an element.
Overflow	Used to specify what to do with content that does not fit in an element box.
verticalAlign	Used to set the vertical alignment of content in an element.
Visibility	Used to set whether or not an element should be visible.
Width	Used to set the width of an element.

These properties have been used in the sub section below to dynamically change content style and layout

5.15.5 Changing Content style and Layout Dynamically

As discussed it by using JavaScript with DHTML and accessing Web page elements using HTML DOM it is possible to dynamically Changing Content Style and the layout. To change the style the current HTML element, use the statement:

```
style.property=new style
```

or more correctly:

```
this.style.property=new style
```

Example 22: Let's change the style of the current element

```
<html>
<body>
    <p id="para1" onClick="this.style.color='red'">Just click
    to change my color</para1>
```

```
</body>
</html>
```

Output: As you click on the paragraph text its color of text changes to red

Just click to change my color

In the above example this object refers to the current object which is a header. The style has been used to change color.

5.15.6 Changing Style of Specific HTML Elements

To change the style of a specific HTML element, use the statement:
document.getElementById(*element_id*).style.*property=new*
style

Example 23: Changing the style of an element as user clicks on the header element

```
<html>
<body>
<h1 onmouseover="style.color='red'" onmouseout=
"style.color='green'">
Just move your mouse here and see change in
color</h1>
</body>
</html>
```

Output:

Just click to change my color

If you click the header above, my colr changes to yellow

Example 24: Check change in color as the cursor moves over it.

```
<html>
<body>
<h1 onmouseover="style.color='red'" onmouseout=
"style.color='purple'">
Just move your mouse here and see change in color</h1>
</body>
</html>
```

Just move your mouse here and see change in color

5.15.7 Changing Visibility of an Element of JavaScript

Visibility of an element can be changed by setting visibility option to hidden. Check out the following example:

Example 25: Changing the Visibility of an element

```html
<html>
<body>
<p id="para1">Just make me invisible and play hide and
seek!!!!!!!!!!!!!!!!!!!!!!</p>
<input type="button" value="Hide Text"
onclick="document.getElementById('para1').style.visibility='hidden'"
/>
<input type="button" value="UnHide text"
onclick="document.getElementById('para1').style.visibility='visible'"
/>
</body>
</html>
```

Output: Following output will be displayed on browser before user clicks on any button

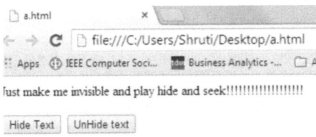

Following output will be displayed as user clicks on the hiding text button

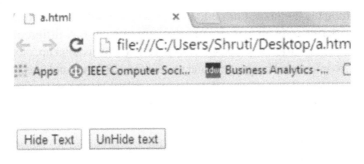

You can see that the text has become invisible in the browser window.

Note: Usage of JavaScript

JavaScript and HTML DOM can be used together to manipulate Web page objects. They together provide capability for changing content, style layout dynamically.

Test Your Progress

1.   *What do you understand by JavaScript DOM?*
2.   *What do you understand by Style Object?*
3.   *What do you mean by properties and methods of an object?*
4.   *How can you generate random numbers in JavaScript?*

5.16   Some Facts About JavaScript

5.16.1 History revisited

When World Wide Web (WWW) was first created in early 1990s all Web pages were static. When a Web page is viewed you saw exactly what page was set up to show you and there was no other way for you to interact with the page.

Being able to interact with Web page - have it do something in the response to the actions - required the addition of some form of the programming language to "instruct" the page how it should respond to your actions. In order to have it respond immediately without having to reload Web page this language needed to be able to run on same computer as the browser displaying the page.

There were two browsers, which were popular, Netscape Navigator and Internet Explorer. Netscape was first to bring out a programming language, which allow Web pages to become interactive, and called it Livescript. It was integrated into browser (the browser would interpret the commands directly without requiring the code to be compiled and without requiring a plug in to be able to run it). Anyone using latest Netscape browser would be able to interact with pages that made use of this language.

The other programming language called Java (that required a separate plug in in order to run) became very well known, and Netscape decided to try to cash in on this by renaming the language built into their browser to JavaScript. Although some Java and JavaScript code appear similar, they are two entirely different languages that serve completely different purposes. Internet explorer was soon updated to support not one but two integrated languages; one was called VBScript and was based on the BASIC programming language and the other was called JScript and was very similar to JavaScript. If you were very careful what commands you used you could write code, that would be able to be processed as JavaScript by the Netscape Navigator and as JScript by Internet explorer.

At the time Netscape Navigator was more popular browser, and thus later versions of Internet Explorer implemented versions of the JScript that were more and more like JavaScript. By the time the Internet Explorer became dominant browser. JavaScript had become the standard for writing interactive processing to be run in the Web browser.

The scripting language importance was so high, that to leave the future development in the hands of the competing browser developers and thus, in 1996 JavaScript was handed over to an international standards body called ECMA, which then became responsible for subsequent development of language, and this language was officially renamed ECMAScript or ECMA-262 but most people still refer to it as JavaScript.

5.16.2 Difference between JavaScript and Jscript

Netscape developed the original version of JavaScript for the second version of their popular browser. Netscape 2 was initially the only browser, to support the scripting language and that language (which was originally going to be called LiveScript) was given the name JavaScript in an attempt to cash in on some of publicity that Sun's Java programming language was getting at that duration. While JavaScript and Java are superficially alike they are completely different languages and this naming decision has caused numerous problems for beginners with both languages who continually get them confused. Just remember that JavaScript is not Java (and vice versa) and you will avoid a lot of confusion. Microsoft was attempting to capture market share from Netscape at that duration and so with Internet Explorer 3 they introduced two scripting languages. These they based on Visual Basic and was given the name VBscript. The second was a JavaScript look alike which Microsoft called JScript. In order to try to out do JScript, Netscape had a number of additional commands and features available, which were not in JavaScript and had interfaces to Microsoft's ActiveX functionality as well. Since Netscape 1, Internet Explorer 2, and other early browsers did not understand either JavaScript or JScript it became a common practice to place all of the content of the script inside of an HTML comment so as to hide the script from older browsers. New browsers even if they could not handle scripts were designed to recognize the script tags themselves and so hiding the script by placing it in a comment was not required for any browsers released after IE3. Unfortunately by that time the extremely early browsers ceased to be used people had forgotten the reason for the HTML comment and so many people new to JavaScript still include these now completely unnecessary tags. Including the HTML comment can cause problems, since if you use XHTML instead of HTML including code inside a comment like that will have the effect of making the script a comment rather than a script. Many modern Content Management Systems (CMS) will do the same. Over time JavaScript and JScript, both were extended to introduce new commands to improve their ability to interact with Web pages. Both the languages added new features that worked differently than the corresponding feature (if any) in the other language. They were similar enough that it was possible to use the browser sensing to work out whether browser was the Netscape or the IE and thus to run the appropriate code for that browser. As the balance shifted toward the IE gaining an equal share of browser market with Netscape this incompatibility needed a resolution. Netscape's solution, was to hand over control of the JavaScript to the European Computer Manufacturers Association (ECMA). The Association formalized JavaScript standards under the name ECMAscipt. At that time, World Wide Web Consortium (W3C) commenced work on a standard Document Object Model (DOM), which would be used to allow JavaScript and other scripting languages full access to manipulate all of the content of the page instead of the limited access that it had up until that time, and before the DOM standard was complete, both Netscape and Microsoft released their own versions. Netscape 4 came with its own document.layer DOM and the Internet explorer 4 came with its own document.all DOM. Both of these document object models were made obsolete, when people ceased using either of those browsers as all the browsers since then have implemented the standard DOM. ECMAscript and introduction of the standard DOM in all of version five and more recent browsers removed most of the incompatibilities between JavaScript and JScript. While these two languages still have their differences, it is now possible to write code, which can run both as the JScript in the Internet Explorer and as JavaScript in all of the other modern browsers. Support for the specific features may vary between browsers but it can be tested for those differences by makin use of a feature built into both the languages from the start that allows us for testing if the browser supports a specific feature. By testing the specific features that not all browsers support we will be able to determine what code is appropriate to run in the current browser. The main difference now between JScript and JavaScript are all of the additional commands which JScript supports, that allow access to ActiveX and local computer. These commands are intended for use on the intranet sites where you know the configuration of all of the computers, and that they are all running Internet explorer. These extensions in the JScript should not be used on the Internet I will not be covering any of them in this book. There are still a few areas left, where JavaScript and JScript differ in the means that they provide to perform a particular task. We will look at both the JavaScript and the JScript processes and how to combine them both into code that will work across all modern browsers. Except in these situations, two languages can be considered to be equivalent to one another, and so unless otherwise specified all of references to the JavaScript can also be taken to include JScript.

People got into the habit of using browser detection **JavaScript**s for testing, if the browser was the Internet Explorer or the Netscape Navigator not only to process appropriate code for those browsers but also made the assumption that either no one was using any other browser or that those browsers did not properly support **JavaScript**. While the assumption was originally correct, other browsers were gradually introduced which did support the **JavaScript** and which duplicated either the the Internet Explorer or the Netscape Navigator was of interacting. In order to run the **JavaScript** that these browsers could understand but which the Web pages did not cater for these browsers lied to the **JavaScript** as to what browser that they actually were and many browsers were released that would report themselves in browser sensing scripts as either Internet Explorer or Netscape Navigator.

Today almost all the browsers can be configured to report themselves as the Internet Explorer, and usually need to be set that way in order to handle the many antiquated scripts that are yet to be updated in old Web pages as well as the many scripts still being written by the people who copy antique coding methods assuming that those irrelevancies are still the right way of writing JavaScript.

5.16.3 Tasks JavaScript cannot do

While there are many things that the JavaScript can be used to enhance your Web pages and improve your visitors experience with your site, there are also a few things that JavaScript cannot do. Some of the limitations are due to the fact that the script is running in the browser window and therefore cannot access the server while others are as a result of security that is in place to stop Web pages from being able to tamper with your computer. There is no way to work around these limitations and anyone who claims to be able to perform any of the following tasks using JavaScript has not considered all of the aspects of whatever it is that they are trying to do.

- JavaScript cannot write to files on the server without the help of a server side script. Using Ajax, JavaScript can send a request to the server. This request can read a file in XML or plain text format but it cannot write to a file unless file called on the server actually runs as a script to do the file written for you.

- JavaScript cannot access the databases unless you use Ajax and have a server side script perform the database access for you.

- JavaScript cannot read from or write to files in the client. Even though JavaScript is running on client computer the one where the Web page is being viewed) it is not allowed to access anything outside of the Web page itself. This is done for the reasons of security since otherwise a Web page would be able to update your computer to install who knows what. The only exception to this are files called cookies which are small text files that JavaScript can write to and read from. The browser restricts the access to cookies so that a given Web page can only access cookies created by the same site.

- JavaScript cannot close a window if it did not open it. Again this is for security reasons.

- JavaScript cannot access the Web pages hosted on another domain. Even though the Web pages from different domains can be displayed at same time, either in separate browser windows or in the separate frames within the same browser window, the JavaScript running on a Web page belonging to one domain cannot access any information about a Web page from a different domain. This helps to make certain that private information about you that may be known to the owners of one domain is not shared with other domains whose Web pages you may have open concurrently. The only way for accessing files from another domain is to do an Ajax call to your server and have a server side script access the other domain.

- JavaScript cannot protect your page source or the images. Any images on the Web page are downloaded separately to the computer displaying the Web page so the person viewing the page already has a copy of all of the images by the time they view the page. The same is true actual HTML source of the Web page. The Web page needs to be able to decrypt any Web page that is encrypted in order to be able to display it. While an encrypted Web page may require JavaScript to be enabled in order for the page to be able to be decrypted in order for it to be able to be displayed by the Web browser, once the page has been decrypted anyone who knows how can easily save the decrypted copy of the page source.

5.16.4 JavaScript Tools

The first tool that you need to write JavaScript is a plain text editor (or at least an editor capable of saving what is typed into it as plain text). If you are using Windows then Notepad is an appropriate choice. On the Mac you could use Simpletext. Linux of course provides lots of plain text editors many of which are probably installed on your system so you just need to choose your favourite one. If you want to get a bit fancier than a plain text editor then check out the options available in your Web editor. Many of them can be used to enter JavaScript as plain text in the same way that they can be used to enter HTML as plain text. Using this option to write and edit your JavaScript may have at least one advantage over the plain text editors, come with the operating system, and the editor can recognize JavaScript. Thus is able to color code JavaScript, which is written using different colors to indicate JavaScript keyword. The built-in objects and the string content makes it easier to see if accidentally a closing quote is omitted, or similar from the code which would have taken a long time to find. The another type of program, which writes own JavaScripts is the Web browsers for testing them in. By the Web browser it does not mean that whichever version of Internet Explorer using that came preinstalled on the Windows operating system or whichever version of Safari came preinstalled on the Mac. To make certain that as many as possible for the visitors, will see the Web page the way intend it to look with JavaScript functionality in place it need to test JavaScript in at least three different Web browsers. There are four different groups of Web browsers, which are used by people to make them worth testing. Internet Explorer is still built on antiquated Trident rendering engine, Netscape, Firefox, and Mozilla are built on Gecko rendering engine. Opera is on Presto rendering engine, and Safari and Konqueror use KHTML rendering engine. Basically rendering engine forms core of the browser, which controls the way that browser converts HTML, stylesheets, and JavaScript into interactive Web pages. The browsers that use same rendering engine will perform in basically same way when it comes to processing the code (assuming of course that they are running same version of rendering engine). Browsers which use a different rendering engine may behave differently when they process exactly same code. For this reason the ideal minimum setup for the testing Web pages would be to test on one browser, which uses each of four different rendering engines (testing on the multiple versions is a better option, but it would take longer for progressively less benefit for the most instances). So why three browsers , while there are four different rendering engines. The problem is that, while it can be tested with all four on windows (that support Firefox, Internet Explorer, Opera, and Safari, and many other browsers) there is no other way to test all the four if you are using a Linux or Mac. Since demise of the Internet Explorer on the Mac back in 2003 (which in any case did not use Trident) there has been no version of Internet Explorer that runs on any other operating system except Windows. In any case Trident itself is so closely embedded into Windows itself, and it cannot be used on other operating system anyway. This means that say Firefox, Opera, and Safari on a Mac or Firefox, Opera, and Konqueror on Linux would be the three browsers that can be tested with and you have to rely on someone with access to Windows to test it in Internet Explorer for you. Internet Explorer runs JScript while the other browsers run JavaScript. The other Web browsers also follow the standards much more closely than Internet Explorer does so the best plan of attack when writing and testing a JavaScript is to test in the any browser other than Internet Explorer first. Continue testing in whatever browsers is available apart from Internet Explorer until it is ensured that your JavaScript works. Only then you should test on the Internet Explorer and make any changes required to code to allow it to function as both the JavaScript and the JScript. Test the script thoroughly before uploading it to your site and then test it again to make sure that it is uploaded correctly.

5.17 Key Terms

- **Events:** Events can be defined as actions that can be detected by JavaScript. By using JavaScript you have the ability to create dynamic Web pages. Each element on a Web page has some event from which JavaScript functions can be triggered. These functions can then be used to perform a specific task.

- **Functions:** A block of code, which performs specific job and return a value.

- **HTML DOM:** The HTML DOM defines standard set of objects, way to access and manipulate them in the HTML documents. The HTML elements, and their text and attributes, can be accessed through the DOM. The contents can be updated or deleted, and new elements can be created.

- **JavaScript:** This is an Interpreter based language, that can be used with HTML.

- **JavaScript Popup Boxes:** It has the ability to pick up user input or display the small amount of the text to user using dialog boxes. The type of popup boxes: Confirm box, Alert box, and Prompt box. These dialog boxes appear in separate windows, and the content depend on information, which given by the user.

- **JavaScript String Object:** In JavaScript string is declared as an object. The String object can be used to manipulate a stored piece of data.

- **JavaScript Array:** JavaScript arrays are implemented as objects. The Array object stores multiple values in a variable.

- **JavaScript Date Object:** This works with dates and times. It provides capability to retrieve, manipulate and display date and time.

5.18 Summary

In this Chapter JavaScript has been discussed in detail. JavaScript is a scripting language which is compliant to W3C standards. In this Chapter you have learnt the use of JavaScript for adding interaction between user and Web page content. The advantages of JavaScript over HTML/DHTML have been discussed in detail. You must have seen that JavaScript can easily be incorporated in an HTML document. JavaScript provides basic programming techniques and has powerful set of operators and programming constructs which include conditional checking and different control loops. JavaScript enables implicit variable declaration and automatically performs type casting as and when required. It provides three easy ways to use dialog boxes for improved interactivity with the user. JavaScript supports functions like major programming languages. There are built-in functions like eval(),parseInt(), parseFloat() which are frequently used. Function can be written in the head or the body of the document. JavaScript also supports recursive functions. JavaScript is an object oriented language. It includes built-in objects like String, Math, and Date object. It supports user defined objects and provides easy syntax for creating an object. JavaScript has the capability of handling events that are defined using HTML tags. Event handlers can be interactive or non-interactive depending on the role of user in the triggering of the event. The popular event handlers are onMouseOver, onMouseClick, onClick, onAbort, etc. JavaScript efficiently supports HTML Document object model. JavaScript together with DHTML and HTML DOM provides flexibility to dynamically change content and style layout in the Web page. Various examples of the same have been discussed in the Chapter.

5.19 Test Yourself

1.   Fill in the blanks:

a.   JavaScript is a _____language.

b.   eval() function used to evaluate _____.

c.   Event handler of JavaScript are of _____ types.

d.   parseInt() used for _____.

e.   _____ is object of JavaScript.

Ans 1. a. Interpreted **b.** <Script>...</Script>. **c.** Variable **d.** Local, Global **e.** Expressions

2.   True or False

a.   **JavaScript** is not a scripting language.

b.   You cannot use script tag more then once in a HTML document.

c. You can place `<script>` tag only in the `<head>` tag in a HTML document.

d. Events cannot be defined using **JavaScript**.

e. An object can have many properties.

Ans 2. a. True **b.** True **c.** False **d.** False **e.** True

3. What is the software required to create and edit JavaScript programs?

Ans 3. Notepad

4. Discuss the different ways in which JavaScript can be used in a HTML document.

Ans 4. JavaScript can be written inside the HTML document or it can be linked with the document. Inside a document **JavaScript** can be written at head or at body section of document.

a. Writing JavaScript in the body section

```
<html>
<body>
<script language="JavaScript"> document.write("<B>JavaScript
written in the head section</b>"); </script>
</body>
</html>
```

b. Writing JavaScript in the head section

```
<html>
<head>
<script language="JavaScript"> document.write("Coding using
JavaScriptpt"); </script> </head> <body> | |
</body>
</html>
```

c. Using an external JavaScript

```
<html> <head> </head> <body> <script src="java_code.js"> </
script> <p> HTML doc is linked to external JavaScript file
"java_code.js".</p> </body> </html>
```

5. What are the different ways of writing comments in a JavaScript document?

Ans 5. Comments in JavaScript can be either single line or multiple line comments. Both single line and multi-line comments can be used to prevent execution of a statement. They are writtem as follows:

1. Single line comments are written using //.

2. Multi-line comments are written using /*...*/.

```
<html>
<body>
<script language="JavaScript">
// Writing the content in italic
/*This is multi-line comments
Code will display content in bold*/
document.write("<i>Welcome</i>");
</script>
</body>
</html>
```

6.   Write a JavaScript code to dsisplay today's day (e.g. today is Friday).

Ans 6.

```
<html>
<body>
<script language="Javascript">
    var b=new Date();
    var weekday=new Array(7);
    weekday[0]="Sunday";
    weekday[1]="Monday";
    weekday[2]="Tuesday";
    weekday[3]="Wednesday";
    weekday[4]="Thursday";
    weekday[5]="Friday";
    weekday[6]="Saturday";
    document.write("Current day of the week:" +
    weekday[b.getDay()]);
</script>
</body>
</html>
```

7.   Write a JavaScript code to display an alert box as user clicks on the header data.

```
<html>
<head>
<script type="text/JavaScript">
function show_alert()
{
    var a=document.getElementById("header1");
    alert(a.innerHTML);
}
</script>
</head>
<body>
```

```
<h1 id="header1" onclick="show_alert()">Click this header</
h1>
<p>You will get alert as you click on the header</p>
</body>
</html>
```

8.   **Create a script, which takes input user name, and then greets user with "Hello" and user name at the page.**

```
<script type = "text/Javascript">
    var n = prompt("Please enter your name.", "");
    /* This will create the variable n and prompts the user
    for a name.*/
    document.write ("Hello "+n);
</script>
```

9.   **Create a script, which prompts user for a number. It needs to count from 1 to that number and only displays odd numbers.**

```
<script type = "text/Javascript">
function CountNow()
{
    var n =parseInt(prompt('Enter a Number from where to
    start count down','10'),10)
    for(j = n; j >= 0; j-) //Create a for loop for counting
    {
        if (i%2==1)
        {
            document.write(i+" ") //(You need to write only
            the odd number)
        }
    }
    document.write("</body></html>");
}
</script>
<input type="button" onclick="CountNow()">
```

10.   **Write JavaScript to greet user on basis of time.**

```
<script type = "text/JavaScript">
current = new Date()
if ((current.getHours() >=4) && (current.getHours() <=12))
{
    document.write("Good Morning !")
}
if ((current.getHours() >12) && (current.getHours() <=18))
```

```
{
    document.write("Good afternoon.")
}
if ((current.getHours() >18) && (current.getHours() <=23))
{
    document.write("Good evening!")
}
</script>
```

Section II: Exercise

1. How data is stored in a JavaScript?
2. How browser recognize JavaScript code?
3. What is the difference between Java and JavaScript?
4. Can we use HTML tags with JavaScript? How to insert comments in a JavaScript?
5. A script, which get executed when the user clicks mouse button is called?
6. Explain the purpose of enclosing the script within a HTML comments?
7. What you understand by local and global variables?
8. Which of the given below is not a valid JavaScript variable name?

    a. 4rita   b. _ram

    c. richirich

9. Write the result of the JavaScript expression 31 + "Hello Delhi"

Section V Previous Year Questions with Answers

Q. 1. Write a JavaScript function for E-mail address validation, i.e., to check if the content has the general syntax of e-mail or not? **[UPTU 2010]**

Solution: Take a text input in HTML and a button input like this.

```
<input type='text' id='txtEmail'/>
<input type='submit' name='submit'
onclick='JavaScript:checkEmail();'/>
```

When the button is clicked then the JavaScript function SubmitFunction() will be called. Now write the bellow code in this function.

```
<script language="Javascript">
function checkEmail()
{
    var email = document.getElementById('txtEmail');
    var filter= /^([a-zA-Z0-9_\.\-])+\@(([a-zA-Z0-9\-
    ])+\.)+([a-zA-Z0-9]{2,4})+$/;
    if (!filter.test(email.value))
```

```
    {
        alert('Please provide a valid email address');
        email.focus;
        return false;
    }
}
</script>
```

Q. 2. Develop an HTML and JavaScript document to evaluate the roots of a quadratic equation. Explain each step clearly. [UPTU 2008]

Solution: JavaScript Code for Quadratic Equation:

```
<script type="text/Javascript">
function quad()
{
    var a=document.getElementById("av").value;
    var b=document.getElementById("bv").value;
    var c=document.getElementById("cv").value;
    var d=(Math.pow(b,2)-(4*a*c));
    var x1=(-b + Math.sqrt(d)) / (2*a);
    var x2=(-b - Math.sqrt(d)) / (2*a);
    document.getElementById("r1").value=x1;
    document.getElementById("r2").value=x2;
    if(document.getElementById("r1").value == "NaN")
    document.getElementById("r1").value="imag";
    if(document.getElementById("r2").value == "NaN")
    document.getElementById("r2").value="imag";
}
var check=true;
function isNumberKey(id)
{
    var no=eval('"'+id+'"');var number= document.
    getElementById(no).value;if(number.length==1)
    {
        check=true;}if(number.length>1)
        {
            var dd = number;
            if(dd.substring(dd.length,(dd.length-1))=='-')
            {
                if(check)
                {
                    check=false;
                }
                else
                {
```

```
                    dd = dd.substring(0,(dd.length-1));
                    document.getElementById(no).value = dd;
                }
            }
        }
        if(!number.match(/^[0-9-]+$/) && number
        !=""){document.getElementById(id).value="";
        document.getElementById(id).focus();}else{
        var dd = number;if(dd.substring(dd.length,(dd.length-
        1))=='-')
        {
            if(check)
            {
                check=false;
            }
            else
            {
                document.getElementById(id).value="";
                document.getElementById(id).focus();
            }
        }
    }
}
</script>
```

HTML Code

```
<html>
<body>
<form name="qfrm">
<table>
<tr>
<td><input type="text" name="av" id="av" size="3"
onkeyup="isNumberKey(this.id)">x<sup>2</sup>+</td>
<td><input type="text" name="bv" id="bv" size="3"
onkeyup="isNumberKey(this.id)">x+</td>
<td><input type="text" name="cv" id="cv" size="3"
onkeyup="isNumberKey(this.id)"></td></tr>
<tr rowspan="2"><td colspan="3" align="center"><input
type="button" value="Calculate" onclick="quad()"></td></tr>
</table>
<table>
<tr rowspan="2"><td colspan="3" align="center">Result</td></tr>
<tr><td>Root 1<input type="text" name="r1" id="r1" size="10"
readonly></td>
```

```
<td>Root 2<input type="text" name="r2" id="r2" size="10"
readonly></td></tr>
</table>
</form>
</body>
</html>
```

Q. 3. **Show the usage of JavaScript in form validation like date and time checking.** **[GGSIP UNIV 2009]**

Solution:

```
<script type="text/Javascript">
function checkForm(form)
{
    // regular expression to match required date format
    re = /^\d{1,2}\/\d{1,2}\/\d{4}$/;
    if(form.startdate.value != '' && !form.startdate.
    value.match(re))
    {
        alert("Invalid date format: " + form.startdate.value);
        form.startdate.focus(); return false;
    }
    // regular expression to match required time format
    re = /^\d{1,2}:\d{2}([ap]m)?$/;
    if(form.starttime.value != '' &&
    !form.starttime.value.match(re))
    {
        alert("Invalid time format: " + form.starttime.value);
        form.starttime.focus(); return false;
    }
    alert("All input fields have been validated!"); return
    true;
}
</script>
```

Q. 4. **What are client side scripting languages? How do you write a program in JavaScript? Explain the following in JavaScript:**

    a.   **Frame object**

    b.   **Document Object**

    c.   **Form Object** **[GGSIP UNIV 2009]**

Solution:

The server-side environment that runs a scripting language is a Web server. A user's request is fulfilled by running a script directly on the Web server to generate dynamic HTML pages. This HTML is then sent to the client browser. It is usually used to provide interactive Websites that interface to databases or other data stores on the server.

This is different from client-side scripting where scripts are run by using Web browser, usually in JavaScript.

a. *JavaScript Frame Object*

Frame Object Properties

The JavaScript Frame object is the representation of an HTML Frame which belongs to an HTML Frameset. The frameset defines the set of frame that make up the browser window. The JavaScript Frame object is a property of the window object.

Properties

* frames - An array of frames in a window or frameset.
* name - The name of the frame. It is defined using the name attribute of the <frame> tag.
* length - The length of the frames array.
* parent - The parent of the current frame.
* self - The current frame.

Frame Object Methods

* `blur()`
* `focus()`
* `setInterval()`
* `clearInterval()`
* `setTimeout(expression, milliseconds)`
* `clearTimeout(timeout)`

JavaScript Document Object

The JavaScript Document object is the container for all HTML Head and Boby objects associated within the HTML tags of an HTML document.

Document Object Properties

* `alinkColor` - The color of active links.
* `bgColor` - Sets the background color of the Web page. It is set in the <body> tag.
* `cookie` - Used to identify the value of a cookie.
* `domain` - The domain name of the document server.
* `embeds` - An array containing all the plug-ins in a document.
* `fgColor` - The text color attribute set in the <body> tag.
* `fileCreatedDate` - Use this value to show when the loaded HTML file was created.

- `fileModifiedDate` - Use this value to show the last change date of the loaded HTML file.
- `lastModified` - The date the file was modified last.
- `layers` - An array containing all the layers in a document.
- `linkColor` - The color of HTML links in the document. It is specified in the `<body>` tag.
- `title` - The name of the current document as described between the header Title tags.
- `URL` - The location of the current document.
- `vlinkColor` - The color of visited links as specified in the `<body>` tag.

b. *Document Object Methods*

- `clear()` - This is depreciated.
- `close()` - Close an output stream that was used to create a document object.
- contextual() - It can be used to specify stype of specific tags.
- `elementFromPoint(x, y)` - Return the object at point x, y in the HTML document.
- `getSelection()` - Get the selected text (if any is selected).
- `open([mimeType])` - Open a new document object with the optional `MIME` type.
- `write(expr1[,expr2...exprN])` - Add data to a document.
- `writeln(expr1[,expr2...exprN])` - Add the passed values to the document appended with a new line character.

c. *JavaScript Form Object*

The JavaScript Form Object is a property of the document object. This corresponds to an HTML input form constructed with the `FORM` tag. A form can be submitted by calling the JavaScript submit method or clicking the form submit button.

Form Object Properties

- action - This specifies the URL and `CGI` script file name the form is to be submitted to. It allows reading or changing the `ACTION` attribute of the HTML `FORM` tag.
- elements - An array of fields and elements in the form.
- encoding - This is a read or write string. It specifies the encoding method the form data is encoded in before being submitted to the server. It corresponds to the `ENCTYPE` attribute of the `FORM` tag. The default is "`application/x-www-form-urlencoded`". Other encoding includes text/plain or multipart/form-data.
- length - The number of fields in the elements array, i.e., the length of the elements array.

- method - This is a read or write string. It has the value "GET" or "POST".
- name - The form name. Corresponds to the FORM Name attribute.

  target - The name of the frame or window the form submission response is sent to by the server. Corresponds to the FORM TARGET attribute.

Form Objects

Forms have their own objects.

- button - An GUI pushbutton control. Methods are click(), blur(), and focus(). Attributes:
  o name - The name of the button.
  o type - The object's type. In this case, "button".
  o value - The string displayed on the button.
- checkbox - An GUI check box control. Methods are click(), blur(), and focus(). Attributes:
  o checked - Indicates whether the checkbox is checked. This is a read or write value.
  o defaultChecked - Indicates whether the checkbox is checked by default. This is a read only value.
  o name - The name of the checkbox.
  o type - Type is "checkbox".
  o value - A read or write string that specifies the value returned when the checkbox is selected.
- FileUpload - This is created with the INPUT type="file". This is the same as the text element with the addition of a directory browser. Methods are blur(), and focus(). Attributes:
  o name - The name of the FileUpload object.
  o type - Type is "file".
  o value - The string entered which is returned when the form is submitted.
- hidden - An object that represents a hidden form field and is used for client/server communications. No methods exist for this object. Attributes:
  o name - The name of the Hidden object.
  o type - Type is "hidden".
  o value - A read or write string that is sent to the server when the form is submitted.
- password - A text field used to send sensitive data to the server. Methods are blur(), focus(), and select(). Attributes:
  o defaultValue - The default value.
  o name - The name of the password object.

o   type - Type is "password".

o   value - A read or write string that is sent to the server when the form is submitted.

o   reset - A button object used to reset a form back to default values. Methods are click(), blur(), and focus(). Attributes:

o   name - The name of the reset object.

o   type - Type is "reset".

o   value - The text that appears on the button. By default it is "reset".

Methods :- reset(), submit()

Q. 5.   What is an event? How events are handled in JavaScript? Write a program to build up a clock using JavaScript.
[UPTU 2010]

Solution:

JavaScript's interaction with HTML is handled through events that occur when the user or browser manipulates a page.

When the page loads, that is an event. When the user clicks a button, that click, too, is an event. Another example of events are like pressing any key, closing window, resizing window, etc.

Developers can use these events to execute JavaScript coded responses, which cause buttons to close windows, messages to be displayed to users, data to be validated, and virtually any other type of response imaginable to occur.

Events are a part of the Document Object Model (DOM) Level 3 and every HTML elements have a certain set of events which can trigger JavaScript Code.

Program to build up a clock using JavaScript is as follows:

```
<!DOCTYPE html>
<html>
<head>
<script>
function startTime()
{
    var today=new Date();
    var h=today.getHours();
    var m=today.getMinutes();
    var s=today.getSeconds();
    m = checkTime(m);
    s = checkTime(s);
    document.getElementById('txt').innerHTML = h+":"+m+":"+s;
    var t = setTimeout(function(){startTime()},500);
}

function checkTime(i)
```

```
{
    if (i<10) {i = "0" + i}; // add zero in front of numbers
    < 10
    return i;
}
</script>
</head>

<body onload="startTime()">

<div id="txt"></div>

</body>
</html>
```

Q. 6. Write a JavaScript that finds the smallest of given *n* integers?   (UPTU B.TECH 2008/2009)

Solution:

```
<!DOCTYPE html>
<html>
<body>
<p>Click the button to return the lowest number of 5 , 1, 2,
6, 7.</p>

<button onclick="myFunction()">Try it</button>

<p id="demo"></p>

<script>
function myFunction()
{
    document.getElementById("demo").innerHTML = Math.min
    (5 , 1, 2, 6, 7);
}
</script>

</body>
</html>
```

Chapter 6
An Introduction to PHP

This Chapter has been basically explains the introduction of PHP. The content and flow of the Chapter is designed mainly for the Web programming and developing purpose. Here you will go with the basic introduction of each essential element used for Web Development.

6.1 Introduction

The original meaning of the acronym is 'Personal Home Page'. It is the most popular language and environment in use on the Web today. PHP is a very powerful language. It is able to access files and execute commands. PHP (Personal Home Page, it now stands for Hypertext Preprocessor which is a recursive backronym) open network connections on the server, it may be included in a Web server as a module or executed as a separate CGI binary. It can also be used for writing CGI programs with correct selection of compile-time and runtime configuration options. PHP is designed to be a more secure language.

PHP is server-side scripting system. Its syntax is based on Perl, Java, and C. It is very good for creating dynamic content. Now it is under the Apache Software Foundation and Licensed under the GPL. PHP is free to use. It is a popular server-side technology available for Apache Web servers. It is available on various Web servers, such as IIS, Nginx (act as a reverse proxy server), etc., and operating systems (UNIX, Linux, Windows, Mac OS, etc.). PHP supports a lot of databases: MySQL, Oracle, ODBC (for Microsoft Access and the SQL Server), SQLite, etc.

PHP is an interpreter-based scripting language. PHP code is executed on the Web server while JavaScript which is executed by the Web browser. The PHP file can have text, HTML tags and scripts. PHP can be embedded alongside HTML code which is the main strength of it. Following example shows how easily PHP can be integrated inside HTML:

```
<html>
<title><? print "DELHI"; ?></title>
</html>
```

And DELHI will be displayed in the Web page title bar.

6.1.1 Script Tags

By mistake several text editors will interpret PHP code as HTML code , through which Web page development process can be interfered. The following escape tags can be used to eliminate the problem:

```
<script language="php">
    print "Welcome to PHP session!";
</script>
```

It can be summarized that PHP is an embedded server-side Web scripting language which help developers quickly and efficiently to build dynamic Web applications. It resembles closely both grammatically and syntactically to the C programming language. Developers have integrated many features from a multitude of languages, including Java, C++ and Perl. Many of the valuable borrowed features from Java, C++ and PERL have been included, such as powerful array-handling capabilities, regular expression parsing, an object-oriented methodology, and also vast database support.

6.1.2 What actually can PHP do?

Major areas where PHP scripts can be used are:

- **Server-side scripting:** PHP is a very popular server-side scripting language. To run PHP one needs to have the PHP parser (server module or CGI), a Web browser and a Web server. After completing PHP installation, once you run the Web server you can access the PHP program output a Web browser.

- **Command line scripting:** It is possible for you to run a PHP script without any server or browser. For this one needs to use PHP parser. Such usage is ideal for scripts which are regularly executed using cron (on Linux) or Task Scheduler (on Windows). Such scripts are also used for simple text processing tasks.

- **Writing desktop applications:** For creating a desktop application with a graphical user interface, PHP is not the best language. However, you can use advanced PHP features in your client-side applications to create cross-platform applications.

> **Note:** Official PHP Website
>
> PHP's official Website is http://php.net/
>
> Print resolution = 150 or 300
>
> Film Resolution = 600

Test Your Progress
1.   *Write full form of PHP?*
2.   *What can PHP do?*
3.   *What are script tags?*

6.2 Characteristics of PHP

PHP provides the necessary tools to the programmer to get the job done in a quick and efficient manner. Following are PHP's five important characteristics:

- *Familiarity*
- *Simplicity*
- *Security*
- *Flexibility*
- *It's free!*

Let us discuss each of them in brief.

Familiarity

PHP code is very similar from typical C or Pascal program. This makes it easy to learn.

Simplicity

A PHP script may contain lines varying from 1 to 10,000 or more. It does not require inclusion of libraries or special compilation directives. The PHP engine simply starts executing the code after first escape sequence (<?) and continues until it passes the closing escape sequence (?>).

Efficiency

Efficiency is a very important concern for working in the multiuser environment, such as the WWW. In addition to session management system, PHP 4.0 introduced resource allocation mechanisms and good support for object-oriented programming.

Security

PHP provides administrators and developers a fexible and efficient set of security safeguards. These safeguards can be categorized as follows:

- System level
- Application level

System-Level Security Safeguards

PHP provides maximum amount of freedom and security if it is properly configured. PHP limits user's attempts to exploit its implementation in many important ways when it is run in safe mode. Limits can also be placed on memory usage and maximum execution time, which will have adverse affects on server performance, if not controlled.

Application-Level Security Safeguards

Several encryption options are supported in PHP's predefined functions set. Through the browser PHP source code is not viewable as the script is parsed completely before it is sent back to the requesting user. The loss of creative scripts to users is prevented by the PHP's server-side architecture. That is enough knowledgeable to execute a 'View Source'.

Flexibility

As PHP is an embedded language, it is very exible towards meeting the developer's needs.

Free

PHP is open-source software and it is free. It can be used freely to copy, study it and change the software in any way and is licensed. People are encouraged to voluntarily improving the design of the software as source code is openly shared.

Test Your Progress
1.   *Describe the characterstics of PHP.*
2.   *Describe script tag with example.*
3.   *List the databases supported by PHP.*

6.3   Variables and Data Types

Variable always starts with $ and variable name begin with letter or underscore (_). It can be composed of numbers, underscore and letter.

Some examples are:

```
$my_var = 10;
$x = "Delhi";
```

Remember:

- It is not required to declare the variables and their data types.
- Variables are sensitive to cases, while function names are not.
- To define constants define keyword is used and capital letters are used for name.

```
define("MIN", 50.00);
define("HEADING", "<h1>My COUNTRY</h1>");
```

A semicolon (;) is used to terminate statements.

PHP supports six general data types, which are as given below:

- Integers
- Floating-point numbers
- Strings
- Arrays

- Objects
- Booleans

These data types are briefly described below.

1. **Integer Values:** Integers are represented as a sequence of one or more digits. Following are some examples of integers:

   Octals and Hexadecimals: Octal number consists of digits from 0-7. Some examples of octal integers are:

   > 0123

   > 0576

   Hexadecimal number consists of digits from 0 - 9 and letters a(A) to f(F). 0x or 0X precedes all hexadecimal integers. Examples of hexadecimal integers:

   > 0x3AA

   > 0X45xyz

2. **Floating-Point Numbers:** Floating-point numbers are used to represent values that require a more accurate representation, such as temperature or monetary figures. PHP supports two floating-point formats:

   > ➤ Standard notation

   > ➤ Scientific notation

   Standard Notation: Standard notation is used for real numbers. Some examples are as given below.

   > 5.67

   > 87.7

   Scientific Notation: To represent very large and very small numbers, such as atomic measurements, interplanetary distances, scientific notation is used. Examples are given below:

   > 2e68

   > 3.8863e12

3. **String Values:** A group of characters that are represented as a single entity but can also be examined on character-by-character basis are known as string values. Examples of strings are given below:

   > Mumbai

   > 45saba

   > ABC

   It can be used to represent both single and multiple character sets.

Assignment of String

There are two ways in which string can be delimited, using either double quotation marks (" ") or single quotation marks (' '). String will be replaced with their respective values if variables are in double quotes, whereas the single quoted strings will be interpreted exactly as it is, even if variables are enclosed in the string. Same result is produced by the two strings:

```
$city = "Bombay";
$city = 'Bombay';
```

However, the result of the following two declarations is different:

```
$sentence = " I have to go to $city";
$sentence2 = 'I have to go to $city';
```

Notice how the variable $city is automatically interpreted:

I have to go to Bombay.

Whereas $sentence2 will be assigned the string as follows:

I have to go to $city.

Delimiters is used to represent special characters, such as the newline or tab characters.

Character Representation

\n	Newline
\r	Carriage return
\t	Horizontal tab
\\	Backslash
\$	Dollar sign
\"	Double-quotation mark
\[0-7]{1,4}	Octal notation regular expression pattern
\x[0-9A-Fa-f]{2,4}	Hexadecimal notation regular expression pattern

Character Handling

Strings can be accessed character-by-character, such as a sequentially indexed array.

PHP starts array position counting from 0.

4. **Arrays:** An array is a list of elements. All the elements in the array are of the same type.

● Arrays can contain any type of value and can have any size.

● Array those can be accessed in accordance with the index position, where the elements are positioned.

Examples:

```
$abc[0] = 5;
$abc[1] = "D";
```

- PHP arrays are **associative arrays.** Element values are allowed to be stored in relation to a key value rather than a linear index order.

  ```
  $State["IN"] = "Delhi";
  ```

  Associative arrays are accessed by a key value.

  Arrays are of two types:

  o   Single-dimensional

  o   Multi-dimensional

6.3.1 Single-Dimensional Array

To denote the position of the requested value, an integer subscript is used in single-dimensional array.

Syntax of a single-dimensional array is:

```
$ename[index1];
```

6.3.1.1 Initialization and printing content of an array

A single-dimension array can be created as given below:

```
$color[0] = "white";
$color[1] = "red";
$color[2] = "green";
```

When the command is executed as:

```
print $color[1];
```

The following will be output to the browser:

  Red

Other way to create arrays is PHP's `array()` function. This function can be used to create the same `$color` array as the one in the example above:

```
$color = array("white", "red", "green");
```

It is also possible to assign values to the end of the array simply by assigning values to an array variable using empty brackets. Therefore, another way to assign values to the `$color` array is as follows:

```
$color[] = "white";
$color[] = "red";
$color[] = "green";
```

6.3.1.2 Single-Dimensional Associative Array

Though the associative arrays have difference in their index yet they are very similar to numeric arrays in functionality terms. You can establish a strong association between key and values as the index of associative array are string. Associative arrays are particularly convenient when it makes more sense for mapping an array using words rather than integers.

Example 1: Method to create Associative arrays

```
/* First method */
$esalary['ranu']= 20000;
$esalary['sonia']=30000;

/* Second Method */
$salary= array(
    "ranu"= >20000,
    "Sonia"=>30000
);
```

echo "Salary of Sonia is:". $Salary['sonia']; will display the salary of Sonia.

> **Note:** This would greatly reduce the time and code required displaying a particular value through the use of this associative array. Necessary output would be produced by a simple call to the pairings array.

6.3.2 Multi-Dimensional Indexed Array

Prima facie Multi-dimensional indexed arrays are similar to their single-dimensions counterparts, but more than one index array is used to specify an element. As such dimension size is of no limit but it unlikely that anything beyond three dimensions would be used in most applications.

Syntax of a multi-dimensional array is:

```
$ename[index1] [index2]..[indexN];
```

An element of a two-dimensional indexed array could be referenced as follows:

```
$eposition = $checks[5][5];
```

6.3.3 Multi-Dimensional Associative Array

Multidimensional associative arrays are also possible and quite useful in PHP.

Example 2: Creating multi-dimensional associative arrays

```
$smarks=array(
    "ranu "=> array
    (   "DBMS"=>88,
        "OS"=>80,
        "DS"=.900,
    ),
    "Sonia" => array
    (   "DBMS"=>70,
        "OS"=>79,
        "DS"=>88
    )
);
```

The objects and Boolean data types will be discussed later in this Chapter.

6.4 Various operations with an Array

Various Operations with an array are:

1. Accessing values of multi-dimensional array

   ```
   Echo " Sonia's marks of DS:";
   ```
   `Echo $emarks['sonia']['DS']. ;` given in a program will display the DS marks of Sonia.

2. Pull values out of an array:

   ```
   $colors = array("white", "red", "green");
   list($c1, $c2) = $colors;
   print("$c1 and $c2"); // prints "white and red".
   ```

3. Delete from an array:

   unset(`$colors[1]`); // $colors now contains white and green at indexes 0 and 2.

4. To extract array keys and values:

   ```
   $state = array_keys($capital); // $state is ("CO")
   $citie = array_values($capital); // $citie is ("Denver")
   ```

5. Treat an array like a stack:

   array_push(`$heroe, 'He Man'`); // Pushed onto end of array

   `$h = `**array_pop**(`$heroe`); // Pops off last element (He Man)

6. To calculate size of an array:

   `$n_items = `**count**(`$colors`); // returns 3

7. To sort an array:

   sort(`$colors`); // Now colors are in alphabetical order (lowest to highest)

   rsort(`$colors`); // Reverse alphabetical order (highest to lowest)

Test Your Progress
1. What is an array?
2. What do you understand by multi-dimensional Array?
3. What are different operations one can perform with an array?

6.5 Objects

An object must be explicitly declared contrary to the other data types contained in the PHP language. This can act as a template for creating objects having specific characteristics and functionality. Therefore, before an object is declared a class must be defined. An example of class declaration and subsequent object instantiation follows:

```
class abc
{
    var power;
    function set_power($on_off)
    {
        $this->power = $on_off;
    }
}

$blender = new appliance;
```

6.5.1 Boolean Data Type

The Boolean data type returns only two values True and false.

An example of Boolean variable is as given below.

```
        if ($sum == 10) :
```

Either value true or false is evaluated. $sum is either equal to 10, or it does not. If $sum does equal 10, then the expression is evaluate to true. Otherwise, the result is false. Boolean values can also be determined as given below.

Example 3: Determining the Boolean values using if statement

```
$flag = true;
if ($flag == true) :
print "Flag is true";
else :
print "Flag is false";
endif;
```

It prints the appropriate statement. If the variable $flag has been set to true, otherwise, an alternative statement is printed. 1 and 0 are also used to represent true and false. The above given example can be restated as given bellow.

```
$flag = 1;
if ($flag == true) :
print "The flag is true";
else :
print "The flag is false";
endif;
```

Test Your Progress

1. *Describe data type used in PHP with examples.*
2. *What do you understand by an object?*
3. *Write code to sort an array in PHP.*

6.6 Identifiers

An identifier is a general term used for various other user-defined objects, variables, and functions. Some of the properties, PHP identifiers must abide by are:

● An identifier may have one or more characters and should begin with an alphabetical character or an underscore. An identifier may only consist of letters, numbers, underscore, and other ASCII characters from 127 to 255.

Some of the examples are given below.

Valid	Invalid
`sum_function`	This&that
`size !counter`	
`_abc 5ward`	

● Identifiers are case-sensitive. Therefore, a variable `$city` is different from variables `$city`, `$nAme`, or `$namE`.

● Identifiers can be any length.

● A name of identifier can not be identical to any of PHP's predefined keywords.

Test Your Progress
1. *What are identifiers in PHP?*
2. *Write down naming rules for PHP identifiers.*
3. *Give example of valid and invalid identifiers.*

6.7 Operators

Different operators in PHP are:

Operator	Purpose
( )	Precedence ordering
`new`	Object instantiation
! ~	Boolean NOT, bitwise NOT
++ −	Auto increment, auto decrement
@	Error concealment
/ * %	Division, multiplication, modulus
+ − .	Addition, subtraction, concatenation
<< >>	Shift left, shift right (bitwise)
< <= > >=	Less than, less than or equal to, greater than, greater than or equal to
== != === <>	Is equal to, is not equal to, identical to, is not equal to
& ^ |	Bitwise AND, bitwise XOR, bitwise OR
&& ||	Boolean AND, boolean OR
?:	Ternary operator

Following are some examples:

$ABC = 9; // It assign integer value 9 to the variable $ABC

$ABC = "9"; // It assign string value "9" to the variable $ABC

$city = "Mumbai"; // assign "Mumbai" to the variable $city

$sum++; // increment the variable $sum by 1

6.7.1 Operator Precedence

Precedence of operator is a characteristic of operators that determines the order in which they will evaluate the surrounding operands surrounding. The standard precedence rules used in elementary school math class is followed by PHP. Let's consider a few examples:

$total_cost = $cost + $cost * 0.06;

is the same as writing:

$total_cost = $cost + ($cost * 0.06);

The addition operator has lesser precedence than the multiplication operator.

Test Your Progress
1. *Discuss some PHP operators.*
2. *What do you understand by operator precendece?*
3. *Solve following statement using Operator precendence:*
$net_cost =$cost + ($cost*10)

6.8 Comments

Comments can be given in the following three ways:

```
// for single line comment
# for single line comment
/* for multiple lines comments */
```

Test Your Progress
1. *Describe various ways of writing comments in PHP.*
2. *How can you write single line comments in PHP?*
3. *Give an example of Multi-line comment.*

6.9 Control Structures

Following are some control structures available:

1. if, else, elseif
2. while, do-while
3. for, foreach
4. switch, break, continue

6.9.1 `if...else`

The `if` statement is a selection statement which evaluates an expression and based on the truth or falsehood of the expression, will (or will not) execute a block of code.

Following is the structure:

```
if (expression)
{
    statement block
}
```

6.9.2 `if...elseif`

Let us discuss the following example.

```
if ($a > 0)
$b= 5; // {} is not needed for only one statement
```

if else

```
if (expression)
{
    statement block
}
else
{
    statement block
}
```

Let us discuss an example given below.

```
if ($a) { // It tests if $a is true or non-zero or a non-
empty string
    print($a);
    $a++;
}
else
print($b);
```

elseif

The `elseif` statement provides further level of evaluation for `if` control structure, adding depth to the number of expressions that may be evaluated:

```
if (expression)
{
    block of statement
}
elseif (expression)
{
```

```
      block of statement
}
```

Let us discuss the following example.

```
if ($x > $y)
print "x is bigger than y";
elseif ($x == $y) // use "elseif" or "else if"
print "x is equal to y";
else
print "x is smaller than y";
```

Multiple Expression Evaluation

Several expressions in a control structure can be simultaneously evaluated.

```
if ($a == 0)
{
    echo "a equals 0";
}
elseif ($a == 1)
{
    echo "a equals 1";
}
elseif ($a == 2)
{
    echo "a equals 2";
}
```

6.9.3 while Loop

To repetitively execute syntax included in the loop, while structure is used. The number of iterations of the statement block depends on the number, the expression evaluates to true.

Structure of the while loop:

while (expression):

```
block of statement
```

endwhile;

Let us consider the following example:

```
while ($n < 20)
{
    print("$n ");
    $n++;
}
endwhile
```

6.9.4 `do...while`

A `do...while` structure works in the same way as the `while` structure does not the only difference is that the expression is evaluated at the end. This loop will always execute at least once, and a `while` loop may not execute at all if the condition is first evaluated before entering the loop is false.

```
do :
block of statement
while (expression);
```

Example below shows how `do...while` loop works.

```
do
{
    print("$n ");
    $n++;
}
while ($n <10);
```

6.9.5 `for` Loop

The only difference from the `while` loop is in the way fact that the iterative value is updated in the statement itself.

```
for (initialization; condition; increment )
{
    statement block
}
```

Let us discuss the following example:

```
for ($i = 1; $i < 10; $i++)
print("$i ");
```

6.9.6 `foreach`

Syntax:

```
foreach (array_expression as $val)
Statement
foreach (array_expression as $key=>val)
Statement
```

Let us discuss the example given below.

```
foreach(array(1,2,3,) as &$val)
{
    $val = $val * 5;
}
print("$val<br />"); // It prints all the three values in
order.
```

6.9.7 `switch`, `break`, `continue`

switch

The switch statement is used to select one of many given blocks of code to be executed. The default statement is used if no match is found.

```
switch ($i)
{
    case 0:
        echo "i equals 0";
        break;
    case 1:
        echo "i equals 1";
        break;
    case 2:
        echo "i equals 2";
        break;
    default:
    echo "no match is found";
}
```

break

To exit out from the `while`, `for`, or `switch` structure, `break` is used.

Syntax:

```
break n;
```

The n in the `break` statement denotes how many levels of control structures will be terminated. Let us say, if a break statement is nested within two `while` statements, both `while` statements would be exited, if the `break` statement is preceded by 2, one of then would contain the default value of *n*.

continue

Control goes at beginning, by execution of a continue in an iterative loop and will bypass the rest the statement. The syntax of `continue` is given below.

```
continue n;
```

Test Your Progress

1. What is difference between `while` and `do..while` loop?
2. Describe `for` loop with example.
3. How to define `break` statement with switch structure?

6.10 Functions

A section of code with a specific purpose that is assigned a unique name is called function. It can be called at various points in a program whenever required and it allows function name to be repeatedly executed as needed. The advantage of function is that the section of code is written only once and can be easily modified whenever required.

6.10.1 Function Definition and Invocation

PHP function can be created in a program at any point of time. For the organizational purposes, at the very top, the script file exists. It is convenient to place all functions intended for use in a script. To promote code reuse and reduce redundancy, the functions are placed in a separate file (also known as a *library*). In this way without having redundant copies and thus risk errors due to rewriting, functions can be repeatedly use in various applications.

A function definition generally consists of three components:

- The function name.
- An optional set of comma-delimited input parameters are enclosed within parentheses.
- The function's body is, enclosed in curly brackets { }.

General form of a PHP function is as under:

```
function function_name (optional $arg1, $arg2, ..., $argn)
{
/*code section*/
}
```

The name of the function should follow the lexical structure conditions as specified in, "Variables and Data Types."

Data type of the input parameters is not needed to specify.

6.10.2 Returning Values from a Functions

Return a value from a function is useful which is done by assigning the function call to a variable. Any type of value can be returned from a function, it also may include lists and arrays.

- Let us assume that a few values have been set, such as some product sales tax, $tax and price, $price.
- Function cost_calculation() is declared. The function accepts two parameters, the tax and price of the product.
- Total cost is to be calculated and return back calculated cast to the caller.
- Call cost_calculation(), value is returned from the function is set to $total_cost.
- A relevant message can be displayed.

A function for calculating sales tax

```
$prod-price = 10;
$tax = .07;
```

```
function cost_calculation($tax, $prod_price)
{
    $sales_tax = $tax;
    return $prod_price + ($prod_price * $sales_tax);
}
```

6.10.3 Recursive Function

A recursive function calls are useful for performing repetitive task. For example, recursively sum of all numbers between 1 and 5.

Example 4: A recursive function to sum numbers between 1 and 5

```
function summation ($count)
{
    if ($count != 0) :
    return $count + summation($count-1);
    endif;
}
$sum = summation(5);
print "Sum = $sum";
```

Execution of the above produces the results as shown below:

Output:

Sum = 15

Speed is improved in a program by using functional iteration (recursion) .

6.10.4 Variable Function

Execution of variable functions is also possible in PHP. A variable function is a dynamic call function. Name of the variable function is determined at the time of execution. Although in the most Web applications, it is not necessary that variable functions may significantly reduce code size and complexity, often eliminating unnecessary if conditional statements.

The form of a variable function is as given below.

```
$function_name();
```

6.10.5 Building of Function Libraries

One of the most efficient ways to save time when building applications are Function libraries. For example, if one has to write function for array, one could use these functions repeatedly in various applications. It is much more convenient to place all relevant sorting functions into a separate file altogether instead of continually rewrite or copy and paste these functions into new scripts.

Example 5: A function library (array_sorting.inc)

```
<?
// file: array_sorting.inc
// A library which contains various functions used for
sorting arrays.
function merge_sort($array, $temparray, $right, $left)
{
    . . .
}
function bubble_sort($array, $n)
{
    . . .
}
function quick_sort($array, $right, $left)
{
    . . .
}
?>
```

Array_sorting.inc, function library, acts as a receptacle for all of array sorting functions. Once custom function library is built, you can use PHP's `include()` and `require()` statements (functions) to include the entire library file to a script, thus making all of the functions available.

Syntax of both statements:

```
include(path/file name);
require(path/file name);
```

Another Syntax for the same:

```
include "path/file name";
require "path/file name";
```

where "`path`" refers to absolute or relative location of the file name.

Assume you want to use the library array_sorting.inc in a script, it could be included in the library, as shown below.

6.10.6 Including a Function Library in a Script

You need to keep the array_sorting.inc library in same folder as script:

```
include ("array_sorting.inc");
// Now you can use any function in array_sorting.inc.
$s_array = (50,11,22, 24);
// make use of the bubble_sort() function
$sorted_array = bubble_sort($s_array, 5);
```

`$_GET, $_POST, $_Request`

User entered data will be transferred to the PHP engine, when a user submit, a form on your Web server, and that will make the submitted data available to your PHP script for processing in pre-defined arrays:

- `$_GET`: An associative array that stores form data submitted with the GET method.

- `$_POST`: An associative array that store form data submitted with the POST method.

- `$_REQUEST`: An associative array which store form data submitted with either GET or POST method. `$_REQUEST` also contains the cookie values received back from the browser.

6.11 File Handling in PHP

Opening and Closing Files

fopen is used to open file in PHP. The command takes two parameters, name of the file which you want to open, and the mode in which the file to be opened. If successful the function returns a file pointer, otherwise it returns zero (false). For example,

```
$fp = fopen("emp.txt", "r");
```

If **fopen** is not able to open the file, it returns 0, which can be used to exit from the function, and a required message can be used. For example

```
if ( !($fp = fopen("emp.txt", "r") ) )
exit("Unable to open the file.");
```

File Modes

The following Rable shows, various modes, in which the file may be opened.

Mode Description

r	Read Only mode, file pointer, at the start of the file.
r+	Read/Write mode, file pointer, at the start of the file.
w	Write Only mode. Truncates the file (effectively overwriting it). fopen() will attempt to create the file, if file does not exist.
w+	Read/Write mode. Truncates the file (effectively overwriting it). If the file doesn not exist, fopen() syntax will attempt to create the file.
a	Append mode, file pointer, at the end of the file. Syntax fopen() will attempt to create the file, if the file doesn't exist.
a+	Read/Append, file pointer, at the end of the file. Syntax fopen() will attempt to create the file, if the file does not exist.

Closing a File

Syntax **fclose()** function closes a file. For example,

```
fclose($fp);
```

Reading from Files

A file can be read by opening in r, r+, w+, and a+ modes. To determine the end of the file function feof() is used. For example,

```
if ( feof($fp) )
echo "End of file reached <br>";
```

The function feof() can also be used in a while loop to read the file until the end of file is reached. **fgets()** function can be use to read a line at a time.

```
while( !feof($fp) )
{
    // It reads one line at a time, maximum up to 254
    characters. Every line ends with a newline.
    // PHP defaults to the length of 1024, if the length
    argument is omitted.
    $XYZ = fgets($fp, 255);
    echo $XYZ;
}
```

To read a single character at a time from a file, function **fgetc()** can be used.

```
while( !feof($fp) )
{
    // Reads a character at a time from the file.
    $c = fgetc($fp);
    echo $c;
}
```

Function **fscanf()** can be used to read a single word at a time from a file. This function can takes number of parameters which may vary, and the first two parameters are mandatory. The file to be handled is the first parameter and the second parameter is a C-style format string.

Example 6: Open a file using feof() function

```
$empFile = emp.txt";
if (!($fp = fopen($empFile, "r")))
exit("Unable to open $empFile.");
while (!feof($fp))
{
    // Assign the variables to optional arguments
    $buffer = fscanf($fp, "%s %s %d", $e_name, $e_title,
    $e_age);
    if ($buffer == 3) // The $buffer contains the number of
    items which it was able to assign.
    print "$e_name $e_title $e_age<br>\n";
}
```

Output:

abc.txt:

Ranu programmer 44

Illa designer 22

Sonu designer 29

Roma programmer 29

Variables can also be stored in an array, if we omit the optional parameters in **fscanf()**.

```
while (!feof($fp))
{
    $buffer = fscanf($fp, "%s %s %d"); // for Assigning
    variables to an array
    // It use list function to move the variables from the
    array into variables
    list($name, $title, $age) = $buffer;
    print "$name $title $age<br>\n";
}
```

Function **fread()** can be used to read the entire file. From a file it reads a number of bytes or till the end of the file (whatever comes first).

The function **filesize()** returns size of the file in bytes, and it can be used with the function **fread()**.

Let us consider the following example:

```
empFile = "emp.txt";
if (!($fp = fopen($empFile, "r")))
exit("Notable to open the input file, $empFile.");
$buffer = fread($fp, filesize($empFile));
echo "$buffer<br>\n";
fclose($fp);
```

The **file()** function can be used to read the entire contents of a file into an array rather than using **fopen()** to open a file.

```
$array = file('emp.txt');
```

From the file, each array element contains one line, where new line is used to terminate the reading the file.

Writing to Files

The function **fwrite()** is used to write a string. It can also be used for writing part of a string to a file. The function takes three parameters i.e. the file to be handled, the string to be written, and the number of bytes to be written. If the number of bytes is omitted, the whole string is written to the file. If the lines to be appeared on separate lines in the file, use the \n character. Windows requires the carriage return character as well as a new line character, terminate the string with \r\n.

Test Your Progress
1.   *Explain various file modes in PHP.*
2.   *Explain* fopen() *and* fread() *with example.*
3.   *Explain* fwrite() *function with example.*

6.12 Running PHP through XAMPP

XAMPP implies Cross-Platform (X), Apache (A), MySQL (M), PHP (P) and Perl (P).

XAMPP is a simple, lightweight Apache distribution. It includes everything to create a Web server application- (Apache), database (MySQL), and scripting language (PHP). It works equally well on Linux, Mac and Windows, it is called cross-platform.

XAMPP includes following four components:

1. **Apache**: It is a Web server application through which Web content to a computer can be processed and delivered.

2. **MySQL:** Every Web application needs a database for storing collected data. MySQL is not only open source but also world's most popular database management system.

3. **PHP:** It is server-side scripting language that powers some of the most popular Websites in the world which includes Facebook and WordPress. It is an open source.

4. **Perl:** Perl is a high-level and dynamic programming language. It is used

extensively in network programming, system administration, etc.

Many versions of XAMPP include additional component, such as phpMyAdmin, OpenSSL (open source implementation of cryptographic protocols, such as Source Sockets Layer and Transport Layer Security), etc.

Steps to Install XAMPP

Follow these steps for installing XAMPP:

1. Start the installation process by double-clicking on the XAMPP installer. You need to click 'Next' after the splash screen.

2. Either select the components you want to install or choose the default selection and click 'Next'.

3. Just choose the folder where you want to install XAMPP. Now this folder will hold all the Web application files.

Testing XAMPP Installation

Check out the installation of XAMPP by following these steps:

1. In the XAMPP control panel, click on 'Start' under 'Actions' for the Apache module, which instructs XAMPP for starting the Apache Web server.

2. Open the Web browser and then type in: http://localhost or 127.0.0. The XAMPP home page on the screen will be appeared

Test Your Progress
1. *What is XAMPP?* 2. *Explain XAMPP installation process.*

6.13   Key Terms

6.14   Summary

PHP was developed by Lerdorf in 1995. The original meaning of the acronym is 'Personal Home Page'. It is the most popular language and environment in use on the Web today. PHP is server-side scripting system. Its syntax is based on Perl, Java, and C. It is very good for creating dynamic content. PHP, a very powerful language, is able to access files, commands are executed and network connections can be opened on the server. It can be included whether in a Web server as a module or executed as a separate CGI binary. Now it is under the Apache Software Foundation. It is free and licensed under the GPL. It is available on a variety of Web servers (ISS, Apache, NGINX, etc.) and operating systems (Linux, Windows, Mac, UNIX, OS X, etc.). Various databases supported by PHP are: MySQL, Oracle, ODBC (for Microsoft Access and SQL Server), SQLite, etc. PHP is a interpreter-based scripting language. PHP file may contain HTML tags, text and script. PHP provides support for general six data types: string, integers, floating point numbers, boolean arrays, objects. Variable of PHP always starts with $ and variable name begin with letter or underscore. It can be composed of numbers, underscore and letter. An identifier is a general term used for variables, functions, and various other user-defined objects, PHP uses some control structures: if, else, elseif, while, do-while, for, foreach, switch, break, continue. A function is a section of code that has a specific purpose. A variable function is a dynamic call for a function. Name of a variable function is determined at the time of execution. XAMPP implies Cross-Platform (X), Apache (A), MySQL (M), PHP (P) and Perl (P). XAMPP is a simple, lightweight Apache distribution. It includes everything to create a Web erver application - (Apache), database (MySQL), and scripting language (PHP). It is called cross-platform as it works equally well on Linux, Mac and Windows.

Do you Know?

Rasmus Lerdorf, founder of PHP was born in 22 November 1968 (age 45) in the Qeqertarsuaq, Green Land. His Alma Mater is University of Waterloo. He has worked as a Distinguished egineer, Etsy. His Website is http://lerdorf.com.

6.15 Test Yourself

Section I: Exercise

1. Explain PHP data types with example.
2. Write following code using PHP switch case.

```
if ($i == 0)
{
    echo "i equals 0";
}
elseif ($i == 1)
{
    echo "i equals 1";
}
    elseif ($i == 2)
{
    echo "i equals 2";
}
```

3. Explain various loops used in PHP.

4. Describe various types of arrays in PHP with example.

5. Write a short note on variable scope in PHP functions.

Section II: Review with Ease

1. What is PHP?

   The original meaning of the acronym is 'Personal Home Page'. PHP is an open source server-side scripting language that is used for the Web development. Dynamically generated Web pages are allowed by PHP to be written efficiently and quickly. Syntax of PHP is based on Perl, Java, and C. It is very good for creating dynamic content. It is now under the Apache Software Foundation.

2. What is the difference between `echo()` and `print()` functions?

   `echo()` and `print()` are are used to output strings. Both the statements have almost same speed.

   Multiple expressions can be taken by `echo()` while multiple expressions cannot be taken by `print()`. True or false are returned by `print()` function based statement on its success or failure while true or false are not returned by echo() function.

3. Write difference between $city and $$city in PHP.

   $city is a variable with a fixed name. $$city is a variable whose name is stored in $city.

   If $city contains "Delhi", $$city is the same as $Delhi.

4. What is a Session in PHP?

   Sessions allow data to be transferred from one page to another page. Information about session is temporary and until the user is using the Website, information is valid. A unique ID, UID to each visitor is assign by a session.

   A session of PHP session is started by using:

   ```
   <?php session_start(); ?>
   ```

5. Describe associative array with example.

   An array is associative array in which a value is associated with each ID key. For example,

   ```
   $e_ages = array("sonia"=>25, " ranu"=>35);
   ```

Section III Practice with Ease for Examination

Chapter 7
ASP.NET and JSP

7.1　Introduction to ASP.NET

ASP.NET server-side technology that gives users to build Web applications. It is syntax compatible with Active Server Pages (ASP). It helps you to develop dynamic and robust Web application. .NET framework allows the features of the advanced to ASP.NET by providing Common Language Runtime (CLR), such as inheritance, type safety, and language interoperability therefore code can be written in a different version. It is a great extent to ASP having the support for XML, controls and various services.

7.1.1　ASP.NET Framework and Application Development

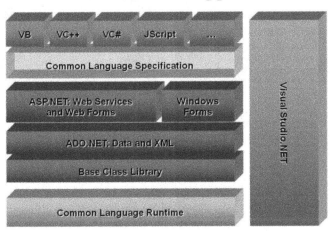

Figure 7.1: ASP.NET Framework

.NET Web application framework developed by Microsoft which is group of several technologies that helps the developers to create different type of applications. .NET Framework is the successor to Microsoft's Active Server Pages (ASP) technology, and was first released in January, 2002.

ASP.NET Framework provides components (See Figure 7.1):

- .NET Languages
- Common Language runtime
- .NET Class Library
- Engine that hosts the Web
- Visual studio as development tool

ASP.NET Web pages provide a dynamic support and solution as these Web forms contained in files with a ".aspx"; this contains HTML, and server-side Web controls.

- Boolean Conditions
- Automatic Garbage Collection
- Properties and events
- Delegated and Event Management
- Indexers
- LINQ and LAMBDA expression
- Generics
- Conditional Compilations

7.1.2 Building and Running the Applications using ASP.NET

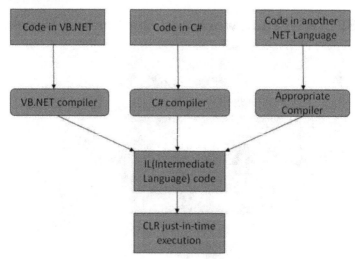

Figure 7.2: Compiling and Running the Applications using ASP.NET

When a building a new project in Web Application through ASP.NET C# that contains a default set of files with name <default.aspx> which is set as default to execute but you can modify the startup page by configuring of Startup project

For application the **Run** command in toolbar or the **Project** menu, or by pressing **F5** function key. This compiles application and loads it up in default Web browser. Figure 7.2 shows how code is compiled and executed in ASP.NET applications, like all .NET applications.

Two stages of compilation of .NET Framework:

1.   The C# codes written and first compiled into an intermediate language which is called Microsoft Intermediate Language (MSIL). This compilation automatically runs when the page is first requested to server.

2.   Then code in Intermediate Language is compiled into low-level native machine code and process known as Just-in-Time (JIT) compilation. By having compiling stages, we can generate a compiled assembly with .NET code and divide this to more than one platform in your Web applications and services. Figure 7.2 shows the two-step compilation process.

7.2   Steps to Install PWS

7.2.1   Installing Personal Web Server (PWS) on Windows 98

Personal Web Server is in built-feature of Windows : Windows 95, 98, and NT. PWS for developing and testing Web applications including ASP for dynamic server support to localhost.

1.   Insert Windows 98 CD in drive.

2.   Explore CD-ROM Drive.

3.   Open "add-ons" folder, open "pws" folder, run "setup.exe".

4.   Install "Personal Web Server".

After installation of PWS, there is PWS icon on your desktop and "Start PWS". To check the PWS is running or not, open your Internet Explorer go to URL and enter http://127.0.0.1. Now PWS is opened.

7.2.2   To Install IIS on Windows

How to Install IIS on Windows XP and Windows 2000

Follow these steps to install IIS:

1. On the Start menu, click Settings and select Control Panel
2. Double-click Add or Remove Programs
3. Click Add/Remove Windows Components
4. Click Internet Information Services (IIS)
5. Click Details
6. Select the check box for World Wide Web Service, and click OK
7. In Windows Component selection, click Next to install IIS

After you have installed IIS, make sure you install all patches for bugs and security problems. (Run Windows Update).

Figure 7.3 shows the connection between IIS (Web Server) and application domain. .NET introduces the concept of an application domain which acts as a container fox code and data, and boundary (a process).

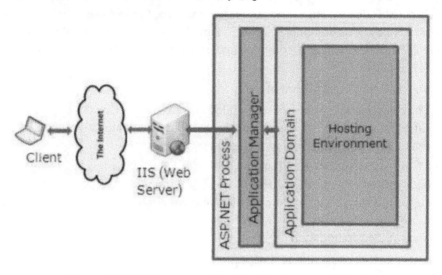

Figure 73: IIS Server on Hosting Environment Windows

How to Install IIS on Windows 7 and Windows Vista

Follow these steps to install IIS:

1. Open the Control Panel from the Start menu
2. Double-click Programs and Features
3. Click "Turn Windows features on or off" (a link to the left)
4. Select the check box for Internet Information Services (IIS), and click OK

After you have installed IIS, make sure you install all patches for bugs and security problems. (Run Windows Update).

7.3   Basic Syntax

a.   As per syntax rules for ASP follows the HTML tags to be defined opening and closing % mark within starting and ending tags <>.

b.   Syntax for creating Web controls is given below:

```
Default.aspx  X
Client Objects & Events                                          ▾   (No Events)
    <%@ Page Title="Home Page" Language="C#" MasterPageFile="~/Site.master" AutoEventWireup="true"
        CodeBehind="Default.aspx.cs" Inherits="WebApplication1._Default" %>

    <asp:Content ID="HeaderContent" runat="server" ContentPlaceHolderID="HeadContent">
    </asp:Content>
    <asp:Content ID="BodyContent" runat="server" ContentPlaceHolderID="MainContent">
        <h2>
            Welcome to ASP.NET!
        </h2>
        <p>
            To learn more about ASP.NET visit <a href="http://www.asp.net" title="ASP.NET Website">www.asp.net</a>.
        </p>
        <p>
            You can also find <a href="http://go.microsoft.com/fwlink/?LinkID=152368&amp;clcid=0x409"
                title="MSDN ASP.NET Docs">documentation on ASP.NET at MSDN</a>.
        </p>
    </asp:Content>
```

7.3.1 ASP Page Life Cycle

Figure 7.4 illustrates ASP.NET page life cycle which specifies how ASP.NET processes pages to produce dynamic output using a hierarchical tree of all the controls on the page.

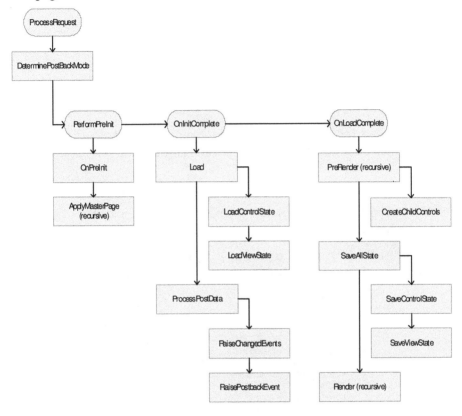

Figure 7.4: Life Cycle of ASP

ASP.NET RAZOR: Embedding server code into ASP.NET Web pages is done by RAZOR as simple markup. RAZOR has the powerful features of traditional ASP.NET

ASP.NET File extensions:

i.   ASP.NET files with RAZOR C# syntax(.cshtml)

ii. ASP.NET files with RAZOR VB syntax (.vbhtml)

7.3.2 Application State

Figure 7.5 shows the hierarchy of state management in ASP.NET which overcomes the limitation of traditional Web programming and helps you preserve data using features, such as View State, Hidden fields, Query strings, Control State etc.

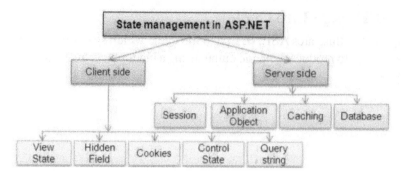

Figure 7.5: Hierarchy of State Management in ASP.NET

There is a **lazy initialization** for creating the application domain when the request is received by server. The categories of Application life cycle in several stages. These can be:

● *Step 1:* User first requests the resource from the Web server.

● *Step 2:* Application receives first request from the application.

● *Step 3:* Application objects are created.

● *Step 4:* An HTTP Application object is assigned.

● *Step 5:* And the request is processed by the HTTP Application (a base class which defines the methods, properties and events).

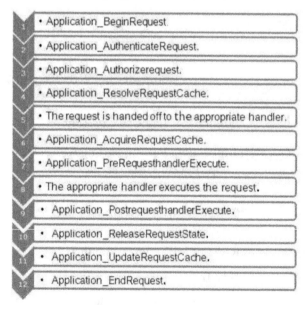

Figure 7.6: State of Applications

Figure 7.6 shows the HTTP Application Events which use members to raise events (client machine), and are handled at the server machine. For example, Authorize

Request event occurs when a security module has verified the user authorization.

7.3.3 Cookies in ASP

Cookie is used to identify the user. It is a file that server embeds on the user's computer. Clients or users request a page with a browser and it will send the cookie with ASP.

Cookies is to be used

- For authentication,
- User's preferences,
- Identification of a user session,
- Shopping cart contents.
- For travelling of the data from one page to other.

```
protected void Button1_Click1(object sender, EventArgs e)
{

    //First Way
    HttpCookie StudentCookies = new HttpCookie("StudentCookies");
    StudentCookies.
}
```

| Domain |
| Equals |
| Expires |
| GetHashCode |
| GetType |
| HasKeys |
| HttpOnly |
| Name |
| Path |

HttpCookie class has a list of some properties, let us outline them.

- Domain: It contains the domain of the cookie.
- Expires: It contains the expiration time of the cookie.
- HasKeys: It contains True if the cookie has subkeys.
- Name: It contains the name of the cookie.
- Path: It contains the virtual path to submit with the cookie.
- Secure: It contains True if the cookie is to be passed in a secure connection only.
- Value: It contains the value of the cookie.
- Values:

7.3.4 Form Validation

There is a group of Web controls that enable us to perform form validation.

i.   CompareValidator uses to validate the data in a form for a fixed value or other form field.

ii. CustomValidator enables to validate the data by using a custom subroutine.

iii.   `RangeValidator` provides validate data in a form field against a minimum and maximum values.

iv.   `RegularExpression` Validator validates the data against a regular expression.

vi.   `ValidationSummary` that displays a summary of validation error messages on a page.

Figure 7.7 illustrates the flowchart of validation trigger process of client-side and server-side. The ASP.NET validation controls validate the input (from user side) which ensure that unauthenticated data will not get stored.

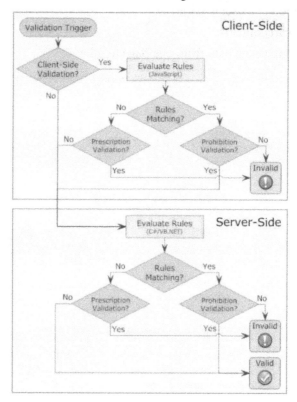

Figure 7.7: Validation Trigger Process in Client-Side and Server-Side

7.4   Introduction to Classic ASP vs ASP.NET

Active Server pages which is known as Classic ASP, introduced in 1998 as Microsoft's first server-side scripting engine.

1.   ASP.NET pages are compiled pages, that makes them faster than Classic ASP.

2.   ASP.NET is advanced generation technique which is not compatible with ASP class, but ASP.NET may include Classic ASP.

3.   User controls in ASP.NET can be used in different languages, including C++ and Java.

4. ASP.NET provides better language support, XML-based components, and integrated user authentication.

ASP.NET Session State:

Session provides functionality to store information on server. It also provides a support to any type of object to store with our own custom objects. For client the session data is stored as per client basis.

Figure 7.8 illustrates the process of mainintaing the client and server sessions.

In ASP.NET, session modes available:

- **InProc**
- **StateServer**
- **SQLServer**
- **Custom**

Figure 7.8: Clients and Web Server Sessions

For every session state the Web.config files in ASP, there is a Session Provider in Web application. Figure 7.9 gives you a brief of session architecure.

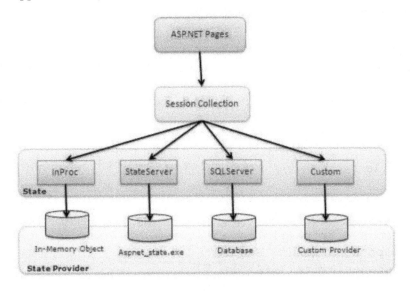

Figure 7.9: Session state architecture

#include Directive:

With this #include Directive this is possible to add the content of ASP file into another ASP file before the server executes.

The #include directive is used to create header, functions, footers, or elements that will be reused on multiple pages.

Syntax for Including Files:

```
<!-#include file ="somefilename"->
```

The included files are inserted before the scripts are executed.

Using loops in ASP.NET:

Loop uses when run the same statements repeatedly.

In ASP. NET various kinds of loops used :

FOR loop is used for counting up or counting down.

Example 1: Displaying 1, 2, 3, 4, 5, using For loop

```
Set the loop to execute 5 times (1, 2, 3, 4, 5)
The counter variable is incremented by one each time.
Dim Counter as Integer
For Counter = 1 To 5
Response. Write( "The loop Counter value is " & Counter
& "<br>")
Next
```

While loop is typically used to add, subtract from a variable used for counting.

Example 2: Executing 1, 2, 3, 4, 5, 6, 7 using while loop

```
Set Counter as 4
Counter = 4
'Set the loop to execute 7 times ( 1, 2, 3, 4, 5, 6, 7 )
while Counter <= 4
Response.Write ("The value of the loop counter is " & Counter
& "<br>")
'Increment value of variable by two
Counter = Counter + 3
End While
<%
    Dim i as integer = 1
    While (i<=90)
    response.Write(i)
    response.Write(". Shahid")
    response.Write("<BR>")
    i= i + 1
End While
%>
```

For Each loop is used when we work with a collection or an array.

Example: For Each loop through the array

```
Dim Dog As String
'Create array
Dim MyPets(1) As String
MyPets(0) = "Rocky"
MyPets(1) = "Jacky"
'Loop through the array collection
For Each Dog In MyPets
    Response.Write(Pets & "<br>")
Next
```

7.4.1 ASP Application Object

The feature provided with Application object is used to bind the files together for performing various purposes.

It is like the Session object, the Application object uses to store and access variables from any page.

This Application object holds information which can be used by pages in the application like in database connection information.

7.4.2 Generating Web Application

a. ASP.NET Web forms can be built on CLR and provide runtime managed execution and inheritance.

b. ASP.NET Web forms maintain state of page and controls between requests are managed with session of state management.

c. This will provide an extensible model that develops own control or add third party controls to the application.

d. Web forms provide a rich set of server controls that having functionality required for a Web application with built-in server controls.

7.4.4 Store and Retrieve Application

The variables can be stored and retrieved by any page in an application by following.

a. Create Application variables in "World.asa" like this:

Code:

```
<script language="vbscript" runat="server">
Sub Application_OnStart
application("vartime")=""
application("users")= 3
End Sub
</script>
```

Created Application: "vartime" and "users".

b. Accesing these variable:

There are active connections.

```
<%Response.Write(Application("customers")) %>
```

Questions based on ASP.NET :

Q1. What is an "interpreted" scripting language?

Q2. By giving any typical example, show the difference between the application variable and the session variable.

Q3. Explain any three advantages that, why session causes performance issue for heavy traffic sites ?

Q4. How can you be able to work and develop program in ASP.NET?

Q5. ASP server scripts are surrounded by delimiters. Why?

Q6. How do you write "Hello Mam" in ASP? Explain it with the help of coding.

Q7. Explain session state architecture in ASP.NET.

7.5 JSP

7.5.1 Introduction

Java Server Page (JSP) is a server-side programming technology that enables the creation of platform-independent and dynamic method for developing Web-based applications. JSP is mainly used for developing Web pages that include dynamic content. Not like a plain HTML page, which includes only static content that always remains the same, a JSP page can modify its content based on any number of changeable items, including identity of the user, the user's browser type, data made available by the user, and selections made by the user. JSP can use the entire family of Java APIs, even the JDBC API to access enterprise databases.

JSP elements can be used for a variety of purposes, such as accessing information from a database or registering user preferences. When a user requests for a JSP page, the server will execute the JSP elements, combines the results with static parts of the page, and sends the dynamically constructed page back to the browser.

Pages of Java server allow special tag and embeded the Java code to the HTML files. These embedded tags and codes will be processed by the Web server to dynamically produce a standard HTML page for the browser.

JSP and HTTP

JSP specification extends the idea of Java servlet API, to provide a robust framework to developers of Web applications for creating dynamic Web content. Currently, JSP or servlet technology supports only HTTP. However, a developer may extend the idea of servlet or JSP to implement other protocols, such as FTP, or SMTP. Since JSP uses HTML, XML, and Java Code, the applications are fast, secure, and independent of server platforms.

Features of JSP

JSP provides an ideal platform for developing Web applications conveniently. It supports various features that make Web application development easy.

Some of these features are:

1. **Platform and Server Independence**

   As JSP is Java based, so it supports "write once, run anywhere" rule according to which JSP Technology can run on various Web servers including Apache, WebSphere, WebLogic etc and various tools from different vendors.

2. **Environment**

   JSP Technology lets user separate presentation logic from business logic by accessing component from layout. This is done using Java Beans technology with JSP.

3. **Extensible JSP Tags**

   JSP uses various scripting tags to create a dynamic Web page for user. It can even extend the existing tags available. Through JSP you can create a custom tag libraries, so that even more functionality can be included.

4. **Reusability Across Platform**

   JSP pages can collaborate with components such as EJB, Java Beans, or custom JSP tags, which are reusable. These reusable components help in keeping the page simple and thus run fast.

5. **Easier Maintenance**

   JSP Applications are easier to maintain. This is because JSP is component based and therefore components are easier to update and revise as compared to scripting. As JSP make applications platform independent, therefore these applications are easily upgraded and switched without affecting the usability of end users.

7.5.2 Need of JSP

In the starting days of the Web, the Common Gateway Interface (CGI) was the only tool for developing dynamic Web pages. But CGI is not an efficient method. For every request that is generated, the operating system in the Web server has to create a new process, load an interpreter and corresponding script, execute the script, and then scrap that process all down again. This becomes very expensive for the server and does not scale well when the amount of traffic increases.

Numerous CGI substitutes and improvements, such as mod_perl from Apache, FastCGI, ISAPI from Microsoft, NSAPI from Netscape, and Java Servlets from Sun Microsystems, have been produced over the years. While these solutions provide improved scalability and performance, all these technologies go through a common problem: they create Web pages by inserting HTML directly in programming language code. This forces the creation of dynamic Web pages exclusively into the sphere of programmers. JSP, however, modifies all that.

JSP tackles the problem from the other direction. Instead of inserting HTML in programming code, JSP lets you insert special active elements into HTML pages. These elements look analogous to HTML elements, but at the back they are componentized Java programs that the server executes when a user sends request for the page.

7.5.3 Advantages of JSP

Following are the list of advantages of JSP over the other technologies:

a. **Vs. Active Server Pages (ASP):** Advantages of the JSP are two fold. Firstly, Java is used for writing the dynamic part, not Visual Basic or other Microsoft specific language, that is why it is more powerful and easier to use. Secondly, its portatobility to the other operating systems, and non-Microsoft Web servers.

b. **Vs. Pure Servlets:** It is easy to write and modify regular HTML rather than to have plenty of `"println"` statements that generate the HTML.

c. **Vs. Server-Side Includes (SSI):** It is intended for simple inclusions, and not for "real" programs, which use form input, create database connections, and like.

d. **Vs. JavaScript:** It dynamically generates HTML on the client but, it hardly interacts with Web server, for the complex jobs, such as image processing and database access, etc.

e. **Vs. Static HTML:** Regular HTML cannot have dynamic information, but JSP can have.

7.5.4 JSP Engines

It is clear that to process JSP pages, a JSP engine is needed. This JSP Engine is typically connected with a Web server or can be integrated inside a Web server or an application server. Many such servers are freely available and can be downloaded for evaluation and/or development of Web applications. Some of them are Tomcat, Oracle iPlanet Web Server, WebLogic, and WebSphere.

Once you have downloaded and installed a JSP-capable Web server or application server in your machine, you need to know where to place the JSP files and how to access them from the Web browser using the URL. We shall use the Tomcat JSP engine from Apache to test our JSP pages.

1. **Tomcat**

    TOMCAT implements servlet 2.2 and JSP 1.1 specifications. It is easy to install and can be used small stand-alone server for developing and testing servlets and JSP pages. For large applications, it is integrated into the Apache Web Server. Appropriate version of Tomcat can be downloaded from the Apache site http://tomcat.apache.org.

    In this book Tomcat is used for testing examples.

2. **Oracle iPlanet Web Server**

Oracle iPlanet Web server, (formerly Sun Java system Web server) by Oracle is a leading Web server that delivers secure infrastructure for medium and large business technologies and applications. Oracle claims that it delivers 8x better performance than Apache 2.0 with Tomcat. It is obtainable on all major operating systems and supports a wide range of technologies, such as JSP, PHP, Java Servlet technologies, and CGI.

3. **WebLogic**

WebLogic by BEA Systems of San Jose, California, is J2EE application server and also an HTTP server for Microsoft Windows, UNIX/Linux, and other platforms. WebLogic supports DB2, Oracle, Microsoft SQL Server, and other JDBC-compliant databases. Data mapping functionality and the business process management are also included in WebLogic Server Process Edition.

4. **WebSphere**

IBM attempted to develop a software to set up, operate, and integrate electronic business applications that can work across multiple computing platforms, using Java-based Web technologies. The result is WebSphere Application Server (WAS). It includes both runtime components and the tools that, can be used for developing robust and versatile applications that will run on WAS.

7.5.4 How JSP Works?

7.5.4.1 JSP Architecture

The Web server needs a JSP engine which is nothing but container to process JSP pages. The JSP container is responsible for receiving requests for JSP pages. In this Chapter Apache Web server is used which has a built-in JSP container to support JSP pages development.

A JSP container works along with Web server to offer the runtime environment and other services that JSP needs. It knows how to understand and process the special elements that are part of JSPs.

Figure 7.10 demonstrates the role of JSP container and JSP files in a Web Application.

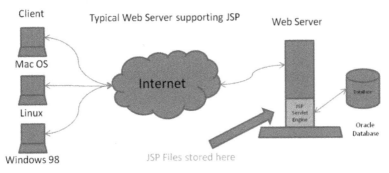

Figure 7.10: JSP Architecture

7.5.4.2 JSP Processing

The following steps demonstrate how the Web server creates the Web page using JSP:

a.   Just like a normal page, user's browser sends an HTTP request to the Web server.

b.   The Web server is able to recognize the HTTP request for the JSP page, and forwards it to the JSP Engine. This uses the URL of JSP page that ends with **.jsp** rather than .html.

c.   JSP engine loads JSP page from the disk and translates it into servlet content. This translation is very straightforward inthat all the template text is converted to the `println( )` statements and all JSP elements are converted to the Java code, that implements the corresponding dynamic behavior of the page.

d.   The JSP engine compiles the servlet into an executable class and forwards the original request to a servlet engine.

e.   A part of the Web server in which servlet engine loads the `Servlet` class and then executes it. After execution, output of this servlet is in HTML format, which the servlet engine forwards to the Web server inside an HTTP response.

f.   The Web server returns HTTP response to user's browser in terms of static HTML content.

g.   Finally Web browser receives the dynamically generated HTML page inside the HTTP response in a way similar to a normal static page.

All the above mentioned steps are shown in the Figure 7.11:

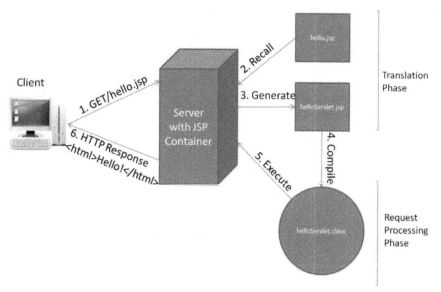

Figure 7.11: JSP Processing

The JSP engine checks to find that servlet for a JSP file exists and whether modification date on the JSP is older than servlet. In case the JSP is older than its generated servlet, the JSP container presumes that the JSP did not change and that the generated servlet is still equivalent to the JSP's contents. This makes the process more efficient and fast than with anyother scripting languages, such as PHP (Hypertext Preprocessor, a recursive backronym).

So it is clear that a JSP page is just another way for writing a servlet without having to be a Java programming proficient. Except for translation phase, JSP page is processed exactly like a regular servlet.

7.5.4.3 *JSP Life Cycle*

JSP life cycle can be defined as a entire process from its creation till the destruction which is same as a servlet life cycle with an additional step, that is required to compile a JSP into servlet.

Paths followed by a JSP are discussed below (See Figure 7.12)

i.   Compilation

ii.   Initialization

iii. Execution

iv.   Cleanup

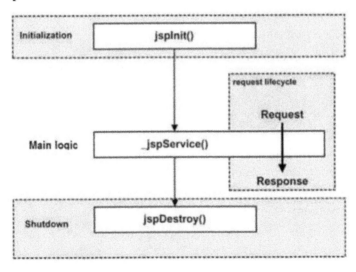

Figure 7.12: Methods used in compiling a JSP into Servlet

javax.servlet.jsp package defines two interfaces:

1.   JSPPage

2.   HttpJspPage

These interfaces define three methods used inside the compiled JSP page. These three methods are:

1.   `jspInit()`

2.   `jspDestroy()`

3.   `_jspService(HttpServletRequest request,`
`HttpServletResponse response)`

The above mentioned methods are available in the compiled JSP file (See Figure 7.12). Programmer can give definition for `jspInit()` and *jspDestroy()* methods, whereas the method *_jspService(HttpServletRequest request, HttpServletResponse response)* is created by the JSP engine.

Four paths are described as below.

i.   **JSP Compilation:**

If the browser asks for a JSP, the JSP engine checks to see whether it is required to compile that page. If the page is to be compiled for the first time, or if the JSP has been changed since it was last compiled, or JSP engine will compile that page.

The compilation process encloses three steps:

1.   Parsing the JSP.

2.   Turning the JSP into a servlet.

3.   Compiling the servlet.

ii.   **JSP Initialization:**

When JSP container loads a JSP it calls the `jspInit()` method before giving service to any request.

```
public void jspInit()
{
    // Initialization code...
}
```

Normally initialization is done only once and as with the servlet `init` method, user generally initializes database connections, open files and generate lookup tables in `jspInit()` method.

iii.   **JSP Execution:**

This phase of the JSP life cycle corresponds to all interactions taking place with requests until the JSP is scraped. When any browser requests for a JSP and page has been loaded and, initialized, JSP engine calls the **_jspService()** method in the JSP.

The `_jspService()` method takes input an **HttpServletRequest** and an **HttpServletResponse** as its arguments as shown below.

```
void _jspService(HttpServletRequest request,
HttpServletResponse response)
{
    // Service handling code...
}
```

The `_jspService()` method of JSP is invoked once for the each request and, it is responsible for generating the response for request and, the method is also responsible for generating the responses to all seven of HTTP methods, i.e., `POST`, `GET`, and `DELETE`, etc.

iv. **JSP Cleanup:**

The destruction phase of JSP life cycle corresponds to a situation when a JSP is being removed from use by a container. The **jspDestroy()** method is basically the JSP equivalent of the destroy method for available servlets. It is mainly overridden to perform any cleanup services, such as closing or opening files or releasing database connections.

The `jspDestroy()` method is written as follows:

```
public void jspDestroy()
{
    // Your cleanup code goes here.
}
```

7.5.5 JSP Application Design

7.5.5.1 Anatomy of JSP Page

A JSP page basically consists of two parts: HTML/XML markups and JSP constructs. A large percent of your JSP page, in many cases, just consists of static HTML/XML components, known as template text. As a consequence, we can create and maintain JSP pages using traditional HTML/XML tools. We use three primary types of JSP constructs in a typical JSP page: directives, scripting elements, and actions.

7.5.5.2 JSP Syntax

The syntax of JSP is almost similar to that of XML. All JSP tags must conform to the following general rules:

1. Tags must have their matching end tags.
2. Attributes must appear in the start tag.
3. Attributes values in the tag must be quoted.

White spaces within the body text of a JSP page are preserved during the translation phase. To use special characters such as ' % ', add a ' \ ' character before it. To use the ' \ ' character, add another ' \ ' character before it.

7.5.5.3 JSP Components

In JSP, components can be divided into four types. These are:

● **Directives**

Using the directives user can import the packages, define the error handling pages or the session information of JSP page.

- **Declarations**

  Declaration tag is used for defining the functions and variables to be used in the JSP.

- **Scriplets**

  Using Scriplet tag user can insert any amount of the valid Java code, and these codes are placed in `_jspService` method by the JSP Engine.

- **Expressions**

  This tag is used to output any expression or data on the generated page. These expressions are automatically converted to string and printed on the output stream.

7.5.5.4 JSP Directives

The JSP directive affects structure of the servlet class. It generally has the form as shown below.

```
<%@ directive attribute="value" %>
```

There are three types of directive tag.

Directive	Description
`<%@ page ... %>`	Defines page dependent attributes, such as error page, scripting language, and the buffering requirements.
`<%@ include ... %>`	Includes a file during translation phase.
`<%@ taglib ... %>`	Declares a tag library, that containing custom actions used in page.

i.   **page Directive:**

Page directive is used for providing instructions to the container which, pertain to the current JSP. Page directives can be coded anywhere inside JSP. Conventionally, page directives are inserted at the top of the JSP.

Following is the fundamental syntax of `page` directive:

```
<%@ page attribute="value" %>
```

ii. **include Directive:**

The directive "`include`" is used to include a file during the translation phase. This directive will direct the container to merge content of the other external files with the current JSP during the translation phase.

Following is the fundamental syntax of `include` directive:

```
<%@ include file="relative url" >
```

iii. **taglib Directive:**

Java server pages API allows to define custom JSP tags which, look as HTML or XML tags and a tag library which is a set of user-defined tags that implement the custom behavior. The directive `taglib` declares that your JSP uses a set of custom tags, specifies location of library and, provides a means for identifying the custom tags in your JSP page.

Following is the fundamental syntax of `taglib` directive:

```
<%@ taglib uri="uri" prefix="prefixOfTag" >
```

7.5.5.5 JSP Declaratives

Syntax of JSP Declaratives is:

```
<%!
//java codes
%>
```

JSP Declaratives begins with `<%!` and ends with `%>`.User can embed any amount of Java code in the JSP Declaratives. Variables and functions which are defined in the declaratives are class level and can be used anywhere in JSP.

Example 4: Incrementing cnt value using ++ operative and `getCount()` method

```
<%@page contentType="text/html" %>
<html>
<body>
<%!
int cnt=0;
private int getCount()
{
    //increment cnt and the value is return
    cnt++;
    return cnt;
}
%>
<p>Values of Cnt are:</p>
<p><%=getCount()%></p>
<p><%=getCount()%></p>
<p><%=getCount()%></p>
<p><%=getCount()%></p>
<p><%=getCount()%></p>
<p><%=getCount()%></p>
</body>
</html>
```

7.5.5.6 JSP Scriplets

Syntax of JSP Scriptles are:

```
<%
//java codes
%>
```

JSP Scriptlets begins with `<%` and ends `%>` .

Example 5:

```
<%
//java codes
String userName=null;
userName=request.getParameter("Name");
%>
```

7.5.5.7 JSP Expressions

Syntax of JSP Expressions are:

```
<%= "Anything"    %>
```

JSP Expressions start with `<%=` and ends with `%>`. Between these symbols user can put anything which will be finally converted to String and displayed on the Web page. For example,

```
<%="Hello JSP World!" %>
```

Above code will display 'Hello JSP World!'.

7.5.5.8 Comments

Comments in JSP are like following:

```
<%- Comment -%>
```

Or

```
<% /*= map.size()*/ %>
```

HTML also provides a method to declare a comment.

```
<!- This is output comment ->
```

7.5.6 Scope of JSP Objects

In a JSP objects may be created using directives, actions, or scriplets. Every object created in a JSP page has a scope. The scope of a JSP object is defined as the availability of that object for use from a particular place of the Web application. There are four types of scopes possible for any object in JSP: request, session, page and application.

i. **Page**

Objects having page scope can be accessed only from within the same page where they were created. JSP implicit objects exception, out, pageContext, response, config, and page have 'page' scope.

ii. **Request**

A request can be served by more than one page. Objects having request scope can be accessed from any page that serves that request. The implicit object request has request scope.

iii. **Session**

Objects having session scope are accessible from the pages, which belong to the same session from where they were created. The implicit object session has the session scope.

iv. **Application**

JSP objects that have the application scope can be accessed from any page that belongs to the same application. Implicit object *application* has this scope.

7.5.6.1 JSP Implicit Objects

JSP sustains nine automatically defined variables, which are also called implicit objects. These variables are:

request	It is **HttpServletRequest** object which is associated with the request.
response	It is **HttpServletResponse** object associated with response to the client.
out	It is the **PrintWriter** object used to send output to the client.
session	It is the **HttpSession** object associated with the request.
application	It is the **ServletContext** object associated with application context.
config	It is the **ServletConfig** object and associated with the page.
pageContext	It encapsulates use of the server-specific features, such as higher performance **JspWriters**.
page	This is a synonym for **this**, and, is used to call the methods defined by translated servlet class.
Exception	The **Exception** object allows exception data to be accessed by the designated JSP.

7.5.6.2 Sharing Data between JSP Pages

All the JSP participate in an HTTP session unless session attribute of the page directive is set to false. An HTTP session is represented by the implicit object *session*. This session object has session scope and is thus shared among all the pages within the session.

This session object can be used as shared repository of information, such as beans and objects among JSP pages of the same session. For example, login.jsp page may store the user name in the session, while the subsequent pages, such as home.jsp can use it. Consider the following code in "login.jsp":

```
String user=request.getParameter("user");
Session.setAttribute("user", user);
```

Now the code inside "home.jsp":

```
String user= (String)session.getAttribute("user");
```

7.5.6.3 Java Bean with JSP

In this section Java Bean will be discussed including one example that illustrates the procedure of handling session and prints a "Hello world" using Java Bean. A

Bean is reusable code, transferable and is platform independent component, which is written in a Java programming language.

In a Bean, for every entity following methods are defined:

1. **getName ( )** - This method is used to return value of the entity which is represented by the Class object as a String.

<jsp.useBean>

1. The next step is to generate a JSP page. Inside this **setName ( )** - used method is to hold value of the Class object as a String.

JSP page, bean is used by **<jsp.useBean>** tag. It is used for locating or instantiates a Java Bean component. An attempt is made for locating an instance of the Bean within the scope.

Attributes used in useBean

1. **id** - This is to identify the Bean in the scope.
2. **scope** - It represents the scope of the Bean. It can be page request, session or the application. Default scope of the Bean is page.

    1. **page:** It specifies that this Bean can be used within the JSP. It is the default scope.
    2. **request:** It specifies that this Bean can be used from any of the JSP that processes the same request. Its scope is wider than page.
    3. **session:** It specifies that this Bean can be used from any of JSP in the same session whether processes same request or not. Its scope is wider than the request.
    4. **application:** It specifies that, this Bean from any JSP in the same application and, has wider scope than the session.
3. **class** - This is used to instantiate the specified bean class.

<jsp.setProperty>

The <jsp:useBean> element has a <jsp:setProperty> element, which is used to set property values in the Bean. Property values can be set in various ways like-

1. Passing all the values which are entered by a user and stored as parameter in request and matches properties of the Bean.
2. Passing for the specific value, such as "Hello" and user enters into a specific property in the Bean.

<jsp:getProperty>

The <jsp:useBean> element has a <jsp:getProperty> element which is used to return the value stored in set property.

The JSP page is saved as the UseBean.jsp. For running this UseBean.jsp, place this file inside TOMCAT HOME\Webapps\UseBean directory and start Tomcat. Once

Tomcat server is started, type this URL in the browser and run application.

Understand with Example

The code given in Example 5 helps to understand the concept of Java Bean. Create a package "my" and then inside this package, define a class "MyBean".

Example 5: Creating MyBean.java and UseBean.jsp files.

MyBean.java

```
package my;
public class MyBean {

    private String name=new String();

    public String getName() {
    return name;
    }
    public void setName(String name) {
    this.name = name;
    }
}
```

UseBean.jsp

```
<html>
<title>Java bean example in jsp</title>
<head>
<h1>Java bean example in jsp</h1>
<hr><hr>
</head>
<body>
<jsp:useBean id="mybean" class="my.MyBean" scope="session">
<jsp:setProperty name="mybean" property="name" value="Hello world"/>
</jsp:useBean>
<h1><jsp:getProperty name="mybean" property="name"/></h1>
</body>
</html>
```

Output:

Java bean example in jsp

Hello world

In this example a package `"bean"` is defined which includes a class `"Employees"`. Inside the class, declare a String variable `FirstName`, `LastName` and `Address`. The `getAddress`, `getFirstName`, `getLastName` return the value from a `bean` in JSP. The JSP uses get property of `bean` and return the value stored in it.

Consider code given in "getproperty.jsp".

Example 6: Creating getproperty.jsp and Employees.java files

```
<html>
<body>
<h1>Get Value from bean</h1>
<jsp:useBean id="emp" class="bean.Employees"/>
<table>
<tr><td>First Name :
<jsp:getProperty name="emp" property="firstName"/>
</td></tr>
<tr><td>Last Name :
<jsp:getProperty name="emp" property="lastName"/>
</td></tr>
<tr><td>Address :
<jsp:getProperty name="emp" property="address"/>
</td></tr>
</table>
</body>
</html>
```

Employees.java

```
package bean;
public class Employees {
    protected String firstName;
    protected String lastName;
    protected String address;
    public String getAddress() {
        address = "Delhi";
        return address;
    }
    public String getLastName() {
        lastName = "Singh";
        return lastName;
    }
    public String getFirstName() {
        firstName = "Komal";
        return firstName;
    }
}
```

Output:

Get Value from bean

First Name : Komal

Last Name : Singh

Address : Delhi

7.5.7 Session Tracking

Since HTTP is a stateless protocol, Web server cannot remember previous requests. Consequently the Web server cannot relate the current request with previous one. This creates problem for some applications that require a sequence of related request-response cycles. Example includes online examination systems, e-mail checking systems, and banking applications. A session ID is a token number that is unique and assigned to a specific user for the duration of that user's session.

a. **Hidden Fields**

In the hidden form fields, the HTML entry will be like this:

```
<input type ="hidden" name = "name" value="">
```

This means, when the form is submitted, then the name and value which are specified will be included in GET or POST method. Along with this, session ID information would be embedded within form as a hidden field, and submitted with the HTTP POST command.

Following is the program where you want to hide the variable.

```
<form action="anotherPage.jsp" method="GET">
<input type="hidden" id="thisField" name="inputName" value="hiddenValue">
<input type="submit">
</form>
```

Then on 'anotherPage.jsp' page you recuperate the value by calling the getParameter(String name) method of the implicit request object:

<% String hidden = request.getParameter("inputName"); %>
The Hidden Value is <%=hidden %>

The output of the above given script will be:

The Hidden Value is hiddenValue

b. **URL Rewriting**

URL rewriting can be used where we do not want to use cookies. It is used to sustain the session. Whenever the browser throws a request then it is always understood as a new request because HTTP protocol is a stateless protocol as it is not persistent. Now if we want that our request object should stay alive till we decide to end it, then we need to use the concept of session tracking. In session tracking initially a session object is generated when the first request goes to the server. Then server generates a token which will be used to sustain the session. The token is transferred to the client by the response object, and gets stored on the client machine. Normally the server creates a cookie by default and then that cookie gets stored on the client machine. But URL Rewriting can be used where we the cookies are disabled. It is a preferred to use URL Rewriting. In this technique, a string is appended.

Consider a program "encodeURL.jsp" that accepts input from user.

Example 7: Creating a program encode URL.jsp

```
<html>
    <head>
        <title>How to use encodeURL in jsp</title>
    </head>
    <body>
        <form method = "post" action = "EncodeURLProgram.jsp">
        <font size = 6>Enter your name  :
        <input type = "text" name = "name"></font>
        <br><br>
        <font size = 6>Enter your password  :
        <input type="password" name = "pwd" ></font>
        <br><br>
        <input type = "submit" name = "submit" value = "submit" >
        </form>
    </body>
</html>
```

Output:

User gives name and password in above form and submit it. After submitting above code following program "EncodeURLProgram.jsp" will be executed.

Example 8: Creating a program EncodeURL Program.jsp

```jsp
<%@ page session ="true" %>
<%
  String name = request.getParameter("name");
    String password = request.getParameter("pwd");
    if(name.equals("Williams") && password.equals("abcde"))
    {
        session.setAttribute("username",name);
        String string = response.encode
URL("NextPageAfterFirst.jsp?name="+name+"&password="+password");
        %>
        <font size = 6><p>Please click here to go forward : </p></font>
        <font size = 8>
        <a href ='<%= string %>'>WelcomeEncodeURL.jsp</a>
        </font>
    <% } else {
        String string = response.encode
URL("encodeURL.jsp?name="+name+"&password="+password");%>
        <font size = 6><p>
        You have entered a wrong value  : Click here to go back : </p>
        </font>
        <font size = 6>
        <a href ='<%= string %>'>encodeURL.jsp</a></font>
<% } %>
```

This program will take request parameters name and password, and according to their value forms a URL along with name and password will also be sent. If value is correct then page with hyperlink having link to page "WelcomeEncodeURL.jsp" is displayed, otherwise page with hyperlink having link to page "encodeURL.jsp" is displayed.

Code for program "WelcomeEncodeURL.jsp" is given in Example 9.

Example 9: Creating a program WelcomeEncodeURL.jsp

```html
<html>
    <head>
    <title>Welcome to the program of URL rewriting
    </title>
    </head>
    <body>
    <font size = 6>Hello</font>
    <%= session.getAttribute("username")%>
    </body>
</html>
```

Output:

When the value is correct, following page is displayed:

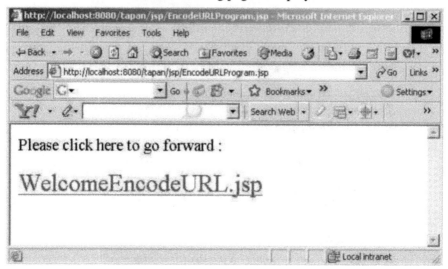

On clicking above link, page "WelcomeEncodeURL.jsp" is displayed.

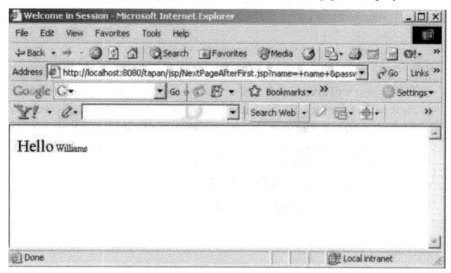

c. **Cookies**

Cookies are short pieces of data, sent by Web servers to the client browser. The cookies are saved on client's hard disk in the form of small text file. Cookies help the Web servers to identify Web users that using them server tracks the user. Cookies play very significant role in the session tracking.

In JSP, cookies are the object of the class "javax.servlet.http.Cookie". As cookie's value can uniquely identify a client, they are commonly used for session management. A cookie includes name, single value, and optional attributes, such as path and domain qualifiers, comment, maximum age, and version number. The "getCookies()" method of the "request" object returns an array of Cookie objects. Cookies can be created using the following given code:

Cookie (java.lang.String name, java.lang.String value)

Here is the code of the form for "cookieform.jsp' which prompts the user to enter his/her name.

Example 10: Creating a form cookieform.jsp

```
<%@ page language="java"%>
<html>
<head>
<title>Cookie Input Form</title>
</head>
<body>
<form method="post" action="setcookie.jsp">
<p><b>Enter Your Name: </b>
<input type="text" name="username">
<br>
<input type="submit" value="Submit">
</form>
</body>
```

User input is posted to the setcookie.jsp file, which initializes the cookie's attributes. Code inside "setcookie.jsp" file is shown in Example 11.

Example 11: Creating a file setcookie.jsp

```
<%@ page language="java" import="java.util.*"%>
<%
String username=request.getParameter("username");
if(username==null)
        username="";
Date now = new Date();
String timestamp = now.toString();
Cookie cookie = new Cookie ("username",username);
cookie.setMaxAge(365 * 24 * 60 * 60);
response.addCookie(cookie);
%>
<html>
<head>
<title>Cookie Saved</title>
</head>
<body>
<p><a href="showcookievalue.jsp">
Next Page to view the cookie value</a><p>
</body>
```

Above code initializes the cookie and then displays a link to view contents of cookie page. The code to display cookie page inside "showcookievalue.jsp" file is shown below.

Example 12: Creating a program to display cookie page inside .jsp file

```jsp
<%@ page language="java" %>
<%
String cookieName = "username";
Cookie cookies [] = request.getCookies ();
Cookie myCookie = null;
if (cookies != null)
{
for (int i = 0; i < cookies.length; i++)
{
if (cookies [i].getName().equals (cookieName))
{
myCookie = cookies[i];
break;
}
}
}
%>
<html>
<head>
<title>Show Saved Cookie</title>
</head>
<body>


<%
if (myCookie == null) {
%>
No Cookie found with the name <%=cookieName%>
<%
} else {
%>
<p>Welcome: <%=myCookie.getValue()%>.
<%
}
%>
</body>
```

d. **Session API**

First we have a form, let us call it "GetName.html".

```
<HTML>
<BODY>
<FORM METHOD=POST ACTION="SaveName.jsp">
What's your name?
<INPUT TYPE=TEXT NAME=username SIZE=20>
<P><INPUT TYPE=SUBMIT>
<FORM><BODY>
<HTML>
```

The target of the form is "SaveName.jsp", which saves the user's name in the session.

```
<%
String name = request.getParameter( "username" );
session.setAttribute( "theName", name );
%>
<HTML>
<BODY>
<A HREF="NextPage.jsp">Continue</A><BODY>
<HTML>
```

The SaveName.jsp saves the name of the user in the session, and provides a link to another page, "NextPage.jsp". NextPage.jsp demonstrates how to retrieve the saved name.

```
<HTML>
<BODY> Hello,
<%= session.getAttribute( "theName" ) %>
<BODY>
<HTML>
```

7.5.8 Application Database Connectivity

Following is the introduction to connectivity to MySQL database using JSP. Take an example of "Books" database. This database has a Table named "books_details". This Table contains three fields which are "ID", "Book_Name" and "Author".

Table books_details:

ID	Book Name	Author
1.	Java I/O	Tim Ritchey
2.	Java & XML, 2 Edition	Brett McLaughlin
3.	Java Swing, 2nd Edition	Dave Wood, Marc Loy,

Program shown in Example 13 "*BookEntryForm.jsp*" contains HTML and JSP code for user interface and accessing data from back end that is MySQL.

```jsp
<%@ page language="java" import="java.sql.*"%>
<%String driver = "org.gjt.mm.mysql.Driver";
Class.forName(driver).newInstance();
Connection con=null;
ResultSet rst=null;
Statement stmt=null;
try{
String
url="jdbc:mysql://localhost/books?user=<user>&password=<password>";
con=DriverManager.getConnection(url);
stmt=con.createStatement(); }
catch(Exception e){
System.out.println(e.getMessage());
}
if(request.getParameter("action") != null){
        String bookname=request.getParameter("bookname");
        String author=request.getParameter("author");
        stmt.executeUpdate("insert into books_details(book_name,author)
values('"+bookname+"','"+author+"')");
        rst=stmt.executeQuery("select * from books_details");
%>

<html><body><center>
<h2>Books List</h2>
<table border="1" cellspacing="0" cellpadding="0">
<tr>      <td><b>S.No</b></td>
          <td><b>Book Name</b></td>
          <td><b>Author</b></td>
</tr>
<%        int no=1;
          while(rst.next()){%>
<tr>      <td><%=no%></td>
          <td><%=rst.getString("book_name")%></td>
          <td><%=rst.getString("author")%></td>
</tr>
<%        no++;}
          rst.close();
          stmt.close();
          con.close();%>
</table></center></body></html>
```

```
<html><body><center>
<h2>Books List</h2>
<table border="1" cellspacing="0" cellpadding="0">
<tr>      <td><b>S.No</b></td>
          <td><b>Book Name</b></td>
          <td><b>Author</b></td>
</tr>
<%        int no=1;
          while(rst.next()){%>
<tr>      <td><%=no%></td>
          <td><%=rst.getString("book_name")%></td>
          <td><%=rst.getString("author")%></td>
</tr>
<%        no++;}
          rst.close();
          stmt.close();
          con.close();%>
</table></center></body></html>

<body>
<center><form action="BookEntryForm.jsp" method="post" name="entry"
onSubmit="return validate(this)">
<input type="hidden" value="list" name="action">
<table border="1" cellpadding="0" cellspacing="0">
<tr><td><table>
    <tr><td colspan="2" align="center"><h2>Book Entry Form</h2></td></tr>
    <tr><td colspan="2"> </td></tr>
    <tr><td>Book Name:</td>
        <td><input name="bookname" type="text" size="50"></td></tr>
    <tr><td>Author:</td>
        <td><input name="author" type="text" size="50"></td></tr>
    <tr><td colspan="2" align="center">
        <input type="submit" value="Submit"></td></tr>
</table></td></tr>
</table></form>
</center>
</body></html><%}%>
```

Output:

Fill the Book Name and Author fields, and press Submit button. A page will be displayed which contains a table of Book Name and Authors as shown below.

Books List

S.No	Book Name	Author
1	Java I/O	Tim Ritchey
2	Java & XML,2 Edition	Brett McLaughlin
3	Java Swing, 2nd Edition	Dave Wood, Marc Loy, James Elliott, Brian Cole, Robert Eckstein
4	Java Cookbook, 2nd Edition	Ian F. Darwin
5	Java Web Services Unleashed	Robert J Brunner, Frank Cohen
6	Core Java Data Objects	Sameer Tyagi, Michael Vorburger
7	Java in a Nutshell	David Flanagan
8	Java Web Services in a Nutshell	Kim Topley
9	The Java AWT Reference	John Zukowski

Explanation of above Program (Example 13):

Declare variables: Java is a strongly typed language which means that all variables must be declared explicitly, before use and must be declared with the correct data types. In above example following variables are declared:

```
Connection con=null;
ResultSet rst=null;
Statement stmt=null;
```

The objects of type `connection`, `ResultSet` and `Statement`, are associated with java.sql package. "`con`" is a variable which is object of type `Connection`. "`rst`" is a variable which is an object of type `ResultSet`. It will hold a resultset returned by a database query. "`stmt`" is a variable which is an object of type `Statement`. `Statement` Class methods allow to execute any query.

Connection to database: The first task of this programmer is to load database driver. This is accomplished using the single line of code:

```
String driver = "org.gjt.mm.mysql.Driver";
Class.forName(driver).newInstance();
```

Next task is to make connection. This is accomplished using single line of code:

```
String url="jdbc:mysql://localhost/
books?user=<userName>&password=<password>";
con=DriverManager.getConnection(url);
```

When `url` is passed into `getConnection()` method of `DriverManager` class it returns Connection object.

Executing Query for Accessing data from database: This is done using following given code:

```
stmt=con.createStatement(); //create a Statement
object
rst=stmt.executeQuery("select * from books_details");
```

stmt is the statement type variable name and **rst** is the ResultSet type variable. A query is always implemented on a Statement object. A Statement object is created by invoking createStatement() method on connection object **con.**

The most important methods of this statement interface are executeQuery() and executeUpdate(). Whenever the executeQuery() method is executed on an SQL statement, it returns a single ResultSet object. Whereas the executeUpdate() method is executed on an insert, update, and delete SQL statement. This method returns a number of records affected by SQL statement execution.

After creating a Statement, a method executeQuery() or executeUpdate() is called on statement object **stmt** and a SQL query string is passed in method executeQuery() or executeUpdate(). After execution this stmt object will return a ResultSet **rst** corresponding to query string.

Reading values from a ResultSet:

```
while(rst.next())
{
    %> <tr><td><%=no%></td><td><%=rst.getString
    ("book_name")%></
    d><td><%=rst.getString("author")%></td></tr>
    <%
}
```

The ResultSet represents a table like database result set. Inside ResultSet object, there is a cursor which points to its current row of data. Initially, the cursor is located before the first row. Therefore, to retrieve the first row in the ResultSet, use next() method. This method moves the cursor to the next record and returns true if the next row is valid, and false in case there are no more records left in the ResultSet object.

Other important methods are getXXX(), where XXX is data type returned by the method at the specified index, including int, long, double and String. The indexing in ResultSet starts from 1. For instance, to obtain the second column of type String, following code can be used:

```
resultSet.getString(2);
```

One can also use getXXX() method that accepts a column name instead of a column index. For instance, the following code can be used to retrieve the value of the column "book name" of type String.

```
resultSet.getString("book_name");
```

7.6   Some Miscellaneous JSP Examples

Let us discuss a program to displaying browser information of the client making request.

When an HTTP client, such as Web browser sends a request to a Web server, at that time along with the request it also sends some HTTP variables like Content type, Remote host, Remote address, etc. In some cases these variables are used by the programmers.

Code given in Example 14 demonstrates the use of the .jsp file to print the HTTP request information.

Example 14: Creating a program to print the HTTP request information

```
<%@page contentType="text/html" import="java.util.*"%>
<html>
<body>
<p><font size="5" color="#800000">Request Information:</font><p>
<div align="left">
<table border="0" cellpadding="0" cellspacing="0" width="70%" bgcolor="#EEFFCA">
<tr>
<td width="33%"><b><font color="#800000">Request Method:</font></b></td>
<td width="67%"><font color="#FF0000"><%=request.getMethod()%></font></td>
</tr><tr>
<td width="33%"><b><font color="#800000">Request URI:</font></b></td>
<td width="67%"><font color="#FF0000"><%=request.getRequestURI()%></font></td>
</tr>

<tr>
<td width="33%"><b><font color="#800000">Request
Protocol:</font></b></td>
<td width="67%"><font
color="#FF0000"><%=request.getProtocol()%></font></td>
</tr><tr>
<td width="33%"><b><font color="#800000">Path Info:</font></b></td>
<td width="67%"><font
color="#FF0000"><%=request.getPathInfo()%></font></td>
</tr><tr>
<td width="33%"><b><font color="#800000">Path
translated:</font></b></td>
<td width="67%"><font
color="#FF0000"><%=request.getPathTranslated()%></font></td>
</tr><tr>
<td width="33%"><b><font color="#800000">Query
String:</font></b></td>
<td width="67%"><font
color="#FF0000"><%=request.getQueryString()%></font></td>
</tr>

<tr>
<td width="33%"><b><font color="#800000">Content length:</font></b></td>
<td width="67%"><font
color="#FF0000"><%=request.getContentLength()%></font></td>
</tr><tr>
<td width="33%"><b><font color="#800000">Content type:</font></b></td>
<td width="67%"><font
color="#FF0000"><%=request.getContentType()%></font></td>
</tr><tr>
<td width="33%"><b><font color="#800000">Server name:</font></b></td>
<td width="67%"><font
color="#FF0000"><%=request.getServerName()%></font></td>
</tr><tr>
```

```
<td width="33%"><b><font color="#800000">Server port:</font></b></td>
<td width="67%"><font
color="#FF0000"><%=request.getServerPort()%></font></td>
</tr><tr>
<td width="33%"><b><font color="#800000">Remote user:</font></b></td>
<td width="67%"><font
color="#FF0000"><%=request.getRemoteUser()%></font></td>
</tr>
<tr>
<td width="33%"><b><font color="#800000">Remote
address:</font></b></td>
<td width="67%"><font
color="#FF0000"><%=request.getRemoteAddr()%></font></td>
</tr><tr>
<td width="33%"><b><font color="#800000">Remote host:</font></b></td>
<td width="67%"><font
color="#FF0000"><%=request.getRemoteHost()%></font></td>
</tr><tr>
<td width="33%"><b><font color="#800000">Authorization
scheme:</font></b></td>
<td width="67%"><font
color="#FF0000"><%=request.getAuthType()%></font></td>
</tr>
</table>
</div>
</body>
</html>
```

Example 15: Retrieving the data posted to a JSP file from HTML file

Consider an HTML page that prompts the user to enter his/her name. Save it as "getname.html".

```
<html>
<head>
<title>Enter your name</title>
</head>
<body>
<p> </p>
<form method="POST" action="showname.jsp">
<p><font color="#800000" size="5">Enter your name:</font>
<input type="text" name="username" size="20"></p>
<p><input type="submit" value="Submit" name="B1"></p>
</form>
</body>
</html>
```

The target of form is "showname.jsp", which displays the name entered by the user. In order to retrieve the value entered by the user, use following code:

```
request.getParameter("username");
```

Here is the code of "showname.jsp" file:

```
<%@page contentType="text/html"%>
<html>
<body>
<p><font size="6">Welcome : 
<%=request.getParameter("username")%>
</font></p>
</body>
</html>
```

Some Miscellaneous Quotes about JSP

1. JSP is server-side scripting language. All processing is executed at the server end.

2. JSP adds dynamic behavior to the static HTML.

3. Comment means those statements written inside code but are never executed when the application runs. They are used for writing explanations about code for developer.

7.7   Some Solved Questions

Q. 1.   What are implicit objects?

Answer: Implicit objects are the object that are created by Web container provides to a developer to access them in their program using JavaBeans and Servlets. These objects are called implicit objects because they are automatically instantiated and are by default available in JSP. They are: request, response, pageContext, session, and application, out, config, page, and exception.

Q. 2.   Identify the advantages of JSP over Servlet.

Answer:

a.   Embedding of Java code in HTML pages

b.   Platform independence

c.   Creation of database-driven Web applications

d.   Server-side programming capabilities

Q. 3.   What are all the different scope values for the `<jsp:useBean>` tag?

Answer: `<jsp:useBean>` tag is used to access any Java Bean object in the JSP. Here are the scope values for `<jsp:useBean>` tag:

a.   page   b.   request

c.   session   d.   application

Q. 4. What types of comments are available in the JSP?

Answer: Two types of comments are allowed in the JSP. These are `hidden` and `output` comment. A `hidden` comment does not appear in the generated output in the HTML, while `output` comment appears in the generated output.

Example of `hidden` comment:

```
<%- This is hidden comment -%>
```

Example of `output` comment:

```
<!- This is output comment ->
```

Section V: Previous Year Questions with Answers

ASP.NET Questions

Q. 1. Discuss the working of CLR and CLS. [UPTU 2009-2010]

Solution: CLR is the Common Language Runtime where all .NET application are executed in. The CLR is an implementation of the CLS, Common Language Specification. It is a standard that needs to be followed to be considered to be .NET platform.

The above only defines the runtime and basic types.

Net Framework provides runtime environment called Common Language Runtime (CLR). It provides an environment to run all the .Net Programs. The code which runs under the CLR is called as Managed Code. Programmers need not to worry on managing the memory if the programs are running under the CLR as it provides memory management and thread management.

Programmatically, when our program needs memory, CLR allocates the memory for scope and de-allocates the memory if the scope is completed. Language Compilers (e.g. C#, VB.Net, J#) will convert the code/program to Microsoft Intermediate Language (MSIL), and this code/program will be converted to Native Code by CLR.

Common Language Specification (CLS) it specifies a set of rules that needs to be adhered or satisfied by all language compilers targeting CLR. It helps in cross-language inheritance and cross-language debugging.

It describes the minimal and complete set of features to produce code that can be hosted by CLR. It ensures that products of compilers will work properly in .NET environment.

Q. 2. Explain the term authentication with respect to ASP.NET security. [BSc IT October 2013 Mumbai university]

Solution: ASP.NET supports the following three authentication providers:

- Forms Authentication: Using this provider causes unauthenticated requests to be redirected to a specified HTML form using client-side redirection. The user can then supply logon credentials, and post the form back to the server. If the application authenticates the request (using application-specific logic), ASP.NET issues a cookie that contains the credentials or a key for reacquiring the client identity. Subsequent requests are issued with the cookie in the request headers, which means that subsequent authentications are unnecessary.

- Passport Authentication: This is a centralized authentication service provided by Microsoft that offers a single logon facility and membership services for participating sites. ASP.NET, in conjunction with the Microsoft® Passport Software Development Kit (SDK), provides similar functionality as Forms Authentication to Passport users.

- Windows Authentication: This provider utilizes the authentication capabilities of IIS. After IIS completes its authentication, ASP.NET uses the authenticated identity's token to authorize access.

Q. 3.　Explain the role of view state and session state in ASP.NET.
[BSc IT October 2013 Mumbai university]

Solution: Session State contains information that pertains to a specific session (by a particular client/browser/machine) with the server. It is a way to track what the user is doing on the site across multiple pages, for example the contents of a particular user's shopping cart is session data. Cookies can be used for session state.

View State on the other hand is information specific to particular Web page. It is stored in a hidden field so that it is not visible to the user. It is used to maintain the users illusion that they remember what they did on it the last time.

Q. 4.　Explain the event Life cycle of ASP.NET?
[BSc IT April 2013 Mumbai university]

Solution: ASP.NET life cycle specifies, how

- ASP.NET processes pages to produce dynamic output.
- The application and its pages are instantiated and processed.
- ASP.NET compiles the pages dynamically.
- The ASP.NET life cycle could be divided into two groups: (i) Application Life Cycle, (ii) Page Life Cycle.

ASP.NET Application Life Cycle

The application life cycle has the following stages:

- User makes a request for accessing application resource, a page. Browser sends this request to the Web server.
- A unified pipeline receives the first request and the following events take place:
  o　An object of the class `ApplicationManager` is created.
  o　An object of the class `HostingEnvironment` is created to provide information regarding the resources.
  o　Top-level items in the application are compiled.
- Response objects are created. The application objects, such as `HttpContext`, `HttpRequest` and `HttpResponse` are created and initialized.

- An instance of the `HttpApplication` object is created and assigned to the request.
- The request is processed by the `HttpApplication` class. Different events are raised by this class for processing the request.

ASP.NET Page Life Cycle

When a page is requested, it is loaded into the server memory, processed, and sent to the browser. Then it is unloaded from the memory. At each of these steps, methods and events are available, which could be overridden according to the need of the application. In other words, you can write your own code to override the default code.

The `Page` class creates a hierarchical tree of all the controls on the page. All the components on the page, except the directives, are part of this control tree. You can see the control tree by adding `trace= "true"` to the page directive. We will cover page directives and tracing under 'directives' and 'event handling'.

The page life cycle phases are:

- Initialization
- Instantiation of the controls on the page
- Restoration and maintenance of the state
- Execution of the event handler codes
- Page rendering

Understanding the page cycle helps in writing codes for making some specific thing happen at any stage of the page life cycle. It also helps in writing custom controls and initializing them at right time, populate their properties with view-state data and run control behavior code.

Following are the different stages of an ASP.NET page:

- Page request - When ASP.NET gets a page request, it decides whether to parse and compile the page, or there would be a cached version of the page; accordingly the response is sent.
- Starting of page life cycle - At this stage, the `Request` and `Response` objects are set. If the request is an old request or post back, the `IsPostBack` property of the page is set to true. The `UICulture` property of the page is also set.
- Page initialization - At this stage, the controls on the page are assigned unique ID by setting the `UniqueID` property and the themes are applied. For a new request, postback data is loaded and the control properties are restored to the view-state values.
- Page load - At this stage, control properties are set using the `view` state and `control` state values.
- Validation - Validate method of the validation control is called and on its successful execution, the `IsValid` property of the page is set to true.

- Postback event handling - If the request is a postback (old request), the related event handler is invoked.

- Page rendering - At this stage, `view` state for the page and all controls are saved. The page calls the `Render` method for each control and the output of rendering is written to the `OutputStream` class of the `Response` property of page.

- Unload - The rendered page is sent to the client and page properties, such as `Response` and `Request`, are unloaded and all cleanup done.

ASP.NET Page Life Cycle Events

At each stage of the page life cycle, the page raises some events, which could be coded. An event handler is basically a function or subroutine, bound to the event, using declarative attributes, such as `Onclick` or `handle`.

Following are the page life cycle events:

- `PreInit`- `PreInit` is the first event in page life cycle. It checks the `IsPostBack` property and determines whether the page is a postback. It sets the themes and master pages, creates dynamic controls, and gets and sets profile property values. This event can be handled by overloading the `OnPreInit` method or creating a `Page_PreInit` handler.

- `Init` - `Init` event initializes the `control`property and the control tree is built. This event can be handled by overloading the `InInit` method or creating a `Page_Init` handler.

- `InitComplete` - `InitComplete` event allows tracking of `view` state. All the controls turn on view-state tracking.

- `LoadViewState` - `LoadViewState` event allows loading `view` state information into the controls.

- `LoadPostData` - During this phase, the contents of all the input fields are defined with the `<form>` tag are processed.

- `PreLoad` - `PreLoad` occurs before the postback data is loaded in the controls. This event can be handled by overloading the `OnPreLoad` method or creating a `Page_PreLoad` handler.

- `Load` - The `Load` event is raised for the page first and then recursively for all child controls. The controls in the control tree are created. This event can be handled by overloading the `OnLoad` method or creating a `Page_Load` handler.

- `LoadComplete` - The loading process is completed, control event handlers are run, and page validation takes place. This event can be handled by overloading the `OnLoadComplete` method or creating a `Page_LoadComplete` handler

- `PreRender` - The `PreRender` event occurs just before the output is rendered. By handling this event, pages and controls can perform any updates before the output is rendered.

- `PreRenderComplete` - As the `PreRender` event is recursively fired for all child controls, this event ensures the completion of the pre-rendering phase.

- `SaveStateComplete` - State of control on the page is saved. `Personalization`, `control` state and `view` state details are saved. The HTML markup is generated. This stage can be handled by overriding the `Render` method or creating a `Page_Render` handler.

- `UnLoad` - The `UnLoad` phase is the last phase of the page life cycle. It raises the `UnLoad` event for all controls recursively and lastly for the page itself. Final cleanup is done and all resources and references, such as database connections, are freed. This event can be handled by modifying the `OnUnLoad` method or creating a `Page_UnLoad` handler.

Q. 5. What is the state management? Explain Sessions in ASP.NET?

[BSc IT April 2013 Mumbai university]

Solution: HyperText Transfer Protocol (HTTP) is a stateless protocol. When the client disconnects from the server, the ASP.NET engine discards the page objects. This way, each Web application can scale up to serve numerous requests simultaneously without running out of server memory.

However, there needs to be some technique to store the information between requests and to retrieve it when required. This information, i.e., the current value of all the controls and variables for the current user in the current session is called the State.

ASP.NET manages four types of states:

- `View` State
- `Control` State
- `Session` State
- `Application` State

View State

The `View` state is the state of the page and all its controls. It is automatically maintained across posts by the ASP.NET framework.

When a page is sent back to the client, the changes in the properties of the page and its controls are determined, and stored in the value of a hidden input field named `_VIEWSTATE`. When the page is again posted back, the `_VIEWSTATE` field is sent to the server with the HTTP request.

The `View` state could be enabled or disabled for:

- The entire application by setting the `EnableViewState` property in the `<pages>` section of Web.config file.
- A page by setting the `EnableViewState` attribute of the `Page` directive, as `<%@ Page Language="C#" EnableViewState="false" %>`
- A control by setting the `Control.EnableViewState` property.

It is implemented using a `view` state object defined by the `StateBag` class which defines a collection of `view` state items. The state bag is a data structure containing attribute value pairs, stored as strings associated with objects.

Control State

Control state cannot be modified, accessed directly, or disabled.

Session State

When a user connects to an ASP.NET Website, a new session object is created. When `session` state is turned on, a new `session` state object is created for each new request. This `session` state object becomes part of the context and it is available through the page.

`Session` state is generally used for storing application data, such as inventory, supplier list, customer record, or shopping cart. It can also keep information about the user and his preferences, and keep the track of pending operations.

Application State

The ASP.NET application is the collection of all Web pages, code and other files within a single virtual directory on a Web server. When information is stored in application state, it is available to all the users.

To provide for the use of application state, ASP.NET creates an application state object for each application from the `HTTPApplicationState` class and stores this object in server memory. This object is rerpresented by class file global.asax (the ASP.NET application file).

`Application` State is mostly used to store hit counters and other statistical data, global application data like tax rate, discount rate, etc., and to keep the track of users visiting the site.

Chapter 8

Electronic Commerce

Key Topics

- *E-Commerce Environment*
- *Electronic Data Interchange*
- *Secure Electronic transactions*
- *Electronic cash and payment schemes*
- *Building E-commerce site*

8.1   Introduction

In this Chapter you will learn about basic concepts of e-commerce. After learning the basics of e-commerce, you will learn about history associated with e-commerce and advance perspectives towards advantages and disadvantages from buyer and seller prospective. As the chapter progress, you will learn about different categories of e-commerce. To have a better understanding of the subject, success stories of Dell and eBay will be discussed as an example. Later on in the lesson, important concepts of EDI (Electronic Data Interchange) and SET (a standard protocol for securing credit card transactions over insecure networks) will be covered. In the final Section of this Chapter, important topics like electronic payment systems and their related security measures will be discussed which will end with an overview of e-business Website designing.

8.2   Understanding E-Commerce

Lets understand what is commerce first. According to dictionary "commerce" refers to "Transactions (sales and purchases) having the objective of supplying commodities (goods and services)" or "the exchange or buying and selling of commodities on a large scale involving transportation from place to place "

Major players of Commerce

Any commerce activity can involves these types of people (See Figure 8.1):

1. **Buyers** – They are the people or individual with money having intention to purchase goods or services.

2. **Sellers** – They are the people or individual who offers goods and services to others (here buyers). Sellers could be of two types:

1. Retailers who sell directly to consumers.

2. Wholesalers/distributors who sell to retailers.

3. **Producers** – They are the people/Individual who create the products and services that are later on being offered by sellers to the buyers. They are also known as manufacturers. In many cases, a producer is the seller as well as for some businesses, manufacturing and selling business are done at their own level.

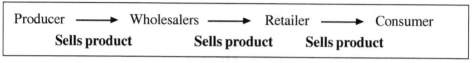

Figure 8.1: Flow of Transactions (Selling and Purchasing)

So you now have a basic idea about commerce. Commerce can be anything from selling a fruit juice on the streets to selling of branded clothes in malls and all these activities involves buyers, sellers and manufacturers.

E-Commerce

E-Commerce implies buying and selling of products or services over electronic systems, such as the Internet and other computer networks.

Note: In an e-commerce activity online monetary transaction is involved.

E-commerce typically uses the World Wide Web, at least at some point in the transaction's life cycle, although it can include a wider range of technologies, such as e-mail as well. As you progress through the Chapter, you will learn more about this. Let us understand the history of e-commerce in the coming Section.

8.2.1 History

Today's e-commerce what you see is much polished version, which has changed over couple of decades. Initially, electronic commerce was meant for facilitation of commercial transactions electronically, using technology, such as Electronic Data Interchange (EDI), Electronic Funds Transfer (EFT), etc. Aforesaid were introduced in few decades before, allowing businesses to send commercial documents like purchase orders, bills, invoices, acknowledgements, electronically. Industry also observed rapid growth and acceptance of credit cards, Automated Teller Machines (ATM) and telephone banking in the 1980s, also forms of electronic commerce. Another major stepping stone in revolution of e-commerce industry was, when airline reservation system was introduced in US/UK. Online shopping originally, was invented in the UK in 1979 by Michael Aldrich and during the 1980s it was used extensively particularly by following auto giants Ford, Peugeot, General Motors and Nissan. 1990s onwards, electronic commerce started to include Enterprise Resource Planning (ERP) systems, data mining and data warehousing features.

During quondam arena, one of example for electronic commerce in physical goods was the Boston Computer Exchange, marketplace for used computers launched in 1982. The first online information marketplace, including online consulting, was likely the American Information Exchange, during erstwhile stage of the Internet system introduced in 1991. Also, IBM in 1997 launched an e-business marketing campaign directed at selling services to companies that needed to connect their current electronic systems to the Web.

Although the Internet became popular worldwide in 1994, it took almost half-decade to introduce security protocols and broadband technologies, like DSL allowing continual connection to the Internet cloud. And towards end of 2000, numerous European and American business companies offered their services through the World Wide Web. Since then people started having confidence with term called "e-commerce" especially with the ability of purchasing various goods through the Internet using secure protocols and electronic payment services.

Success of any business is potential customers, Imagine taskforce of online users, estimated Internet Users is 1, 463, 632, 361 for Q2 2008 (Source: internetworldstats.com/stats.com), wow! what whooping number, which are potential e-commerce customers.

8.2.2 How E commerce works?

Unless you are living in forest/caves, you would hear and also experienced flavor of the Internet. Then, famous stuff you already played by now includes e-mail, chat, etc., and also during last decade new hype "e-commerce", started ruling famous jargons. But later is not as easy to understand, as compared to former ones. Lets explore how this fancy thing works.

To make things simple, let's start with an example, the activity is the sale of some product by a retailer to a customer: It is also comprised of number of steps, do not worry it is not rocket science. Firstly you must have a **product or service** to offer. The product can be anything from foot-ball to supercomputer. Like traditional commerce, you may get your products directly from a producer, or you might go through a distributor/retailer to get them, or also possibly you may produce the products yourself.

You must also have a **place** from which to sell your products (similar to shop-keepers which own shop to sell goods). For most physical products we tend to think of the place as a store or shop of some sort. You need to chalk out a way to get people to come to your place. This process is known as **marketing/advertisement**. If no one knows that your place exists, you will never be able to sell anything. Some of advertisement techniques, we have seen hoardings, newspapers/magazines, posters, etc., and not to forget "word of mouth" is biggest source to spread information.

Then its 'money', i.e., you need a way to accept **orders**. At most of shopping malls, you can use cash, check or credit cards to pay for goods. B2B transactions often use purchase orders. There are some product or service where you do not pay at the time of delivery, and they are delivered continuously (mobile, water, gas, electricity and pagers are like this); these are charged per cycle-say on monthly basis, which comes under radar of **billing** and **collections**.

Also, you need a way to deliver the product or service, often known as **fulfilment**. Also, sometimes customers do not like what they bought, so you need a way to accept **returns**. You may or may not charge certain fees for returns, and you may or may not require the customer to get authorization before returning anything, depends on customer/product too. Sometimes a product breaks, so you need to abide by warranty claims. Usually for retailers this part of the transaction is often handled by the producer. Many products/services in today's next generation world are so complicated that they require **customer service** and **technical support** departments to help customers use them. Computers/laptops/printers/scanners are few good examples. Then, products like mobile phone service may also require regular customer service force, as customers want to switch/add/delete service they receive over time.

In an e-commerce world, sales channel you find all of these elements as well, but they change slightly. You must have the following elements to conduct e-commerce:

- A product/good or service parse
- A place to sell the product – for example Website/portal to showcase products in some way
- A way to get people to come to your Website, i.e., its reachable to anyone on Internet
- A mechanism to accept orders – database to track this, customer wise information
- A way to accept money, i.e., online payment methodology
- A facility to ship/transport products to customers
- A way to accept returns (if it happens!)
- A procedure to handle warranty claims, if necessary
- A well-being state of customer service process, i.e., after sales support could be through e-mail, online-chats, forms, FAQs series, etc.
- Also process/tool, where customer could track delivery/shipment of good ordered

  Whoosh and you thought selling goods online was is child's play.

8.2.3 Advantages and Disadvantages

Advantages:

Table 8.1 summarizes the advantages of e-commerce

Table 8.1: Advantages of E-Commerce

Seller Prospective	Buyer Prospective
Playground in all online users.	Wide choice, as usually your search used to end up.
Lowers selling cost, as not many taxes involved, apart from basic rules.	Information could be searched precisely as per requirement.
Market is open 24×7×365.	Market is open 24×7×365.

Without much investment you can sell products across continents.	You can buy products across globe.
Buyer/seller have same platform.	Try your luck in auctions, reverse auctions to save money.

Disadvantages:

Table 8.2 summarizes the disadvantages of e-commerce

Table 8.2: Disadvantages of E-commerce

Seller Prospective	**Buyer Prospective**
Every year, we hear new technology.	Security, biggest threat for transactions.
Still many countries have deficient communication infrastructures.	In bulk deals / costly goods lack of trust with sellers.
Language, big barrier at times.	Even in digital era, many want to touch/feel before buying.
Currency conversions.	Not enough knowledgably about currency/tax rules.
Security issues for online transactions.	Concerned over warranty, support issues when bought online.

8.2.4 Models of E-commerce

E-commerce can be spilt into four major categories: B2B, B2C, C2B, and C2C.

- **B2B (Business-to-Business)**

  Organizations/Companies doing business with each other, such as manufacturers selling to distributors and wholesalers selling to retailers. For example, bulb manufacturing company dealing with car manufactures. Pricing/terms and conditions are based on quantity of order. Examples: shop2gether, metalsite, etc.

- **B2C (Business-to-Consumer)**

  Businesses selling to the public directly, usually through catalogs utilizing shopping cart software. In race of maximum volume category B2C is undoubted leader. Buying air ticket, hotel booking across continent, book purchase all are very easy. Examples: makemytrip.com, amazon.com, etc.

- **C2B (Consumer-to-Business)**

  Consumer publish his/her project with a set budget online and within hours companies review the consumer's requirements and bid for the project. The consumer checks the bids and selects the company that will complete the project. Examples: reverseauction.com, priceline.com, etc.

- **C2C (Consumer-to-Consumer)**

  Consumer sells directly to consumers. There are numerous sites offering free classifieds, auctions, and forums where individuals can buy and sell thanks to online payment systems like PayPal where people can send and receive money online with ease. eBay's auction service is a classic example of same.

8.2.5 Main players on this playground

Table 8.3 summarizes the Websites/portals doing online business.

Table 8.3: List of Online Business Websites/Portals

Best Overall	Name of Website / Portal	Some glimpse over same
	Amazon.com	A third of the people who buy online shop at Amazon.com.
	Dell	The pioneer of direct computer sales online is selling $30 million worth of gear a day from its Website, so it is obviously doing something right.
	IQVC	You might expect the king of TV-based shopping to make a seamless leap to the Internet, having distribution and customer service already in place.
Best Auctions	EBay	It is not just the never-ending cavalcade of inventory — 250, 000 new items are put up for auction every day here — that keeps its 5.6 million registered users hooked. eBay figured out that trust means everything to e-commerce.
	OnSale	Part outlet store and part liquidator's auction, the best feature of the auction half is that it never refers to people who purchase products as "buyers" but rather as "winners."
Best Shopping	MySimon	The "Simon" character on this shopping but looks like the kind of doll that would become animated and go homicidal in a horror movie.
	shopdashonline	If you were a corporation, Dash would be your vice president in charge of discounts. When you sign up for Dash, you get rebates from its participating merchants.

8.2.5 Dell E-Commerce Strategy

The Dell Example (B2C)

Things You Should Know about Dell (source:www.dell.com)

- Every Fortune 100 company does business with Dell.
- The Del is (i) PC provider in the US and (ii) Worldwide.
- The Dell is preferred desktop and laptop of enterprises in the US and Europe.
- It has been no. 1 PC supplier to small and medium businesses in the US for 10 years in a row.
- The Dell was considered as the world's leading provider of flat panel displays.
- About 140, 000 systems shipped per day, on average – that is more than one every second.
- Nearly 2 billion interactions with Dell customers every year.
- The Dell company won more than 400 product awards in 2007.
- More than 55, 000 customers have posted ratings and reviews on Dell.com.
- Customers have also offered more than 9, 100 ideas on Idea Storm that have been promoted more than 617, 000 times.
- Customers have generated and confirmed more than 7, 000 accepted solutions to their technology challenges.
- 24 of the world's top supercomputer run on Dell.
- The 10 largest US companies run on Dell.
- The top 6 Internet service companies run on Dell.
- The top 5 US commercial banks run on Dell.

Yes, one of the most successful e-commerce companies: Dell.

Dell sells custom-configured PCs to consumers and businesses. Dell during initial phase, started as a mail-order company that advertised in the back of magazines and sold their computers over the phone. Dell's e-commerce presence is widely publicized, as Dell is able to sell so much merchandise over the Web. According to IDG, Dell sold something like $14, 000, 000 in equipment every day in 2000, and 25 percent of Dell's sales were over the Web.

If Dell were to lose 25 percent of its phone sales to achieve its 25 percent of sales over the Web, then it is not clear that e-commerce has any advantage, right ! Dell will not be selling computers, then. Only if the transaction cost on the Web is lower, or if the presentation of merchandise on the Web is more inviting and encourages larger transactions, then moving to the Web is productive for Dell.

In building Website to attract these buyers, Dell may be able to lure away customers from other vendors who do not offer such a service. This gives Dell a competitive advantage over its competitors that lets it increase its market share.

There is also a widely held belief that once a customer starts working with a vendor/manufacturer, it is much easier to keep that customer than it is to bring in new customers. So if you can build brand loyalty for Website early stages, it gives you an advantage over other vendors who try to enter the market later. Dell implemented its Website very early, and that presumably gives it an advantage over the competition.

8.2.6 eBay(C2C)

eBay Inc.: A Short History (source-www.ebay.com)

eBay was born over Labor Day weekend in 1995, when Pierre Omidyar, a computer programmer, wrote the code for an auction Website that he ran from his home computer.

Today, Omidyar's hobby is known as **eBay**, the world's largest online marketplace - where practically anyone can sell practically anything at any time. It is an idea that Business Week once called "nothing less than a virtual, self-regulating global economy."

With a presence in 39 markets, including the US, and approximately 84 million active users worldwide, eBay has changed the face of Internet commerce. In 2007, the total value of sold items on eBay's trading platforms was nearly $60 billion. This means that eBay users worldwide trade more than $1, 900 worth of goods on the site every second.

The benefit to consumers is clear: eBay provides an open trading platform where the market determines the value of items that are sold. Over the years, the site has become a cultural barometer of sorts, providing a view into what objects consumers want most at any time.

Since its initial public offering in 1998, the company has continued to innovate and connect people - and not just through its marketplaces. Two critical acquisitions have made eBay Inc. a global leader in online payments and communications as well.

PayPal enables any individual or business with an e-mail address to securely, easily and quickly send and receive payments online. Acquired by eBay Inc. in October 2002, PayPal builds on the existing financial infrastructure of bank accounts and credit cards and uses the world's most advanced proprietary fraud prevention systems to create a safe payment solution. Today, PayPal is a global leader in online payment solutions: It has 149 million registered users and is accepted by millions of merchants worldwide - on and off eBay. PayPal's Q1 2008 global total payment volume of $14.4 billion accounted for nearly 9 percent of worldwide e-commerce.

Acquired by eBay Inc. in October 2005, **Skype** is the world's fastest-growing Internet communication company that has revolutionized the way people talk online. With more than 309 million registered users as of early 2008, Skype allows people everywhere to make unlimited voice and video calls online for free using its software. Skype is available in 28 languages and is used in almost every country on Earth. This business unit generates revenue through its premium offerings, such as calls (using its software) made to and from landline and mobile phones; voicemail; call forwarding; and personalization, including ringtones and avatars. In addition to its presence on eBay, Skype has relationships with a growing network of hardware and software providers.

Other key acquisitions have strengthened eBay Inc.'s portfolio of e-commerce companies, including **shopping.com**, a pioneer in online comparison shopping; **Stub hub**, a leading online marketplace for the resale of event tickets; **rent.com**, the most visited online apartment listing service in the US; **Stumble Upon**, an online solution that helps people discover and share content on the Web; and market-leading **online classifieds** sites including LoQUo.com, Intoko, and Netherlands-based Marktplaats.nl. The company has also grown its classifieds business through **Kijiji**, which launched in the US in 2007.

8.2.7 Future of E-commerce

Industry experts predict a promising and glorious future of e-commerce in the 21st century. In the foreseeable future e-commerce will further confirm itself a major tool of sale, at least past results shows it will!! Successful e-commerce will become a notion absolutely inseparable from the Web, because e-shopping is becoming more and more popular. At the same time severe rivalry in the sphere of e-commerce services will intensify their development. Thus prevailing future trends of e-commerce will be the growth of Internet sales and evolution.

Each year number of e-commerce deals grows enormously. Sales volumes of online stores are more than comparable with those of "brick-and-mortar" ones. And the tendency will continue, because a lot of people are "jugged" by work and with personal priorities, while Internet saves a lot of time and gives opportunity to choose goods at the best prices. Present-day Internet sales boom is the foundation for magnificent e-commerce future.

The "quantity to quality" tendency of e-commerce is also becoming more and more obvious, as the Internet has excluded geographical factor from the sale. So it does not matter any more whether your store is situated in UK/US/India or in a small town. To survive, sellers/merchants will have to adapt rapidly to the new conditions. To attract more customers e-store owners will have not only to increase the number of available services, but to pay more attention to such elements like attractive design, user-friendliness, appealing goods presentation, they will have to opportunely employ modern technologies for their businesses to become parts of e-commerce future.

In the study, small businesses with annual revenues of less than $10 million saw average improvements of 40 percent to 50 percent in financial performance.

The US Department of Commerce has also released statistics, which document the increasing impact of business on our lives. The online sales figures for the third quarter indicate that total online retail sales reached nearly $6.4 billion for the quarter ended Sept. 30. That a 15.3 percent increase from the previous quarter, and the biggest increase since the department started tracking e-commerce numbers a year ago.

Mail-order companies have superior database-marketing and customer-intimacy practices. Brick-and-mortar retailers boast huge customer bases and powerful brands. Pure-play Net retailers, however, can not match that kind of retail experience. They want it, but they can not afford it in today's venture capital environment.

Jupiter estimates that a total of 35 million people in the US will purchase gifts online this holiday season, compared with the 20 million who shopped online last year. This will likely translate into $11.6 billion being spent this season, compared with $7 billion during the same period last year.

More shoppers are also expected to buy clothes and shoes online this year, in addition to safer online purchases, such as books, CDs and computer gear. This shows that consumers are becoming increasingly comfortable buying online.

8.2.8 Factors affecting Growth of E-commerce

a. **Security**

Without iota of thought it is on mind of everyone who even thinks to do business online. Today hackers have become so personal, that it takes minutes to conquer / take over Website having loop holes. Firewall, IDS, encryptions, digital signatures all have same endeavor to provide secure and peaceful life over Internet cloud.

b. **Scalability**

It relates to your capability to run show, no matter what how large business gets. Usually new players/ freshers to e-commerce community do not have strong vision. Most silly mistake players do, they under-estimate growth rate, never forget your playground is spread across globe. From day one, you should keep your seats belts tighten. One example in past, where we saw failure was "alladvantage.com" They failed to anticipate the network effect, and the company found its business model did not scale with unanticipated customer growth. They added one million customers within three months of launch; their revenue model was based on selling demographic data to advertisers.

c. **Perceived Risk with Product/Service**

If there are thousands of e-commerce savvy personnel's, lets not forget there are millions of others, who do not agree too much with concept due to risk with final product/service they will get after buying online. Different people, different perception some are scared with fraud, some worried about delivery schedules, some say there is no meaning of warranty when you buy goods online.

Test Your Progress
1. *What is e-commerce?*
2. *How it is different from e-business?*
3. *What are the factors affecting e-commerce?*

8.3   Electronic Data Interchange

EDI the inter-organization exchange of well-defined business transactions in standardized electronic form directly between computer applications. Focused on Business-to-Business community. Also, EDI can be stated as collection of standard message formats to exchange data between organizations computers via any electronic service.

Domains EDI covers: traditional business facets: inquires, planning, purchasing, acknowledgments, pricing, order status, scheduling, test results, shipping and receiving, invoices, payments, and financial and business reporting. Additional standards: interchange of data relating to security, administrative data, trading partner information, specifications, contracts, distribution.

8.3.1   EDI History

- Electronic transmission started during 1960s.

- Initially main focus was for road and rail transport industries.

- In 1968, the United States Transportation Data Coordinating Committee (TDCC) was formed to coordinate the development of translation rules among existing four sets of industry-specific standards.

- Later, the X12 standards of the American National Standards Institute (ANSI) gradually extended and replaced those created by the TDCC.

- At the same time, the UK Department of Customers and Excise was developing standards for documents used in international trade. These extended by the United Nations Economic Commission for Europe (UNECE) as GTDI (General-purpose Trade Data Interchange).

- A United Nations Joint European and North American working party (UN-JEDI) addressed the harmonization between the two sets of standardized documents. They developed EDI for Administration, Commerce, and Transport (EIFACT) document translation standards.

- Although EDI technology works well, until now this technology has been expensive to implement.

- Today, EDI messages are coded in a standard data format based on X12 and EDIFACT specifications.

> **Note:** EDI technology has matured.
>
> EDI has been growing in the past, although the penetration is still low.
>
> In spite of its moderate success, EDI has failed to gain total acceptance and become ubiquitous in industry.

8.3.2 EDI Advantages and Disadvantages

Table 8.4 summarizes the advantages and disadvantages of EDI.

Table 8.4: EDI Advantages and Disadvantages

Advantages	Disadvantages
Automating existing business procedures in inventory management, transport and distribution, also in administration, and cash management.	Managerial problems in the support, maintenance and implementation of EDI transactions.
Cost saving in - document preparation, postage, and handling of mainstream transactions reduced errors and exceptions handling.	Each entity may have a different method of delivery, ranging from dial-up BBS systems mailing hard media, such as CD-ROM or tape backup.
Faster handling of transactions results in increased cash flow.	Lack of strict standards across implementations, transactions and methods.
Improve customer services and enhance the business process and operations.	One single computer application cannot handle all health care entities. Though this may not be necessary, it can lead to an obvious management headache as a company attempts to register itself with various EDI partners.

8.3.3 EDI History

Let's first give quick glimpse to how EDI is setup. There are several ways to set up EDI.

- A dedicated PC link to the EDI network.
- A group of computers via modems are linked to the EDI network, and A dedicated server is linked to the EDI network.

Communication link could be: dial-up phone line (such as ISDN line or switched digital services) - a dedicated link to the network's local hub point.

Required software:

- Application software - Message translator.
- Routing manager.
- Communication handler Migration to Open EDI.

The Internet and the transition to open EDI will change the economics of EDI by reducing setup and rollout costs.

Migration groups:

- A nonuser becoming a private network/VAN user.

- A current EDI user who wishes to make a transition to Open EDI.
- A non-EDI user who can make a direct transition to Open EDI.
- EDI transactions across the Internet in two ways:

E-mail and FTP

The benefits:

- Reduction of the cost of transferring EDI messages.
- Increase the performance.
- Supporting e-commerce.
- Increase the interoperability of networks increasing the usability of EDI.

The Problems and Challenges:

- Security issues.
- Many companies using EDI based on VANs. Not all VANs have connections to the Internet.

Test Your Progress
1. *What do you understand by EDI?*
2. *What are the basic steps for conducting EDI?*
3. *What is VAN?*

8.4 SET (Secure Electronic Transaction)

When it comes to e-commerce, first thing which pings someone mind is security. Industry gurus have been putting heart and soul, in order to address this concern. SET was one of endeavor on same lines.

Secure Electronic Transaction (SET) is a standard protocol for securing credit card transactions over insecure networks, more specifically addressing transactions over Internet. Please note clearly, SET is not itself a payment system, but rather a set of security protocols and formats that enables users to employ the existing credit card payment infrastructure on an open network in a secure fashion.

SET was developed by Visa and MasterCard (Credit card leaders)involving other companies, such as GTE, IBM, Microsoft, Netscape, RSA and Revising starting in 1996. SET is based on X.509 certificates with several extensions. [X.509 is an ITU-T standard for a Public Key Infrastructure (PKI) for single sign-on and Privilege Management Infrastructure (PMI).]

SET makes use of cryptographic techniques, such as digital certificates (an document used to prove ownership of a public key) and public key cryptography to allow parties to identify themselves to each other and exchange information securely. SET uses a blinding algorithm that, in effect, lets merchants substitute a certificate for a user's credit card number. This allows traders to credit funds from clients' credit cards without the need of the credit card numbers. The public key cryptography is a cryptographic system that uses two keys - a public key known to everyone and a private (secret) key known only to the recipient of the message.

SET was intemperately publicized in the late 1990's as the credit card approved standard, but failed to win market share. Reasons for this include:

- Network effect - need to install client software (an e-wallet).

- Cost and complexity for merchants to offer support and comparatively low cost and simplicity of the existing, adequate SSL based alternative.

- Client-side certificate distribution logistics.

SET was said to become the de-facto standard of payment method on the Internet between the merchants, the buyers, and the credit card companies. When SET is used, the merchant itself never has to know the credit card numbers being sent from the buyer, which provides a benefit for e-commerce.

The SET Protocol

People today pay for online purchases by sending their credit card details to the merchant. A protocol, such as SSL or TLS keeps the card details safe from eavesdroppers/hackers, but does nothing to protect merchants from dishonest customers or vice-versa. SET addresses this situation by requiring cardholders and merchants to register before they may engage in transactions. Every cardholder has to register by contacting a certificate authority, supplying security details and the public half of his/her proposed signature key. Registration allows the authorities to validate an applicant, who if approved receives a certificate confirming that his/her signature key is valid. All orders and confirmations bear digital signatures, which provide authentication and could potentially help to resolve disputes.

8.4.1 How it Works?

SET purchase involves three parties: the cardholder, the merchant, and the payment gateway (fundamentally a bank). The cardholder shares the order information with the merchant but not with the payment gateway. He shares the payment information with the bank but not with the merchant. A set dual signature accomplishes this partial sharing of information while allowing all parties to confirm that they are handling the same transaction. The method is simple: each party receives the hash of the withheld information. The cardholder signs the hashes of both the order information and the payment information. Each party can confirm that the hashes in their possession agree with the hash signed by the cardholder. In addition, the cardholder and merchant compute equivalent hashes for the payment gateway to be compared. He/she confirms their agreement on the details withheld from him/her.

SET is a family of protocols. The five main ones are cardholder registration, merchant registration, purchase request, payment authorization, and payment capture. There are many minor protocols, for example to handle errors. SET is enormously more complicated than SSL, which merely negotiates session keys between the cardholder's and merchant's Internet service providers. Because of this complexity, much of which is unnecessary, the protocol is hardly used. However, SET contains many features of interest:

- The model is unusual. In the registration protocols, the initiator possesses no digital proof of identity. Instead, he/she authenticates himself/herself by filling a registration form whose format is not specified. Authentication takes place outside the protocol, when the cardholder's bank examines the completed form.

- The dual signature is a novel construction. The partial sharing of information among three peers leads to unusual protocol goals.

- SET uses several types of digital envelopes. A digital envelope consists of two parts: one, encrypted using a public key, contains a fresh symmetric key K and identifying information; the other, encrypted using K, conveys the full message text. Digital envelopes keep public key encryption to a minimum, but the many symmetric keys complicate the reasoning. Most verified protocols distribute just one or two secrets.

Key features

To meet the business requirements, SET incorporates the following features:

- Confidentiality of information
- Integrity of data
- Cardholder account authentication
- Merchant authentication

Participants

A SET system includes the following participants:

- Cardholder
- Merchant
- Issuer
- Acquirer
- Payment gateway
- Certification authority

Transaction

The sequence of events required for a transaction is as follows:

1. The customer obtains a credit card account with a bank that supports electronic payment and SET.

2. The customer receives an X.509 v3 digital certificate signed by the bank.

3. Merchants have their own certificates.

4. The customer places an order.

5. The merchant sends a copy of its certificate so that the customer can verify that it is a valid store.

6.   The order and payment are sent.

7.   The merchant requests payment authorization.

8.   The merchant confirms the order.

9.   The merchant ships the goods or provides the service to the customer.

10. The merchant requests payment.

Dual Signature

An important innovation introduced in SET is the dual signature. The purpose of the dual signature is the same as the standard electronic signature: to guarantee the authentication and integrity of data. It links two messages that are intended for two different recipients. In this case, the customer wants to send the Order Information (OI) to the merchant and the Payment Information (PI) to the bank. The merchant does not need to know the customer's credit card number, and the bank does not need to know the details of the customer's order. The link is needed so that the customer can prove that the payment is intended for this order.

Test Your Progress
1.   *What do you understand by SET?*
2.   *What are key features of SET?*
3.   *What do you mean by dual signature?*

8.5   Electronic Cash Payment Schemes

8.5.1 Basics

Before jumping to e-com related jargons, let's spend a while on basics on banking /payment systems. Banking originated in ancient era, where royal palaces, temples were used as secure place for safekeeping of grain and other commodities. Receipts for stored commodities were used for transfers not only to the original depositors but also to third parties, including tax gatherers and traders.

Bank notes were introduced during 1694 by Bank of England as central banking system. On following steps during 1775 continental congress issued paper money to finance revolutionary war. Thereafter in 1800s and early 1900 saw issuance of state bank notes, gold certificates. And finally in 1913 Federal Reserve act was created to further structure roadmap.

Table 8.5 summarizes the list of modes of payment.

Table 8.5: Modes of Payment

Cheque	It is written order on a bank or other financial institution to pay money belonging to the owner of cheque to cheque presenter. Personal cheque is drawn on individual bank account, while cashier cheque is drawn on financial institution.

Money Order	It is an order for the payment of a specified amount of money, usually issued and payable at a bank or post office. It is feasible for people who do not have back account or circumstances where cheques are not accepted in payments.
Credit Card	It is a valuable piece of plastic, i.e., plastic card used instead of cash or cheques to pay for buying goods/services. Credit card companies send monthly statement of charges made by credit card. Users can make full payment or partial payment, later one comes with interest/finance charges attached to same.
Debit Card:	It is also plastic used to procure good/services, but it is important to note it is linked to bank account. Bank deducts transactions made directly from account. It good workaround for people, who for contend (i.e., not to fell in trap of credit card companies). And want to avoid carrying actual cash with them.

Now, let's start rolling the e-related stuff!

The twenty-first century way to pay is by electronic or digital cash (or one can say virtual cash also), which allows consumers to pay for goods/services by transmitting a number from one computer to another. These numbers function much like the serial numbers on "real money", they are unique and represent a specific amount of actual cash.

Unlike credit card transactions, electronic-cash transactions are anonymous. E-cash works just like paper cash. Once it is withdrawn from an account it does not leave a trail of digital crumbs. E-cash by its nature is portable and therefore more convenient for mobile commerce (Internet-capable cell phones and personal digital assistants).

Couple of well known players in industry on this domain:

PayPal - US-based system that allows individuals in the United States to send money to each other via e-mail.

First-E - European, Internet-only bank.

Mondex - Electronic cash that is made available via "smart card."

eCash (formerly DigiCash) - One of the early developers of electronic payment systems.

Although there are various options of electronic payments, most common consumer choice is use of credit, debit and charge cards. In order to accept these cards, an e-business, must have a merchant account, payment-processing software and procedure to safeguard its customers and itself against fraud, i.e., in basic terms "security".

8.5.2 Requirement for running E-commerce Business

Merchant Accounts :

When you want to have credit card, you fill up form/details and submit same to financial institution, on similar lines when some want to start e-business/online transactions (which need online transaction through credit, debit, charge cards), one must step up a merchant account.

Couple of FAQ asked by financial institution while accepting aforesaid request:

i.   Type/category of goods/services being sold.

ii.   How old is business?

iii. Which all type of cards (Visa/MasterCard) to be accepted?

iv.   How many transactions accepted on regular basis?

v.   What should be limit of transaction per individual?

vi.   How much transaction fees should be marked?

vii. Terms and conditions for end customers.

Charges for keeping merchant account could be one time entry fee, as registration cost and then followed with charges with every transaction (% attached to same), or on monthly basis, it also varies from institutions to institutions !

Working of Pay flow Gateway works (See Figure 5.2):

● Your Online Store

● Payment Gateway

● Internet Merchant Account

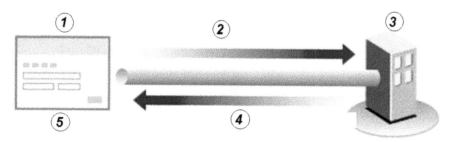

Figure 8.2: Cyclic Flow of Payment Gateway

1.   Your customer inputs credit card information on Your Online Store.

2.   The Payment Gateway encrypts data and securely sends it to your Internet Merchant Account.

3.   The transaction is reviewed for authorization.

4.   The result is encrypted and sent back through the Payment Gateway.

5.   You get the results and decide whether or not to fulfil the order.

Payment Processing Software

Its usually third party organization, which provides payment processing software, for example, monetra, verifone, etc. It is used for getting card transactions authorized and further processed. E–business usually pays monthly fees for processing services. Also its extremely vital, for any online transactions e-business must provide adequate security for the card information being transmitted.

Security, it is like heart-beat for online transactions!

If you want your business to survive, its extremely essential to build up security mechanisms for online transactions. Couple of noteworthy security features includes:

Cyptography : Is process to safeguard data by encrypting same.

Encryption : Is process for translating data into secret code called cipher text.

Cipertext : Is process for transmitting data to destination and then decrypted to plaintext.

SSL : Is protocol which is agreed upon for e-transactions. It provides server-side encrypted transactions for electronic payments and other forms of secure internet communications. Please note URL for secured Web pages start with **https :** //instead of normal http://, indicating transaction is transmitted over SSL or Secure Socket Layer protocol.

Verisign : Industry leaders in SSL certificates.

8.5.3 Other Electronic Payment Forms

Electronic Cheques : It is electronic cheque of a paper cheque. It contains similar information, and contains same legal info is also. It is important to know, e-cheque is less expensive for institutions then traditional ways.

Screen below shows comparison sheet from ICICI Bank on different payment systems.

6. **What are the advantages of doing an online Funds Transfer (eCheques)?**

Let us take a look at the comparison table for a better understanding. (for Inter A/c transfer)

Payment system	Speed	Cost	Effort	Portability	Acceptance	Security
Cash	Low	High	High	Low	High	Low
Cheque	Low	High	High	High	High	Medium
Money order	Low	High	High	High	High	High
Telegraphic (or wire) transfer	High	High	High	High	High	High
ICICI Bank eCheque	High	Low	Low	High	High	High

Top

7. I want to know more about

a. Funds Transfer (eCheques) between my own a/c's

You can transfer funds to your own linked a/c's instantaneously or you can even schedule the transfer for a future date.

Top

7. I want to know more about

b. Funds Transfer (eCheques) to a third party a/c in ICICI Bank

For doing a third party transfer in ICICI Bank, you will have to register the payee.

Smart Cards: It is a size similar to credit card that contains electronic money.

Apart from storing cash, it is also does value adds like storing medical records, generating network identification. One of leading service providers in this arena Mondex is on contrary one of disadvantage of using smart card, it needs additional device to be attached to PCs, to read the card.

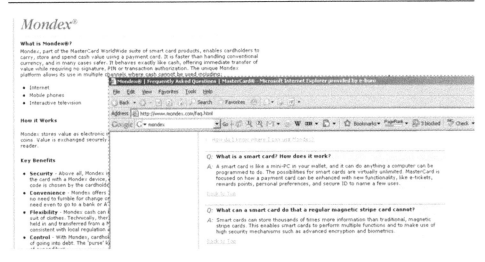

Electronic Cash: Its method that allows online buyers to pay for goods/services using unique electronic number/code that carries a specific value. Couple of advantages for using this system is low processing cost and no special credit card type authorization.

Some analysts predict electronic cash will only chip away at the dominance of the credit card as preferred online payment method in near future. Example: digicash.

8.5.4 Case Study-PayPal

An exciting new world of online cross-border opportunities awaits you. With PayPal, you can send and receive money in 18 currencies from anyone with an eimail address in 190 countries and regions. As a global leader in online payments, with 150 million accounts worldwide and growing, we empower you by removing hurdles and accelerating the pace of online transactions across borders.

Whether you are a buyer or seller, PayPal offers an outstanding array of benefits for international transactions:

● Attract an international audience to your e-commerce Website.

● Send money to family or friends around the world.

● Welcome regional or global buyers to your eBay listings.

● Buy online from another country with minimal fuss, hassle and cost.

This section presents a framework for discussion of electronic payment schemes. A comprehensive index of such schemes and a brief overview of their relationship to the framework is provided. The framework consists of two axes, the levels of abstraction at which the protocol is analyzed and the payment model considered.

A Layered Protocol Model

A three layer model is used to compare payments schemes.

Policy: Its represents semantics of the payment scheme. This includes refunds policies, and the liabilities incurred by customers, merchants and financial institutions.

Data flow: It represents requirements for storage of data by and communications between the parties. This includes not only the data flows for payments themselves but also for refunds, account enquiries and settlement.

Mechanism: It represents methods by which the necessary security requirements for messages and stored data are achieved.

All three abstraction levels are tightly coupled since policy makes requirements of data flow and data flow makes requirements of mechanism.

Payment Protocol Models

Cash: Cash consists of a token which may be authenticated independently of the issuer. This is commonly achieved through use of self authenticating tokens or tamper proof hardware.

Cheque: Cheques are payment instruments whose validity requires reference to the issuer.

Card: Card payment schemes provide a payments mechanism through the existing credit card payment infrastructure. Such schemes have many structural similarities to cheque models except that solutions are constrained by that structure. A key feature of card payment systems is that every transaction carries insurance.

Test Your Progress

1. *What is e-cheque?*
2. *What is Momdex?*
3. *What are different ways for conducting online transactions?*
4. *How is cheque different from money order?*

8.6 Building E-commerce Site

8.6.1 Why to build E-commerce Site?

Not only with e-commerce Website, but one should always ask himself/herself during start of new project/process/business, why we are doing this adventure. As everything in today's fast moving world is linked to TEM (Time/Energy/Money), one should take every step to avoid landing into pitfall.

Now let's spend a minute focusing on e-commerce stuff. Before jumping into, this new adventure, its good to have quick look on following FAQ:

i. What is wish list on products/services?

ii. Should allow customers to order products/services on the fly?

iii. Technical support for products/services.

iv. How will be advertise our products/services and Website itself?

v. Collect information about current and potential customers.

vi. Skilled/ technical manpower requirement for running show.

vii. Build e-business image and brand.

viii. Also showcase links to related Websites.

ix. Capex and Opex calculations?

8.6.2 What will be Website/portal structure?

Need of hour in today's fast moving era, "how fast and accurate you are able to provide information to customers"; one has to believe this after Google grand success.

Similarly for e-commerce Website, we must organize the information/content very carefully and how fast/quickly you are able to provide information to information seekers/potential customers. Some of noteworthy things to pull upon:

i.   Name of new baby, i.e., e-commerce's name.

ii.   Your identify marks, logo/trademarks.

iii. Database for capturing customer information.

iv.   Search option, to dig out information quickly.

v.   Vision and mission statement.

vi.   Contact us.

vii. Site map.

viii. Copyright information.

ix.   No. of visitors of day.

x.   Forms for registration process.

xi.   Press release and testimonies.

xii. Offers on the shelf.

xiii. Careers.

xiv. Link to associate Websites.

xv.   Domain name registration and Web space.

Apart from aforesaid stuff, one must follow two simple principles: (i) Your Website should provide what speaks for, (ii) Keep it as simple as possible! Multiple layers of associated Web links/pages make things complicated, which could eventually frustrate customers.

Also creating logically like with flowchart in hand to set navigation would be really helpful. Registration forms should be kept very handy and ask to the point information.

8.6.3 Techniques to be Used

Basic Techniques:

-   Maintain consistency in flow.

-   Internal hyperlink to connect different pages.

-   Navigation bar for quick search.

-   Using Splash pages – Some Websites need showy entrance, with animations and sound effects to highlight the effects.

-   Text and icon hyperlinks can be positioned in body of a Web page to help viewers navigate a Website.

-   Using color, its critical as it should have showcase theme and concept.

-   Font to be carefully as Arial for headings, Times New Roman for text, etc.

-   Background images, small images are preferred then large ones.

- Adding thumbnail is also trendy concept these days.

- Frames and form to be kept simple, and also to the point questions.

8.6.4 Web Development Tools

Web development has been one of the fastest growing industries, courtesy popularity of Internet cloud. Since 1995 there were fewer than 1 000 Web development companies in the US alone, but by 2005 there were over 30, 000 such companies (officially registered). The Web development industry is expected to grow over 20% by 2010. The growth of this industry is linked with e-commerce, as it opens global market to push selling products /services.

In addition, cost of Website development and hosting has dropped dramatically during this time, mainly due to too many players joining boat. Smaller Website development companies are now able to make Web design accessible to both smaller companies and individuals further fueling the growth of the Web development industry.

Speaking about, Web development tools and platforms there are many options on plate, many available to the public free of charge to aid in development. A popular example is the LAMP (Linux, Apache, MySQL, PHP), which is usually distributed free of charge. This fact alone has manifested into many people around the globe setting up new Websites daily and thus contributing to increase in Web development popularity

Web Development can be split into many areas and a typical and basic Web development hierarchy might consist of Client-sides and Server-sides.

Client-Side Coding

- AJAX Provides new methods of using JavaScript, PHP and other languages to improve the user experience.

- Flash Adobe Flash Player is a ubiquitous client-side platform ready for RIAs.

- JavaScript Formally called EMCAScript, JavaScript is a ubiquitous client-side programming tool.

- Microsoft Silverlight Microsoft's browser plug-in that enables animation, vector graphics and high-definition video playback, programmed using XAML and .NET programming languages.

Server-Side Coding

- ASP (Microsoft proprietary)
- Cold Fusion (Adobe proprietary, formerly Macromedia)
- CGI and/or Perl (open source)
- Java, for example J2EE or WebObjects
- Lotus Domino
- PHP (open source)
- Python, for example Django (Web framework) (open source)

- Ruby, for example Ruby on Rails (open source)
- Smalltalk for example Seaside, AIDA/Web
- SSJS (Server-Side JavaScript), for example Aptana Jaxer, Mozilla Rhino
- Websphere (IBM proprietary)
- .NET (Microsoft proprietary)

8.6.5 Website Testing and Maintenance Issues

In technical jargons testing is also popularly known as "AT", i.e., Acceptance Testing.

Success of your Website depends on this factor in major way. You should do self (means self) check in order to cross validate, that all things are working properly, for example:

- Forms filled by users is properly stored in database
- Hyperlinks/associate links to work properly
- Security related stuff, encryption/SSL etc., totally secure
- Make a accentuate test, to check how much load Website can carry?

Maintenance is ongoing endeavor, which will go long way. After Website is through with testing and works online, it becomes your moral responsibility to nurture this "new kid on the block". One has to constantly monitor traffic and evaluate Website activities. Remember most of knowledgeable visitors, check first thing while visiting Website is "when it was last updated", it gives impression that how serious/ updated seller is about business Also, it is extremely vital to be innovative from time to time, static Websites does not last long, one has to lead with latest Web technologies available and always dig out room for improvements.

When traffic grows, one has to careful do bandwidth/space calculations/server processing speeds which host Websites/DNS entries, etc., slow opening Websites gives bad impression and you might loose potential customers. Keep visitor count tab on Website, in order to track things in professional way.

Last but not least, "value visitor feedback", which can really make wonders for you.

Test Your Progress
1.   *What are basic steps to develop a Website?*
2.   *Define LAMP?*
3.   *What is server-side development tool?*

8.7   Case Studies

8.7.1 Understanding Search Engine E-Commerce

Paid search can now be visualized as a primary business model for Web search engines. The success of search community can be analyzed as shown in screen shot

(Mondex) which show that search has emerged as the most reachable and monetizing category among other popular categories such as News, Sports, Entertainment, etc. Search Engine has emerged as an advertising platform for business and services of companies. Understanding Search engines marketing strategies is much important in order to achieve success in online business. The simplicity of the model lies in the fact that searchers are not disturbed by the visibility of advertisements and their search results are not hampered by the advertising process. Apart from supporting online advertising industry, search engine has also developed a model for getting rich online. This model is based on a simple rule, i.e.,

"Earn pennies at a time in exchange for allowing Search Engine to place advertisements on a personal or small-business Web page".

Major players in this role are Google and Yahoo. The Advertisement publishers are supposed to give permission to search engine to place advertisement in their Website and for every click a user makes on the advertisement the Website owner gets paid by the search engine. People with creative ideas can get rich relatively quickly by permitting advertisers to piggyback on any Website that attracts a lot of viewers. Technology can direct advertisement to more and more specific audiences, rewarding entrepreneurship on the smallest scale. Thus, the only most important factor is the traffic to the Website. If the Website has visitors it is fit for making online income via search engine. Advertisement publishers must be approved through search engine, to ensure that the ads do not subsidize pornography or gambling, or contain material that is racist, violent or related to illegal drugs. Success of the model depends on the cooperation of advertisers, who have to see that their money is well spent, as they pay search engine for each click visitor makes and this revenue is shared then with Advertisement publisher.

The study on revenue generated by Website owner shows that most of the revenue is generated by pay per click strategies like Google's adsense program. Google pays adsense publishers 78.5 cents on the dollar as revenue share. Google never officially disclosed details on revenue sharing but it has been observed that, as per rule Google shares 50 cents of every dollar to partners - and can range up to the full dollar, depending on the size of the relationship. The revenue generated by the program highly depends on the traffic of the Website. It is not only Web publishers search engine also earn through their advertising strategies. Google revealed that last year 41 percent of its revenue, through the network of Websites that host ads through the adsense system. Thus, search engine advertising has emerged as highly promising model for earning online.

The popularity of making money online using search engine model has led to creation of "Made-for-AdSense" Web pages that contain little content and lots of advertisement, which critics say clutter the Internet and divert online searches. Some scraper sites are created for monetizing the site using advertising programs, such as Google adsense. Its also a derogatory term used to refer to Websites that have no redeeming value except to get Web visitors to the Website for the sole purpose of clicking on advertisements. The major problem with such "Made for Adsense" sites is they are considered as sites responsible for spamming search engines and diluting the search results by providing surfers with less than satisfactory search results. The content of such Websites is considered redundant to that which would be shown by the search engine under normal circumstances when no such sites are listed.

8.8   Amazon.com Case Study

Source: http://www.davechaffey.com/E-commerce-Internet-marketing-case-studies/Amazon-case-study

Amazon e-commerce strategy case study prepared for e-business, Internet Marketing and E-commerce lecturers and students for readers of my Internet Marketing and E-business books.

2008 Update on Amazon logistics

"Amazon.com has finished its 13th Christmas season and the results are the best ever season, with its busiest day being December 10. On that day, Amazon customers ordered more than 5.4 million items, which is 62.5 items per second.

Amazon Worldwide 2007 (Including results for the US, UK, Germany, France, Japan and Canada) shipped more than 99 percent of orders in time to meet holiday deadlines worldwide and on the peak day this season, Amazon's worldwide fulfilment network shipped over 3.9 million units to over 200 countries.

Amazon.co.uk received orders for over 950, 000 items on its busiest day in the run up to Christmas this year – at a rate of 11 orders per second – exceeding all previous sales records. At its busiest, Amazon.co.uk shipped over 700, 000 units in one 24 hour period, which represents 375 tonnes of goods. That means that on average, a delivery truck was leaving an Amazon.co.uk distribution centre once every seven minutes."

Amazon Case Study Context

Why a case study on Amazon? Surely everyone knows about who Amazon are and what they do? Yes, well that may be true, but this case goes beyond the surface to review some of the 'insider secrets' of Amazon's success.

Like eBay, Amazon.com was born in 1995. The name reflected the vision of Jeff Bezos, to produce a large scale phenomenon like the Amazon river. This ambition has proved justified since just 8 years later, Amazon passed the $5 billion sales mark – it took Wal-Mart 20 years to achieve this.

By 2008 Amazon was a global brand with other 76 million active customers accounts and order fulfilment to more than 200 countries. Despite this volume of sales, at December 31, 2007 Amazon employed approximately 17, 000 full-time and part-time employees.

In September 2007, it launched Amazon MP3, a la carte DRM-free MP3 music downloads, which now includes over 3.1 million songs from more than 270, 000 artists.

Amazon Vision and strategy

In their 2008 SEC filing, Amazon describes the vision of their business as to:

"Relentlessly focus on customer experience by offering our customers low prices, convenience, and a wide selection of merchandise."

The vision is to offer Earth's biggest selection and to be Earth's most customer-centric company. Consider how these core marketing messages summarizing the Amazon online value proposition are communicated both on-site and through offline communications.

Of course, achieving customer loyalty and repeat purchases has been key to Amazon's success. Many dot-coms failed because they succeeded in achieving awareness, but not loyalty. Amazon achieved both. In their SEC filing they stress how they seek to achieve this. They say:

"We work to earn repeat purchases by providing easy-to-use functionality, fast and reliable fulfilment, timely customer service, feature rich content, and a trusted transaction environment.

Key features of our Websites include editorial and customer reviews; manufacturer product information; Web pages tailored to individual preferences, such as recommendations and notifications; 1-Click® technology; secure payment systems; image uploads; searching on our Websites as well as the Internet; browsing; and the ability to view selected interior pages and citations, and search the entire contents of many of the books we offer with our "Look Inside the Book" and "Search Inside the Book" features. Our community of online customers also creates feature-rich content, including product reviews, online recommendation lists, wish lists, buying guides, and wedding and baby registries."

In practice, as is the practice for many online retailers, the lowest prices are for the most popular products, with less popular products commanding higher prices and a greater margin for Amazon.

Free shipping offers are used to encourage increase in basket size since customers have to spend over a certain amount to receive free shipping. The level at which free-shipping is set is critical to profitability and Amazon has changed it as competition has changed and for promotional reasons.

Amazon communicates the fulfillment promise in several ways including presentation of latest inventory availability information, delivery date estimates, and options for expedited delivery, as well as delivery shipment notifications and update facilities.

This focus on customer has translated to excellence in service with the 2004 American Customer Satisfaction Index giving Amazon.com a score of 88 which was at the time, the highest customer satisfaction score ever recorded in any service industry, online or offline.

Amazon focuses on customer satisfaction metrics. Each site is closely monitored with standard service availability monitoring (for example, using Keynote or Mercury

Interactive) site availability and download speed. Interestingly it also monitors per minute site revenue upper/lower bounds. It is like describing an alarm system rather like a power plant where if revenue on a site falls below $10,000 per minute, alarms go off! There are also internal performance service-level-agreements for Web services where T% of the time, different pages must return in X seconds.

Amazon Customers

Amazon defines what it refers to as three consumer sets customers, seller customers and developer customers.

There are over 76 million customer accounts, but just 1.3 million active seller customers in it is marketplaces and Amazon is seeking to increase this. Amazon is unusual for a retailer in that it identifies "developer customers" who use its Amazon Web Services, which provides access to technology infrastructure, such as hosting that developers can use to develop their own Web services.

Members are also encouraged to join a loyalty program, Amazon Prime, a fee-based membership program in which members receive free or discounted express shipping, in the United States, the United Kingdom, Germany and Japan.

8.9   Key Terms

- **E-Commerce:** Is meant for facilitation of commercial transactions electronically, using technology such as Electronic Data Interchange (EDI), Electronic Funds Transfer (EFT), etc.

- **EDI:** Collection of standard message formats to exchange data between organizations computers via any electronic service.

- **Merchant account:** When you want to have credit card, you fill up form/details and submit same to financial institution, on similar lines when some want to start e-business/online transactions (which need online transaction through credit, debit, charge cards), one must step up a merchant account.

- **Models of e-commerce:** B2B, B2C, C2B and C2B.

- **SET:** A standard protocol for securing credit card transactions over insecure networks, more specifically addressing transactions over Internet.

8.10   Summary

E-commerce which has made this place felt in last decade has lot of potential in coming digital era. Main advantage seller foresees, target audience for his/her goods/services is across globe, which eventually was confined to local geographic area initially. Various categories B2B, B2C, C2B, and C2C, have supported e-commerce facelift its value as there are different cum structured options available to run the show. EDI, the inter-organization exchange of well-defined business transactions in standardized electronic form directly between computer applications, focused on Business-To-Business community.

Secure Electronic Transaction (SET) is a standard protocol for securing credit card transactions over insecure networks, more specifically addressing transactions over Internet. On e-payment front apart from traditional credit and debit cards, other options available e-cheques, smart cards and e-cash. And finally on Web development front we have seen tremendous growth in this arena. This industry has been growing with splendid growth rate.

8.11 Test Yourself

Section I: Review with Ease

Q. 1. Explain various roles in e-commerce.

Ans 1. Different roles of e-commerce are:

a.   Buyers - These are public/people with money who want to purchase goods or services.

b.   Sellers - These are the people/public who offer goods and services to buyers. Sellers could belong to different categories: (i) Retailers who sell directly to consumers (ii) Wholesalers/distributors who sell to retailers and other businesses.

c.   Producers - These are the people who create the products and service those sellers. Offer to buyers, i.e. also known as manufactures.

Q. 2. What are advantages of e-commerce?

Ans 2. Different advantages of e-commerce are:

a.   Lowers selling cost, as not many taxes involved, apart from basic rules.

b.   Market is open 24×7×365.

c.   Without much investment you can sell products across continents.

Q. 3. Explain Models of e-commerce?

Ans 3. Different models of e-commerce are :

a.   B2B (Business-to-Business): Organizations/companies doing business with each other, such as manufacturers selling to distributors and wholesalers selling to retailers. Examples: shop2gether, metalsite, etc.

b.   B2C (Business-to-Consumer): Businesses selling to the public directly, usually through catalogs utilizing shopping cart software. In race of maximum volume category B2B is undoubted leader. Examples: makemytrip.com, amazon.com, etc.

c.   C2B (Consumer-to-Business): Consumer publish his/her project with a set budget online and within hours companies review the consumer's requirements and bid for the project. The consumer checks the bids and selects the company that will complete the project. Examples: reverseauction.com, priceline.com.

d.   C2C (Consumer-to-Consumer): Consumer sells directly to consumers. There are numerous sites offering free classifieds, auctions, and forums where individuals can buy and sell thanks to online payment systems like PayPal where people can send and receive money online with ease.

Q. 4.   Discuss the need of Migration to open EDI.

Ans 4. The need of migration can be summarized as follows:

a.   Reduction of the cost of transferring EDI messages

b.   Increase the performance

c.   Supporting e-Commerce

d.   Increase the interoperability of networks increasing the usability of EDI

Q. 5. What is SET? Describe in detail.

Ans 5. Secure Electronic Transaction (SET) is a standard protocol for securing credit card transactions over insecure networks, more specifically addressing transactions over Internet. SET is not itself a payment system, but rather a set of security protocols and formats that enables users to employ the existing credit card payment infrastructure on an open network in a secure fashion !

Q. 6.   Name different traditional ways of payments?

Ans 6. Cheque, money order, credit card and debit card are famous traditional payment ways.

Q. 7.   Explain SSL.

Ans 7. SSL is protocol which is agreed upon for e-transactions. It provides server-side encrypted transactions for electronic payments and other forms of secure Internet communications. URL for secured Web pages starts with https:// instead of normal http://, indicating transaction is transmitted over SSL protocol (SSL: Secure Socket Layer).

Q. 8.   Why e-commerce Website need regular maintenance?

Ans 8. E-commerce site owners, has to constantly monitor traffic and evaluate Website activities. Remember most of knowledgeable visitors, check first thing while visiting Website is "when it was last updated", it gives impression that how serious/ updated seller is about business! Also, it is extremely vital to be innovative form time to time, static Websites does not last long, one has to lead with latest Web technologies available and always dig out room for improvements.

Section II: Exercises

1.   Fill in the blanks

1.   Various roles in e-commerce are_____.

2.   EFT stands for _____.

3.   B2C is_____.

4.   ebay is _____ site.

5.   SET is set of _____ protocols.

2.   True/False

1.   Estimated Internet Users is approximately 1.4Bn for Q2 2008.

2. Amazon.com falls under B2C model of e-commerce.

3. Security is factor impacting growth of e-commerce.

4. SET stands for Secure Electrical Transactions.

5. Credit card and smart card are same products with different names.

3. Answer the following questions:

1. Explain the evolution of e-commerce in detail.

2. Explain SET in detail.

3. Discuss various models of e-commerce in detail.

4. List down advantages and disadavantages of EDI in detail.

5. Explain SSL Layer.

Chapter 9
Adobe Photoshop

There are 3 key things for good photography: The Camera, Lighting and Photoshop   *~Tyra Banks*

Key Topics

- *Introduction*
- *Getting Started*
- *Creating Files*
- *Using Tools*
- *Layer Management*
- *Using Filters in Photoshop*
- *Linking HTML files*

This Chapter basically deals with the introduction of Adobe Photoshop. The content and flow of the Chapter are designed mainly for the Web designing and developing purpose. Here you will go with the basic introduction of each essential element used for Web Development.

9.1   Introduction

Photoshop is a tool to work with the images. It is one of the powerful and extremely fun applications to use. This is globally accepted tool for image editing. With a name and fame of this tool wikitionary.org has given meaning for "Photoshop", that is "to digitally alter a picture or photograph". This tool gives you a different color and lighting correction, historically occurrence of events or task, filtering options, painting options, layering and masking and many more. This tool allows you to take a certain image editing process to the next level.

Where to use?

- *For **image correction** by using its lighting options.*
- *For **image enhancement** by adding blur and soften options.*
- *For **image composition** by using two or more images in one.*

- For **artistic effects** by using different filters.
- For **painting** by using a different type of brushes.
- For **adding text** to a certain image.
- For **creating images** of the Web and mobile devices.

Where not to use:
- For textual work or word processing.
- For creating presentations and business graphics.
- For text editing or managing.

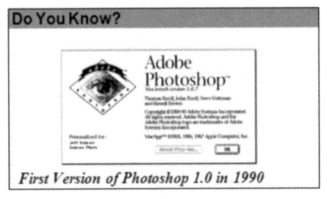

First Version of Photoshop 1.0 in 1990

Test Your Progress
1. Give a brief description about Adobe Photoshop.
2. Where to use Photoshop?
3. Where not to use Photoshop?

9.2 Getting Started

Visit the Interface of Adobe Photoshop 7

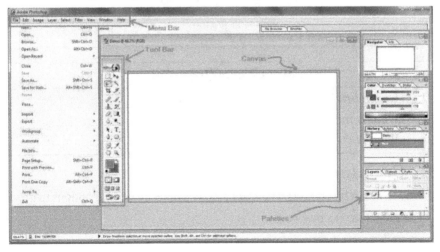

The work area can be unapproachable to work with because of all the composite functionality. A swift breakdow+n of the available elements and their uses, here you will be ready to navigate the work area with ease. Photoshop has the following basic working and appearance:

- **Menu Bar:** This is top most bar/area, you can easily access most of the commands and features.

- **Drawing Area(Canvas):** An area where the image being worked on will appear with different options.

- **Options bar**
  - It exists below the Menu bar.
  - Context sensitive as per tool option (below option image is as per Brush Selection Tool).
  - It changes as different tools are selected from the Tool box.
  - Display using **Window → Options** or by clicking on a tool in the toolbox.

- **Tool box** – Consist of all tools for creating and editing images (display or hide using **Windows → Tools**).

- **Palettes** - To monitor each event and modify images.

Second Version of Photoshop 2.0 in 1991

Test Your Progress

1. *Give a brief description about the Workspace.*
2. *What is the use of Option bar?*
3. *What is the use of Palettes?*

9.3 Creating Files

Now we start by creating a new document. There are several options to go with. Let's discuss one-by-one.

Size: It is the dimensions of your Canvas and can be set using inches, pixels, etc.

Background: It is what your base is, on which you perform your work. It can be Transparent, Colored or White.

Resolution: It is very important. It is dependent upon the purpose of creating image, i.e., for printing, banner, Website, mobile devices or others.

Now, let's start to create a new document. For this, you select **Menu → File → New** or **Ctrl + N**. This opens a window called New dialog box that requires above discussed inputs.

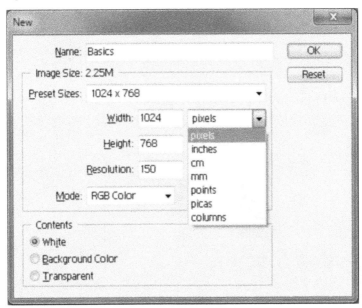

Let us discuss the options available in New dialog box.

Name: Name of the Document. In the above picture, it is "**Basics**".

Present Sizes: We will use **1024 pixels** by **768 pixels**. It is standard form for Web. It is depend on the width and height you select in this box.

Resolution: We will take it **150pixels/inch.**

Note: Resolution specifications
Web Resolution = 72
Print resolution = 150 or 300
Film Resolution = 600

Let's just consider these settings as this will work all over the place, rather than getting into a discussion on the resolution.

Background Color: Here, we will use as a white background. This radio button appears in Contents Section, and is used to set background color.

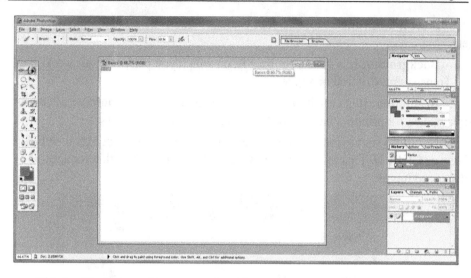

This is all what you have to work with.

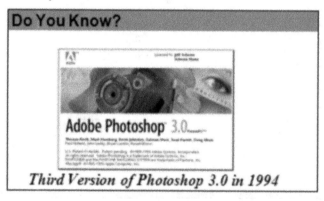

Third Version of Photoshop 3.0 in 1994

Test Your Progress
1. *What are the several options consider for creating a file?*
2. *What are different resolution specifications?*
3. *What are the units under the Image Size: option in New dialog box?*

9.4   Using Tools

Let's start the most important part of Photoshop, i.e. **Tools.**

We have just discussed the basic working of each tool. As for Web development and designing all tools is not that much important.

 The **Marquee Tool** are used for Rectangular, Elliptical, Single Row and Single Column selections.

 The **Move Tool** is mainly used to move the selected region, layers and guides.

The **Lasso Tools** are used to make some Free Hand selection, Polygonal and Magnetic selections.

The **Magic Wand Tool** is mainly used for similar colored area selection.

The **Crop Tool** is used to cut/trim the selected portion.

The **Slice Tool** is used for making slices of image and widely used in Web development.

The **Healing Brush Tool** is used to renovate the imperfection by painting it with its similar type of textures.

The **Brush Tool** is for Paint Brush strokes over the canvas.

The **Clone Stamp Tool** is used for paint similar to specific region.

The **History Brush Tool** is used to paint a copy of the selected region or image into current image window.

The **Tool Eraser** is used to erase pixels and also restores parts of an image to a previously stored image.

The **Gradient Tools** is used to create the Radial, Angle, Straight Line, Reflected and Diamond Blend between colors.

The **Blur Tool** is used to blur hard edges in an image.

The **Dodge Tool** is for lighting the areas in an image.

The **Path Selection Tool** is for some shapes or some segment selections by showing the anchor point, direction lines and direction points.

The **Type Text Tool** is used to create text over an image.

The **Pen Tools** is used to draw smooth-edged paths.

The **Rectangle Tool** is used to make a rectangular shape, and it also contains different types of shape lists.

The **Annotations Tool** is used to make some notes and also audio annotations that can be attached to an image.

The **Eye Dropper Tool** is used pick the color from the selected region or sample color in the image.

 The **Tool Hand** is used to move the selected portion of an image within its own window.

 The **Zoom Tool** is used to magnify and reduce the selected portion of image view of the image.

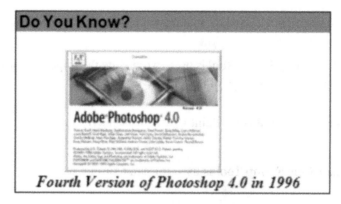

Do You Know?

Adobe Photoshop 4.0

Fourth Version of Photoshop 4.0 in 1996

Test Your Progress
1.   *Why we use Healing Brush Tool?*
2.   *Why we use Lasso Tool?*
3.   *Why we use Clone Stamp Tool?*

9.5   Layer Management

The most efficient way to work with Photoshop is to know how to deal with layers. Working with multiple layers is an asset to the Photoshop users. You can perform as many numbers of operations using layers with its usability. Layers are basically like a "Glass". Working on layer is like working on transparent Glass. Every glass layer has its own usability and it is also visible over one another. It will be easy to move with the basics to reduce beginner's confusion.

Layers Pane

The layers pane has the maximum usability so it is good to keep visible at all times. It exists as one of the components of pallets. If you are unable to see it when you open Photoshop then click on **Window → Show Layer** and it will be automatically restored.

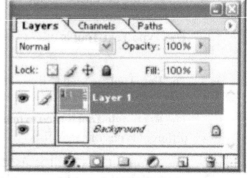

The Appearance of the Layers Pane is shown in the screen.

Working With Already Exist file as a Layer

If you open any image in Photoshop then you will find, there is only one layer named as **"Background"**. This **"Background"** layer have a Lock icon which represents that it is locked. If you want to unlock it then double click on the particular layer name and change its name. That layer is now unlocked and you can now make any changes in that particular image. It will be good enough to leave this layer and perform your work on other layers.

Adding New Layers

We discussed earlier that the layers are like Glass / clear pages overlaying each other. The layers emerge in the layers pane as similar as they are organized in the document.

To Create a New Layer

Click on **Layer → New Layer** or click on the dog eared icon at the bottom of the layers pane. Type any name for this layer & click enter. Now it appear in the layers pane, where there will be no sign of it. To perform this you can select the Brush Tool from the Tool bar and then paint anything on the image.

Selecting Layers

Select the Type Tool and type a little. You can observe that the type appears on top of the image. It is very similar to the Glass Slab. The layer which is above is more vibrant and visible. Now, you can use these two layers to learn how to use the layers pane.

For beginners, on the top text layer in Layer Panel, click the eye icon. It toggles the layer between Show and hide. When you click on the Paint Brush, which symbolizes that this is the layer you are working on currently. Now you click on the name of the layer below. You will notice that the Paint Brush now shows on the new active layer.

You can click on the empty Paint Brush box to lock and unlock layers, and can avoid unwanted modifications.

Arranging Layers

You can manually arrange the layers. For this, you click and drag your text layer under the original image layer. You will notice that the text no longer appears. That is because it is located behind the opaque image layer.

Delete Layer

If you want to delete a particular layer then you can either select the layer and click the Trash icon or right click on any layer. Click on delete layer or drag to the Trash icon at the bottom of the layers pane.

Combining or Merging Layers

Several times you will need to merge the contents of two layers onto one layer. For this, select the particular layer which you want to be on the top of the new merged layer. After this, make sure that the other layer you had like to merger is directly under it and then select **Merge Down** from the **Layer** menu. Now, you will notice that the two layers are now become one. If you wish to merge down an entire file of the layers then select **Flatten** image from the layers menu and then all the layers will be merged into one.

When it is merged or flatten layers, which contain the text layers, then you will be asked whether you'd like to rasterizing that text, i.e., convert it to the image and lose the ability to edit it. You will observe that it is a good idea to copy any layers and hide them before you rasterizing and merge.

Do You Know?

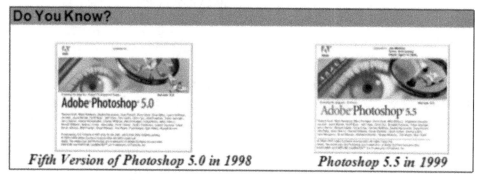

Fifth Version of Photoshop 5.0 in 1998   *Photoshop 5.5 in 1999*

Test Your Progress

1.   *What is Layer Pane?*
2.   *How to create a new layer?*
3.   *Give a brief description about Select, Arrange, Delete and Merge Layers.*

9.6   Using Filters in Photoshop

Filters are mainly used to alter the look of an image, layer or selected area in Photoshop. We will discuss some common filters, and also demonstrate you how to use them.

Figure 9.1 : Normal View

Filters in Photoshop are kind of like special effects. With the help of filters you can easily add some Artistic view. There are ample of ways to get creative using filters. So they are positively significant understanding in Photoshop!

For demonstrating filters, we will consider the below image as a sample. Here we will discuss some of the filters and also show you its effect. After that you can try other filters to make some innovative artwork.

Now, you can start using filter by selecting Filter option from Menu bar and choose the desire option to apply.

Example:

Filter→Artistic→Cutout→OK. By using this option the above image will look like abstract piece of artwork.

Figure 9.2 : Using Artistic Cutout

Now we get into some of the more common filters used frequently in Design:

Blur Filters (Filter→Blur)

The Blur Filter makes it easy to create a realistic Lens Blur effect in Photoshop.

Figure 9.3 : Using Blur Filter

Noise Filters (Filter→Noise)

Noise Filters are perfect for adding or reducing noise and provide grain effect in photographs. You may get filters, such as the **Reduce Noise Filter** very practical if you work with old, damaged or filthy images that need get repair work done to them. **Add Noise Filter** can also come in versatile, and has some resourceful applications of its own.

Figure 9.4: Using Noise Filter

Sharpen Filters (Filter→Sharpen)

The **Sharpen Filters** are great for correcting some imperfections in images as well as putting emphasis on significant elements in a design. If you are working with blurred images then a Sharpen Filter can be used to illuminate and enhanced edges by increasing contrast between pixels.

Figure 9.5: Using Sharpen Filter

These are some of Filter effects we will discuss here. You can also try your hands on this so that it will enhance your capability to illustrate images.

Sixth Version of Photoshop 6.0 in 2000

Test Your Progress
1. *What are Filters in Adobe Photoshop?*
2. *How to perform Artistic cutout?*
3. *How is Sharpen Tool different from Noise Tool?*

9.7 Linking HTML Files in Photoshop

Linking HTML files and Web address is done by the help of Slice Tool. It is a most important tool for Web developer and designer. Slicing Tool helps you to divide a image into as many slices and also create a HTML Web page by linking all slices.

Here whole process is discussed into total seven steps. It is very handy way to demonstrate all the flow to create such document. Let's discuss all the steps one-by-one:

- Open Adobe Photoshop and Create or select the image to which you want to add a link.

- Slice your developed image using the Slice Tool from the toolbox. Now, this will select the region of the image you desire to turn into a link. You can select the complete image or definite portions of it. To use this Slice Tool, you have to hold down the mouse button while you drag over the portion of your choice.

- Select the slice you desire to link using the Slice Select Tool from the toolbox. To open the Slice Options box you have to double-click on the selected slice.

- Type any name for the slice along with the full Website address or the HTML file address. Name should be where you want to move after clicking it. Always remember to add the **http://** in front of your desired Website address inside the URL text box or total path for HTML file address.

- In the Target text box enter your target. It will inform the browser how to open the link. [For an example, a **_blank** will open a new Web browser whenever you click on the link.] Click the OK button when you complete.

- Now, save the file and optimize for the Web. You can perform this by selecting **File→Save for Web.** Select the image optimization options which you want to submit an application to the file. The most common options are to save the file as a GIF, PNG or JPEG image file. For most uses, a **JPEG** will be a complete choice. The **JPEG Options** box appears which allows you to choose the size of the file and the quality level. For most of the time, the default settings here should be sufficient. Click OK when complete.

● Name this file and select this file type as **.html** under the **Save as Type** menu. Ensure that **All Slices** option is turned on and click **Save** when complete.

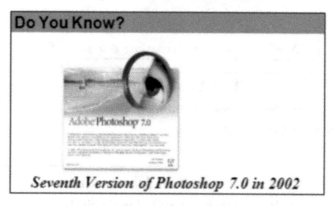

Do You Know?

Seventh Version of Photoshop 7.0 in 2002

Test Your Progress
1.   *Give a brief description about the Workspace.*
2.   *What is the use of Option bar?*
3.   *What is the use of Palettes?*

9.8   Key Terms

1. **Healing Brush Tool:** Healing brush tool is used to renovate the imperfection by painting it with its similar type of textures.

2. **Layers Pane:** The layers pane has the maximum usability so it is good to keep visible at all times. It exists as one of the components of pellets.

3. **Lasso Tools:** Lasso Tools are used to make some free hand selection, polygonal and magnetic selections.

4. **Magic Wand Tools:** Magic Wand tools used for similar colored area selection.

5. **Marquee Tools:** Marquee Tools are used for rectangular, elliptical, single row and single column selections.

6. **Move Tool:** The Move Tool is used to move the selected region, layers and guides.

7. **Noise Filters:** Noise filters are perfect for adding or reducing noise and provide grain effect in photographs.

8. **Photoshop:** A program made by Adobe used to manipulate images.

9. **Sharpen Filters:** Sharpen filters are used for correction some imperfections in

images as well as putting emphasis on significant elements in a design.

10. **Slice Tool:** Slice Tool is used for making slices of image and widely used in Web development.

9.9   Summary

Photoshop is great tool to work with images. It is globally accepted tool for image editing. There are several options for creating a file. These are Size, Background, Resolution, etc. There are several Tools helpful for creating the file. These are Marque, Move, Lasso, Magic Wand, Crop, Slice, Healing, Brush, Clone, History Brush, Eraser, Gradient, Blur, Dodge, Path Selection, Text and many more. The most efficient way to work with Photoshop is to know how to deal with layers. Working with multiple layers is an asset to the Photoshop users. You can perform as many numbers of operations using layers with its usability. Layers are basically like a "Glass". Working on layer is like working on transparent Glass. Every glass layer has its own usability and it is also visible over one another.

Filters are mainly used to alter the look of an image, layer or selected area in Photoshop.

Linking HTML files and Web address is done by the help of Slice Tool.

9.10   Test Yourself

Section I: Review with Ease

1. What is the main use of Adobe Photoshop?
   - For image correction by using its Lighting options
   - For image enhancement by adding Blur and Soften options
   - For image composition by using two or more images in one
   - For artistic effects by using different filters
   - For painting by using different type of brushes
   - For adding text to certain image
   - For creating images of the Web and mobile devices

2. Explain the Work Space in Photoshop?

   The workspace in Photoshop consists of Application Bar, Options Bar, Tools Panel, Panel Dock and Document Window.
   - Application Bar contains menu bar with many controls, such as zoom and buttons for viewing extras.
   - Tools Panel contains all set of tools for selecting and manipulating images.
   - Options Bar contains various options available for particular selected tool.
   - Document Window holds the current working file.
   - Panel Dock has several panels to edit or modify the images. As by default there are layer, adjustment and style panels.

3. What are size guide and resizing images in Photoshop?
    ●   Most of time images need to resize to suit a particular purpose of the application.
    ●   Unit measurement of pixels is 1 cm = 28 pixels.
    ●   You can adjust units by using Edit→Preferences→Units and Rulers.
    ●   Options to modify the size of canvas are types of picture, Background resolution, Size of Pixels. Standard picture usually of size 200 × 200 appears in Title Bar. Then Select Image→Image Size menu item.

4. How to crop an image in Adobe Photoshop?
    Cutting out of a particular portion of an image is known as cropping.
    ●   Any part of the image can be selected for cropping.
    ●   Preview of the cropped image is visible at the right side of the panel.
    ●   The process to crop is as follows:
        1. Select any part of the image.
        2. Select a shape of cropping tool from the menu.
        3. Hold Shift key and drag it to select the marquee to a square or a circle.
        4. Hold a Marquee from its center, hold down Alt after dragging.
        5. Select Image→Crop menu item.

5. How to organize layers in Adobe Photoshop?
    ●   A layer shows an image/picture.
        ●   Multiple layers are used to place separate images/pictures.
        ●   Place various images in separate layers.
        ●   Lock the unused layers.
        ●   Unlock the layer that is in use.
        ●   When two or more layers need to be changed, unlock the layers.
        ●Ensure that at least one layer is unlocked.

Section II: Exercises

1. Make 3D sphere with Photoshop.
2. Design a Web page in Photoshop.
3. Develop a HTML Web page in Photoshop.
4. Implement different types of filter to create a background image.
5. Create different types of image files formats and implement in HTML Page.

Chapter 10
Adobe Flash

The best way for the beginner to write for Animation is to closely watch animated films, then read the screenplays for them afterwards   *- Douglas Wood*

Key Topics

- *Introduction*
- *Masking*
- *Guide Layer*
- *Layer Management*
- *Animation*
- *Button Creation*
- *Motion Tween*
- *Shape Tween*

10.1 Introduction

"**Macromedia Flash**" is also known as Adobe Flash/Shockwave Flash. It became a popular program to create advertisements, animations, Web pages and presentations since it has been started in 1996. It is also used to program games and Internet applications. Flash contains a scripting language known as ActionScript. Flash was the brainchild of **Jonathan Gay**. He developed the idea in college and then developed the main software while working for the Silicon Beach Software.

Flash is a great animation tool for creating movies that run on your computer. It also works fine on the Internet using the Flash player. Flash is now widely used all over the world. You can easily create animated and interactive advertisements for the Web pages in Flash. These kinds of advertisements are additional successful than static advertisement because of the animation as well as sound and music. Flash can create a whole Web page and it is livelier than plain HTML.

You can easily make your own cartoon shows for own enjoyment and share them with the Internet users. Educators also started building interactive classroom to teach the students almost any subject, such as Mathematics, Physics, Biology,

Chemistry, language. Standalone interactive games or video games that can be played on the Internet are also created. You can also program all those interactive games.

Do You Know?
Jonathan Gay, Annie Awards, Robert Tatsumi and Gary Grossman were awarded with the Ub Iwerks Award. These computer programmers developed the Flash. This is animation and interactive content software that helped ignite an animation revolution. Flash is used by 13.9% of all the Websites.

Test Your Progress
1. Give a brief description about Adobe Flash.
2. Why we use Flash?
3. Describe the advantages of Adobe Flash.

10.2 Masking

What mask layers are?

To use the spotlight effects and transitions, make use of a mask layer to create a hole through which underlying layers are visible. A mask item can be filled shape, type object, instance of a graphical representation, or a movie clip. You can group multiple layers under a single mask layer to create classy effects.

- To generate dynamic effects, animate **Mask Layer.**
- For a filled shape, use **Shape Tweening**.
- For a type object, graphic, or movie clip, use **Motion Tweening.**
- Implementing a movie clip as Mask, animates the **Mask along a Motion Path.**

To make a Mask Layer, place a mask item over the layer to use as a mask. As a replacement of having stroke use the mask item acts as a window and, that reveals the area of linked layers below it. The other part of the Mask Layer conceals everything except that shows through the mask item. Mask Layer can include only one mask item. Mask Layer is never used inside a button. One cannot apply a mask to another mask.

To create a Mask Layer from a movie clip, use ActionScript. A Mask Layer created with ActionScript can be applied only to another movie clip.

Note: The 3D tools cannot be used on objects on Mask Layer. Layers containing 3D objects cannot be used as Mask Layer.

Steps to Create Mask Layer:

- Select/Create a layer containing the objects (to be appeared inside the mask).
- Select Insert → Timeline → Layer to create new layer. A Mask Layer masks the layer immediately beneath it.

- Create Mask Layer in the correct place.
- Place filled shape, text, or symbol on Mask Layer.

  Flash ignores bitmaps, colors, gradients, transparency, and style in Mask Layer. Any filled part is completely transparent in the mask. Any non-filled part is opaque.

- Right click the Mask Layer name in the Timeline and select Mask. Then Masked Layer name is indented and its icon changes to Masked layer icon.
- To display the mask effect in Flash you have to lock the Mask Layer and the Masked Layer.

3-Way to Mask Additional Layers:

1. Drag existing layer straight under Mask Layer.
2. Create new layer under Mask Layer.
3. Select **Modify →Timeline → Layer Properties** and then select **Masked.**

2-Way to Unlink Layers from Mask Layer:

1. Drag the layer over Mask Layer.
2. Select **Modify → Timeline → Layer Properties** and then select **Normal.**

Steps to Animate a Shape, Object or Symbol on Mask Layer:

- Select Mask Layer.
- Unlock Mask Layer by clicking on Lock column.
- Now, do the following:
  - o If the mask object is a shape then apply Shape Tweening.
  - o If the mask object is a object or symbol then apply Motion Tweening.
- When you finish animation operation then click on the Lock column. It helps you to re-lock the layer for Mask Layer.

Steps to Animate a Movie Clip on Mask Layer:

- Select Mask Layer.
- To edit the clip in place and to display the clip's Timeline you have to double-click the clip on the Stage.
- Apply Motion Tweening to clip and, click on the Back button to return to document-editing mode.
- When you finish animation operation then click on the Lock column. It helps you to re-lock the layer for Mask Layer.

Do You Know?

In year 1993 Jonathan Gay, Michelle Welsh, Charlie Jackson had stated FutureWave Software. They made an initial investment of $500, 000 and, set their sights on the emerging market of pen computing.

Test Your Progress

1. *What is masking and Mask Layer?*
2. *Describe the steps to create a Mask Layer?*
3. *Write down the steps to animate Shape on Mask Layer?*

10.3 Guide Layers

Always create Guide layers and align objects on other layers to the objects you create on the Guide layers. It helps in aligning objects when drawing in Flash. It is not exported and do not appear in published SWF file. You can make any layer as Guide layer. A Guide icon is displayed to the left of the layer name for each Guide layers.

You cannot implement a motion tween layer onto Guide layers. You can only drag a normal layer onto Guide layer. This converts the Guide layer to the motion Guide layer and, also links the normal layer to the New Motion Guide Layer.

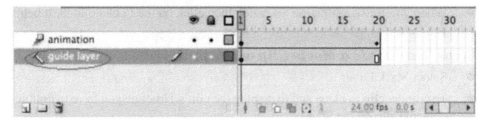

Steps to create a Guide layer:

● Select the layer.
● Right-click and select Guide from context menu.

If you want to change the layer back to the normal layer, again select the Guide option.

Note: To prevent accidentally converting a Guide layer, it is a best practice to place all of the Guide layers at the bottom of the layer stacking order in the Timeline.

To have a control over the movement of objects in a tween animation, it is better to use Motion Guide Layer.

Do You Know?
By the of summer of 1996 the team of Jonathan Gay was ready to give a new version. That version was FutureSplash Animator.

Test Your Progress
1. *What is Guide Layer?*
2. *Is Motion Layer implemented on Guide layer?*
3. *Write down steps to create Guide layers?*

10.4 Layer Management

Layers help you to organize the work in Flash document. You can easily draw and make changes in objects on one layer, without affecting the objects of another layer.

To create any artwork like drawing, painting, or otherwise modifying a layer or folder, then you have to select the layer in the Timeline to make it to start work. You can see Pencil icon next to a layer or folder name in the Timeline. It indicates that the layer or folder is active. You always remember that only one layer can be active at a time. But more than one layer can be selected at a time.

When you start a Flash document then you will notice that it contains only one layer. To organize your work, animation, or any other activity in your document, add more and more layers. It helps you to have a good control over artwork. You may also lock, hide, and rearrange the layers. Layers never increase the file size of your published SWF file. But the objects you place over the layers increase the project's file size.

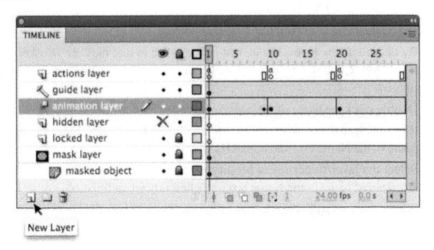

3-Ways to Create a Normal Layer:

1. Click the New Layer icon. It exists in the bottom left corner of the panel.
2. Select **Insert → Timeline → Layer.**
3. Right-click an existing layer. Select **Insert Layer** in the menu.

5-Different types of layers:

1. **Normal layers**: It contains most of your work in a FLA Flash Files (files extension).
2. **Mask layers:** It contain objects used as masks to hide some of the selected portions of layers.
3. **Masked layers**: These are the layers under a mask layer that you correlate with the Mask layer. Some of the portion of the mask layer not sheltered by the mask is mostly visible.
4. **Guide layers:** It contains strokes which are used to guide the arrangement of the objects on other layers.
5. **Guided layers:** These layers are associated with a Guide layer. The objects under the guided layers are arranged or animated along the strokes of the Guide layer.

> **Note:** A guided layer mainly contains Static Artwork and Classic Tweens. But not Motion Tweens.

3-Way to Create a Layer Folder:

1. Select a **layer/folder → Insert → Timeline → Layer Folder.**
2. Right-click on a **layer name →** select **Insert Folder** from the menu. The new folder appears above the layer/folder that you selected.
3. Click on the New Folder icon [icon] exists at the bottom. The new folder appears above the layer/folder that you selected.

3-Way to Rename Particular Layer/Folder:

By default a new layers are named in the order in that they are invoked, i.e., **Layer 1, Layer 2,** and so on. To better reflect their contents you must rename layers accordingly.

1. Double-click the name of the layer/folder and enter any desired name.
2. Right-click on the name of the layer/folder. Select **Properties.** Enter any desired name in the Name box and click **OK** when finished.
3. Select the layer/folder select Modify → Timeline → Layer Properties. Enter any desired name in the Name box and click **OK** when finished.

Steps to Copy Frames from the Single Layer:

•   Select some range of frames in the layer. (To select the entire layer: click **Layer Name** in the Timeline.)

- Then Select **Edit → Timeline → Copy Frames.**
- Now click the frame where you want to begin pasting it.
- Finally select **Edit → Timeline → Paste Frames.**

Steps to Copy Frames from the Layer Folder:

- Collapse the folder (by clicking the triangle to the left of the folder name).
- Click **folder name** to select the entire folder.
- Then Select **Edit → Timeline → Copy Frames.**
- Now to create a folder you select **Insert → Timeline → Layer Folder.**
- Finally click the new folder and select **Edit → Timeline → Paste Frames.**

3-Way to Delete Particular Layer/Folder:

1. Click on **Delete Layer** button in the bottom.
2. Drag the layer/folder to the **Delete Layer** button.
3. Right-click on the layer/folder name and select **Delete Layer** from the menu.

> **Note:** When you delete a particular layer/folder, all the enclosed layers and all their contents are also deleted simultaneously.

Steps to Lock or Unlock One or More Layers/Folders:

- To lock a particular layer/folder you have to click on the **Lock column** to the right of the name. To unlock the layer/folder then click on the **Lock column** again.
- To lock all layers/folders you have to click on the padlock icon and to unlock all layers and folders, click it again.
- To lock or unlock multiple layers/folders you have to drag the **Lock column.**
- To lock all the other layers/folders you have to **Alt+click** on the **Lock column** to the right of a layer/folder name. To unlock all layers or folders then again **Alt+click** on the **Lock column.**

Do You Know?

On January 6th, 1997, Macromedia announced that they had acquired the FutureWave. After that FutureSplash Animator renamed as Macromedia Flash. Then they integrated with the Shock wave family of multimedia players.

Test Your Progress

1. *How we create Layers in Adobe Flash?*
2. *What are different types of layers?*
3. *How to lock and unlock the layers?*

10.5 Animation

Adobe Creative Suite provides some great new features in Flash which makes Flash animation less time-consuming, more attractive and more engaging.

There are several ways to create animations in Flash:

- By creating Motion Tweens
- By creating frame-by-frame animations
- By applying Motion Presets
- By using tween instances
- By copying Action Script 3 code
- By creating Shape Tweens
- By using inverse kinematics
- By writing Action Script code

Create Quick Motion Tweens

It is also known as "**Motion Tween**" and now called as "**Classic Tween**". "**Motion Tween**" in the new Flash is so much easier and more exciting.

You do not have to hand created keyframes. You do not have to write a line of code. Flash has **auto-key framing.** You have to just drag a symbol from the Library to the Stage, i.e., workarea. Take any target object. Drag that object to another part of the Stage and then Flash automatically creates the Motion Tween.

Changing the Motion Path

You will observe the **Motion Path** from the object to the part of the stage that you dragged it to. It is shown in the form of dotted line.

The Motion Path can easily be changeable by raising/lowering the dots on the line. You can easily change the movement of the object from a simple straight movement into different bouncing movements.

Flash animation is now **object-based** instead of **timeline-based.** It helps in cutting down hours of work and making you faster and more productive.

The Motion Editor

The Motion Editor in Flash allows you to control the animation of the object on the Stage. You can easily see the animation within seconds of applying different properties to the target object. Example: scaling the object up or down, X-axis and Y-axis properties, skewing the object and many more.

Easily Save Your Innovative Time!!!!

You can easily add animation to any .FLA file with a few clicks. Apply some prebuilt animations in Flash. This can take place without any prior knowledge of animation and with your little effort.

- Simply select **Preset** in Presets Panel, say the Bounce in 3D Preset.

● Apply it to your target object on the stage for some desired result.

● To create the same effect with a new object you have to just select a new object on the stage and apply the preset to it. There is no need to re-creating animations. You can easily save your time and enjoy your work.

Save Your Complex Custom Animations

Save some of your complex animations under **Custom Presets**. It helps you to use them again and again with different objects. By this you can easily change your target object without recreating the animation. This helps you to save your quality hours of work.

Do You Know?

As per the Adobe, Flash Player is the world's most pervasive software platform. This software is used by over 2 million professionals. The main portion of these professionals use Flash to create interactive content, Websites and rich media advertisements. The emergence of Flash also supported a revolution in character animation.

Test Your Progress

1. *What do you mean by Animation?*
2. *Write down the different ways to perform Animation in Adobe Flash?*
3. *How will you implement animations in HTML Web page?*

10.6 Button Creation

Creating a button that changes its property upon mouse over events is extremely simple. For this the only thing you have to do is to tell Flash how you desire the button to look on different circumstances, i.e.,

1. In normal state.

2. Whenever the mouse moves over the button.

3. Whenever the user clicks the button.

Once you get hands on these 3-step techniques you can create buttons in some seconds. The buttons that you create this way are very simple ones. If you want to create really attractive buttons then you should use a slightly different method based on some movie clips.

Adobe Flash Handles These Three Types of Objects:

1. **Graphics:** You probably noticed that when you edit any graphics objects you have the entire Timeline available for it. So this means that graphics objects are not limited to only static elements. It is easy to create looping animations. It is just possible by creating graphic objects that uses more than one frame.

2. **Buttons:** Buttons are different from graphic objects. Whenever you create a

button object you only require four frames, i.e., button in normal state, button when a mouse-over is detected, button when gets clicked, last frame is used to indicate which portion you want mouse events to react to.

3. **Movie clips:** Movie clips are very much similar to Graphics objects. In both cases you can easily create animations that can be drag onto your movie clips. While animations made as graphics objects loops over and over. You can easily control the Movie clips.

Steps to Create Buttons:

Buttons are graphical symbols that contain four frames. Each of the frames of a button symbol represents a different state of the button, i.e., Up, Over, Down, and Hit. These are the states that determines how a button behaves when the mouse is rolled over it and when it gets clicked.

Steps are as follows:

1. Select **New Symbol** Insert in menu or use shortcut press [Ctrl+F8].
2. Under the **Symbol Properties** dialog box, enter the name for new button symbol
3. Choose Button as the Behavior option.
4. Click OK when gets completed.
5. To create a Up state button image:
    o   Use only drawing tools.
    o   Import the graphic/ place the instance of another symbol on the Stage.
    o   You can use either the movie clip/graphic symbol in the button.
    o   You cannot use another button in the button.
    o   Use any movie clip symbols if you want to create any animated button.
6. Select **second frame then labeled over** and choose **Keyframe** in Insert menu. You will observe that the button image from first frame appears on Stage.
7. Change button image for over state.
8. Repeat Steps 6, 7 and 8 for Down frame and Hit frame.

> **Note:** The Hit frame is not visible on Stage on playback. It totally defines the area of button that responds whenever gets clicked. To make sure that Hit frame graphic is solid area large enough to encompass all graphic elements of Up, Down and Over frames. You will notice that it can also be larger than the visible button. If you unable to specify a Hit frame then the objects in the U state are used as Hit frames.

●   After you totally define those images of the four button states. Now select **Edit → Edit Movie** to exit from symbol edit mode.
●   Now open **Library window** by selecting **Window → Library**.
●   Locate the button in the Library window.

- Drag the button symbol out of Library onto Stage. Finally this step creates instance of button in movie.

Assigning a Simple Action to A Button for Flash

- In Edit Movie mode, select the button instance created in above steps.
- Select **Window→Actions**, it will open Actions panel.
- Under Toolbox list on left side of panel, click basic actions option to display basic actions.

  Now assign any action by any of the mentioned options:

  o   By double-clicking on the action in basics actions option.

  o   By dragging action from basic actions option on left to actions list on the right side of panel.

  o   By clicking the Add (+) button and choose any action from popup menu.

  o   By using keyboard shortcut.

- If any chosen action has any associated parameters then those parameters appears in parameter panel at the bottom of actions panel.
- If the Parameter pane is not visible then click the small triangle in the lower right corner of the panel.
- Select/type the parameters appropriate for that action.
- For example, the gotoAndPlay action contains three parameters, i.e., **Scene, Type,** and **Frame.**

Do You Know?

In the year 1997 launched the first animated series "The Goddamn George Liquor Program". John Kricfalusi is the creator of The Ren & Stimpy Show.

Test Your Progress

1.   What is 3-steps technique to create a Button?

2.   Write down the steps to create a Button in Adobe Flash?

3.   How will you assign a simple action to a Button for Flash?

10.7 Motion Tween

Motion Tween is like tweening an Object or Symbol from one position to another position. To execute Motion Tween you have to do is to provide Object/Symbol's initial position and the end position. Rest is taken care by Adobe Flash. Is not it really simple to implement?

Prerequisites for implementing Motion Tween:

- **Flash Player 7.0** must be installed to view the Flash animation.
- **Flash MX 2004** must be installed to download the **.fla** file.

Steps to Implement Motion Tween:

- Open a new Flash Document by clicking on **File** option or by using shortcut **[Ctrl+N]**.

  New Document window will appear on the screen.

- Select **General panel** and choose Type as **Flash Document**.

- Press **OK** when get completed.

- If timeline window is not visible on the screen then, press **[Ctrl+Alt+T]**.

- This is what you can see on the screen, it is shown as **Layer 1** in your Timeline Window by default.

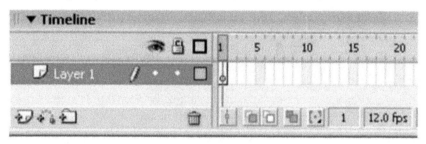

- Select the first frame. Import your Image/Object/Symbol onto stage, upon which you would want to implement Motion Tween.

  File → Import → Import to Stage or press **Ctrl+R** key together.

  Or you can even draw your individual Object. You may choose Rectangular Tool or Oval Tool from the Toolbox to draw your preferred shape.

- Now select your Object on the stage and press **F8** to convert the image to a **Symbol**. Convert to Symbol window will pop-up.

- Give a desired name to the symbol. Say pencil.

- Select Graphic behavior and press OK when completed.

> **Note:** You can create Motion Tween only over the Symbols. So if any object upon which you would want to implement Motion Tween, first convert that object to a Symbol.

- Right now your Symbol is in frame 1 of Layer 1 in the document. Select frame 25 and press **F6** to insert a **New Keyframe**.

- Keeping the playhead on frame 25, place your Symbol to some other position other than the present one.

- Select any frame between, 2 to 25 & click on **Motion** from the **Tween** pop-up menu in the **Property Inspector**.

- Now you will have interface in front of you as shown below.

- Now press **Ctrl+Enter** to view your Tween.

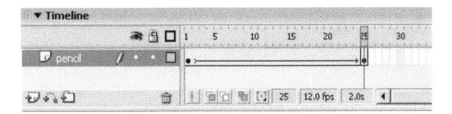

Do You Know?
● *Flash runs the 98% of Internet enabled desktops.*
● *Flash is used to develop 70% of Web games.*
● *Flash Player 10 is used by 95% of Internet videos.*
● *Flash has over 30 million AIR downloads and growing.*

Test Your Progress
1. *What do you mean by Motion Tween?*
2. *What are the prerequisites for Motion Tween?*
3. *Write down the basic steps to implement Motion Tween?*

10.8 Shape Tween

By tweening different shapes, one can create an effect like morphing, making one shape appear to change into a different shape over particular time. Flash can also used to Tween size and color of shapes.

Prerequisites for implementing Shape Tween:

● **Flash Player 7.0** must be installed to view the Flash animation.

● **Flash MX 2004** must be installed to download the **.fla** file.

Steps to Implement Shape Tween:

● Open a new Flash Document by clicking on **File** option or by using shortcut **Ctrl+N**.

New Document window will appear on the screen, Select **General Panel** and choose Type as **Flash Document**. Press **OK** when get completed.

● If timeline window is not visible on the screen then, press **Ctrl+Alt+T** keys together.

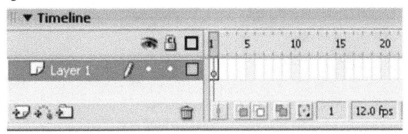

- This is what you can see on the screen, it is shown as **Layer 1** in your Timeline Window by default.
- Now select the first frame. Draw any object on your working area. Let's start with basic shapes, draw a Circle. This is going to be your initial object for the document.
- Select frame 25 and press F6 to insert a new keyframe.
- Still keeping limit on frame 25, delete the object present in your working area.
- Now draw a different object say as square.
- Select any frame between 2 and 24.
- Select shape from the **Tween** pop-up menu in the **Property Inspector**. Now you will have this interface in front of you as shown below.

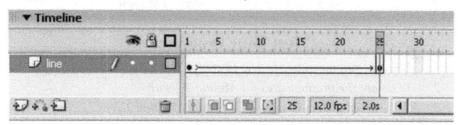

- Now press **Ctrl+Enter** to view your tween.

Do You Know?

Adobe Enterprise solutions are used by:
1. *8 of the 10 global bank holding companies.*
2. *9 of the top 10 global manufacturing companies.*
3. *7 of the World's leading national governments.*
4. *More than half of the top global insurance companies.*
5. *All 10 of the world's largest publically traded companies.*
6. *19 of the top 20 pharmaceutical companies globally.*

Test Your Progress

1. *What do you mean by Shape Tween?*
2. *What is the shortcut for Timeline window?*
3. *Write down the basic steps to implement Shape Tween.*

10.9 Key Terms

10.10 Summary

"Macromedia Flash" It is also known as Adobe Flash/Shockwave Flash. It became a popular program to create advertisements, animations, Web pages and presentations since it is started in 1996. It is also used to program games and Internet applications. Flash contains a scripting language known as ActionScript.

To use the spotlight effects and transitions, make use of a mask layer to create a hole through which underlying layers are visible. A mask item can be filled shape, type object, instance of a graphical representation, or a movie clip. You can group multiple layers under a single mask layer to create classy effects.

Always create Guide layers and align objects on other layers to the objects you create on the Guide layers. It helps in aligning objects when drawing in Flash.

Layers help you to organize the work in Flash document. You can easily draw and make changes in objects on one layer without affecting the objects of another layer.

Adobe Creative Suite provides some great new features in Flash which makes Flash animation less time-consuming, more attractive and more engaging.

Adobe Flash handles these three types of objects: Graphics, Buttons, and Movie Clips. Motion Tween is like tweening an Object or Symbol from one position to another position. To execute Motion Tween you have to do is to provide Object/Symbol's initial position and the end position. By tweening different shapes, one can create an effect like morphing, making one shape appear to change into a different shape over particular time. Flash can also used to tween size and color of shapes.

10.11 Test Yourself

Section I: Review with Ease

1. How to embed Flash movie in HTML?

   To embed flash movie in HTML, to to the Flash program and perform the following steps:

   - Select File→Open. Select the Flash movie.
   - Select File→Export Movie.
   - Name the saved file with .swf extension. Select the location to save the file.
   - Click OK.
   - Open the HTML file.
   - Insert the following code:

```
<object width="500" height="350">
<param name="movie" value="the flash file123.swf">
<embed src="the flash file123.swf" width="500" height="350">
</embed>
</object>
```

2. How to start a graphic animation at a specific frame?

   A graphic can be animated in Flash. The animation is within the selected frame.

   - Select Graphic Symbol properties.

- The Graphic Symbol properties are available in option for graphics drop-down.
- Select the option play once.
- Mention the frame number in the input box by name first.

3. What is Motion Tween in Adobe Flash?

   Motion tween is like tweening an Object or Symbol from one position to another position. To execute Motion Tween you have to do is to provide Object/Symbol's initial position and the end position.

4. Define the use of Shape Tween.

   By tweening different shapes, one can create an effect like morphing, making one shape appear to change into a different shape over particular time. Flash can also used to tween size and color of shapes.

Section II: Exercises

1. Write down the features of Adobe Flash.
2. Implement Masking in Flash.
3. What do you mean by Flash Tweening?
4. What is Animation?
5. Create buttons for HTML page.
6. Create animation using Motion Tween.
7. Create animation using Shape Tween.